Algrove Publishing Limited
1090 Morrison Drive
Ottawa, Ontario
Canada K2H 1C2

Canadian Cataloguing in Publication Data

Crawshaw, Fred D. (Fred Duane), b. 1874
Farm mechanics

(Classic reprint series)
Originally published: Peoria, Ill. : Manual Arts Press, 1922.
Includes index.
ISBN 1-894572-01-7

1. Agricultural mechanics. 2. Farm equipment. 3. Agricultural machinery. I. Lehmann, E. W. (Emil Wilhelm). II. Title. III. Series: Classic reprint series (Ottawa, Ont.)

S675.C73 2000 631.3 C00-900342-8

Printed in Canada
#10400

Publisher's Note

Originally used as a text for university and extension courses, some of the technical information has become dated in the intervening 80 years. It is not so much that the information is inaccurate but that alternatives have been developed for some of the subjects covered. For example, very few aspiring farmers trouble to learn blacksmithing today since they will probably never shoe a horse or forge a plow point. On the other hand, despite the advances in types of cement and methods of treating concrete to increase its strength and durability, virtually anyone would benefit from the very clear explanation of the appropriate use of concrete in this book. The same is true of the treatment of sheet metal work and woodworking. An intelligent person armed with the basics of a craft can develop in it. This book was focussed on providing farmers with the basics in a range of crafts. In an age when we are all specialists, there is a tendency to forget that at one time survival required us to be generalists.

Leonard G. Lee, Publisher
Ottawa
March, 2000

FARM MECHANICS

by

FRED D. CRAWSHAW
Formerly Professor of Manual Arts,
University of Wisconsin

and

E. W. LEHMANN
Professor of Farm Mechanics,
University of Illinois

THE MANUAL ARTS PRESS
PEORIA, ILLINOIS

Printed in the United States of America

PREFACE

THIS book has been prepared to meet the increasing need for a textbook on the mechanical processes commonly taught in agricultural high schools and colleges, and in industrial schools. Many teachers of vocational agriculture who find it difficult to organize suitable projects for their students will find that the exercises in this text have been worked out to meet their needs. The book should also be widely useful as a reference and instruction book on the farm.

The types of work covered, while primarily representing the common branches of mechanical activity required under rural conditions, are, in most cases, applicable to the requirements of the industry upon which each type has a bearing.

Each part of the book deals exclusively and comprehensively with one particular type of work, as woodwork, cement work, forging, etc.; a fact which should contribute to its usefulness, both as a text and as a reference book. Thru further divisions into chapters and numbered topics, a greater possibility of locating, at any time, the various details and descriptions is offered.

The treatment thruout the book is thoroly practical. Emphasis is placed upon the proper use of tools and materials in their application to projects. The projects are selected from the standpoint of the practical application to the needs of the student. The gradation of projects within each of the parts has been kept in mind. The plan has been to treat each topic in such detail that the teacher who has a variety of mechanical work going on in his classes at one time may be largely relieved of the burden of class instruction, and can devote his energies to the needs of the individual pupil. Working drawings and specifications for many of the projects have been given. Each of these projects is analyzed into its sequential operations with numerous references to the previous projects for specific details. Many supplementary projects are provided.

The authors are indebted to their many friends who have given freely of their material and advice. They wish particularly to acknowledge the use of material furnished by the University of Illinois, the University of Missouri, the Iowa State College, the Portland Cement Association, and of cuts furnished by several trade journals and taken from state bulletins.

FRED D. CRAWSHAW.
E. W. LEHMANN.

CONTENTS

PART I

Woodworking

PART II

CEMENT AND CONCRETE

PART III

Blacksmithing

PART IV

SHEET-METALWORK

PART V

FARM MACHINERY REPAIR AND ADJUSTMENT

PART VIII

ROPE AND HARNESS WORK ON THE FARM

PART I

WOODWORKING

CHAPTER I

TREES AND LUMBER

1. **Logging.** The student is familiar with wood in two forms. One is logs and the other is lumber. It is not only desirable as information that you know the common trees, but it is necessary for practical purposes that you know different kinds of wood when you see them in boards.

Timber is first "spotted" by men who go thru the forest to mark with an ax those trees which are to be cut. It is then felled (chopped or sawed down) and trimmed by having all limbs cut off. The body, or trunk, of the tree and the limbs which are large enough to be sawed into boards are cut to board lengths of twelve, fourteen, or sixteen feet, etc., forming logs. These logs are rolled, hauled or skidded into a clearing to be piled up, measured and later transported to a saw-mill.

While in large piles in the clearing, which is an open space in the woods where the logs are said to be "banked," they are scaled. This is measuring and estimating the number of board feet in each log. Each end of the log is measured and marked with the owner's number.

The banking ground is frequently near a river and on a level above that of the water in the river, so that the logs can easily be rolled down into the stream, where they are allowed to drift to some point down stream, to be collected in a bog, or set-back, near a mill, and then to be sorted and later run into the mill and sawed into lumber. In case it is not possible to transport logs in the natural way, as just described, they must be hauled by team or train to the mill.

This description is very brief and is designed merely to give the outstanding facts in the process of felling trees and conveying them cut up to the mill. The reader is referred to Noyes' *Handwork in Wood,* published by The Manual Arts Press, Peoria, Illinois, for an adequate description of this process and for a bibliography on logging.

2. **Milling.** The logs are conveyed from the mill pond or yard into the mill by means of an endless chain and the "jack ladder" which is an inclined platform running from the mill into the water of the mill yard. The endless chain which runs over this inclined platform is fitted with studs which engage with the logs as they are directed toward the jack ladder by men with long spiked poles. The logs are carried end to end into the mill and there are inspected for stones which may be lodged in the bark. A flipper, controlled by steam, throws each log to the side when the operator of the machine throws a lever. The log now rolls down an inclined plane to a stop made of heavy iron which is located at the edge of the saw table. When the operator of the saw wants a log, he releases the stop. This operation permits one log to roll onto the saw table, where it is dogged, or clamped, to the table.

The saw table moves backward and forward. With each passage of the table, a large circular, or band, saw cuts off a board. When two or three boards have been removed from the side, the log is turned completely over and a similar operation is performed on the opposite side.

By easily-controlled machinery, the log is revolved or moved into different positions to be sawed into boards. It is sent from the saw to the edger and the cross-cut, or butting, saw on "live" rollers which revolve on a horizontal table and transmit the boards at a rate of 200 to 250 feet per minute

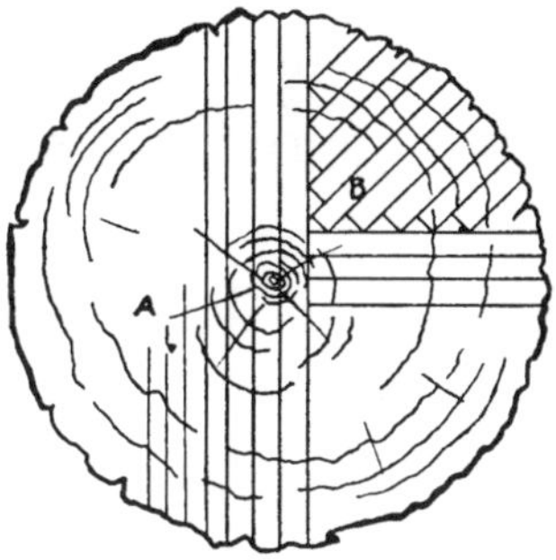

FIG. 1. Methods of sawing lumber. *A*, slash-sawing; *B*, quarter-sawing.

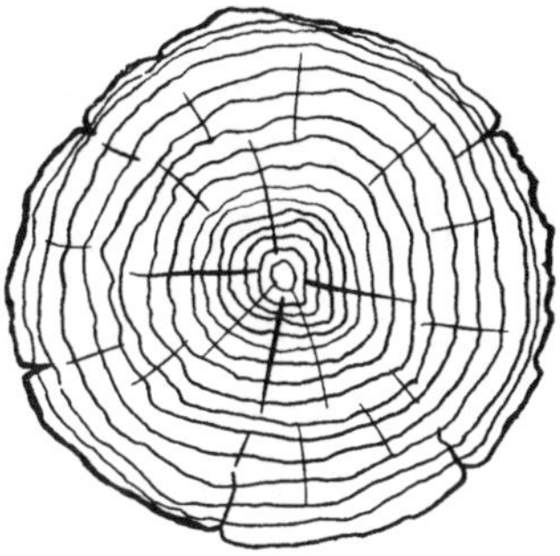

FIG. 2. End of log, showing annual rings and medullary rays.

from one place to another. Finally, the boards, now known as lumber, are transferred to a shed, where they are sorted as to size, quality and cut, and then again transferred out of doors to be piled for air-seasoning until sold for construction purposes.

Boards are usually slash-sawed, the term used for parallel sawing (*A*, Fig. 1). However, they are also rift-sawed or quarter-sawed, which means that the saw cut is radial, as shown in *B*, Fig. 1. The advantage of the radially-sawed board is that the edges rather than the sides of the fiber of the wood form the surface of the board and thereby make a more even grain and one which wears better.

3. Tree Growth. When a tree is sawed down, the sawed end will show concentric rings (Fig. 2). Those near the center are more compact than the ones near the outside. The center portion is called heart wood; the outer portion, sap wood, because it conducts the sap which gives vitality to the tree.

Each ring, if observed closely, will be found to be made up of two layers—one denser than the other. These are called annual rings because one pair of rings is formed each year. The dense portion of the ring is the result of winter growth, and the porous part is that formed in the spring and summer when the growth is most rapid.

Upon closer inspection, it will be observed that these rings are crossed by radial lines running from the center to the bark. These are called medullary rays. In a sense, they help to bind the rings together. When cut at a slant, as they may be in radial- or quarter-sawing, these rays, which are very solid, will appear as light spots in the grain of the wood shown on the surface of a board. The beauty of quarter-sawed wood when polished makes certain kinds of it very desirable for interior finish and furniture construction. One of the woods which has this particular feature emphasized is oak. Other grain irregularities, such as wanes and gnarls, make attractive wood surfaces. Curly birch and bird's-eye maple are conspicuous examples.

4. Seasoning. One of the most important parts of the preparation of wood for construction use is its seasoning or drying. A properly-seasoned board is lighter than one not seasoned. It is stronger and is not subject to change of volume which causes checking and warping. Of the several methods of seasoning, the best is natural-air-drying, which takes from two to six years. In this process, boards are piled up with broad surfaces horizontal and separated one from another by thin strips of wood known as sticks. The boards in a particular layer are placed so that edges will not touch; hence, air is permitted to circulate throughout the pile and come in contact with all surfaces. The piles are set up a foot or more from the ground, one end being a few inches higher than the opposite one. They are covered with boards to protect the drying lumber from rain and sun.

In order to produce lumber quickly for construction use, it is artificially seasoned or kiln-dried. This reduces the moisure of the wood to perhaps five per cent, whereas, in the natural process, ten per cent is the approximate minimum. However, kiln-dried lumber will more quickly re-absorb moisture. As most lumber nowadays is seasoned by some artificial means, it is advisable to pile it in shops as for air-seasoning. In case there is a tendency to warp, it is sometimes advisable to clamp a board to a flat surface, concave surface down, or clamp two boards together with the concave surfaces facing each other.

Whenever a board is dressed, it is well to plane both broad surfaces, especially in the case of air-dried lumber, in order to open the pores, as it were, on both sides and thus make the exposure conditions uniform throughout. If the ordinary means of overcoming warping are not sufficient, it is sometimes possible to straighten a board by heating the convex side and, possibly, at the same time moistening the concave side. The heating can be done by laying the board on top of a furnace.

5. Measurements and Calculations. Lumber is measured by the so-called board foot, which is one foot square and one inch thick.

There are two satisfactory methods of calculating the number of board feet in a board or a number of boards:

Rule 1. Multiply thickness in inches by width in inches by length in feet, and divide by 12. Example: $\frac{2'' \text{ x } 7'' \text{ x } 14'}{12}$ = 16-1/3 board feet.

Rule 2. Multiply the thickness in inches by width in feet by length in feet. Example: $\frac{2 \text{ x } 7 \text{ x } 14}{1 \text{ x } 12 \text{ x } 1}$ = 16 1/3 board feet.

The possibility of cancellation in the second method makes it shorter and, consequently, preferable.

When purchasing lumber, give the dimensions in the order of thickness, width and length, as: 8 pieces 5″ x 9″ x 12′.

In quantities, lumber should be ordered as follows:

Example 1. 1000′ Norway pine dressed two sides to 7/8″, 9″ and up. This makes the minimum width 9″.

Example 2. 1000′ White Pine S4S 7/8″ x 5″ x 12′. This means all boards are to be surfaced on all four surfaces and the dimensions are to be uniform, viz.: 7/8″ thick by 5″ wide by 12′ long.

6. Trees. Trees are divided into two general classes known as the broadleaf, or hardwoods, and the needleleaf, or softwoods. In each of these classes, there are many varieties which are of great value in some one or more forms of construction work. Those listed below are only a few of particular significance, either because of their general use, or because of their prevalence in agricultural or industrial communities:

BROADLEAF OR HARDWOODS

NAME	VARIETY	LOCATION	QUALITIES	USES
Oak.	White.	North Central and East U. S.	Durable, easily worked. Does not warp or check easily. Polishes well.	Cabinet work and Interior finishes.
	Red Oak.	North Central	Same.	Same.
	Burr.	and East U. S.	Same.	Same.
	Black.	East of long. 96, westward to Mo. and Tex.	Same.	Same. Also outdoor construction.
	Live.	West of Rockies.	Durable, tough.	Implements.

Distinguishing Tree Features: Heartwood, light brown to red or dark brown.
Sapwood, light brown to yellow.
Height, 75 feet; diameter, 4-1/2 feet. Rough bark.

NAME	VARIETY	LOCATION	QUALITIES	USES
Ash.	White.	Eastern U. S.	Tough, elastic, straight-grained, brittle.	Cheap interior finish and cabinet work.
	Black.	North and Northeast U. S.	Soft, heavy, tough, not strong.	Same and splints.
	Green	East of Rockies.	Hard heavy, strong, brittle.	Same
	Oregon.	Pacific Coast.	Light, hard, strong.	Furniture, cooperage, carriage frames.

BROADLEAF OR HARDWOODS (*Continued*)

NAME	VARIETY	LOCATION	QUALITIES	USES
Ash (*Cont.*)				

Distinguishing Tree Features: Heartwood, yellow to brown, or reddish-brown.
Sapwood, light yellow.
Height, 65 feet; diameter, 2-1/2 feet.

NAME	VARIETY	LOCATION	QUALITIES	USES
Maple.	Hard.	Northeast and East U. S.	Straight-grained, strong, tough, shrinks.	Furniture, interior finish, implements.
	Silver.	East U. S. Ohio Basin.	Light, brittle, easily worked.	Interior finish, wooden ware.
	Red.	East U. S.	Same.	Cabinet work.
	Oregon.	Western Coast.	Light, hard, strong.	Furniture, tool handles.

Distinguishing Tree Features: Heartwood, light to dark yellow.
Sapwood, white to dark yellow.
Height, 75 feet; diameter, 2 feet.

NAME	VARIETY	LOCATION	QUALITIES	USES
Walnut.	Black.	East and Central U. S.	Heavy, hard, strong, firm, easily worked.	Furniture, fixtures, interior finish.
	White (Butternut).	Northeast and Central U. S.	Light, soft, not strong.	Interior finish, cabinet work.

Distinguishing Tree Features: Heartwood, dark brown to reddish brown.
Sapwood, light brown to dark brown.
Height, 80 feet; diameter, 1 foot and larger.

BROADLEAF OR HARDWOODS (*Continued*)

Name	Variety	Location	Qualities	Uses
Hickory.	Shagbark.	Eastern U. S.	Very tough, elastic, resilient, heavy.	Carriage and implement work, ax handles.

Distinguishing Tree Features: Heartwood, light to dark brown.
Sapwood, ivory to cream.
Height, 85 feet; diameter, 2-1/2 feet.

Name	Variety	Location	Qualities	Uses
Chestnut.		East of Mississippi river except in central portion of this section.	Weak, brittle, durable, easy to work, checks and warps in drying.	Cabinet work and furniture.

Distinguishing Tree Features: Heartwood, brown.
Sapwood, lighter brown.
Height, 65 feet; diameter, 7-1/2 feet.

Name	Variety	Location	Qualities	Uses
Beech.		Eastern and Central U. S.	Hard, heavy, strong.	Ship and wagon work, plane stocks.
	Ironwood (Blue Beach).	Same.	Same.	Liners, tool handles.

Distinguishing Tree Features: Heartwood, light reddish brown.
Sapwood, nearly white.
Height, 55 feet; diameter, 2-1/2 feet. (Dimension of ironwood less.)

Name	Variety	Location	Qualities	Uses
Birch.	White.	Canada, Atlantic Coast to Delaware.	Soft, light, weak.	Small woodenware, cheap furniture.
	Red.	Massachusetts and Florida.	Light and strong.	Furniture and woodenware.

BROADLEAF OR HARDWOODS (*Continued*)

NAME	VARIETY	LOCATION	QUALITIES	USES
Birch (*Cont.*)				
	Yellow.	Eastern U. S.	Same.	Same.
	Sweet.	Northeastern U. S.	Heavy, hard, strong.	Furniture, ships.

Distinguishing Tree Features: Heartwood, light brown.
Sapwood, white to yellow.
Height, 50 feet; diameter, 2 feet.

NAME	VARIETY	LOCATION	QUALITIES	USES
Whitewood.	Yellow.	Eastern Coast.	Light, soft, difficult to season, durable.	Boxes, cabinet work, interior trim. *Note:* The pine of the hardwoods.
	Poplar.	Scattered, Central U. S.	Same.	Same.
	Basswood.	Eastern U. S. Coast.	Tough, weak, very soft.	Boxes, cheap furniture, carriage bodies.

Distinguishing Tree Features: Heartwood, greenish yellow to brownish yellow.
Sapwood, almost white.
Height, 80 feet; diameter, 5 feet.

NAME	VARIETY	LOCATION	QUALITIES	USES
Mahogany.		Central America, West Indies.	Strong, durable, easily warped, beautiful polish.	Furniture, interior trim.

BROADLEAF OR HARDWOODS (*Continued*)

NAME	VARIETY	LOCATION	QUALITIES	USES
Mahogany (*Cont.*)				
	White.	Mexico and Central America.	Same. More yellow.	Same.
	Spanish.	Mexico, Cuba, West Indies.		Same. Veneers.
	Cedar.			

Distinguishing Tree Features: Heartwood reddish brown, darkens easily.
Sapwood, light brown to yellow.
Height, 50 feet; diameter, 3 feet.

NEEDLELEAF OR SOFTWOODS

NAME	VARIETY	LOCATION	QUALITIES	USES
Pine.	White.	North Central and Eastern U. S.	Uniform grain, strong, elastic, light, easily worked, weakest of pines.	General carpentry, boxes and crates.
	Georgia ("Hard," "Yellow" or "Longleaf").	South Atlantic and Gulf states.	Resinous, strong and heavy. Durable.	Heavy and outside construction flooring.
	Norway (Red).	New England and Lake states.	Light, hard, resinous.	Poles, masts, flooring. *Note:* The oak of the softwoods.

Distinguishing Tree Features: Heartwood, yellowish to reddish brown.
Sapwood, white to whitish yellow.
Height, 80 feet; diameter, 3 feet.

NEEDLELEAF OR SOFTWOODS (*Continued*)

Name	Variety	Location	Qualities	Uses
Spruce.	Black.	Eastern U. S.	Soft, light, not durable when exposed.	Structural substitute for white pine.
	White.	Western states.	Close, straight-grain, soft, light.	Lumber, ordinary carpentry.
	Sitka.	Pacific Coast.		Construction, interior finish.

Distinguishing Tree Features: Heartwood, reddish brown.
Sapwood, nearly white.
Height, 75 to 100 feet; diameter, 2-1/2 feet.

Name	Variety	Location	Qualities	Uses
Fir.	Great Silver.	Washington, Oregon, Texas and Mexico.	Soft, easily split.	Interior finish, boxes.
	Red.	Northwestern U. S.	Light, hard, strong.	House trimmings.

Distinguishing Tree Features: Heartwood, light red to brownish yellow.
Sapwood, white to yellow.
Height, 200 feet; diameter, 5 feet.

Name	Variety	Location	Qualities	Uses
Cedar.	Red.	Atlantic Coast, Southeastern U. S.	Fine-grained, light, soft, weak, durable.	Chests, boxes, pencils.
	White.	Northern states, mountains of North Carolina and Tennessee.	Light, soft, weak, durable.	Poles, fencing, railroad ties.

NEEDLELEAF OR SOFTWOODS (*Continued*)

Name	Variety	Location	Qualities	Uses
Cedar(*Cont.*)	Incense	Southeastern U. S.	Same	Furniture, interior finish, shipbuilding.

Distinguishing Tree Features: Heartwood, reddish brown.
Sapwood, nearly white.
Height, 40 feet; diameter, 2-1/2 feet.

Name	Variety	Location	Qualities	Uses
Cypress.		Southern Coast.	Soft, very durable.	Cooperage, carpentry.
	Redwood.	Western Coast. California.	Soft, durable, light weight.	Construction, shingles.

Distinguishing Tree Features: Heartwood, reddish brown.
Sapwood, yellow.
Height, 85 feet; diameter, 3 feet.
Giant, 250 feet; diameter, 25 feet.

The trees above listed are "exogenous," which means that they grow from the inside out. There are a few trees which are "endogenous," or inward-growing. These are the palm, yucca and bamboo, all of which grow in southern countries, principally in the tropical region. They have little value in this country except for novelty furniture and, when shredded into cane, for chair seats, etc.

CHAPTER II

Woodworking Tools

7. Classification. Practically all woodworking tools are listed below under a classification based on use (Figs. 3, 4, 5, 6 and 7). The particular use of each tool is explained in

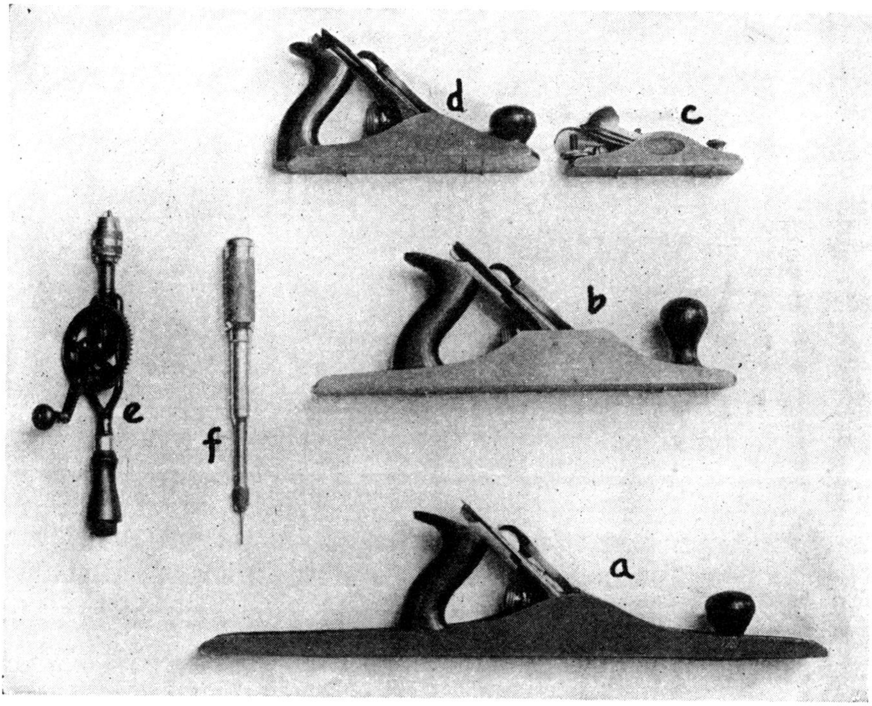

Fig. 3. *a*, jointer plane; *b*, jack plane; *c*, block plane; *d*, smooth plane; *e*, hand drill; *f*, automatic drill.

the instructions given for the several projects. It is believed that one will learn best how to use a tool by actually using it in making something of material value.

Dividing Tools: Planes (jack, smooth, block, jointer, rabbet, moulding, tongue and groove, router),
Chisels (firmer, paring, framing, mortise),
Saws (rip, crosscut, back, turning, compass, dovetail),
Knife,

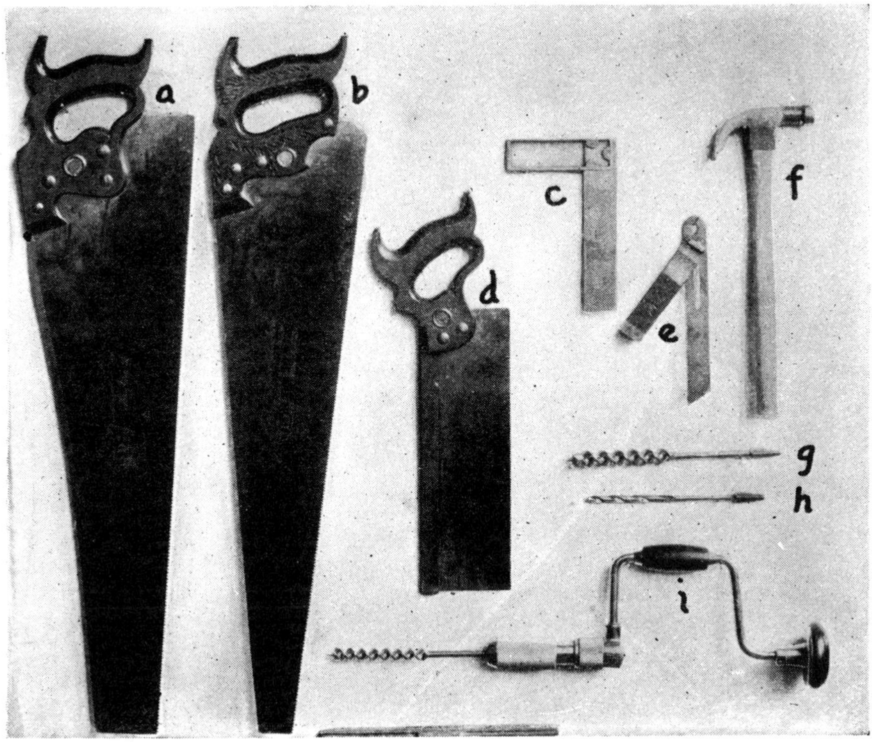

FIG. 4. *a*, rip-saw; *b*, crosscut-saw; *c*, try-square; *d*, jig-saw; *e*, bevel square; *f*, hammer; *g*, auger bit; *h*, drill bit; *i*, brace and bit.

Ax,
Wedge,
Draw-knife,
Spoke-shave.

Boring Tools: Bits (auger, center, Forstner, expansive),
Drills (single- and double-cut),
Gimlet,
Brad-awl,

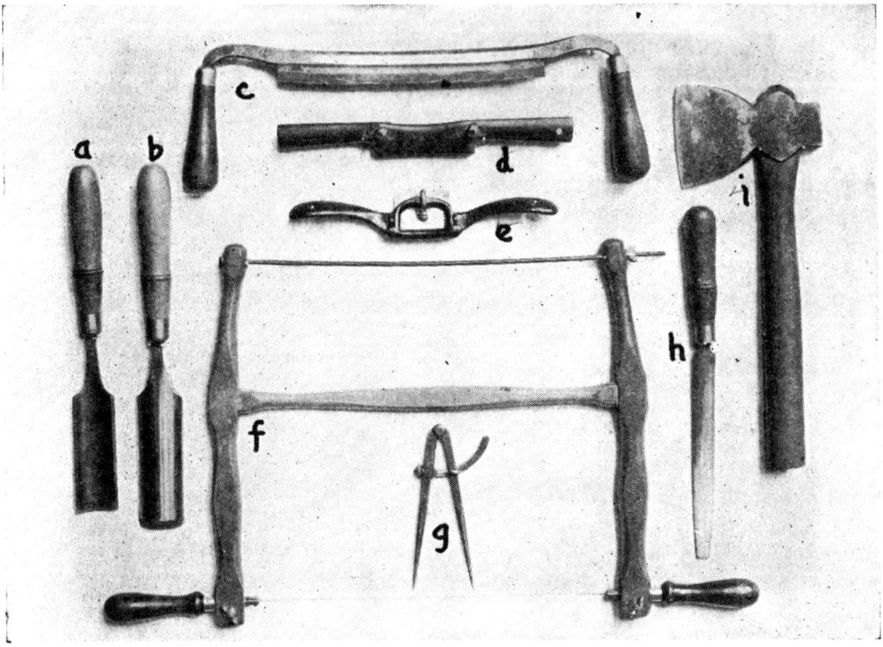

FIG. 5. *a*, gouge (inside ground); *b*, gouge (outside ground); *c*, draw-knife; *d*, spoke-shave; *e*, spoke-shave; *f*, turning-saw; *g*, compass; *h*, wood rasp; *i*, hatchet.

Reamer,
Countersink.

Chopping Tools: Ax,
Hatchet,
Adz.

Scraping Tools: Scraper,
Rasp,
Files (single-cut, blunt, flat, bastard, double-cut, taper, half-round).

Pounding Tools: Hammers (claw, upholsterer's, riveting, veneering),
Mallet,
Nailset.

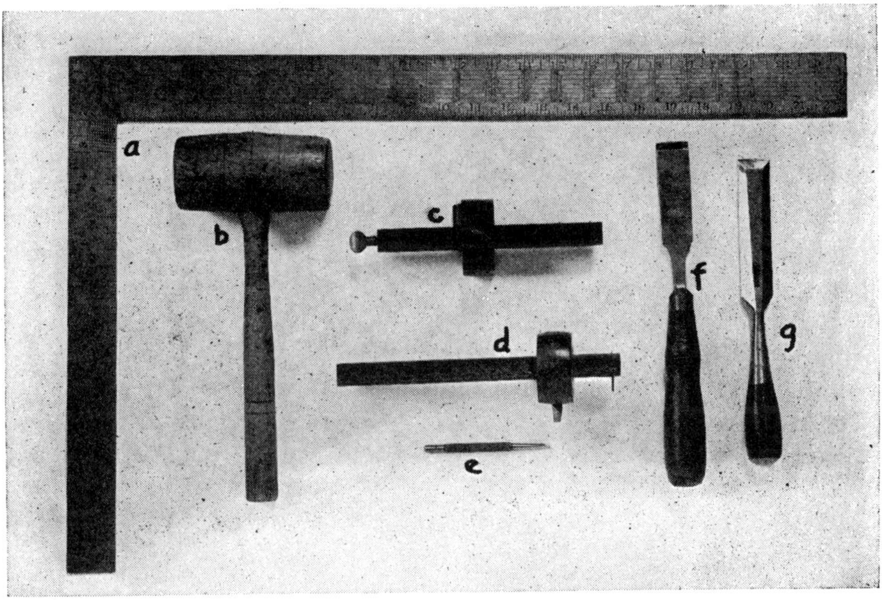

FIG. 6. *a*, carpenter's square; *b*, mallet; *c*, mortise gage; *d*, marking gage; *e*, nailset; *f*, tang chisel; *g*, socket chisel.

Holding Tools: Bench,
Vise,
Saw-horse,
Bench-hook,
Handscrew,
Carpenter's clamps,
Pliers (end-cutting, side-cutting),
Pinchers (nippers),
Bit-brace.

Measuring and Marking Tools: Carpenter's square,
Rule (two-foot, steel or scale),
Try-square,
Bevel square,
Marking gage,
Compass.

FIG. 7. Woodworking bench with the tool rack.

Sharpening Tools: Grindstone,
Grinder,
Slip stone,
Oilstone,
Saw-filing machine.

Cleaning Tools: Broom,
Brush,
Buffer.

CHAPTER III

Saws and Sawing

Suggested Projects:

a) Garden marker (Fig. 8).
b) Flower trellis (Fig. 9).
c) Window stick (Fig. 10).
d) Buggy axle rest (Fig. 11).
e) Peck crate (Figs. 12, 13, 14).

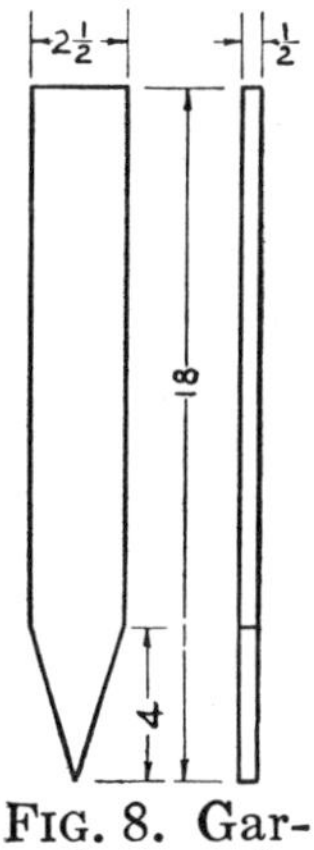

FIG. 8. Garden marker.

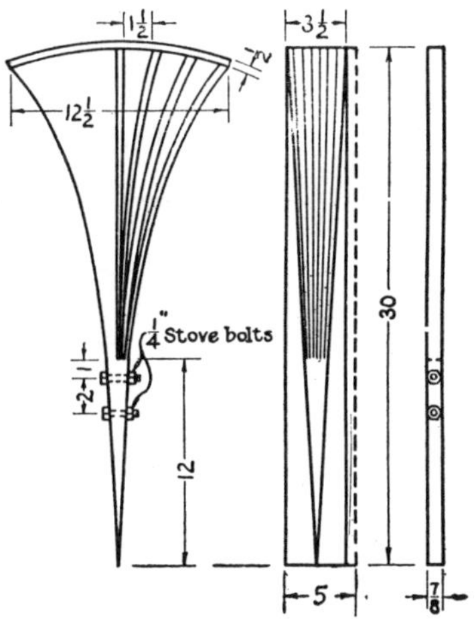

FIG. 9. Flower trellis.

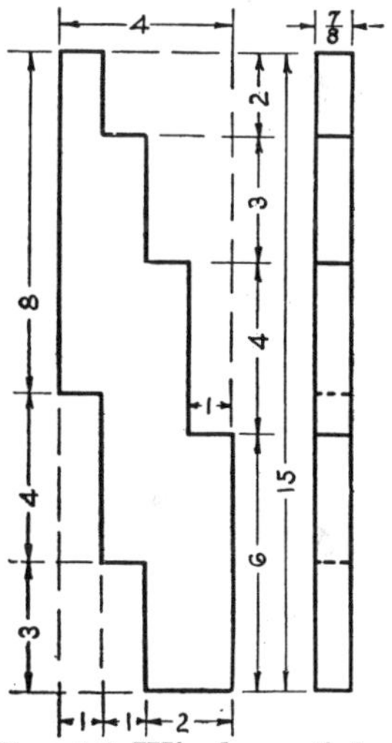

FIG. 10. Window stick.

8. Saws Used. The tools emphasized in this group are the crosscut-saw and rip-saw. Auxiliary tools are the hammer, brace and bit, bevel square, try-square and marking gage.

While there are many saws which constitute a complete equipment, as indicated in the classification of woodworking tools (Sec. 7), there are three only which are used generally —the crosscut-, rip- and back-saws.

9. Rip-saws. The formation of the teeth on a rip-saw is shown in Fig. 15. This saw cuts *with* the grain and, conse-

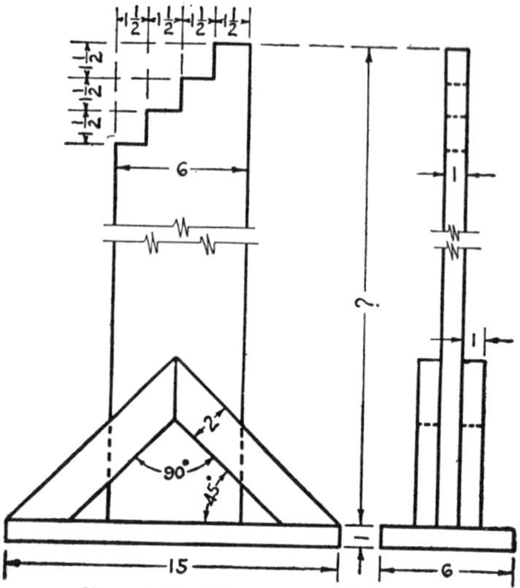

FIG. 11. Buggy axle rest.

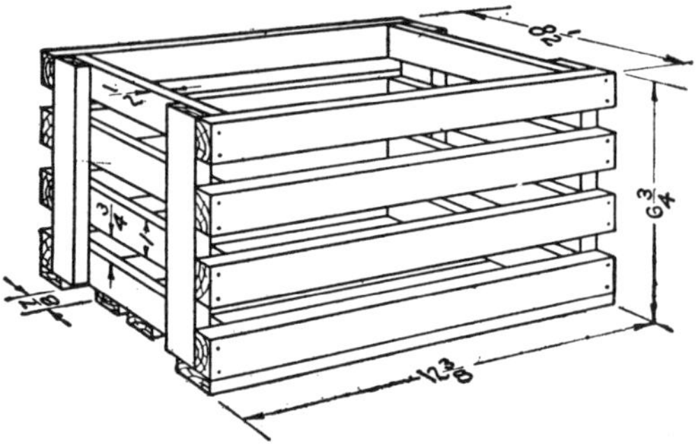

FIG. 12. Peck crate.

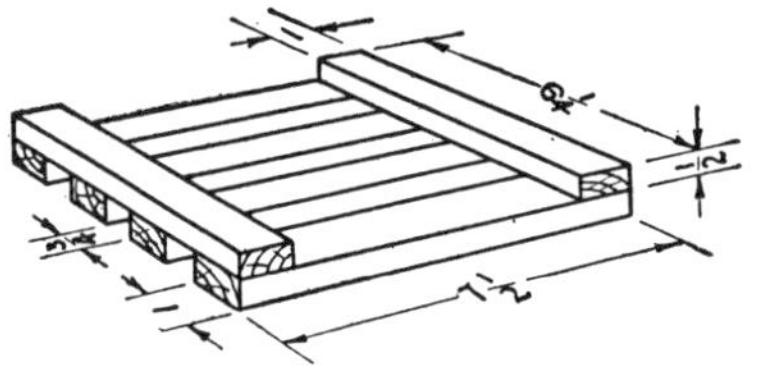

FIG. 13. End of peck crate.

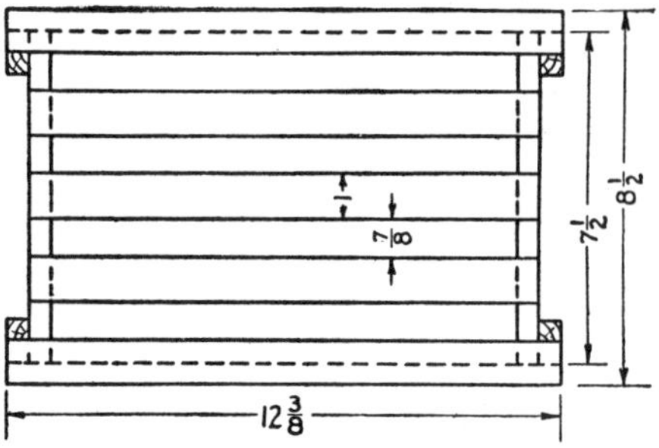

FIG. 14. Bottom of peck crate.

quently, cuts off the ends of the wood fiber (Fig. 16). The teeth, filed squarely across the saw-blade, form a series of chisels. Alternate teeth are set to one side of the blade, one series being set one way and the alternate series the other way (Fig. 15). The saw-blade is thus made thicker on the tooth edge of the blade than elsewhere, permitting the saw to pass thru the wood without binding while it makes its cut, or "kerf".

The back-saw is a combination of the rip and crosscut in tooth formation, and is used for cutting either with or across the grain, particularly where fine sawing is required, as in the making of joints.

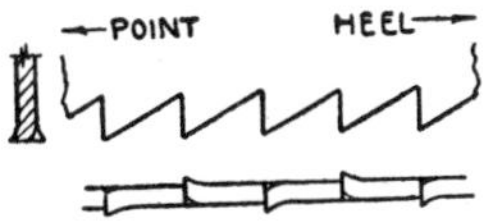

FIG. 15. Shape of rip-saw teeth.

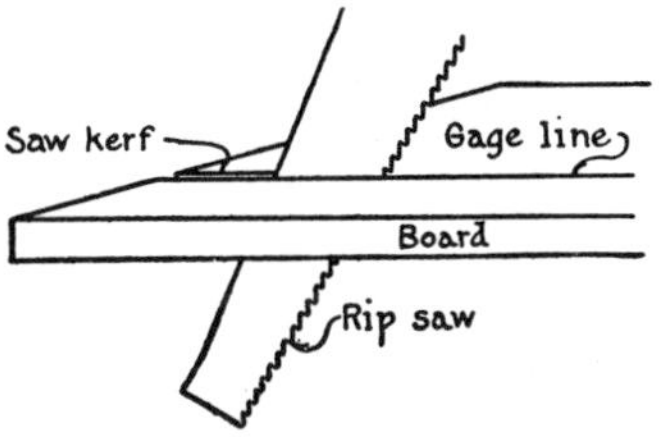

FIG. 16. Position of rip-saw in action.

10. Crosscut-saws. The teeth of a crosscut-saw are filed on both the front and back edges at an angle with the surface of the saw-blade (Fig. 17). This saw cuts *across* the grain, and does its work as it makes its forward stroke. The

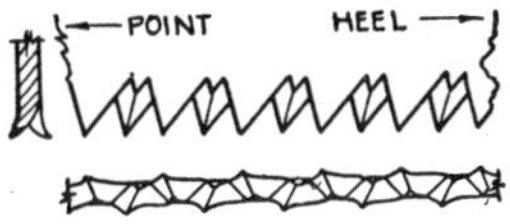

FIG. 17. Shape of crosscut-saw teeth.

saw is "set" by pushing all teeth outward from the sides which are filed. This results, as in the case of the rip-saw, in forming two series of teeth, those of one series being pushed toward one side of the blade, and those of the other in the opposite direction (Fig. 17).

Working Instructions for Flower Trellis.

Stock: 1 piece, 1″ x 5″ x 32″.

Soft, straight-grained wood. (Drawing, Fig. 9.)

11. Rip-sawing. The chief tool exercise in this project is rip-sawing. It is more difficult to make a series of parallel rip-saw cuts than to make an individual one. In this project, the cuts must be made with great care, that one fan strip may not be weakened more than another. The guide lines must be followed accurately.

FIG. 18. Correct position when using rip-saw.

There is a possible element of difficulty in sawing each edge of the trellis stock to a taper. The saw must run at an angle with the grain. The piece should be placed in the vise with the end that goes in the ground at the top, and the taper line to be followed by the saw must be in a vertical position (Fig. 18). The saw should run just outside the line in the waste stock.

12. Squaring and Measuring for Length. Select the best surface (*1*) and the best edge (*2*), as in Fig. 19. With the try-square blade on one face, called the face side, and its beam on one edge, called the joint edge, square a line across the face side near one end (Fig. 19).

With the beam of the try-square on the face side and the blade on the joint edge, run the try-square with the left hand toward the end of the line squared across the face side until the blade touches the blade of the knife held in the right hand, the point of the knife-blade being on the end of this squared line. With the try-square in this position, square a line across the joint edge (Fig. 20).

Measure the board for length from the squared line on the face side and mark a point with the end of the knife-blade

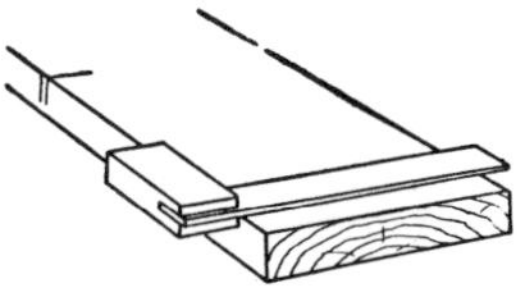

FIG. 19. Position of try-square when squaring face side.

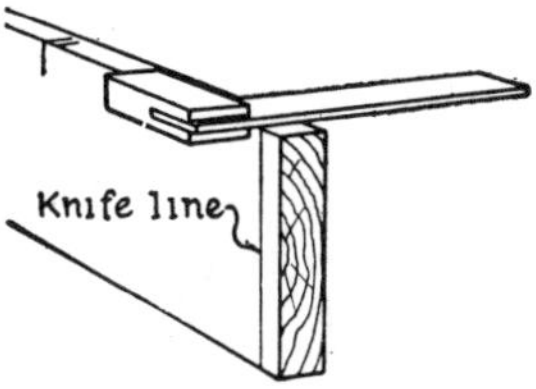

FIG. 20. Position of try-square when squaring edge.

(Fig. 21). Using the try-square as just described and holding the end of the knife-blade in this point, bring the square up to the knife, square a line across the face side, and then, as on the

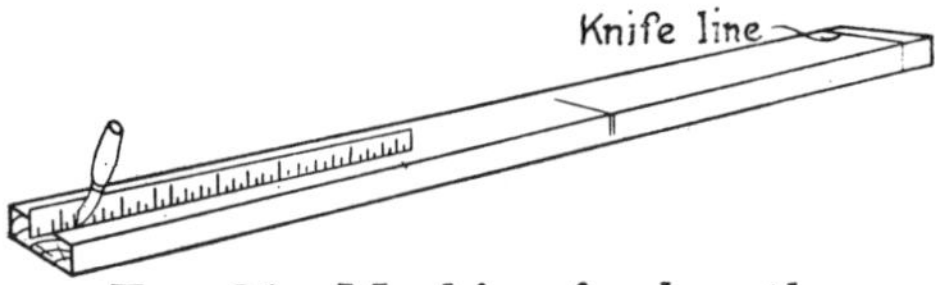

FIG. 21. Marking for length.

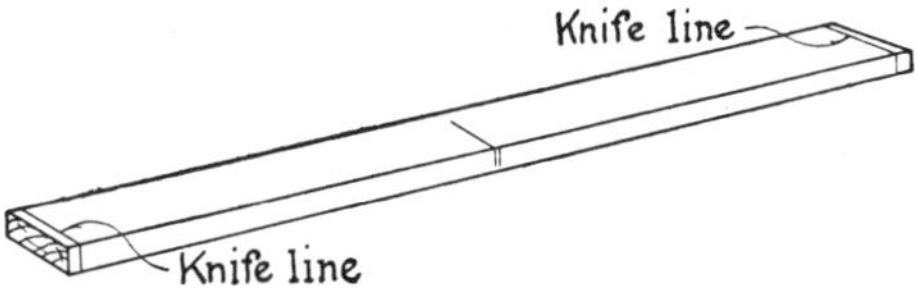

FIG. 22. Board marked for length.

first end, across the joint edge. The board is now marked for length (Fig. 22).

13. Gaging for Width. Gage two lines on the face side —one 3-1/2″ and the other 4″ from the joint edge.

Set the marking gage so that the width of the board is indicated by the distance from the marker to the stop (Fig. 23). This distance should be measured with a ruler before using the gage (Fig. 24). Inspect the marker before setting the gage to see that it protrudes from the beam of the gage about 1/32″ and that it is filed to a knife edge parallel to the surface of the stop (Fig. 25).

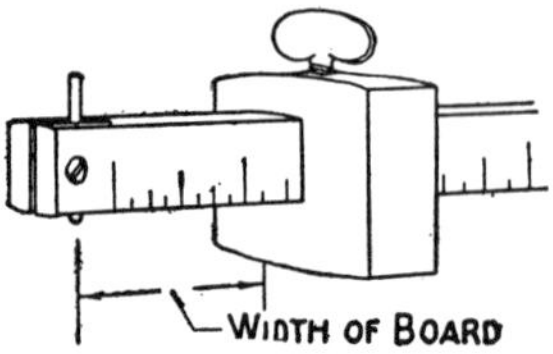

FIG. 23. Setting the marking gage.

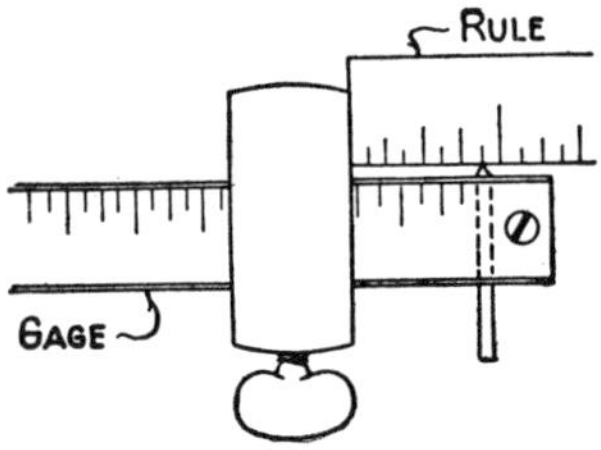

FIG. 24. Testing gage with rule.

Hold the gage on the face side of the wood with the head against the joint edge (Fig. 26), and run the gage from the end of the wood nearest you to the far end, which, in the case of a

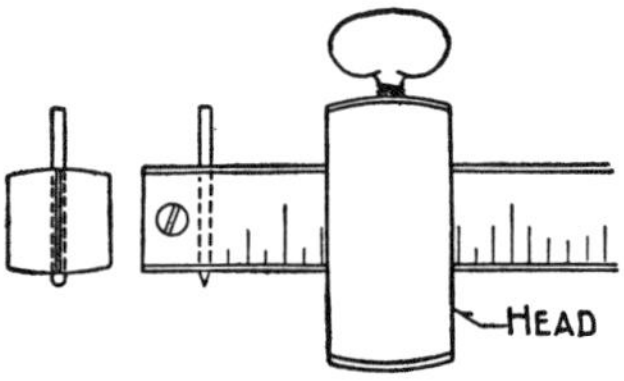

FIG. 25. Correct shape of point of marking gage.

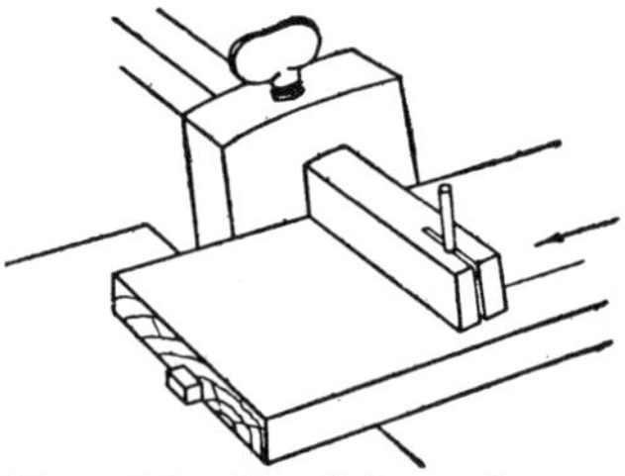

FIG. 26. Position of gage when marking on wide boards.

long piece, may be rested on the bench (Fig. 27). The relative position of the gage and the wood is shown in Fig. 28.

Do not roll the gage as it is pushed over the surface of the wood, as this will make the marker run too deeply into the wood.

The board is now marked for width (3-1/2″), with another mark to guide the rip-saw in its first cut, and to provide a 1/2″ strip along the edge of the board to be used in fastening the fan strips on the end of the trellis (Fig. 29).

14. Marking Fan Strips. Lay off six points on the fan end of the board, 1/2″ apart. Do this by laying the graduated edge of the ruler across the end of the board on the face side, with the end of the ruler against the joint edge and the graduated edge on the squared knife line, and making a point with a sharp pencil at each 1/2″ graduation mark on the ruler (Fig. 30).

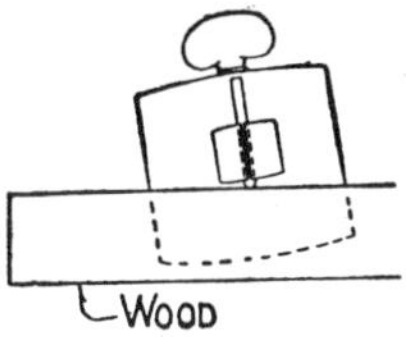

FIG. 28. The correct angle for position of gage.

FIG. 27. Correct method of holding gage and stock.

With a straight edge, connect each one of these points with the center point of the 3-1/2″ strip on the other end of the board. The outside lines only need be drawn the full length.

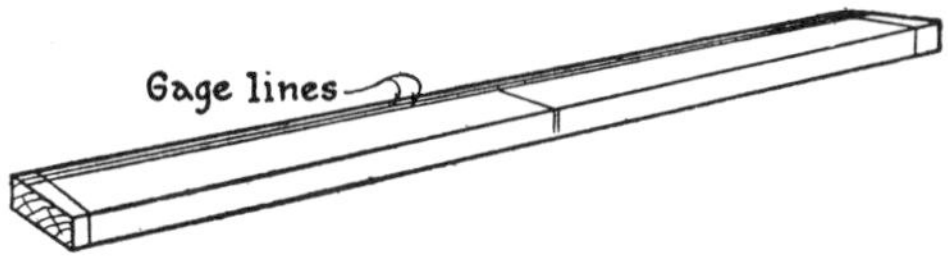

FIG. 29. The board after gage lines have been drawn.

FIG. 30. Measuring for fan strips.

All others should be drawn a distance equal to the depth of the saw cuts for the fan strips (Fig. 31). The bottom of these cuts should be located by a squared pencil line across the face side of the board, as should the position of the center line of each of the bolt holes (Fig. 32).

15. Boring Holes. Place the board edge up in the vise. With a 5/16″ auger-bit in the bit-brace, stand squarely before the board, placed horizontally edgewise in bench vise, with spur of bit on center for one of the holes to be bored for bolts and with bit in a vertical position (Fig. 33). This position may be tested by the use of the try-square (Fig. 34). With left hand on knob and right hand grasping the handle, turn the handle clockwise until about one-half of the hole is bored. Repeat this operation in boring the second hole. Reverse the board in the vise and bore the second half of each hole. Great care must be taken to make all borings straight to secure holes without shoulders near the center.

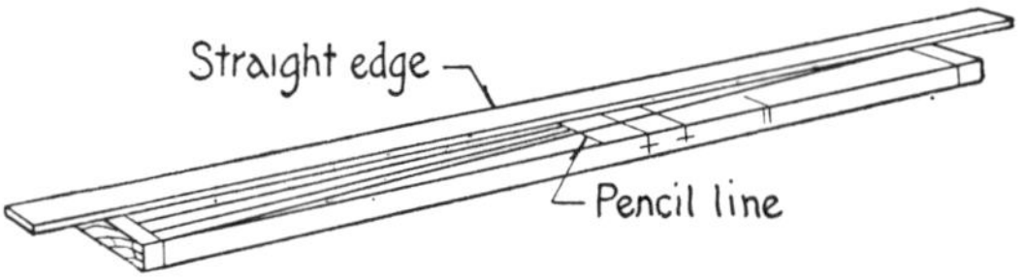

FIG. 31. Laying out rip-saw cuts.

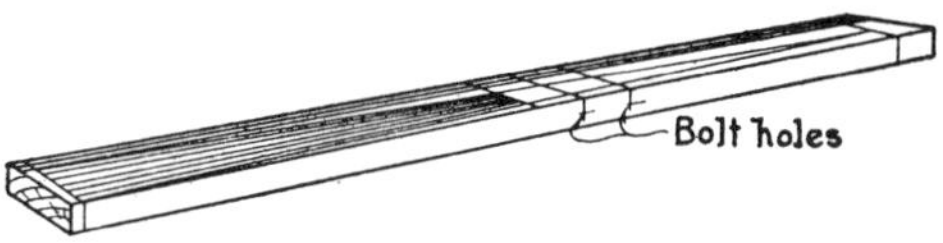

FIG. 32. The board marked for bolt holes.

16. Sawing Ends. The saw works at an angle to the surface of the board (Fig. 35). The strokes are taken the length of the saw without exerting more pressure than to guide the saw. The squared line on the face side should be touched by the saw as it goes across the surface (Fig. 35). The squared line on the joint edge should be touched by the saw as it finishes its cut thru the board. In a similar manner saw to the squared lines on the other end of the board.

When sawing, place the board on the top of wooden horse with its end projecting over the end of the horse and with face side up and joint edge toward operator (Fig. 36.) Hold the stock with left knee and left hand, allowing thumb of left hand to guide the saw when beginning the cut. The first stroke should be upward. Very little pressure is used in downward strokes, and none in upward strokes.

17. **Ripping Off One-half-Inch Strip.** Place the board with long dimension vertical in the vise. Have the gage lines

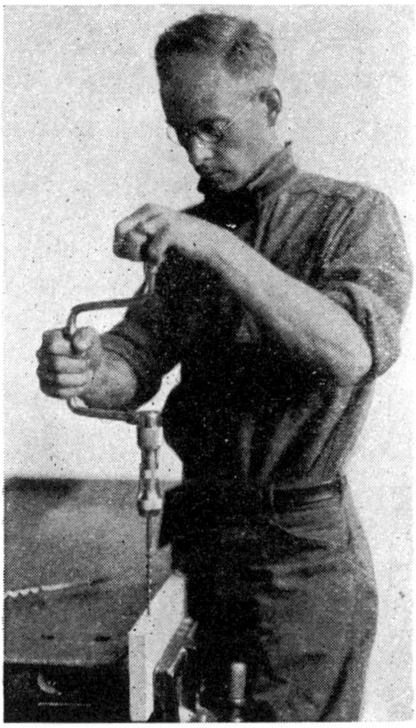

FIG. 33. Correct method of using auger bit.

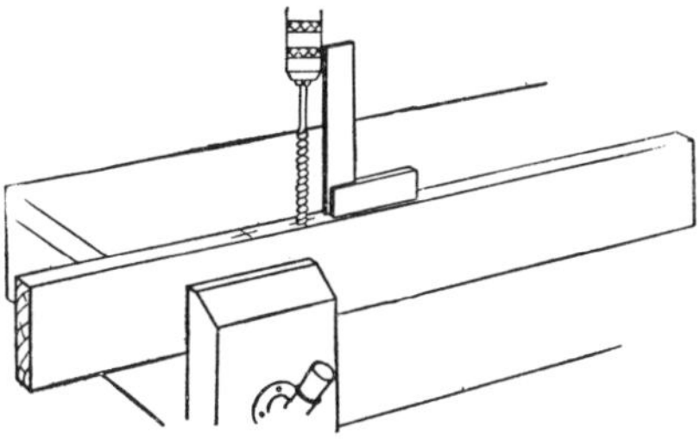

FIG. 34. Testing for squareness when boring.

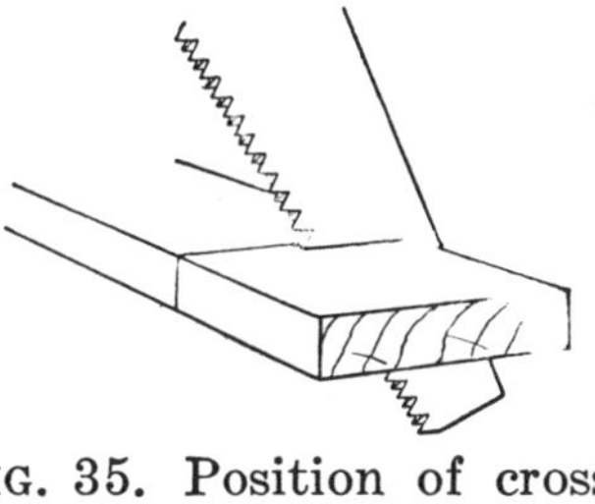

FIG. 35. Position of cross-cut-saw when cutting.

FIG. 36. Correct position of operator using a crosscut-saw.

3-1/2″ and 4″ from the joint edge beyond the end of the bench (Fig. 37). Stand squarely in front of the board with right hand grasping the handle of the rip-saw (Fig. 18), allowing the index finger to rest on the side of the handle. Grasp the upper left-hand corner of the board with the thumb and the first two fingers of the left hand, stand in a bracing position, and place the saw on the upper end of the board in a position to draw it toward you. Pull the saw slightly downward without pressure and guide it against the thumb of the left hand. Make the stroke approximately the length of the saw blade. In a similar manner push the saw from you, slightly upward. Continue this backward and forward motion, gradually bringing the saw to a horizontal position, or nearly at right angles with the surface of the board. The saw should always be cutting so that the angle formed between the cutting edge and the board on the operator's side is less than 90 degrees. In this manner saw on the outside of the vertical gage lines on the left (Fig. 37) in sawing to the 3-1/2″ and 4″ gage lines.

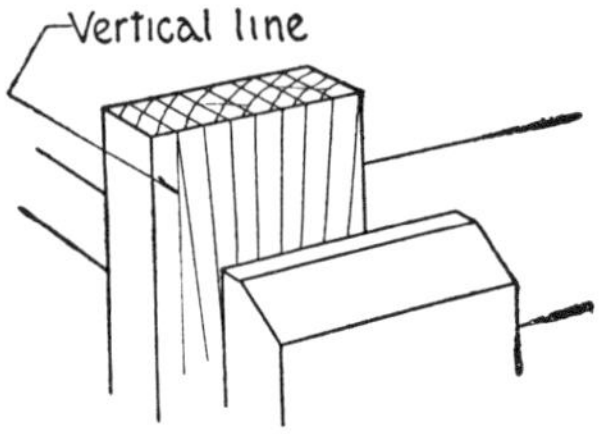

FIG. 37. Stock put in vise for rip-sawing.

18. Ripping Tapered Edges. Place the board vertically in the vise with fan end downward and marked surface toward the front. One of the lines indicating a tapered edge of the trellis must be vertical (Fig. 38). Saw to this line in waste stock, leaving a sufficient amount of stock to plane finished edge on the board. Reset the board in the vise so that the second line making a tapered edge is vertical. Saw to this line as to the first one.

FIG. 38. Rip-sawing at an angle over the grain.

19. Ripping for Fan Strip. Place the board vertically in the vise and carefully saw *on* each line, marking the dividing line between two fan strips so that one-half of the kerf is taken on each side of the line. The end of each of these cuts must be square with the surface of the board, and must be exactly on the pencil line which limits these cuts.

All sawing on the board is now completed. Plane the two tapered edges and the back of the board.

To secure a definite thickness, the board may be gaged for thickness on finished tapered edges before the back of the board is planed.

Insert a stove bolt in each of the holes bored, and fasten in position with a washer under both the head of the bolt and the nut.

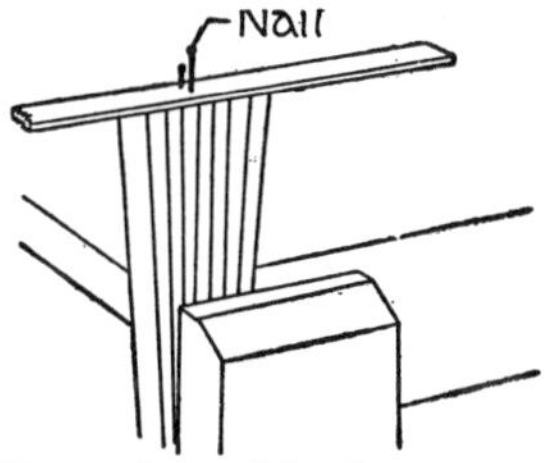

FIG. 39. Nailing the trellis.

Plane the strip which was first sawed from the edge of the board. Saw off 12-1/2″ of it, being certain that each end is square. With try-square and sharp pencil, mark a center cross-line on one edge of the strip. This line locates the center position for the end of the middle fan strip. Similarly on this supporting strip locate the center position for each of the other fan strips. With this line at the center of the middle fan strip and with trellis in natural position in the vise, nail the strip to this middle fan strip at the center of its end with two 1″ brads, each about 3/16″ from the outer surface of the trellis (Fig. 39).

Carefully bend each of the outside fan strips to its proper position, and fasten it with two brads as in the case of the middle fan strip. In like manner, fasten each of the other strips. This work must be done with great care to avoid splitting either the supporting or any one of the fan strips. A wise precaution against such an accident is to bore holes with a brad-awl for each of the nail holes.

Supplementary Instructions.

20. The Buggy Axle Rest and the Measuring Crate require the use of tools not described in instructions for the flower trellis.

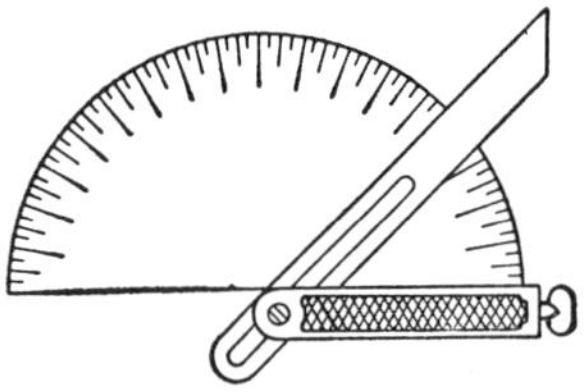

FIG. 40. Bevel square used with a protractor.

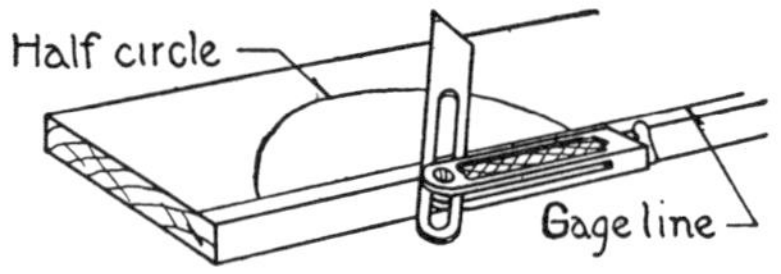

FIG. 41. Bevel square used in geometric construction.

21. The Bevel Square, which is used to lay off the angles of the ends of the braces in the buggy axle rest, is shown in Fig. 4. It has an adjustable blade. It may be set by placing it upon a protractor, as shown in Fig. 40, or for the more com-

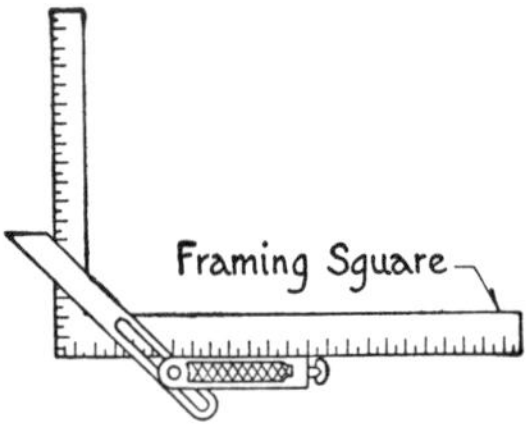

FIG. 42. Setting bevel square to an angle of 45°.

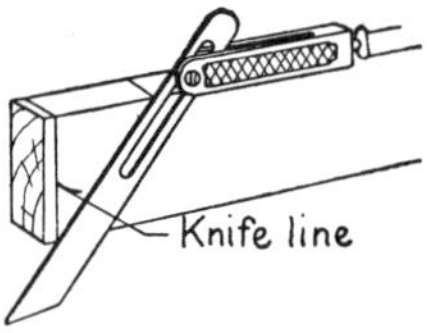

FIG. 43. Laying out with bevel square.

mon angles, it may be set on the edge of a board with a geometrical construction made near this edge with compass and straight-edge, as shown in Fig. 41. The angle of 45 degrees is easily secured by placing the edge of the bevel-square blade thru two equal graduations on the sides of a carpenter square, as shown in Fig. 42. A bevel angle should be laid off with a bevel-square, much as a right angle is with a try-square.

Each end of the brace in the buggy axle rest should be completely defined by making bevel-square lines on edges and try-square lines on broad surfaces (Fig. 43).

22. Nailing. The nailing exercise is the principal one in the construction of the measuring crate, aside from the use of the try-square and crosscut-saw, as it is assumed that lath or strips dressed to dimensions will be used as stock.

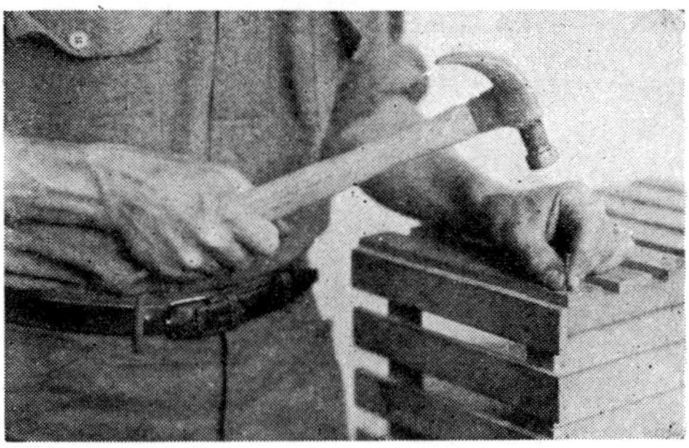

FIG. 44. Proper use of hammer.

The hammer should be grasped in the right hand near the end of the handle and swung freely from the elbow in a vertical plane with but slight wrist and shoulder movement. The thumb and finger of the left hand should hold the nail (Fig. 44).

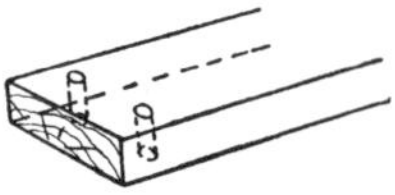

FIG. 45. Jig for nailing.

Where a good many operations are repeated, it is often well to use a form, or jig, to secure uniform results and to avoid waste of time in unnecessary preliminaries in making each individual operation.

Fig. 45 shows jig which might be used in locating and driving nails when fastening crate strips on corners. The holes are sufficiently large so that when the jig is placed over the end of a crate strip in position to nail, and the nail is driven thru the jig hole, the jig may be lifted off, the head of the nail being smaller than the hole in the jig.

CHAPTER IV

PLANES AND PLANING

Suggested Projects:

a) Scouring board for kitchen (Fig. 46).
b) Bread-cutting board (Fig. 47).
c) Bulletin board to hang on wall (Fig. 48).
d) Bill board for filing meat and grocery bills (Fig. 49).
e) Swing board (Fig. 50).
f) Rope wind (Fig. 51).

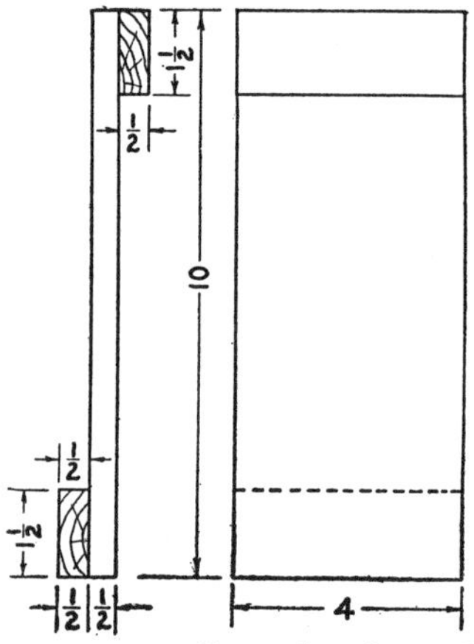

FIG. 46. Scouring board.

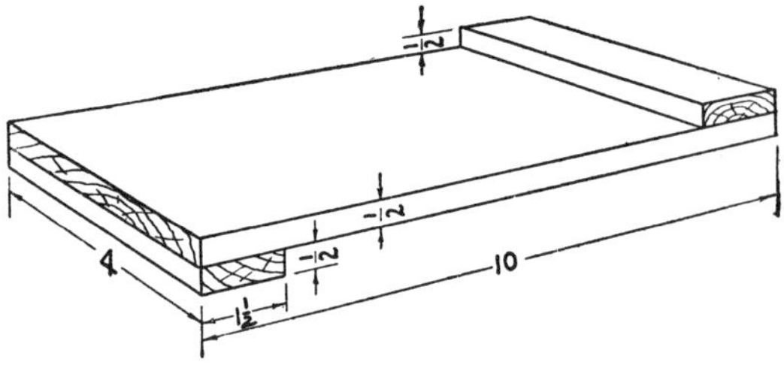

The tool chiefly emphasized in this group of projects is the plane. Other tools needed are the *try-square, ruler, marking gage, crosscut-saw, rip-saw* and, for some of the projects, the *hammer* or *bit* and *bit-brace.*

23. The Plane. There are four principal planes used in a woodworker's kit. They are the jointer, jack, smooth and block. It is not necessary to have all of these in order to do satisfactory work. The jack plane (Fig. 52) shows the plane and its parts.

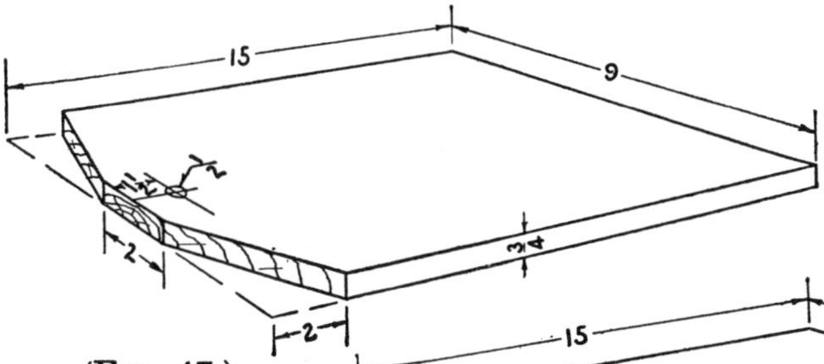

(FIG. 47.)

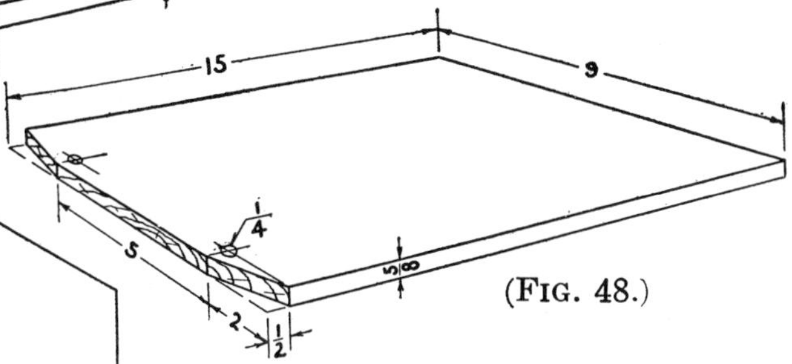

(FIG. 48.)

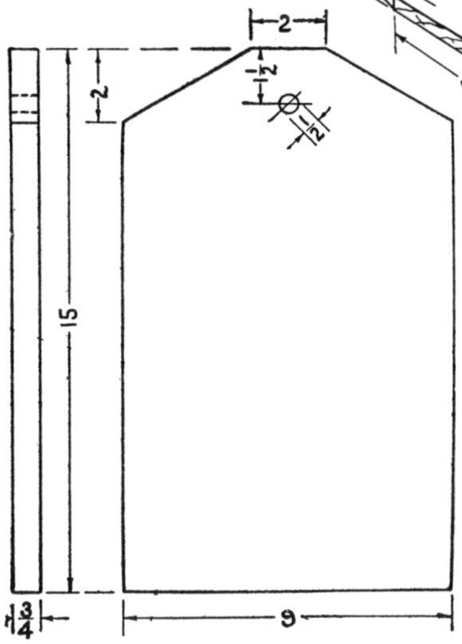

FIG. 47. Bread-cutting board.

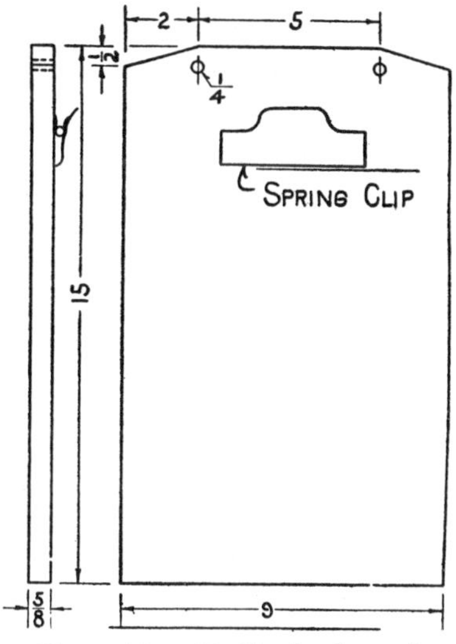

FIG. 48. Bulletin board.

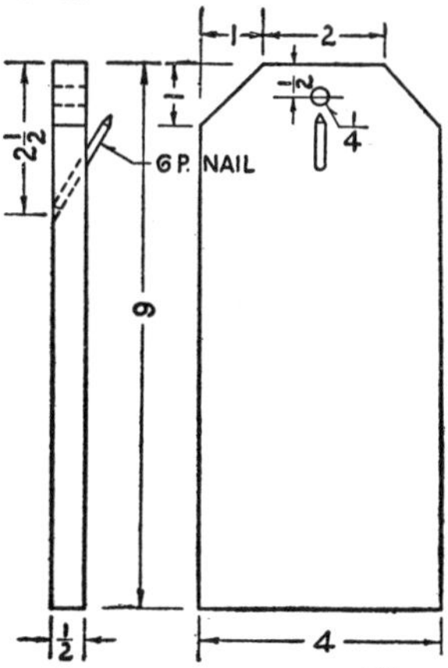

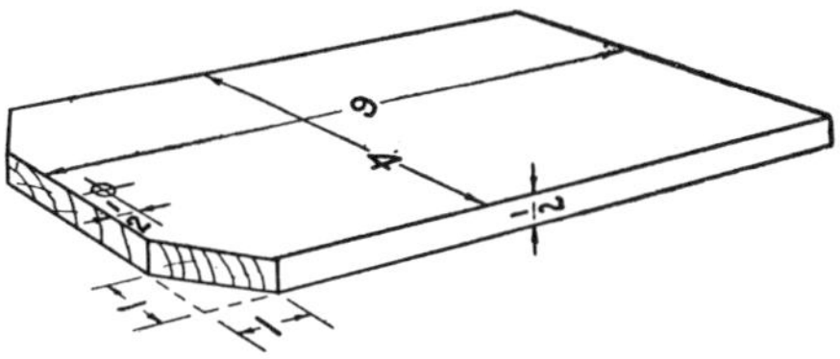

FIG. 49. Bill board.

24. Care of the Plane. The plane-iron must be kept sharp. Grind it when it is very dull or nicked; otherwise, whet it on an oilstone. Fig. 53 gives the position of the plane-iron on a grindstone as held by the operator. Fig. 54 shows the position of the plane-iron on the oilstone as held by the operator.

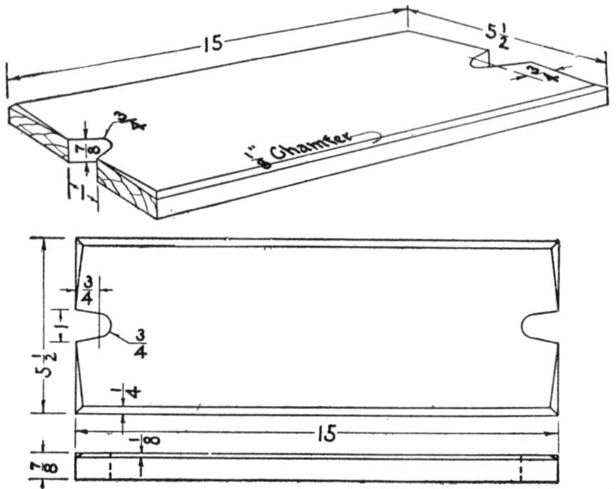

FIG. 50. Swing board.

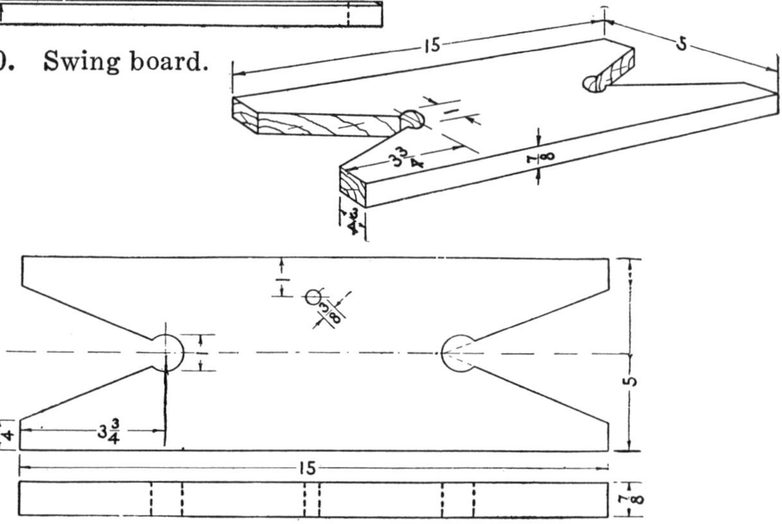

FIG. 51. Rope wind.

25. Grinding the Plane-Iron. To grind the plane-iron, hold it steady and at such an angle that the proper bevel will be secured. Move it back and forth sideways to account for any unevenness in the stone, but do not raise or lower it.

26. Whetting the Plane-Iron. To whet the plane-iron, hold it so that the bevel formed by the grindstone will be in contact with the oilstone. Use a circular motion in whet-

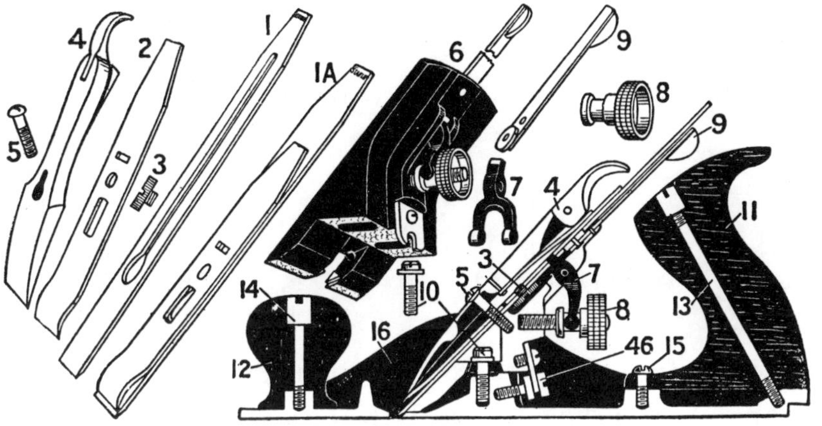

FIG. 52. Parts of jack plane:

1A Double plane-iron.
1 Single plane-iron.
2 Plane-iron cap.
3 Cap screw.
4 Lever cap.
5 Lever cap screw.
6 Frog, complete.
7 "Y" adjusting lever.
8 Adjusting nut.
9 Lateral adj. lever.
10 Frog screw.
11 Plane handle.
12 Plane knob.
13 Handle bolt & nut.
14 Knob bolt & nut.
15 Plane handle screw.
16 Plane bottom.
46 Frog adj. screw.

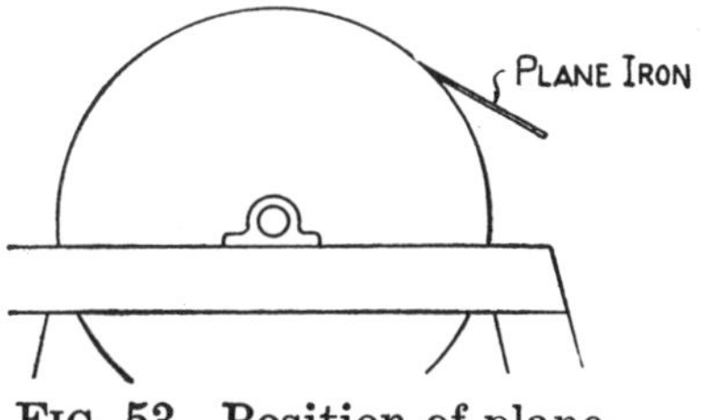

FIG. 53. Position of plane-iron on the grindstone.

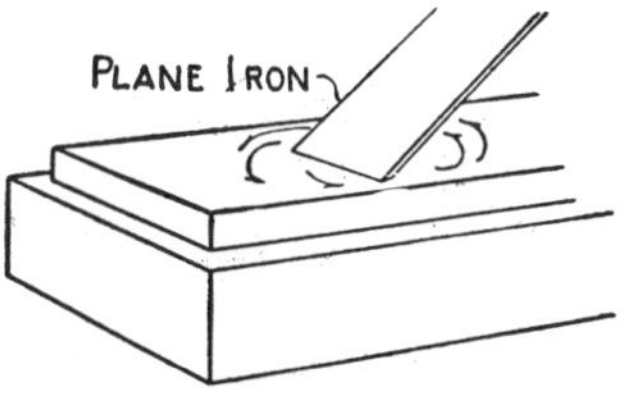

FIG. 54. Position of plane-iron on the oilstone.

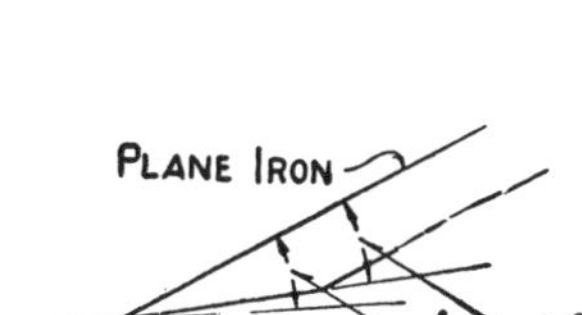

FIG. 55. Difference in angles for grinding and for whetting.

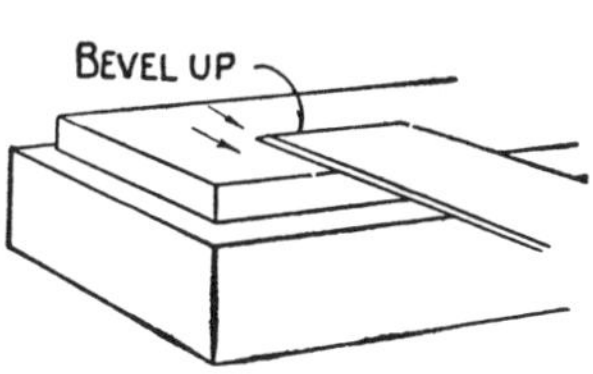

FIG. 56. Whetting the face side of plane-iron.

ting (Fig. 54). Finally, raise the hands, slightly continuing this motion. This will tend to create a whetted bevel made slightly at an angle with the ground bevel (Fig. 55). The plane-iron should be held in this position for a few moments only, when it may be reversed, laid flat on the top of the stone and given a few circular strokes (Fig. 56).

FIG. 57. Shape of cutting edge for general use.

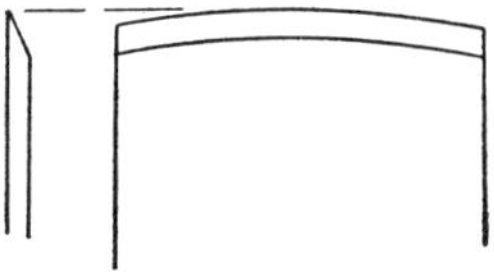

FIG. 58. Shape of cutting edge for jack plane.

The irons for all planes except the jack should be ground at right angles with the edge, with the corners rounded (Fig. 57).

The plane-iron for the jack plane, if used principally as a roughing plane, should be ground rounding on the edge as in Fig. 58. When used as the only plane in a kit, it should be ground very slightly rounding, if at all. The angle for grinding, except when a plane is used exclusively for very hard wood, should be approximately 20 degrees. The whetted bevel should make approximately 5 degrees with the ground bevel (Fig. 55).

FIG. 59. Correct way of holding the plane.

27. Care of Plane. In order to protect the edge of the plane-iron, lay the plane on its side when not in use. Fig. 7 shows the plane and other tools in position on a carpenter's bench, which is a very satisfactory kind to use on the farm.

28. Use of the Plane. To use a plane, the operator stands in front of the bench in a bracing position, the left foot in front of the right and the body turned slightly toward the bench.

Note that the handle of the plane is grasped with the right hand, with the fingers and thumb wrapped about the handle. The palm of the left hand is placed on the knob of the plane (Fig. 59).

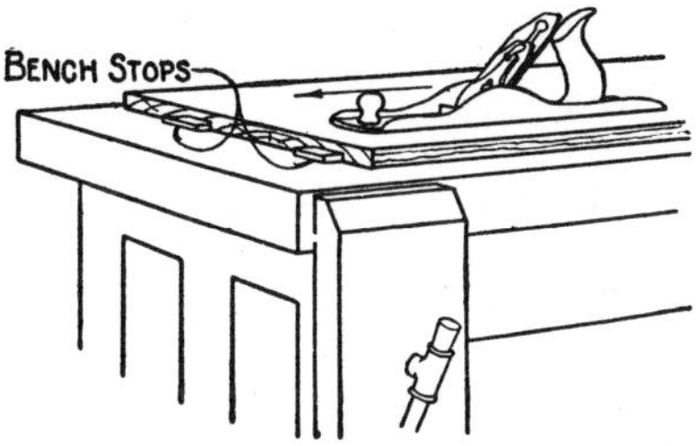

FIG. 60. Planing a wide board.

The plane is placed upon the board so that its bottom is in contact with the surface to be planed. The left hand presses the plane downward, and the right hand pushes it forward. When the plane bottom is fully in contact with the wood, both hands exert an equal pressure. As the plane projects over the end of the board in completing its stroke, the right hand exerts the pressure and the left hand merely serves to hold and guide the plane.

It is customary in planing a surface to begin the planing at the edge nearest the operator, and to finish at the opposite edge. However, if the board is warped or twisted, shavings must first be taken from the high surfaces to establish a flat and true surface. Then the finishing shavings should be taken as suggested.

Working Instructions for Swing Board:

Stock: 1 piece, 1″ x 6″ x 16″.

29. Face Side. Place the board flat upon the top of the bench with one end against the bench stop (Fig. 60). With the plane set to take a light shaving, proceed to surface the stock, as explained in Sec. 28. The planed surface should be tested with the blade of a try-square or other straight-edge, placed in several positions. When testing, place the blade of the try-square across the surface at different points. The amount of light shown between the board and the try-square blade will indicate the low places in the surface. Continue planing either by taking regular shavings across the board or by planing high places only until the straight-edge test shows approximately the same amount of light for all positions of the try-square. Mark this surface 1.

30. Joint Edge. Place the board in the vise with one edge up. Plane this edge until it tests straight lengthwise by the straight-edge test, and straight and at right angles with the face surface by using the try-square, as shown in Fig. 61. The try-square should be placed on the edge at several points, always having the beam of the square against the face side. When edge tests are satisfactory, mark the planed edge 2.

FIG. 61. Testing edge with try-square.

31. Second Edge. Set the marking gage and gage for width of the board, using the method described in Sec. 13.

Plane the second edge of the board as you did the joint edge. Test frequently with the try-square, and keep the amount of wood to be planed off the same in thickness the entire length of the board. Remember, when the gage line is reached, planing must stop and the edge must be straight and square with the face side.

32. Second Surface. From the face side, gage the thickness of the board on both planed edges. Plane the second surface as you planed the first, testing frequently for straightness in width and length so that the surface will be true when the gage lines are reached.

33. First End. Place the board vertically in the vise. First from one edge and then the other, never allowing the plane to take a shaving completely across the end, plane the upper end of the board square with the face side and the joint edge (Fig. 62).

34. Second End. Measure the board for length, and square across the face side and joint edge with knife and try-square. (See Sec. 12 for instructions on sawing and squaring.) Plane the second end according to the directions for planing the first end.

FIG. 62. Planing the end.

Note: The face side, joint edge and first end are surfaces from which all measurements must be taken in securing the dimensions of a board or in making surface measurements.

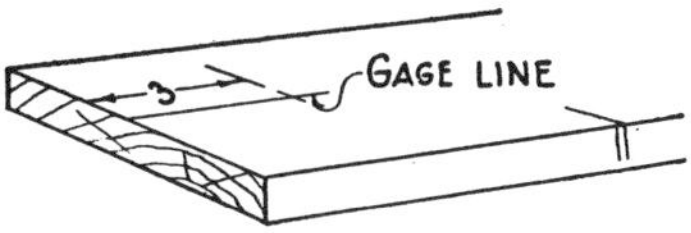

FIG. 63. Layout for boring.

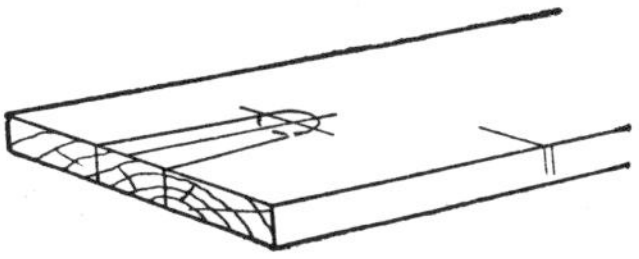

FIG. 64. Lines for rip-sawing.

35. Boring Holes for Rope. With marking gage, make a short, light center line on face side of board from each end thru a point 3″ from each end (Fig. 63). By the use of the try-square and knife, cross each of these center lines with a short knife line at right angles to the joint edge (Fig. 64).

With 3/4″ auger-bit and brace, bore the two holes for the rope, as shown in Fig. 65. A piece of board must be placed on the back of the swing board, opposite the auger-bit, to prevent splintering the fibers of the wood in the swing board, or, the stock must be reversed in the vise as soon as the spur protrudes on the back side of the swing board so that the hole may be finished from the opposite side.

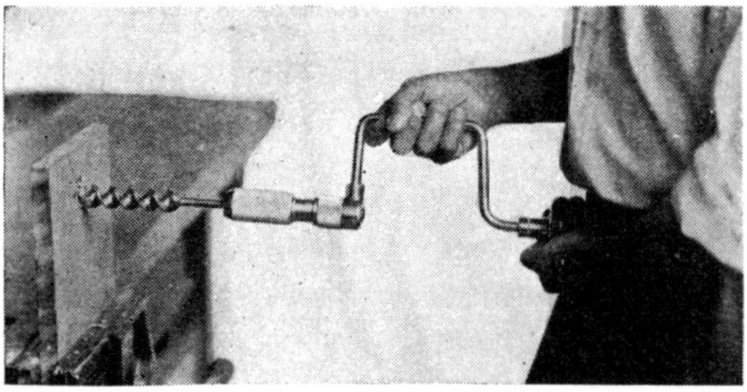

FIG. 65. Boring on broad side of stock.

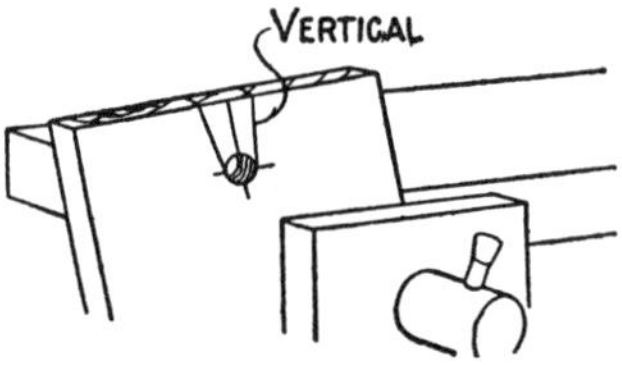

FIG. 66. Position of board for rip-sawing.

36. Sawing End Notches. On each end, measure 1″ in each direction of the center lines, square across the ends at these points and on the face side join the end of each of these lines with the corresponding side of the hole, to form tangents (Fig. 66).

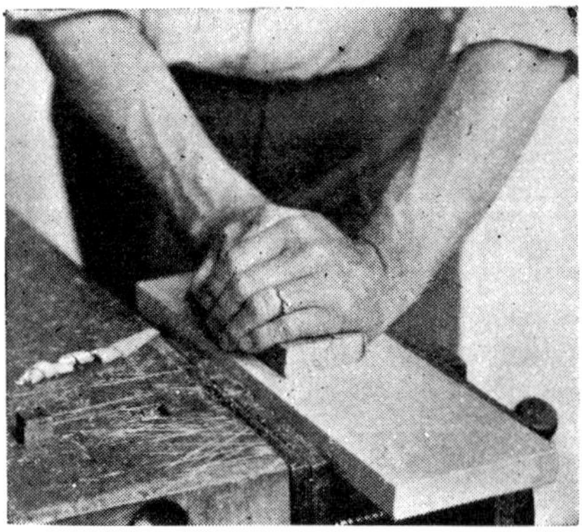

FIG. 67. Sandpapering.

Place the board in the vise so that one of these lines is in a vertical position (Fig. 66).

As previously instructed, saw to this line in waste stock with a rip-saw.

Sandpaper used over a block and run lengthwise of the grain may be used to smooth surfaces of the swing board and round edges slightly (Fig. 67).

Supplementary Instructions:

The "Working Instructions" for the swing board includes practically all those necessary for any one of the suggested projects in this group. However, in the bulletin board and bill board, the following suggestions should be made:

In cutting off the corners on each of these projects, you should work from the center line shown in Fig. 68. By measuring on each side of this line, one will be sure to make the end symmetrical. The lines drawn to show where the corners are to be cut should be drawn on the face side and from each end of these a line should be squared across the joint edge or end of board (Fig. 68).

FIG. 68. Layout for corner cuts.

FIG. 69. Use of hand drill.

To saw each of these lines, put board in vise so that line is in vertical position.

To insert bill-board stake at any particular point on the front of the board, drill or bore a hole slightly smaller than a ten-penny finishing nail thru the board from the front side, as suggested (Fig. 69). If a hand drill is not available, use bit and brace (Fig. 4).

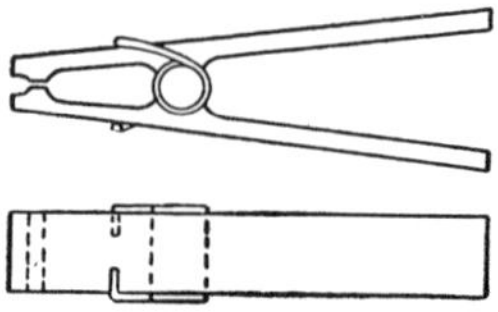

FIG. 70. Clothes pin which may be used with bulletin board.

From the back side of the board, drive thru the hole a ten-penny finishing nail and set the head under the surface of the board by the use of a nailset or second nail.

The bulletin board may be equipped either with a spring clip, as shown in Fig. 48, or with clothes pin (Fig. 70).

CHAPTER V

Estimating Materials; Constructing an Assembly Problem

Suggested Projects:

a) Wash bench (Fig. 71).

b) Chicken coop (Fig. 72).

c) Feed bin or wood-box (Fig. 73).

d) Shipping crate (Fig. 74).

e) Flower box (Fig. 75).

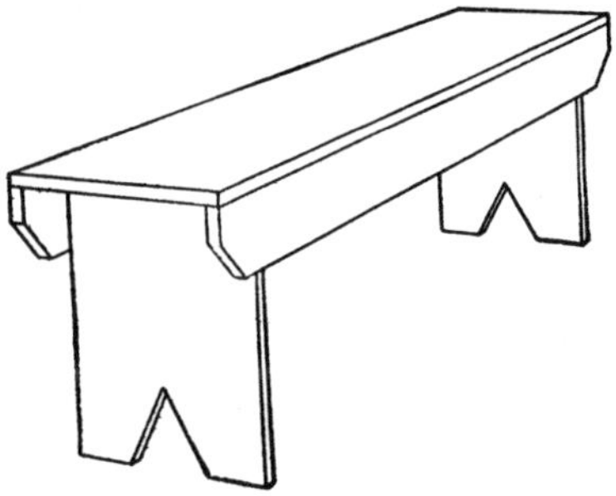

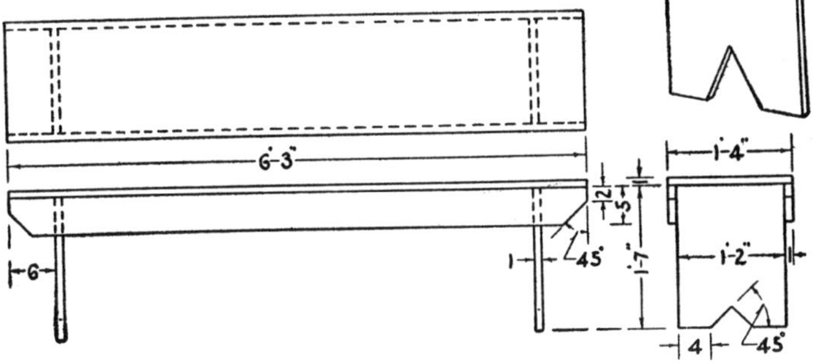

Fig. 71. Wash bench.

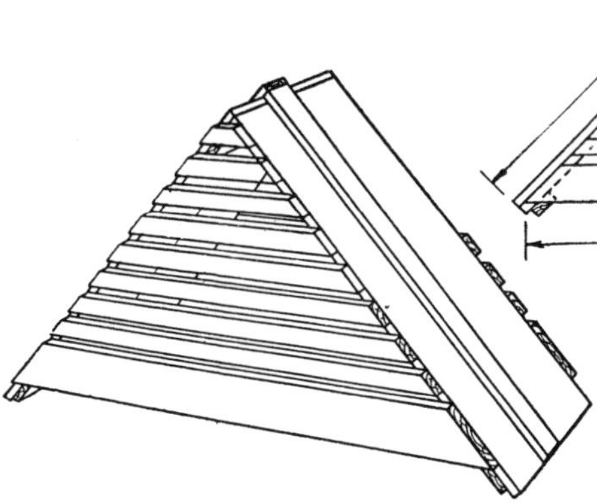

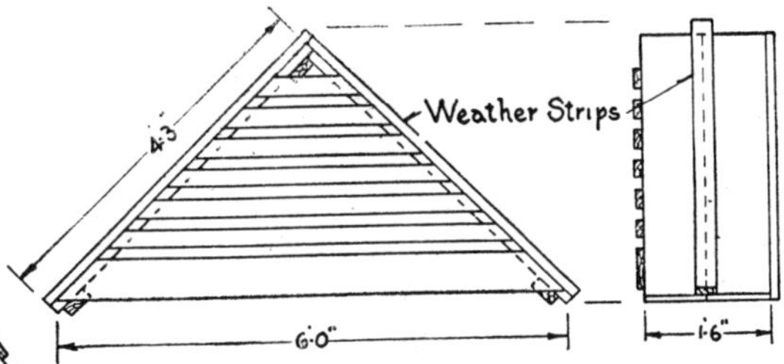

Fig. 72. Chicken coop.

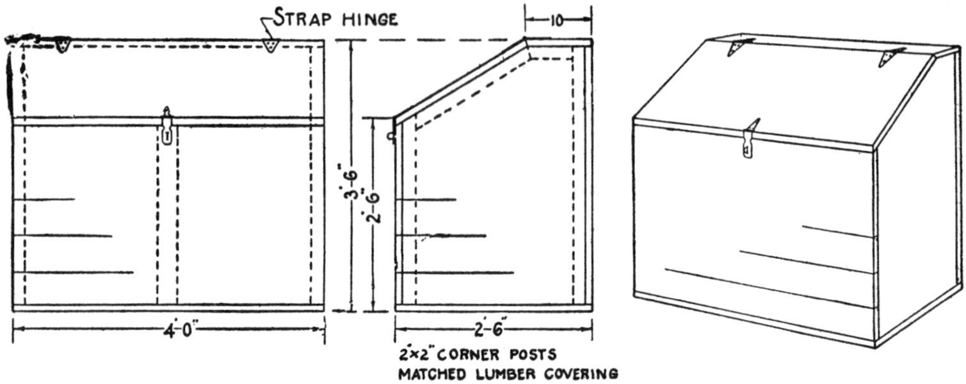

Fig. 73. Feed bin or wood box.

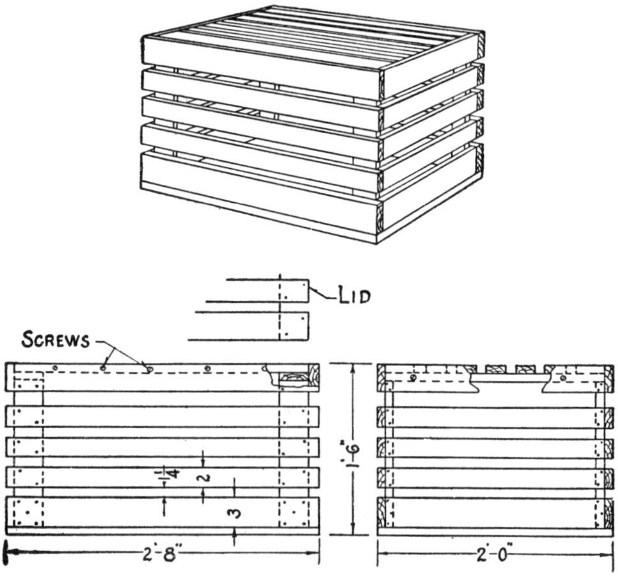

Fig. 74. Shipping crate.

This group of projects does not require the use of tools not already described. It represents, however, a type of project slightly different from any of those included in former groups. The projects in this group are larger and generally include more distinct parts requiring the use of more and larger stock. In a sense, they represent a type of work which is neither carpentry on the one hand nor bench woodwork on the other; they combine the elements of both.

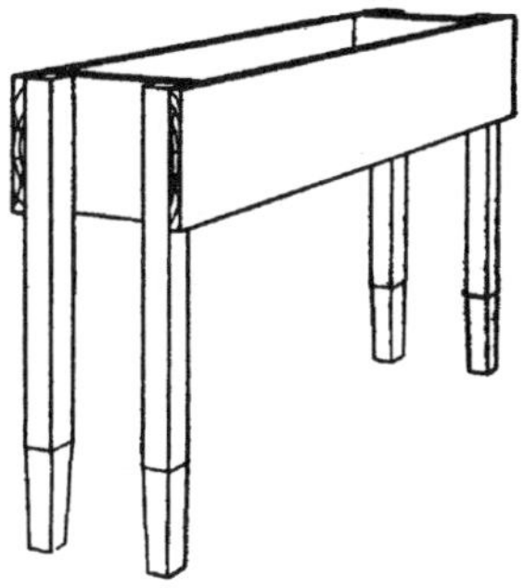

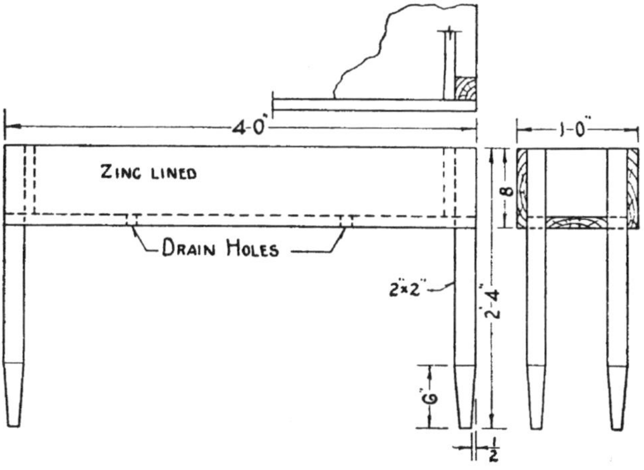

FIG. 75. Flower box.

37. Calculations of Stock. In Sec. 5, rules are given for finding the number of board feet in one or more boards. It is essential that we know how to apply this rule, both to estimate the cost of a project and actually to determine the amount of material that has gone into it. It is equally important to form a judgment of what stock to select before a project is chosen. For example, small pieces of wood may sometimes be used up for the smaller parts of a project, while boards from which pieces for the project may be cut can be selected carefully with a view to wasting as little material as possible.

Think carefully of the means of getting out stock, both to save material and to save time. Be as systematic about your work as possible. When a tool is set for a particular dimension or use, do all that you can with it, not only on one board, but on all which are to have similar work done upon them. Plan ahead so that you know exactly what you should do next, and how you will proceed from step to step. Think thru a problem before you begin construction. If you need to make changes, you can do so better, having once thought out one solution. Whenever possible, make a complete working drawing of the project with dimensions and notes.

Working Instructions for Chicken Coop:

Instructions are given below for making the chicken coop. Use strips of wood, if they can be found, for the slats in the front, and select boards for the roof and back as nearly as possible the desired width. For such a project as this, use old material if available rather than new. Old fence boards are satisfactory for the back.

38. Roof Boards. Secure lumber free from knots which will cut economically to make the roof boards. Example: Two boards, each 9″ wide, or one 12″ and the other 6″ wide, the latter a fence board, possibly. Test the ends of boards for squareness. Use a carpenter's square for this, and in case an end needs to be sawed square, follow the usual method of squaring and sawing, substituting the carpenter's square for the try-square. If two boards are used, find the center in length of each one. Square across thru the center points and saw on lines. Place one 12″ and one 6″ board, or the two 9″

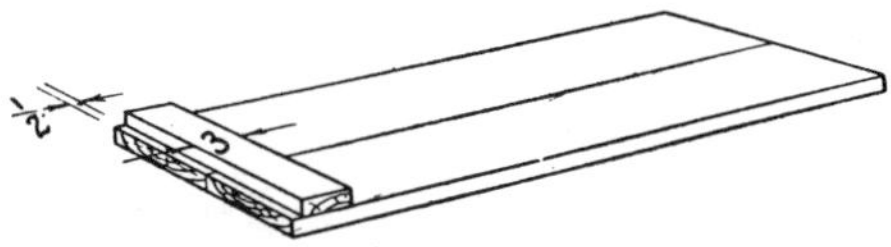

FIG. 76. First cross cleat in place.

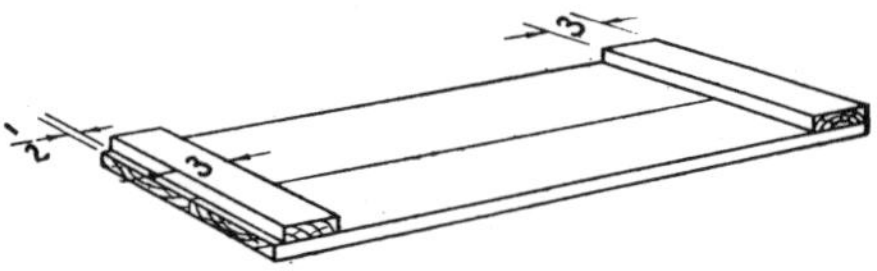

FIG. 77. Second cross cleat in place.

boards edge to edge with ends flush. Nail a 2″ or 3″ strip 1/2″ from one end of the pair of boards (Fig. 76), and another 3″ strip flush with the opposite end (Fig. 77).

Place the remaining two boards together in a similar manner and fasten at one end only with a strip placed 1/2″ from the end.

Nail the unfastened end of one pair to the end of the other

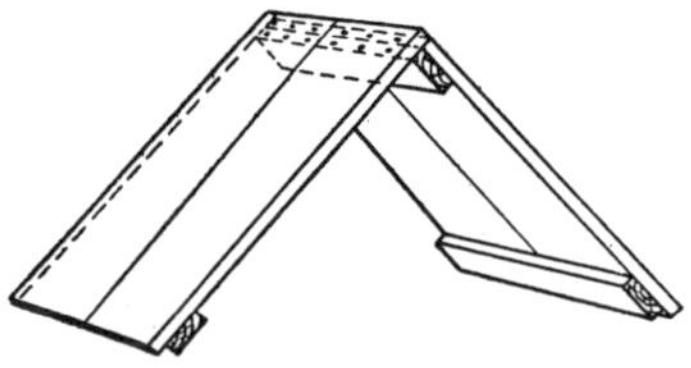

FIG. 78. Roof sections nailed together.

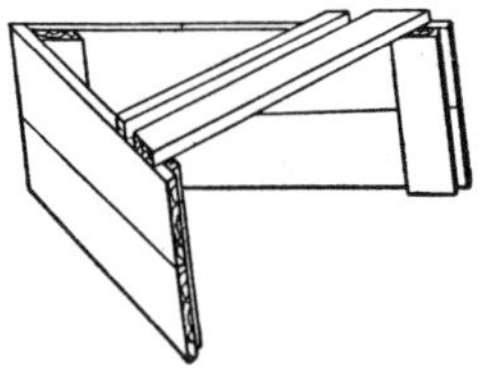

FIG. 79. Attaching side slats.

pair which has the strip attached flush with the end (Fig. 78). This joint forms the ridge of the roof of the coop. The cleat should be on the under side, and nails should enter it as well as the ends of the boards to which it is fastened when the two pairs of boards are nailed together at the ridge.

39. Fastening Front Strips. Place the roof edgewise on the ground and fasten the lower ends together with a 4″ or 6″ strip of siding to form the lower front board of the coop

(Fig. 79). The lower edge of this board should be high enough to permit the coop to set off the ground at least 1-1/2″. A pan of water can then be placed under it and be held by it when the coop is in use. Before fastening the lower front board in place, set a bevel-square to 45 degrees. Mark and saw the ends of the board to come flush with the outside surfaces of the roof boards. A miter box may be used to saw the ends of this board and other boards to be fastened on the front and back (Fig. 80). Stock for remaining cleats may be sawed by using the method of laying out and sawing, as shown in Fig. 81.

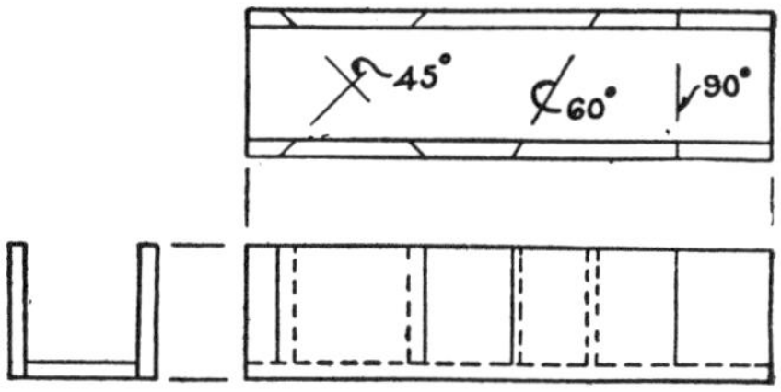

FIG. 80. Miter box.

In a similar manner, mark, saw and nail the remaining front strips which may be laths or narrow strips of wood. A space of from 1″ to 1-1/2″ should be left between adjacent

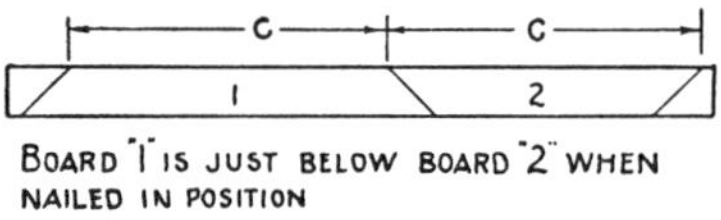

FIG. 81. Method of laying out strips.

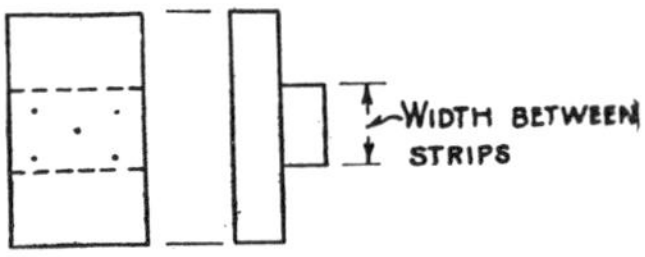

FIG. 82. Gage for spacing slats.

strips, all of which should be parallel. The space can easily be determined by the use of a gage made as shown in Fig. 82.

40. Fastening Back Boards. Turn the coop over, cut and fasten the back boards, beginning at the bottom. Alternate boards should be reversed in order to save lumber by taking advantage of the end cut made at 45 degrees (Fig. 81).

41. Trimming. Place the coop on the floor in its natural position. If it does not set squarely on all bottom edges, plane those which are too low until all surfaces rest on the floor. In case the ends of the front or back boards project over the surface of the roof boards, they should be planed flush with these boards.

42. Checking Estimate. Measure carefully all stock used, and determine the number of board feet of lumber in the project. Compare this amount with the original estimate. If this and the planning at the beginning of a project are both done whenever a project is constructed, you will gain in efficiency in making close estimates and in planning to save both material and time.

CHAPTER VI

CHISELING; MAKING COMMON FRAMING JOINTS

Suggested Projects:

a) Milk stool (Fig. 83).
b) Combination milk stool and pail rest (Fig. 84).
c) Harness rack (Fig. 85).
d) Harness clamp (Fig. 86).
e) Seed tester (Fig. 87).
f) Saw horse (Fig. 88).

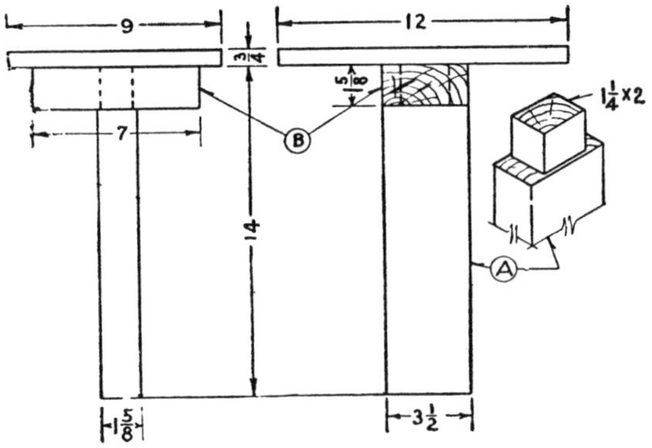

FIG. 83. Milk stool.

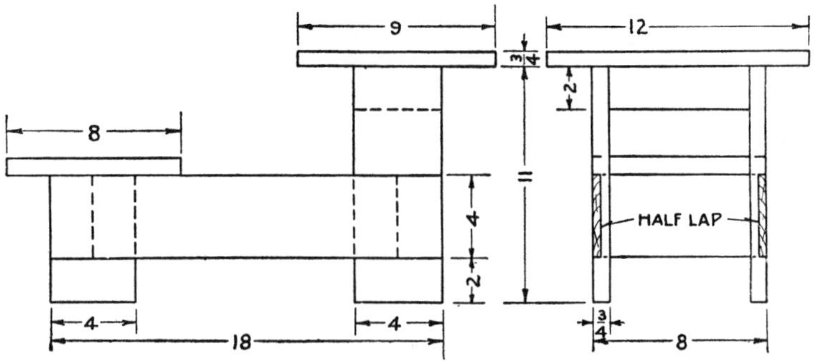

FIG. 84. Combination milk stool and pail rest.

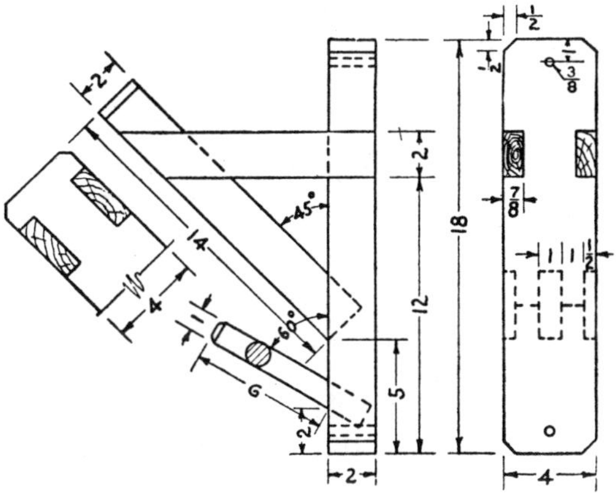

FIG. 85. Harness rack.

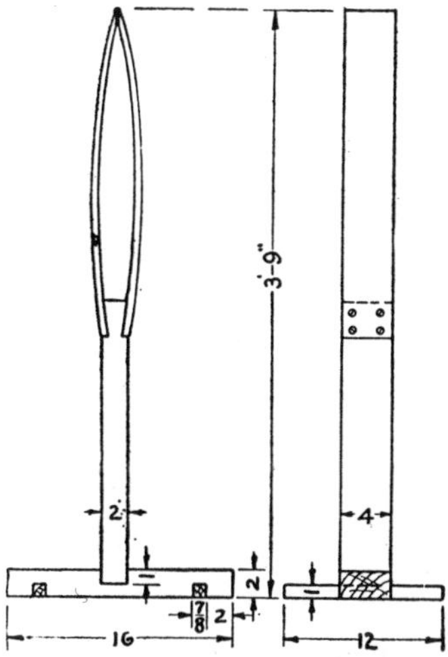

FIG. 86. Harness clamp.

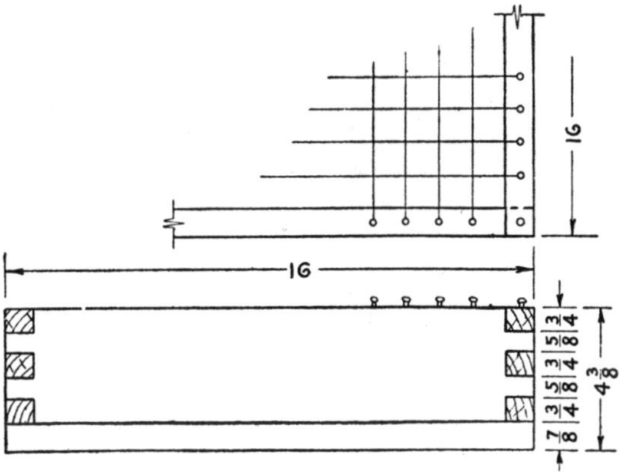

FIG. 87. Seed tester.

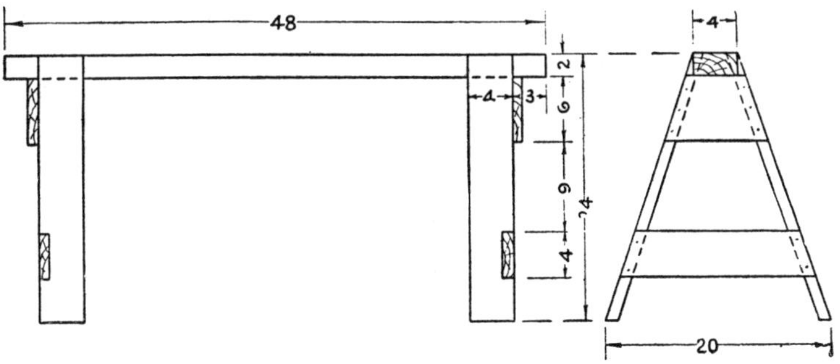

FIG. 88. Saw horse.

43. Tools. The tools emphasized in this group are the different kinds of chisels. (See Classification, page 29.) Auxiliary tools described are the double gage, mallet, and nailset.

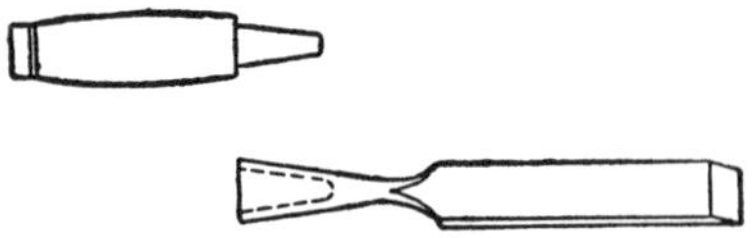

FIG. 89. Socket chisel.

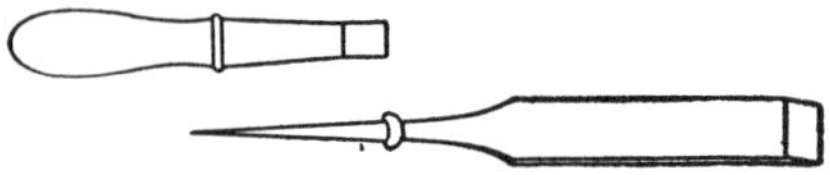

FIG. 90. Tang chisel.

44. Preliminary Instruction. For carpentry work, a heavy chisel is required, one in which the handle fits into a socket in the chisel blade, called the socket chisel (Fig. 89). For ordinary use, however, even tho the handle of the chisel will be struck with a mallet occasionally, but lightly, a chisel with a spike on the end of it (a "tang") which fits into the handle is used (Fig. 90).

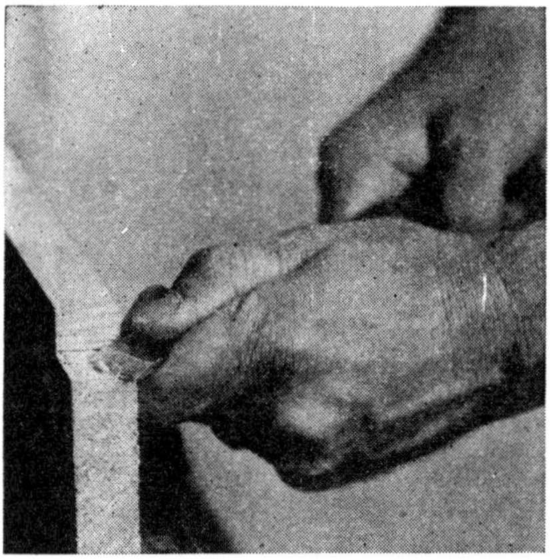

FIG. 91. Paring with chisel.

The work a chisel does is divided into two classes, depending upon the relation of the direction of cutting and the grain of the wood cut. When the chisel cuts with the grain (Fig. 91), it is said to pare off a shaving, and the process is called paring. When a chisel cuts across the grain, whether abruptly or at a sharp angle with the wood fiber, it is said to be cutting crosswise, and the process is called cross-chiseling (Fig. 92). In case one cuts across the grain in a vertical position, the process is called vertical chiseling. It is in cross or vertical chiseling that the mallet is much used to force the chisel across the grain. Such work is illustrated by the cutting of joints such as the tenon and mortise joint, in which the mortise is chiseled out.

A chisel is ground and whetted in the manner described for sharpening a plane-iron (Sec. 26).

Working Instructions for Seed Tester:

Stock: Four 1″ x 3-1/2″ x 6″ hard pine S2S.
Four 1″ x 6-1/4″ x 6″ matched flooring S2S.
Six-penny (6d) nails and 1-1/2″ brads.

45. Purpose of Seed Tester. The following instructions are for the seed tester, or germinating box, which is used to test the fertility of seeds. As the soil must be moist for this purpose, the box must be made strong to withstand the effect of the moisture, which has a tendency to open up joints and change the shape of boards by warping or winding.

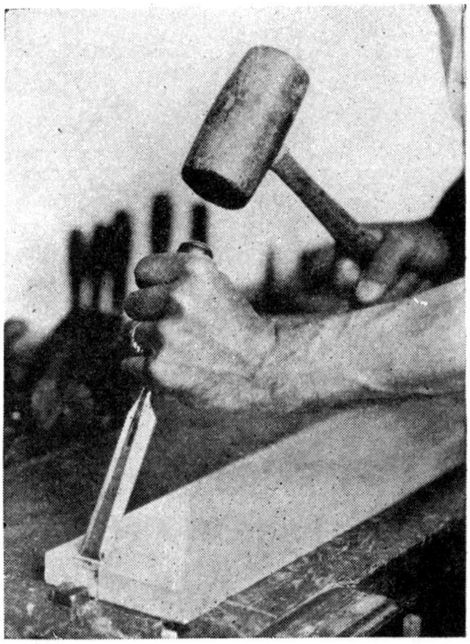

FIG. 92. Chiseling across the grain.

It is for this reason that the corners of the box are made with a lock joint, and that the tongues of the joint are glued and nailed together (Figs. 87 and 93).

The upper surface of the soil is blocked off into squares that each one may be used for an individual seed or a group of seeds. These squares are determined by a cord strung between the opposite sides of the box (Fig. 87).

46. Rough Cutting. If necessary, rip the pieces for the sides of the box from a board, and square and saw each to the required length. Plane each board to width (3-1/2″) and thickness (3/4″).

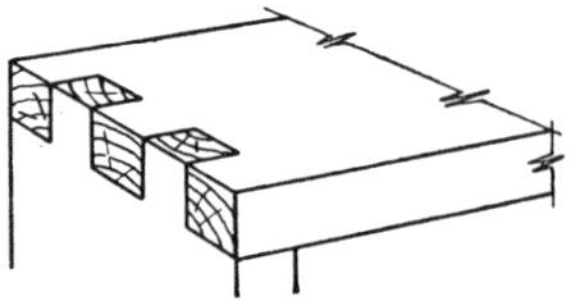

FIG. 93. Corner joint for seed tester.

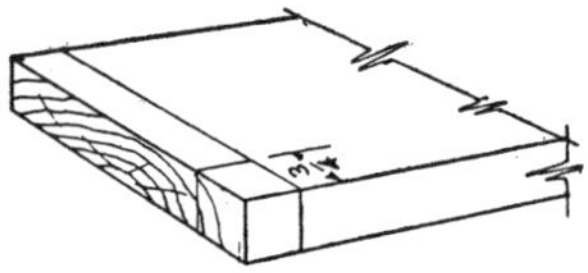

FIG. 94. First step in laying out joint.

47. Laying Out. On the face side of each board, which should become the inside surface of a side of the box, square a knife line 1″ from each end, or a distance equal to the thickness of the stock. Continue this as a fine pencil line around the piece.

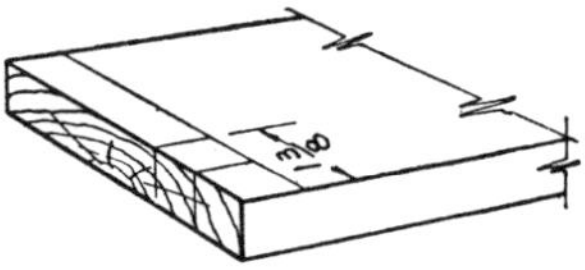

FIG. 95. Second step.

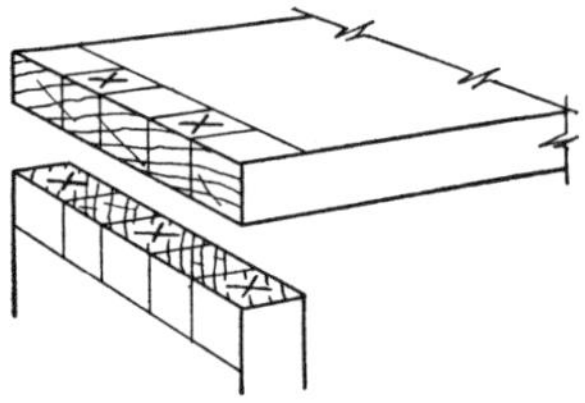

FIG. 96. Waste wood marked for removal.

From the joint edge, which should become the upper edge of a side of the box, gage consecutively on the end and on both surfaces of each end of each board a line 3/4″ from the joint edge to form the first dovetail line (Fig. 94). Reset the gage to 1-3/8″ (3/4″ + 5/8″), and in a similar manner gage the second dovetail line on each end of each piece (Fig. 95). Continue this process of gaging, adding 3/4″ and 5/8″ alternately until all cuts are indicated. On the end of each board, mark with a pencil the parts of the joint to be removed (Fig. 96).

48. Sawing. Saw with the rip-saw to each line in the

stock to be removed. Saw with a crosscut-saw, to the shoulders, those corners to be removed (Fig. 97).

49. Chiseling Joints. Lay each board flat on a wooden surface and chisel out remaining parts of joint to be removed. The chisel should be held at an angle, and the first cut should be made near, but not on the shoulder line (Fig. 98). The last cut should be made by holding the edge of the chisel on this line, perpendicular with the surface of the board, the depth of the cut being about one-half the thickness of the board (Fig. 99). Reverse the board, again place the edge of the chisel on the line, and gently tap the chisel with mallet, or push it with right hand thru to meet the opposite cut already formed. This must be done with great care not to under-cut the joint to any appreciable extent.

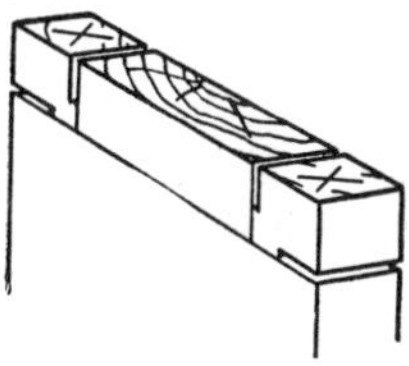

FIG. 97. Sawing the joints.

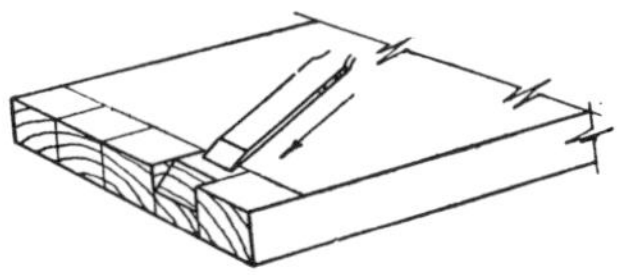

FIG. 98. Chiseling dove tails.

The sides of the tongues formed by the rip-saw cuts should not be touched with a chisel unless the saw has not cut to the gage lines. In this case, the chisel should be used to pare off this superfluous stock (Fig. 91).

50. Fastening Corners. Drive a 1-1/2″ brad thru each projecting piece of the joint, as shown in Fig. 100. Before driving the nails in the corners, cover each sliding surface of each joint with cold or hot glue.

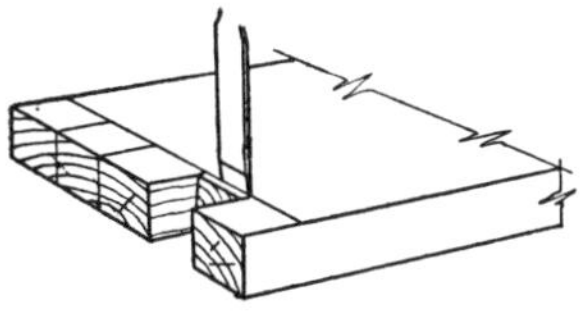

FIG. 99. Finishing the chisel cut.

51. Nailing Bottom. The bottom boards may be nailed onto the lower edges of the sides of the box with six-penny common nails (Fig. 101). Each bottom board should be squared and sawed to length before it is nailed in place.

A more satisfactory box in appearance and in strength, but one more difficult to make, would have the bottom set inside of the sides of the box and nailed from the outside. Such a bottom would be completely fitted and set in place at one time (Fig. 102).

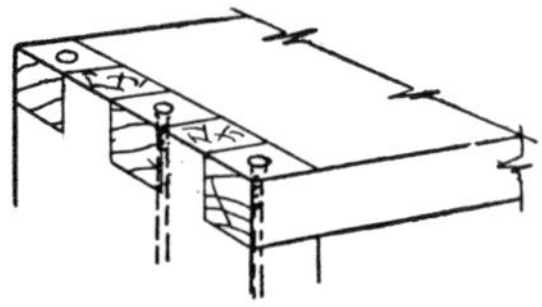

FIG. 100. Position of nails in joints.

52. Marking Edges. With pencil and ruler, divide the length of the inside of each side of the box into equal spaces—1″, 1-1/2″ or 2″—depending upon the distance the strings on the top of the box are to be separated.

Square a light pencil line across the upper edge of each

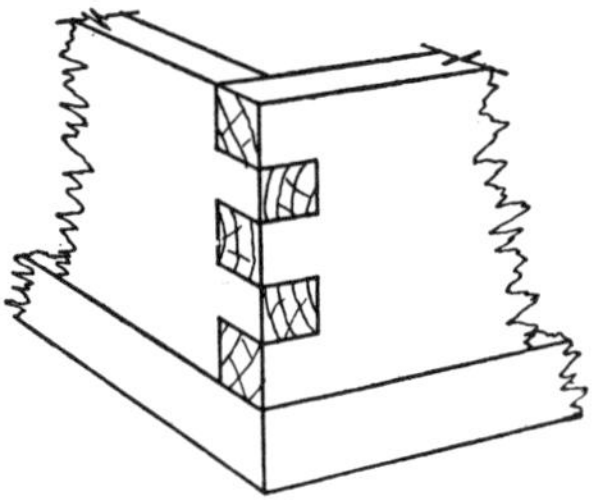

FIG. 101. Method of attaching the bottom.

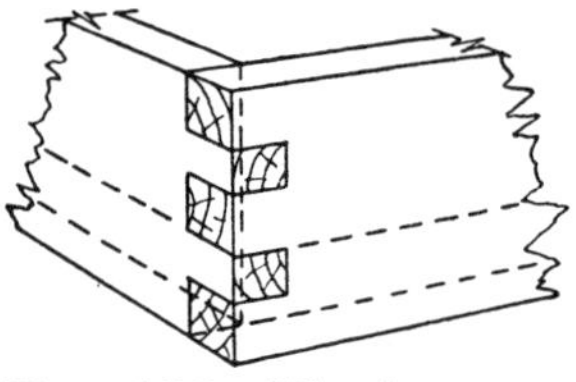

FIG. 102. The bottom fitted inside of side pieces.

board at the points located, and place at the center of each of these lines a 1-1/2″ brad (Fig. 103). The brad should be driven into the wood to allow the head to project 1/4″ above the surface of the wood. Continue the process until all brads are driven in place.

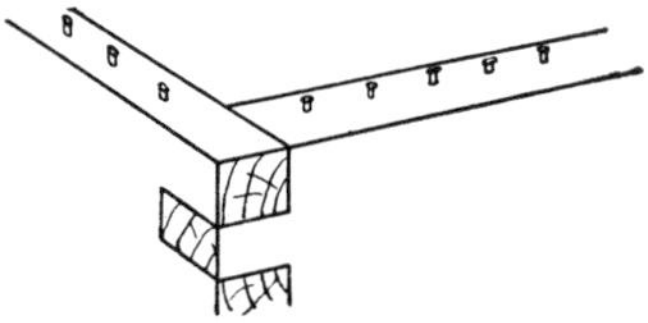

FIG. 103. Location of nails for stringing.

String the cord continuously back and forth between the opposite sides of the box, the cord running between one pair of sides to be at right angles with that strung between the sides of the other pair.

53. Supplementary Instructions. In the instructions for the seed tester, two operations in which the chisel is a principal tool are not fully described, viz.—(*a*) paring a broad surface and (*b*) cutting a mortise. Examples of the former are found in the body of the saw horse, where a recess for the leg is formed, or in the upright of the harness clamp, where supporting surfaces for the barrel staves are formed; while the latter is used in working out and cutting a mortise and tenon for the joint in the milking stool.

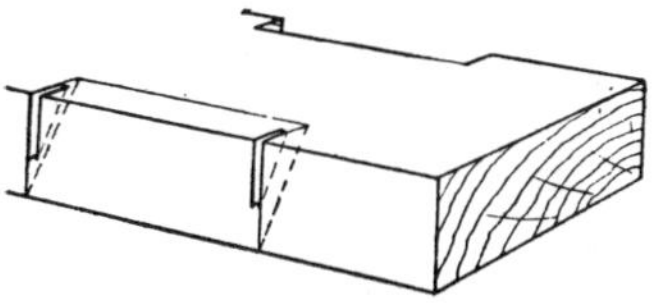

FIG. 104. Making the joints for saw horse.

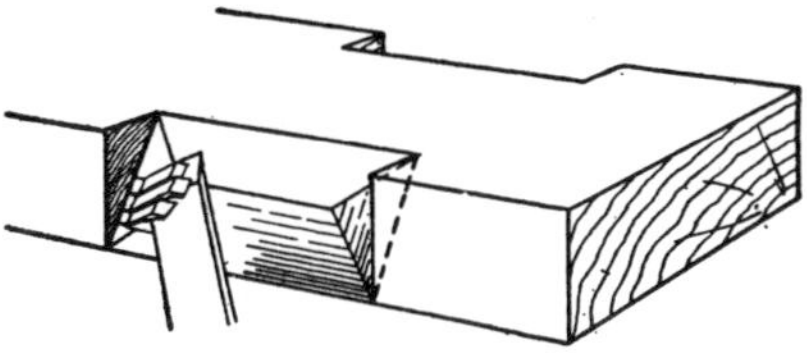

FIG. 105. Method of chiseling joints.

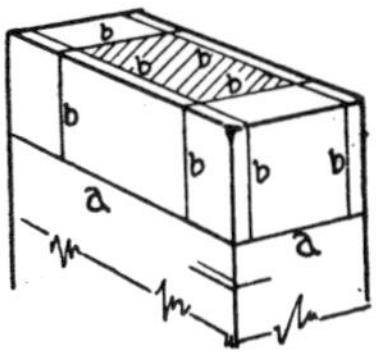

FIG. 106. Layout of joint for milking stool.

54. Special Operations. After the recess for the saw horse leg is laid out in the body of the saw horse, and the shoulders are cut with a crosscut-saw (Fig. 104), the waste stock must be removed. Fig. 105 shows how the chisel is used in taking paring cuts. The waste stock being removed, the surface is finally tested with a try-square blade used as a straight-edge to determine when the surface is perfectly true.

To lay off the tenon on the top of the upright piece in the milking stool, the try-square and single- or double-marking gage should be used and lines drawn, as indicated in Fig. 106.

Parallel lines can be made at one time with the double gage (Fig. 107). The cross-hatched part of Fig. 106 represents the end of the tenon. Saw to lines *a* with crosscut-saw in waste stock. Saw to lines *b* in waste stock with rip-saw.

Fig. 108 shows the joint for the milking stool with the rectangle representing the mortise made up of lines marked *b*, corresponding to similarly-lettered lines on top of upright. The long lines of this rectangular hole should be made on both top and bottom of board with the marking gage, the short lines with knife and try-square. The extension of the short lines marked *b* about the edge of the board suggests how the try-square will be used to secure lines on the under side of the board corresponding to those on the top side.

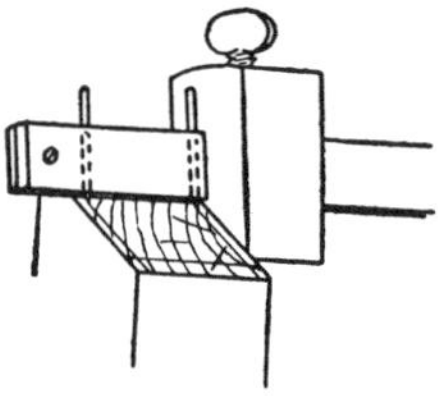

FIG. 107. Gaging joint for milking stool.

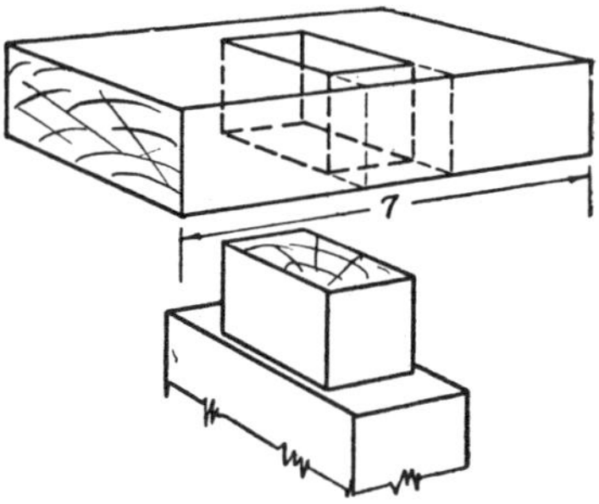

FIG. 108. The joint completed.

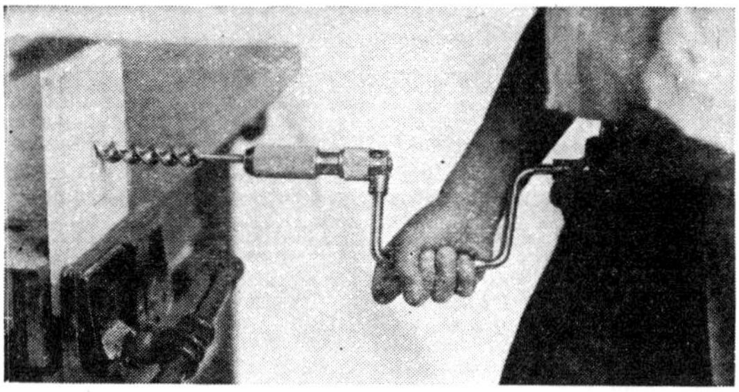

FIG. 109. Boring out the mortise.

The mortise should be bored out by the process illustrated in Fig. 109, the ends of the mortise chiseled as described in Sec. 49, and the sides of the mortise pared out as described in Sec. 44.

CHAPTER VII

USE OF MODELING OR FORMING TOOLS; SHAPING IRREGULAR FORMS

Suggested Projects:

a) Hammer handle (Fig. 110).
b) Hatchet handle (Fig. 111).
c) Neckyoke (Fig. 112).
d) Singletree (Fig. 113).
e) Shoulder carrier (Fig. 114).

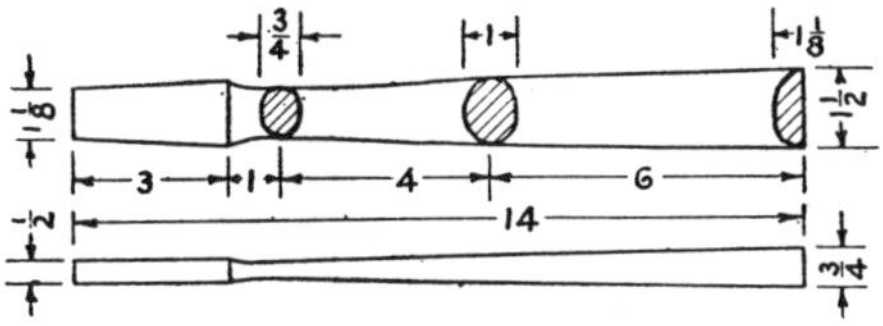

FIG. 110. Hammer handle.

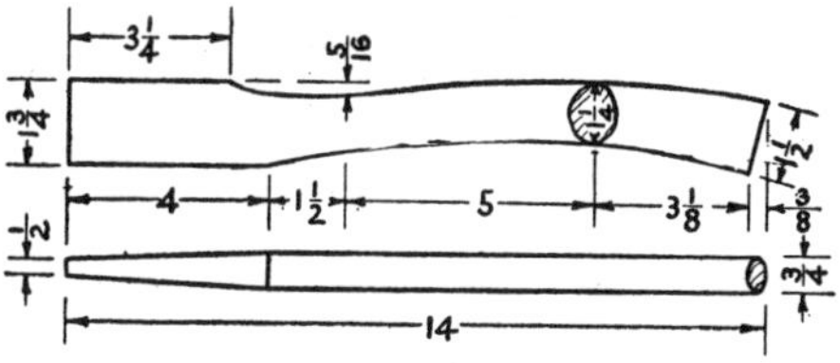

FIG. 111. Hatchet handle.

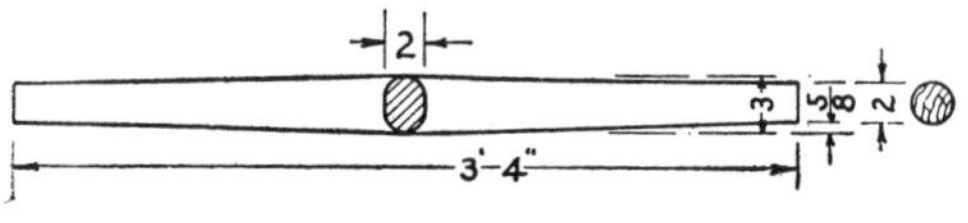

FIG. 112. Neckyoke.

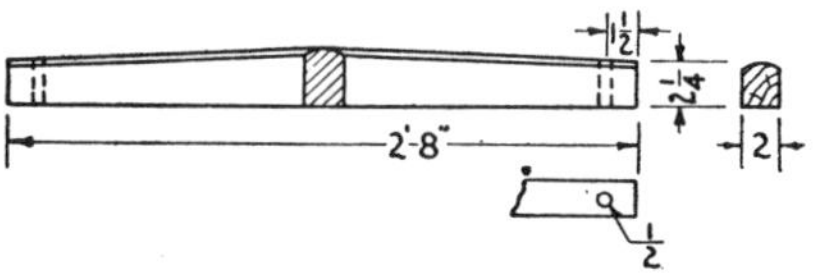

FIG. 113. Singletree.

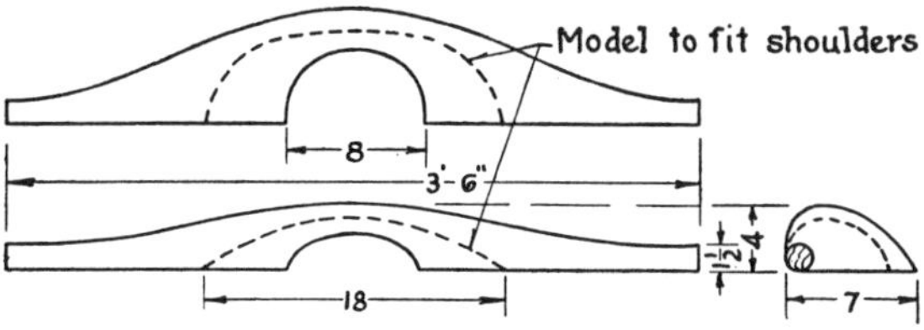

FIG. 114. Shoulder carrier.

55. Modeling Tools. Under the classification of tools (Sec. 7), are listed those in common use. Among these, but not under a single heading, are those which are used principally for fashioning irregular surfaces. In such a group are found the spoke-shave, the draw-knife and similar tools; the hatchet, ax and adz, and also such miscellaneous tools as the turning-saw, woodrasp and gage (Fig. 5).

Perhaps in no place where woodworking hand tools are in common use are the modeling tools more generally used than on the farm, with the possible exception of the cooper shop. The cutting edge of any one of these tools, except the turning-saw and file, is, in form and use, both a chisel and a knife, yet none of them are used either as the chisel or knife.

Both the draw-knife and the spoke-shave (Fig. 5) are chisels with a handle at either end of the cutting edge. In the case of the spoke-shave, the thickness of the shaving is controlled by a gage in an opening in the shoe or bed-plate of the spoke-shave. There is also similarity in construction between this tool and the plane.

On the other hand, the hatchet, ax and adz are chisels, but controlled differently from either the chisel or the spoke-shave and draw-knife. The descriptive matter under heading, "Working Instructions," in the following pages, suggests the use of each of these tools, and should be studied carefully in connection with the illustrations.

The instructions given are for making the hatchet handle. This project includes the principal modeling exercises for the majority of the forming tools herein listed.

Working Instructions for Hatchet Handle:

56. Squaring the Stock—Laying Out. Plane stock to over all dimensions, 3/4″ x 1-1/2″ x 14″.

On the face side, sketch the outline of the handle, as shown in Fig. 115. Taper the front end of the handle to 1/2″ thickness on the end, beginning the taper at a point 4″ from this end, as shown in the edge view of the mechanical drawing of the handle.

57. Using the Turning-saw. Place the stock upright in the vise, one-half its length being above the vise. Stand in front of the vise in position to saw (Fig. 115).

FIG. 115. Correct use of turning saw.

Grasp the turning-saw in hands, as shown in Fig. 115, the teeth pointing toward the operator. Move the saw away from you to start the saw cut, or kerf; then toward you without downward pressure, until the saw blade has begun to cut. Continue to move the saw backward and forward the approximate length of the saw blade, holding the frame vertically except when necessary to vary from this position in order not to have the frame strike the stock. Gradually turn the right hand as forward strokes are made to direct the saw blade on the curve.

Where possible, the saw cut should be taken *over* the grain. However, unless the saw can be removed from stock and started in a new place without much difficulty, it is best to complete a saw cut regardless of relation of wood fiber to saw cut. Continue work with the turning-saw until the complete outline of the handle is sawed out.

58. **Use of the Spoke-shave.** Place the stock in vise, as illustrated in Fig. 116. Stand at end of vise, bending slightly over stock with spoke-shave grasped firmly, but not rigidly, in both hands. Draw or push it *over* the grain, holding the blade square with the face side, but allowing one hand to lead the other slightly, that the shaving may be cut more readily. It may be advisable to shift the position of the stock in the vise from time to time, that the tool may be used with the least difficulty.

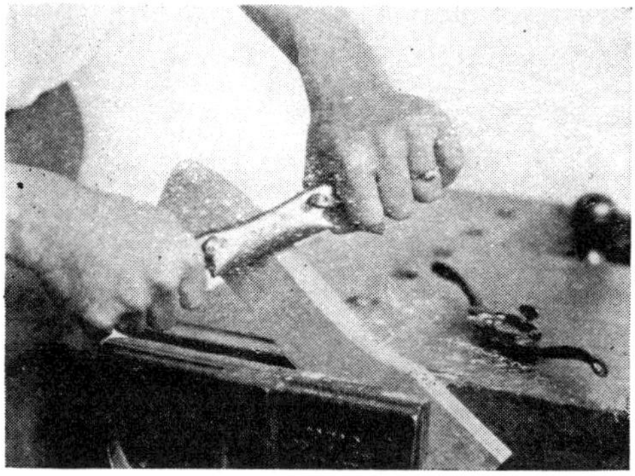

FIG. 116. Using the spoke-shave.

When the spoke-shaved edges are square with the face side, the corners should be taken off to form a cross-section, as shown in Fig. 111 and Fig. 117. Care must be taken to remove no more stock than must be taken off finally to secure a good oval-shaped handle. The oval should be an ellipse.

After the first corners are removed, the process of cutting off corners should be continued, as shown in Fig. 117, to secure the closest approximation to an elliptical cross-section. The front end of the handle may now be modeled to fit the hatchet head. This may

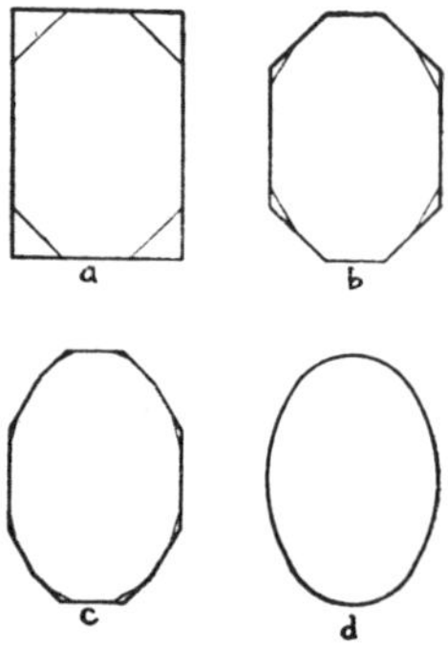

FIG. 117. Steps in modeling handles.

be done with the spoke-shave or the plane, or partly by the use of each.

59. Scraping and Sandpapering. Finally, all irregular surfaces should be scraped with a piece of glass or a steel scraper, and sandpapered, first using the sandpaper on a block and moving the block slowly around the handle as it is moved back and forth lengthwise with the grain. Finally, with the sandpaper in the hand, continue to move the paper lengthwise to secure the finished surface. Cross strokes with the sandpaper may be taken if followed by strokes with the grain.

Supplementary Instructions:

60. The Wood Rasp. In some cases, it is advisable to use a wood rasp (Fig. 5) separately or in conjunction with the spoke-shave, scraper and sandpaper in modeling a piece of wood to an irregular form and shape. If a spoke-shave had not been available for use on the hatchet handle, the same general procedure could have been followed with the wood rasp in modeling the form for each of the different shapes described, viz.—rectangular cross-section, eight-sided cross-section, etc.

The wood rasp is held like a file. It is pushed forward with pressure for the cutting stroke, and lightly drawn back in contact with the wood, or lifted from the wood entirely on the return stroke. As it is pushed, it is rolled slightly and, also, moved lengthwise on the stock, thus avoiding rutting or gouging the wood.

The hatchet, ax or adz may be used to remove a considerable portion of stock to secure roughly the desired form or shape.

Of the projects listed in this group, little or no difficulty should be experienced in securing the result indicated by the drawings, if the instructions for the hatchet handle are followed as a guide.

61. The Shoulder Carrier. The most difficult project to form is the shoulder carrier. This may be modeled from a straight-grained, well-seasoned piece of cord-wood, or from a heavy plank. It is advisable to cut out with the turning-saw the shape of the carrier shown in the top view, or the one you would get if looking down on the carrier as it is placed on one's shoulders. Next, model the upper surface with a draw-knife, spoke-shave and wood rasp. Finally, the under surface should be modeled to fit over the shoulders. This work may be done with an outside ground gouge (Fig. 5). It is pushed into the wood with the grain, and, as the right hand is lowered, the stock is removed and the desired shape is secured. The convex, concave and cylindrical surfaces of the carrier may all be smoothed finally with a wood rasp or sandpaper, or both.

CHAPTER VIII

SUPPLEMENTARY PROJECTS

62. **Sheep Rack and Feed Bunk** (Fig. 118).

Directions:

1) Frame up each end with 1″ x 10″ boards 3′ 0″ long, cleated together on the outside by the two 1″ x 4″ strips, and on the inside by the 1″ x 3″ strip upon which the trough floor is to rest. Flush with the upper edge of this cleat, and with each of the outside edges of the bunk end, fasten the 2″ x 4″ corner posts or legs.

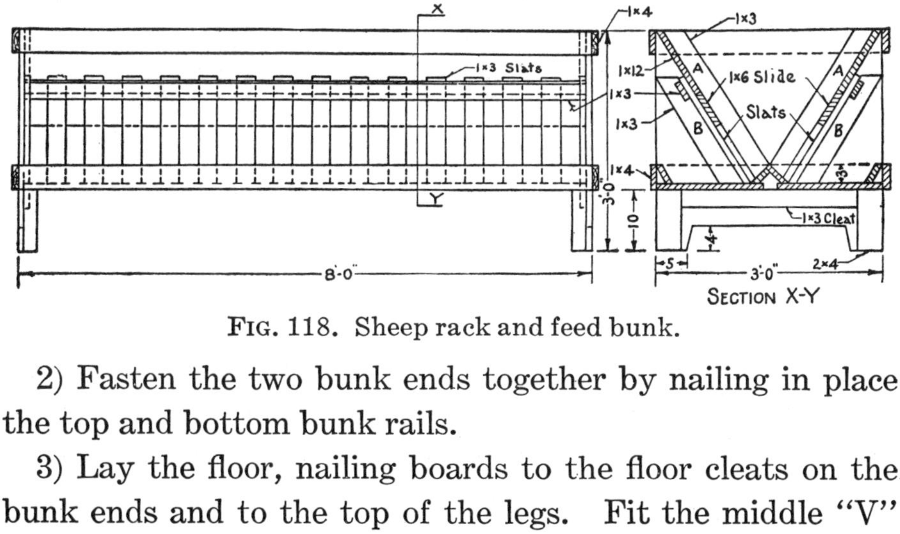

FIG. 118. Sheep rack and feed bunk.

2) Fasten the two bunk ends together by nailing in place the top and bottom bunk rails.

3) Lay the floor, nailing boards to the floor cleats on the bunk ends and to the top of the legs. Fit the middle "V" feed guides and the outside trough edge boards, nailing ends of the same from outside of bunk end.

4) From lower edges of feed guides to upper corners of ends of bunk, draw lines to locate guide boards for the 1″ x 12″ board and rack which hold feed. Construct and nail these guides in place.

5) Cut slats for rack and fasten together at top ends by means of a 1″ x 3″ board, to which all are squarely nailed.

6) Nail 1″ x 12″ feed boards in position to the inside guide boards (*A*).

7) Place feed rack in position, supported by outside guide boards (*B*). Toe-nail the bottom of each rack slat to the "V"

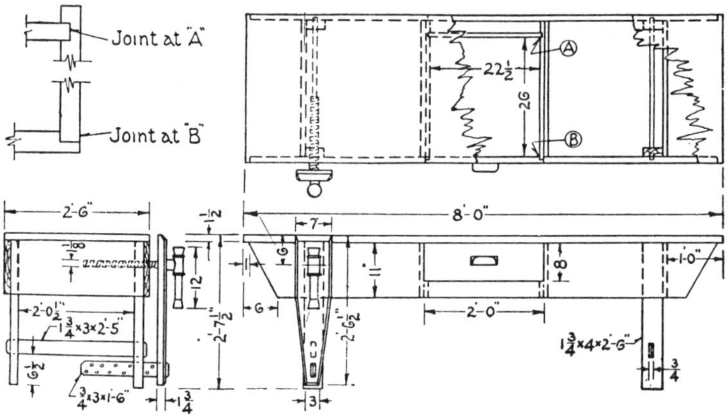

FIG. 119. Woodworking bench.

feed guide board, and nail the top of the rack securely to the 1″ x 12″ feed board, over the lower edge of which they should lap by 3″. This should be done after the 1″ x 6″ slide has been placed in position. This should slide in the openings between the feed rack and the inside end guide boards with difficulty, that it may be held in any particular position by friction, or it should be fastened thru grooves in the end boards of rack by means of wing nut bolts.

63. Directions for Woodworking Bench (Fig. 119).

1) Construct the frame by planing for each end:

2 oak boards (uprights), each 1-3/4″ x 4″ x 2′ 6″.

1 oak board (lower crosspiece), 1-3/4″ x 3″ x 2′ 5″.

1 pine board (upper crosspiece), 1″ x 11″ x 2′ 4″.

2) Lay out and construct the mortise and tenon joints to join the front and back uprights with the lower crosspiece. Tenons may be full width, viz., 3″ wide and 3/4″ thick. Length between tenon shoulders, 2′ 1/2″.

3) Assemble each frame by joining the parts; the lower crosspiece to be fastened to the uprights by gluing joints, and clamped for at least twelve hours, and the upper connecting piece to be nailed in position as soon as clamps are applied to the lower part of the frame.

4) Construct the front of the vise, planing it to dimensions as given in the drawing. Fasten the lower guide piece in with glue and nail it from each edge of the vise board. The staggered holes in guide piece for vise, in which to insert pin to keep the lower portion of the vise board the proper distance from the bench, should each be 1/2″ in diameter, in two rows each about 1″ from the edge of the guide board, holes to be 2″ apart in each row.

5) Nail front and back side boards, or rails, of the bench onto the end sections.

6) Purchase a 1-1/4″ iron vise screw. Bore the holes for this in vise board and bench, and cut the slot for the vise guide board. Assemble vise.

7) Cut the opening for the drawer 2′ x 8″ in upper portion of center of front board, and fasten in place the runner and guide boards for the drawer by nailing or screwing into their ends thru front and back boards.

8) Lay the top boards on. These may be of oak, altho dressed pine will suffice. Joints between boards must be tight. They need not be glued.

9) Construct drawer, as shown by drawer details of joints,

and fit in bench to slide freely. The bottom of the drawer may be nailed onto cleats fastened to the lower inside surfaces of the sides of drawer.

64. Working Directions for Dog House (Fig. 120).

1) Cut 2″ x 4″'s to proper lengths for either sills or plates, and one-half the number of studs.

2) Rip all pieces of 2″ x 4″ into 2″ x 2″ strips.

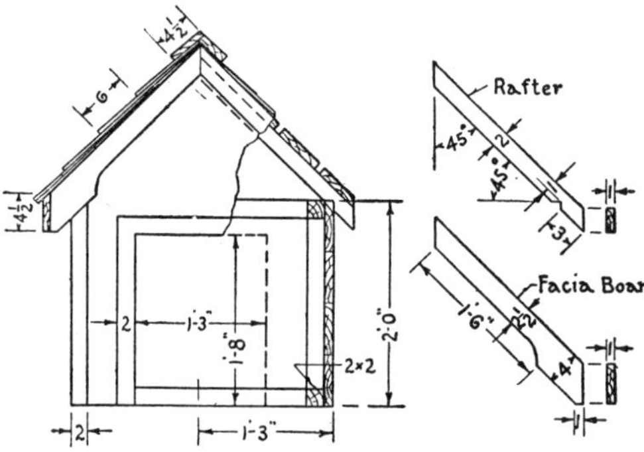

FIG. 120. Dog house.

3) Construct sill and plate frames with horizontal half-lap corner joints, and connect sill and plate frames with studs by nailing thru frames into ends of studs.

4) Nail on sheathing (fence boards), lapping side boards over ends of end boards.

5) Beginning at the bottom, cut and nail on siding on sides and ends.

6) Cut and nail on roof boards (fence boards), allowing space of 1″ between boards.

7) Shingle roof, beginning at eaves and working toward ridge, breaking joints for every two consecutive layers or rows of shingles.

8) Cut, fit and nail ridge, facing, corner, base, and trim boards.

65. Directions for Corn Drier (Fig. 121).

1) Secure pine lumber 1″ thick, 3-1/2″ or 4″ wide, and 16′-0″ long, dressed.

2) Cut each piece to form lengths for parts of drier with least possible waste. Example: 10′ and 6′ or 6′, 6′ and 4′ (2 braces).

3) Nail, as shown in drawing, nailing two pieces together, surface to surface for ends. Toe-nail in braces. Use six-penny and eight-penny common nails.

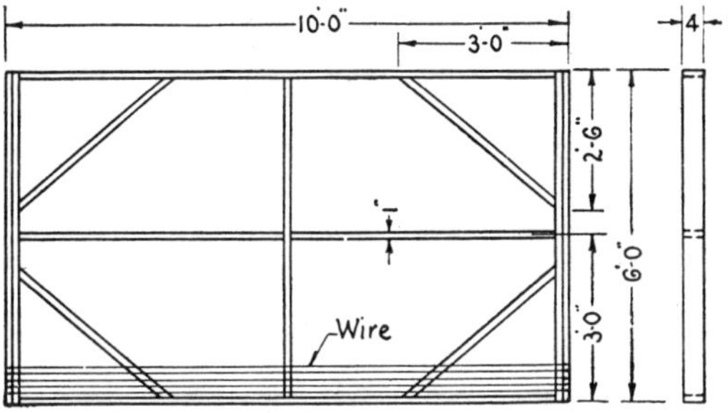

FIG. 121. Corn drier.

4) On end pieces and vertical center piece, with two-foot rule or carpenter's square, lay off points with pencil on front and back for spacing wire. Drive shingle-nail, or 1-1/2″ brad at each point.

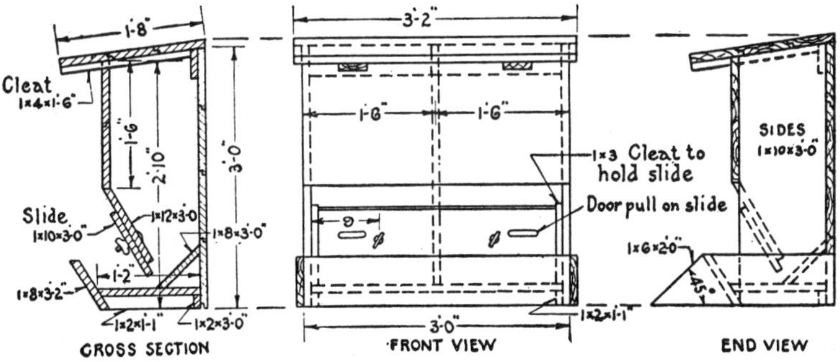

FIG. 122. Self-feeder.

5) Wind wire (1/16″ annealed iron), taking one turn about each nail.

66. Making the Self-Feeder (Fig. 122).

1) Cut ends to dimension—10″ x 3′ 0″—bottom end square

and top end tapered toward the front to make it 2′ 10″ long.

2) Cut center partition to overall dimensions of end boards. Bevel front and back edges of lower end to fit to deflector board on the back, and to the front board, to which the adjustable slide is attached on the front.

3) Nail cleat 2″ wide on inside surfaces of end boards at the bottom, upon which floor will rest; also 1″ x 3″ cleat to hold slide, as marked in front view of drawing.

4) Nail to edges of end and center partition boards ship-lap to form vertical portion of front of feeder and all of back of feeder.

5) Lay floor of ship-lap on inside bottom cleats fastened on end boards of feeder. Cut deflector board and toe-nail into position.

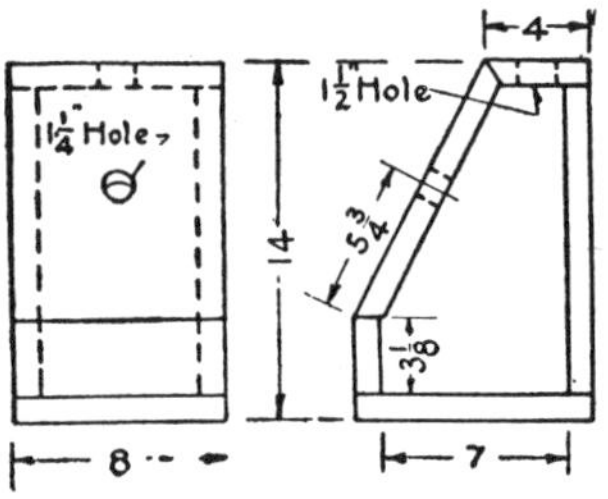

FIG. 123. Egg tester.

6) Cut slanting 12″ board of front of feeder, bore holes for 1/2″ wing-nut bolts and nail board in position to lower front edge of center partition board. Thru end boards of feeder nail into ends of this slanting front board.

7) Cut adjustable slide board to dimensions, cut slots for wing bolts, attach handles and fit board in position.

8) Bevel front edge of floor and attach front board of tray. Nail on end bottom boards.

9) Nail ship-lap to cleats for top. Hinge at rear with two 4″ leaf strap hinges.

10) Paint outside of feeder with brown creosote paint.

67. Making the Egg Tester (Fig. 123).

1) Secure stock from one board 8″ wide, or from more than one board of shorter length, but the same width, to construct the complete box.

2) Cut stock to convenient planing lengths, each to cut finally into a certain number of pieces for the box. A little must be allowed in length for crosscutting and squaring ends.

3) Plane stock to dimensions. Saw to proper lengths and square ends.

4) Taper front edges of side boards.

5) Set bevel-square for angle of front edge of top board and ends of front board. Mark and trim to proper angles.

6) Bore 1-1/2″ hole and 1-1/4″ hole in centers of top and front boards, respectively.

7) Nail box together with six-penny (6d) finish nails in the following order: Back, bottom, front vertical board, top to sides; front slanting board.

68. Constructing a Cow Stanchion (Fig. 124).

1) Select straight-grained hickory, oak or other close-grained, tough wood from 2″ or 1-1/2″ dressed plank.

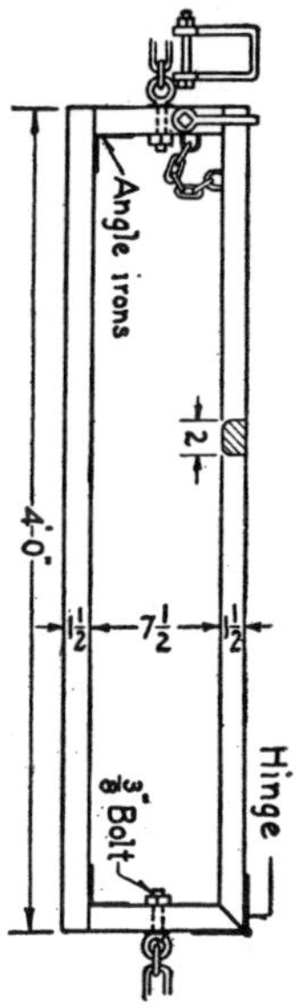

FIG. 124. Cow stanchion.

2) Rip stock to width or thickness to secure strips which will dress to 1-1/2″ x 2″.

3) Plane strips to correct width and thickness.

4) Square and saw strips to correct lengths.

5) Bore 3/8″ holes in center of end pieces for chain bolts.

6) Bore 3/8″ hole in upper end piece for corner fastening clamp. (Position of hole depends on length of clamp.)

7) Bevel lower end piece and one side piece, each on one end to 45 degrees for hinged corner.

8) Fasten corner angle iron with 1″ flathead screws to inside of each end piece to draw tightly to side piece when screwed to it. Drill small holes for screws.

9) Fasten remaining side of each angle iron to side piece. First place in position, mark for screw holes, and then drill for them.

10) Fasten strap hinge in manner similar to that used in fastening angle irons.

11) Drill small holes for staples for corner chain.

12) Fasten chain and corner clamp bolts by setting up nuts over washers and burr ends of bolts slightly.

69. Making Tomato Trellis (Fig. 125).

1) Secure eleven 12′ strips of pine, 3″ or 3-1/2″ wide. Pine

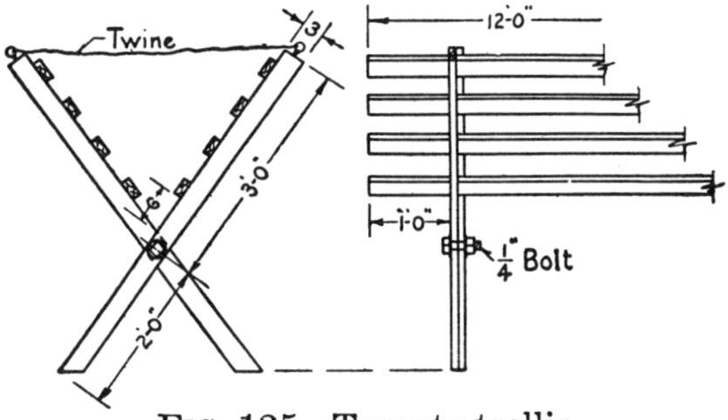

FIG. 125. Tomato trellis.

flooring or 6″ pine fence boards ripped in two will be satisfactory.

2) Cut from each of three strips two pieces 5′ 0″ long.

3) Two feet from one end of each of the 5′ strips, bore a 1/4″ hole in the middle of the stock.

4) Fasten two of the strips together with a 1/4″ bolt, using a washer under the head and under the nut, to form one end of the rack. In like manner, make the remaining two supports, one for the opposite end and one for the middle of the rack.

5) Nail four of the 12′ strips evenly spaced on the 3′ leg of each support, allowing the strips to project 12″ on the end of the frame beyond the end support, and leaving sufficient space below the strip nearest the hinge for the vines. Place the middle support centrally in the frame.

6) Put strong screw-eyes at the top of each bar of each end support, in which to fasten wire or cord to hold the top edges at a fixed position when the frame is in place.

70. Feed Bunk for Cattle (Fig. 126).

1) Construct each trestle or pair of legs by first cutting to

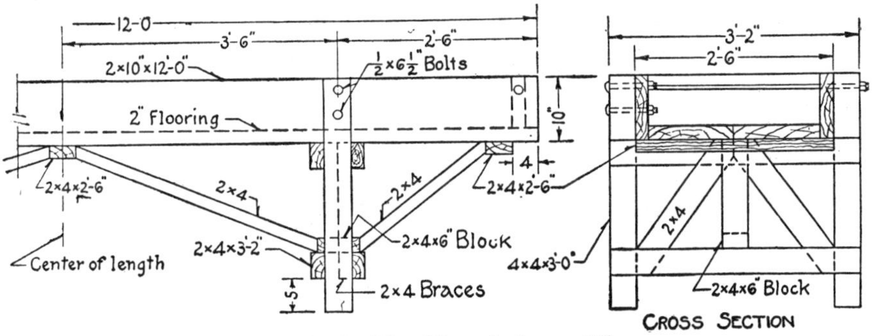

FIG. 126. Feed bunk for cattle.

length the four legs from 4″ x 4″ stock and connecting each pair with the four 2″ x 4″ cross and brace pieces.

First nail in position the two crosspieces on one side of a pair of legs, then insert and nail securely to this pair of crosspieces the two leg frame braces. Now nail on the two remaining crosspieces, both to the legs and the braces. Finally, nail on the 6″, 2″ x 4″ block lengthwise of the bunk in the center of the lower crosspieces, allowing it to rest 1″ on each crosspiece.

2) Construct the frame of the box from 1-1/2″ x 10″ or 2″ x 10″ stock. Bore holes to secure the sides to the end pieces. Note that the end boards of frame rest on floor boards.

3) Turn box bottom side up. Lay and nail floor boards to end boards, and nail on 2″ x 4″ crosspieces.

4) While box is bottom side up, place leg frames in position and bore holes thru legs and side rails of box. Insert and fasten bolts. Fit and nail the four length braces in position, carefully locating center position for them on the crosspieces. The lower ends of these braces butt against the 6″, 2″ x 4″ blocks already nailed to the lower leg frame crosspieces.

5) Place bunk in upright position and insert and tighten end rods.

71. Saw Buck (Fig. 127).

1) Saw legs of frame to lengths from 3″ x 4″ stock.

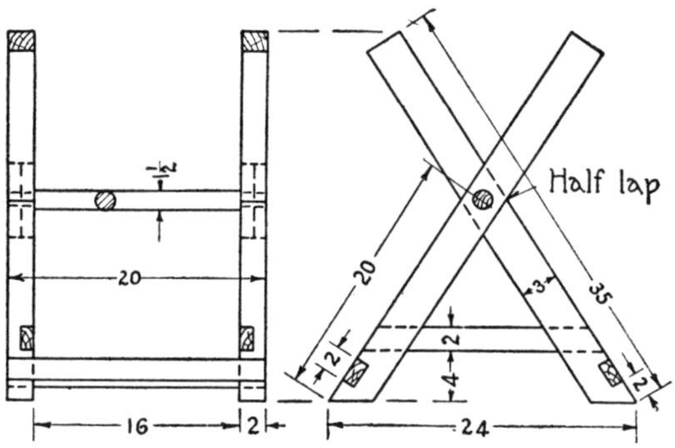

FIG. 127. Saw buck.

2) Locate, lay out and cut half-lap joints for each end of frame.

3) Lay out and cut 2″ notches for thickness and width of connecting braces.

4) Bore holes for center rod in each half-lap joint connecting ends of frame. Do this when each end of frame is halved together.

5) Plane and fit all brace rods.

6) Form center rod, using draw-knife and spoke-shave on

center portion of rod, saw to cut shoulder and use chisel and wood rasp to form ends of rod.

7) Nail cross braces on each end frame and trim ends with plane.

8) Place center rod in position and wedge ends with thin wooden wedge.

9) Nail length braces in place and trim edges.

10) Place saw buck upright on level floor. With open dividers, scribe line for bottom of legs; saw to lines.

72. Chicken Feeder (Fig. 128).

1) Cut nine pieces from 6″ fence boards, each 2′ 6″ long.

2) Construct each of the ends and the partition of the feeder by nailing three of these pieces together with a cleat at the bottom and another at the upper edge 2′ 0″ from the bottom.

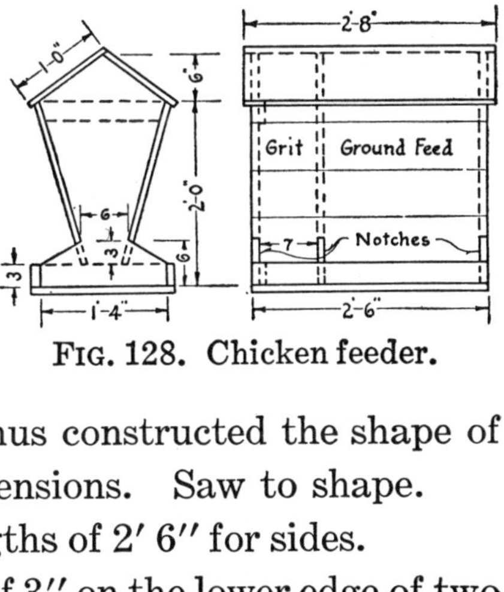

FIG. 128. Chicken feeder.

3) Lay out upon a vertical center line of each end board thus constructed the shape of the feeder end according to dimensions. Saw to shape.

4) Saw 6″ fence boards to lengths of 2′ 6″ for sides.

5) Cut out corners a distance of 3″ on the lower edge of two of the side boards to fit between the end pieces at the bottom of the feed box. Nail each in position for lower board of each side. Nail other side boards on from bottom to top. Dress with plane upper edge of top side boards at roof angle to allow roof boards to fit on same closely.

6) Saw, fit and nail on bottom, roof and side boards for tray. Use 8d. common nails.

73. Garden Marker (Fig. 129).

1) Secure stock as follows:

One 2″ x 4″ x 4′ 0″.

One 1″ x 6″ x 8′ 0″.

Short stock for braces and marking pins may be secured from waste from handle.

2) Plane bed board to dimensions; bevel front edge.

3) Locate centers for marker pin holes on top and bottom surfaces of bed board by means of marking gage and try-square. Angle of pin should be about 15 degrees to a vertical line.

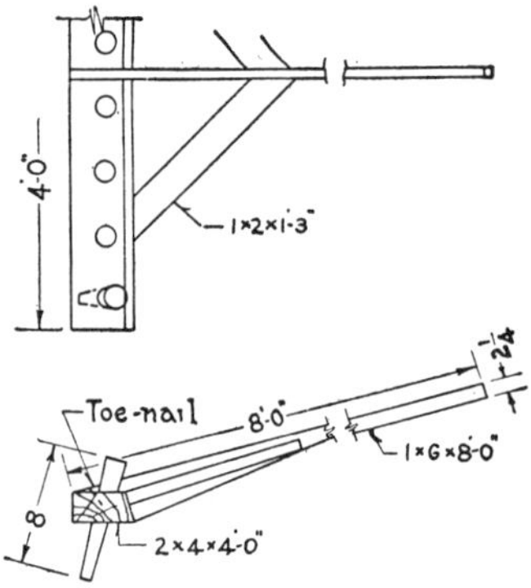

FIG. 129. Garden marker.

4) Bore 1-1/4″ holes for marker pins, working from each side of bed board. With jack-knife, ream out holes on top side to approximately 1-1/2″.

5) Shape handle, nail securely in place, and brace with pieces of stock ripped from handle on under side.

6) From waste stock ripped from handle, or better, from pieces of 2″ x 4″ ripped to 2″ square strips, whittle out marker pins. Drive pins in place and toe-nail from the top, allowing nail heads to project sufficiently so that the nails may be removed with a hammer.

74. Individual Hog Cot (Fig. 130).

1) Frame floor by nailing four 2″ x 4″'s edgewise across the two 2″ x 4″ runners, one at each end, front and back, and the remaining two evenly dividing the remaining space.

2) Cut rafters, three for each side, each 6′ 6″ long. Toe-

nail bottom ends on runners, one at each end and one in the middle. Toe-nail tops of rafters of each pair together.

3) Fasten rafters together on each side by three strips (roof stringers) of 1″ x 3″ stock. These preferably should be set in (housed) to upper edge of rafters. If so, housings should be cut before rafters are placed in position.

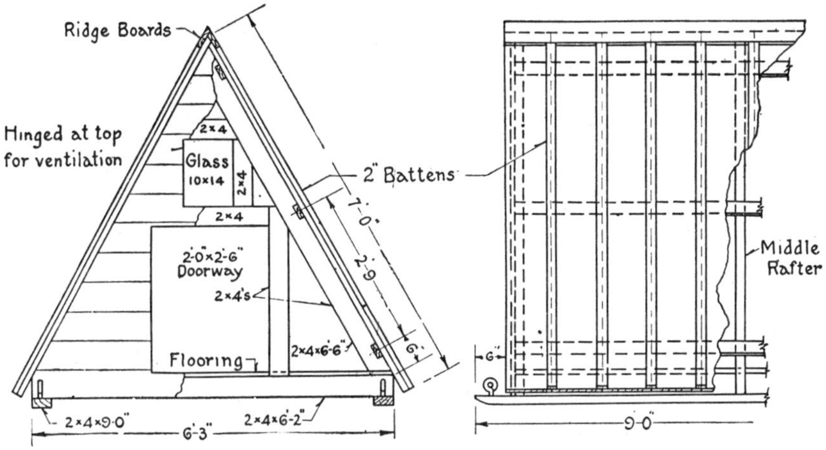

FIG. 130. Hog cot.

4) Lay floor of 1″ x 6″ matched lumber, matching outside floor strips to fit around rafters and come flush with outside edges of them.

5) Erect supports or studs front and back under end rafters to form framing for door and window.

6) Toe-nail window framings between studs.

7) Cover in ends with 1″ x 6″ matched siding, resting bottom edge of bottom boards on top of runners.

8) Cover roof with 1″ x 6″, 1″ x 8″ or 1″ x 10″ boards vertically, nailing each to each roof stringer. Cover each crack with a batten (2″ strip), first placing ridge boards in place.

9) Set window and hinge at top so that it may be opened for

purpose of ventilation. Place framing strips around door and window, if desired, to represent casings.

10) Fasten large eyebolt in each end of each runner to serve as connection in dragging cot from one place to another.

75. Feed Bunk for Sheep (Fig. 131).

1) Cut all 2″ x 4″ stock, viz., four corner posts and two horizontal cross-bar supports for the floor, from a 16′ piece.

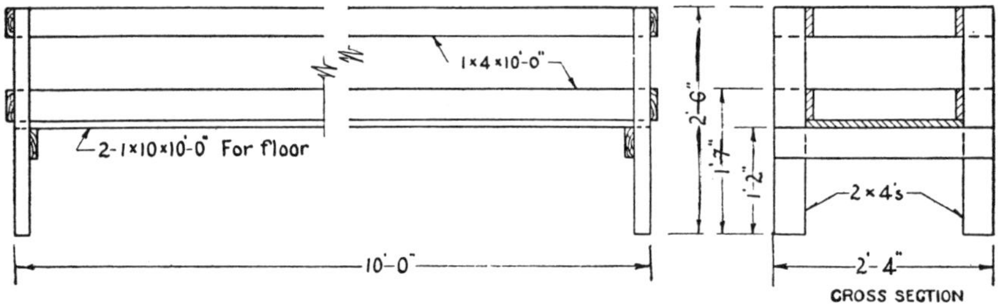

FIG. 131. Feed bunk for sheep.

2) Secure five boards, each 1″ x 4″ x 10′ 0″, and cut from one of them four pieces, each 2′ 4″ long.

3) Frame each end of the bunk.

4) Connect the end frames by nailing the two upper side strips in position.

5) Lay the floor.

6) Nail in position the two lower side strips to form the sides of the feed tray.

76. Plow Doubletree (Fig. 132).

1) Select, from 2″ hickory or straight-grained oak, stock for each of the three parts of the doubletree.

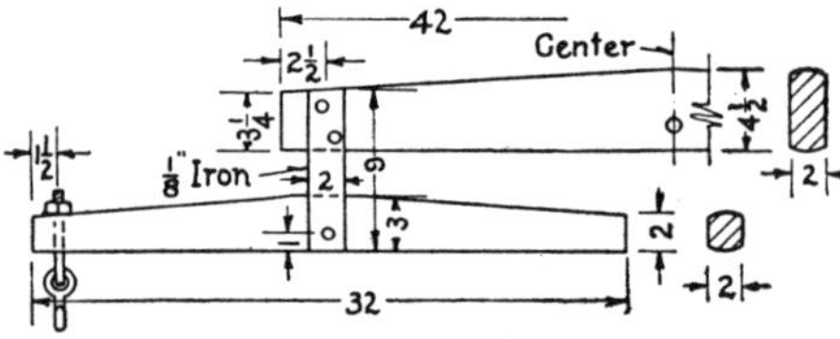

FIG. 132. Plow doubletree.

2) Saw and plane each piece of stock to rectangular shape and to overall dimensions.

3) Plane back edges of each part to the correct taper, first

making lines with straight-edge and pencil defining these edges.

4) Bore holes for metal fittings.

5) Secure in stock, or forge out the tug hooks and bolts to fasten same to wooden parts; also the iron straps to fasten the singletree and doubletree together.

6) Attach metal fittings.

77. Wagon Jack (Figs. 133 and 134).

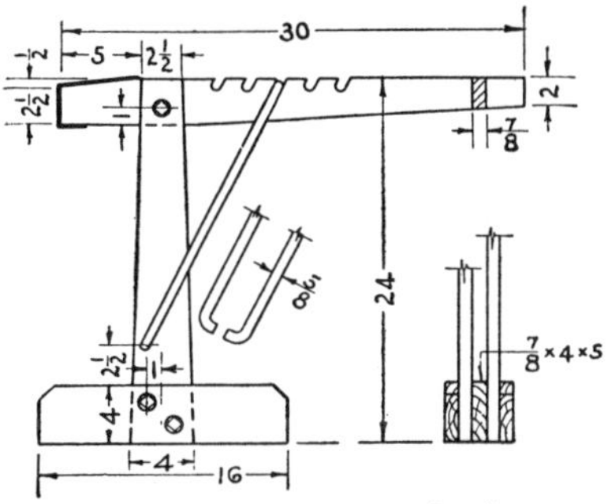

FIG. 133. Wagon jack.

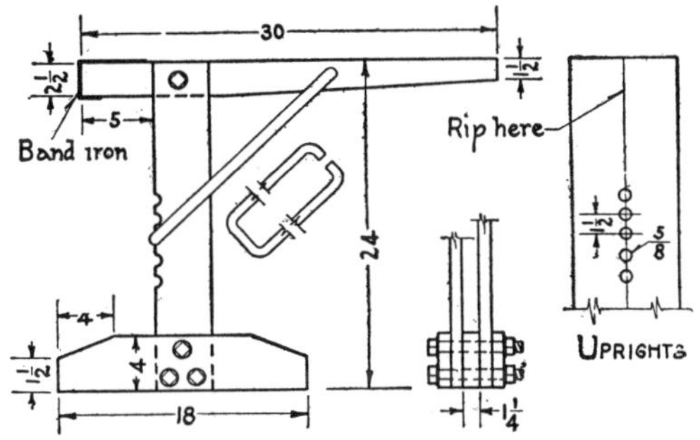

FIG. 134. Another type of wagon jack.

1) Secure hickory, strong, straight-grained oak or other tough wood in following dimensions:

2 pieces 7/8″ x 5″ x 2′ 2″ S2S, uprights.
2 pieces 7/8″ x 4″ x 2′ 6″ S2S, base strips.
1 piece 7/8″ x 3″ x 2′ 6″ S2S, handle.
1 piece 7/8″ x 4″ x 5″ S2S, block at bottom between uprights.

2) Saw and plane each piece of stock to shape and dimensions, as shown in Figs. 133 and 134.

3) Bore series of 5/8″ holes 2″ apart, beginning 12″ from end of handle, each with center 1/2″ from upper edge of handle.

4) Saw notches, as indicated in Fig. 133, saw-cut in each case meeting outer surface of bored hole.

5) With all pieces fastened together in vise or clamp, bore holes for 5/8″ bolts to fasten upright to base strips and handle.

6) Bend 3/4″ band iron around lifting end of handle; drill and countersink holes for 1″ flat-head screws and fasten band iron in place.

7) Assemble all parts of the jack, except the iron rod, to hold the handle in particular positions. The bolts used should be fastened each with a washer under the head and under the nut.

8) Measure with a cord the distance from one hole into

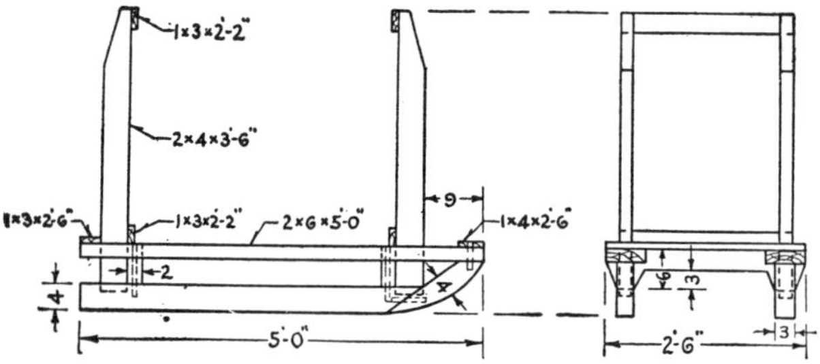

FIG. 135. Farm sled.

which the handle holding iron is to be slipped to the opposite one, thru the first notch from the standard on the handle. In doing this, lower the lifting end of the handle to the lowest desired position. Make allowance for the ends of the handle holding rod, which will slip into the holes in the standard. Add the amount of this allowance to the length of the cord; the total length will be that of the handle holding rod.

9) Cut a 5/8″ round wrought-iron rod to the length of the cord as calculated. Bend the rod to the desired shape by heating portion at bend, and working over end of peen of blacksmith anvil. Cool and spring rod into position.

78. Heavy Farm Sled (Fig. 135).

1) Cut all stock (rough) to overall lengths.

2) Lay out, saw and cut all joints on similar pieces. Example: Two horizontal parts of runners; two front parts of runners; two cross-beams, etc.

3) Frame together the two parts of each runner, driving dowel in with glue, and toe-nailing runner parts together from top and bottom.

4) Put cross-beams in place, driving dowel in place in glue and spiking from under side of runner.

5) Nail long boards of runner frames (bed boards) in position on each cross-beam and on top of runner.

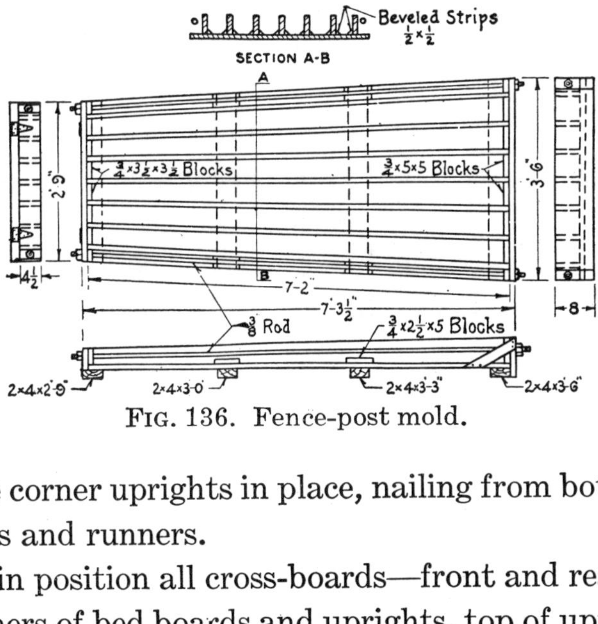

FIG. 136. Fence-post mold.

6) Place corner uprights in place, nailing from both sides of bed boards and runners.

7) Nail in position all cross-boards—front and rear of sled, inside corners of bed boards and uprights, top of uprights.

Note: Letter each set of boards, and use letter in operation steps.

79. Fence Post Mold (Fig. 136).

1) Lay floor on 2″ x 4″ cleats, as shown in cross-sectional side view. Upper surface of flooring material should be sur-

faced, and joints between boards made close, but not absolutely tight if lumber is very dry.

2) Prepare ends by planing one board 4-3/4″ wide and 2′ 9″ long, and the other 6″ wide and 3′ 5-3/4″ long, out of 3/4″ stock. On the first board flush with upper edge, fasten a series of 3-1/2″ x 3-1/2″ blocks, leaving 13/16″ between them. Begin to fix these blocks at the center of the board where a 13/16″ space is to be left for the middle partition. On the second board, fasten 5″ x 5″ blocks in a similar way.

3) Prepare seven partition boards dressed on all surfaces, 3/4″ thick, 3-1/2″ wide at one end, 5″ wide at the other end, and 7′ 2″ long. The ends must be square with the center line of the partition board.

4) Place the two end boards and the partition boards in place on the floor and nail into position the 2-1/2″ x 5″ blocks noted on the top view of drawing.

5) Nail in position end blocks on each end board thru which 3/8″ rods pass. These should touch, but not bend, the outside partition boards. Locate position of holes for rods to come in center of space on end boards outside of the last partition board. Locate position of hinges on small end board.

6) Remove end boards, bore holes for rod, fasten on hinges and replace end boards, inserting side rods and fastening hinges to floor (see end view).

7) Remove partition boards, prepare beveled strips (section *A*), fasten them to the floor, and replace the boards.

8) Cover inside surfaces for each individual mould with linseed oil.

CHAPTER IX

WOOD-FINISHING AND PAINTING

80. Purpose of Wood-Finishing. With few exceptions, all woodwork, whether exposed to the weather or used under cover, is given some sort of surface finish. The object of wood-finishing is twofold, viz.:

First, to preserve the wood. All wood is porous and, consequently, absorbs moisture. With the change of temperature and amount of humidity in the atmosphere, the quantity of moisture taken up by wood will vary. The change in the moisture content of wood causes a change in its shape, known as *warp* (the word used for buckling) and *wind* (the word used for twisting).

The absorption of moisture by wood is accompanied by swelling. As wood dries, it shrinks, thus causing checks and cracks.

Second, to decorate the wood. Decoration may be natural or artificial. Any substance such as oil or wax which, when applied to the surface of wood, brings out its natural markings and colorings, is regarded as a natural decorative agent. Any substance such as colored stain or paint, which covers the grain of wood when applied to it, may be made a decorative agent, but is considered artificial, as it changes the natural appearance.

81. Method of Preservation. Both the natural and artificial wood-finishing agents serve to seal the pores of the wood. All stains have a tendency to enter the wood fibre and to close the pores, but not to fill the cells or larger holes and openings. Paint, on the other hand, covers the entire surface of the wood and, consequently, fills all openings—both pores and cells, as well as such artificial openings as cracks and checks. It must be evident, therefore, that for exposed woodwork, paint is the most satisfactory physical preservative covering. However, besides the fact that it obliterates the material appearance of the wood, it has the possible disadvantage of checking and peeling. On the other hand, when a stain has some inherent preserving quality, chemical or otherwise, it results in both protecting the wood and preserving its natural beauty.

82. Classification of Wood Finishes.

A. *Non-covering agents* may be divided as follows:

1. Oil.
2. Wax.
3. Stain
   - *a.* Water.
   - *b.* Oil.
   - *c.* Chemical.
   - *d.* Creosote.

P. *Covering agents* may be divided as follows:

1. Shellac
   - *a.* White.
   - *b.* Orange.
2. Varnish
3. Filler.
4. Paint.

83. Oil Stain is used on work which does not require a high finish, but which, to present the full effect of the natural grain, needs a light coat of finishing material. Raw linseed oil is generally used for this purpose. That it may penetrate to the greatest extent, the oil should be applied when hot. A soft cloth, cotton waste or a brush may be used. When the oil has evaporated, or has set in the wood, a brisk rubbing will secure a dull polish, which, however, will not long continue except by repeated rubbing, which may be done on inside work in the process of dusting.

Oak, when used outside, as for garden furniture, is protected somewhat from the weather when given coats of hot linseed oil two or three times annually.

84. **Wax.** This may be secured in cans as "prepared wax." It is frequently used to give a natural finish of low gloss. This material is a substitute for oil and serves not so much as a preservative by means of penetration as by virtue of its filling up openings. When rubbed with a soft cloth, it gives a velvet-like polish. Wax hardens with time and, therefore, makes a very satisfactory wood finish, especially if new coats are added from time to time and if the waxed surfaces are rubbed occasionally.

85. **Water Stains** are the simplest of all liquid finishes to apply. They are sold both in powder and liquid form. A water stain is applied with a brush and, before dry, is rubbed with a cloth or with waste. If care is taken in mixing and applying, there is little difficulty in securing a uniform color. Wax or one of the class *B* finishes may be used after the stain has dried.

Before applying a water stain, the wood should be thoroly scraped and sandpapered, and then "wet down" with water. Water raises the grain as would the water stain if applied first.

When the wood surface has dried after the application of the water, it should be thoroly sanded. The application of the water stain will raise the grain slightly, but not sufficiently to require sanding, which, of course, would injure the appearance of the stained wood.

86. Oil Stains; Chemical Stains. These are applied in the manner described for water stains, except that the previous washing is omitted. An oil stain will strike into the wood more freely than will a water stain, and, consequently, because of the variation in the porosity of the average piece of wood, and especially of different pieces of wood assembled in one unit, difficulty is sometimes experienced in getting a uniform color. It may be necessary on particularly porous woods to dilute an oil stain, or to apply a thinner coat than would be used on a less porous part or piece of wood. Wax or one of the class *B* finishes may be used after an oil stain has dried and the surface oil has evaporated thoroly.

Chemical stains, which now constitute the largest part of those to be secured in the open market, are prepared to overcome the disadvantages of poor penetrating qualities of water stains and the uneven penetration of oil stains. They prove quite satisfactory in giving a uniform and well-set color on wood of fairly uniform quality. They may be covered either with wax or the finishes under class *B*.

87. Coal-tar Creosote Oil. The preservation of wood on the farm cannot always be most satisfactorily accomplished by the use of wood finishes already described. Wooden fence posts, bridge and trestle supports, piles or posts used to support roofs for grain and hay stacks, timbers used in silos, wooden shingles for roofs, etc., are neither stained nor painted as a rule; they are frequently left unprotected. Moisture, air and temperature are natural weather elements which permit the development of fungus growths which cause rot and decay. All wooden structures exposed to the weather should, therefore, be protected.

Toxic mineral salts or coal-tar creosote oil is used to protect outside woodwork which it is not desirable to decorate as the common stains and paints do. Coal-tar creosote oil eradicates fungus organisms or suspends their destructive growth. It is insoluble and, therefore, is impervious to moisture. Present practical results of treating wood with it have justified its use.

The two general methods of treatment are known as the pressure processes and the non-pressure processes. The former are used extensively by large corporations, and the latter by small consumers, in which class the farmer would be placed. Of the non-pressure processes, there are two, viz., the open-tank system and the brush method.

88. **The Brush Method** is the one which the conditions of the average farm make entirely possible. It consists of painting refined coal-tar creosote oil, heated to approximately 150 degrees F., on the wood in the same manner as is done with paint, or pouring the heated creosote over the lumber, catching the drippings in pans or basins, or applying the heated creosote with a mop instead of a brush. It is current opinion that in order to make effective the use of coal-tar creosote oil, it must be applied under pressure; nevertheless, the fact remains that the brush method of surface treatment results in a most surprising increase in the life of the material treated, and in a most satisfactory reduction in the annual cost of maintenance of structure.

Two or three coats of coal-tar creosote oil are necessary, and all surfaces exposed or in contact with moisture-collecting materials, such as concrete, should be covered. Particular attention is directed to the covering of surfaces of joints, such as the sides of mortises and tenons, etc.

89. The Open-Tank Process, while not feasible under ordinary farm conditions, is here briefly described, that it may be used where conditions permit. It consists of alternate hot-and-cold treatments of wood with refined coal-tar creosote oil by immersion and continuous soaking in open tanks without artificial pressure, requiring no mechanical apparatus other than tanks, hoist (in some cases), and means of heating the oil.

The procedure is as follows: Season the lumber sufficiently to expel any excess of moisture. When cut for sizes, construction, etc.—that is, when completely framed—immerse lumber in a bath of coal-tar creosote oil maintained at a temperature of from 150 to 210 degrees F. for a period determined as follows: For close-grained wood (naturally resistant to impregnation), one hour in the hot and one hour in the cold, or cooling, bath for each inch of the largest cross-section. For species more susceptible to treatment, one-quarter of an hour for each inch of the largest cross-section, and milled lumber from ten to thirty minutes in each bath; or, if the stock is in the form of boards, an immersion of a few minutes is sufficient. Frequently, heavy-milled stock is not subjected to the cold-bath treatment, but allowed to remain in the hot bath after the source of heat is removed and while the oil cools. On the other hand, boards are not subjected even to a "cooling" bath as suggested by the use of the word immersion above.

A project in creosoting may be selected from the buildings or structures already erected or to be erected. In some cases, the possibility of creosoting is suggested in the instruction given for woodworking projects.

90. **Shellac** is a gum preparation prepared from the secretion of the lac bug. It is procurable in the market in dry flakes, and is dissolved in alcohol. The consistency for satisfactory use should be that of thin syrup. It is applied with a brush, which should be of good quality. Shellac evaporates rapidly; hence, unusual precaution is necessary in applying it to avoid streaking the surface. Long, single strokes with a well-filled brush will produce the best results. The brush should not make a second stroke over the same surface until the first coat of material is dry.

A dry shellacked surface may be sandpapered and again shellacked. By repeated coats and careful sandings, a very smooth and highly-polished surface may be secured which can be improved by a final light rubbing with a piece of felt or burlap wrapped over a piece of cork or wood, and first dipped in a shallow dish of rubbing oil, and then into pumice stone.

91. **Varnish** acts very similarly to shellac. It is the customary finishing material for highly-polished woodwork. It is applied and treated the same as shellac, but dries much slower.

92. **Wood-Filler** is used to fill the pores of the grain of wood. When shellac or varnish is used, both as a filler and as a finish, many coats are required before the grain is filled and a finishing surface is built up. Wood-filler is, therefore, used

to fill holes and level up the surface for the finishing material, which, ordinarily, is varnish.

Wood-filler is silex mixed with linseed oil, japan and turpentine. It should be thinned with turpentine or benzine to the consistency of paste and applied by means of a brush. When it begins to "gray," a sign of its drying, it should be rubbed across the grain with a handful of excelsior, shavings or waste. Before applying shellac, varnish or other finishing material, the filler should dry at least forty-eight hours. Colored fillers are common to produce particular color effects. The white filler may be mixed with dry pigment colors to secure the color desired. In case wood is both stained and filled, the stain should be used first.

93. **Paint** is made from white lead and linseed oil. It may be secured in the market prepared ready for use after being thoroly stirred. It may be made by mixing white lead and linseed oil with a coloring material. The surface of wood to be covered with paint should be clean and smooth. Paint is applied with a brush with the grain of the wood. The brush should be run back and forth over the same surface several times to work the paint into the grain of the wood. Two or three coats are usually necessary to cover the surface properly. Each coat may be sanded carefully when dry before the succeeding coat is applied. Unless a paint has considerable drier in it, or is a cheap substitute for white lead and oil, it needs at least three or four days to dry before it can be smoothed with sandpaper, or a second coat of paint can be applied.

The projects in wood-finishing and painting should be worked in approximately the order given in the "Classification of Wood Finishes" in Sec. 82. The projects may be those given in the several groups under "Woodworking." Upon the completion of a woodworking project, the proper finish may be applied, or all woodworking projects may first be completed and then finished. In this case, there will be an advantage in concentrating attention upon the work, both of using woodworking tools and of applying wood-finishing materials.

Paint is regarded as easier to apply than shellac or varnish; hence, the project in painting may well precede that in shellacking or varnishing.

Always keep a "full" brush of finishing material; that is, have the lower half of the bristles full of the finishing material, but do not allow the upper part of the brush to be covered. As one removes the brush from the material, it should be drawn upward against the edge of the receptacle on each side, that not too much material may be left in the brush, and also that the upper part of the bristles shall be free from material and the brush kept clean.

Brushes when not in use should be kept hanging in the material in which they are used so that the ends of the bristles will be clear of the bottom of the receptacle. Receptacles should be covered to prevent accumulation of dust and dirt. Any wide-necked bottle or fruit jar may be used as a receptacle for brushes, the stopper being made of wood.

The projects given in the woodworking section of this book suggest the finish which each may be given. It is suggested that the finishing of these projects in the order presented be regarded as the desirable wood-finishing projects to secure the necessary knowledge and practice in this subject.

CHAPTER X

Glazing and Screening

94. Definition. Glazing consists of cutting and setting glass in frames. The chief use of this art is in cutting, tacking and puttying panes of glass in window sash, hot-bed frames, etc.

95. Precautions. Window glass may be secured in single- or double-strength thicknesses. Double-strength glass is thicker and stronger than single-strength. Glass also is manufactured in a variety of qualities. That known as common is used for ordinary purposes. Whatever the strength or quality, sheet glass should be handled with care, both to prevent breaking it and to provide against being cut by it. It should be grasped by thumb and fingers of both hands, each taking hold of one of opposite edges. When working upon a pane of glass, it should be laid flat on a plain wood surface, such as the top of a bench or table.

96. Cutting Glass. Clean off a flat wooden surface and lay the glass on it, preferably by sliding the glass upon the surface rather than placing it upon the surface from above. If an irregular piece of glass is to be used, place a straight-edge, preferably of wood, but the edge of a carpenter's square may be used, near one edge and run a glass cutter across the glass and against the edge of the straight-edge with one firm stroke, using moderate pressure. If the glass cutter is sharp and the single operation is done carefully, a cut will appear at all points on the glass where the cutter has run. Slide the glass into a position so that the waste stock projects over the edge of the wooden surface, table or bench top, on which it is placed, and so that the line cut in the glass is directly above this edge. With the left hand placed flat on the surface of the glass which is on the table, and with the thumb and fingers of the right hand grasping the edge of the glass projecting over the edge of the table, gently press downward with the right hand.

The glass should crack or make a clean break on the line made with the glass cutter, thus giving one edge of the piece of glass desired.

Place one leg of carpenter's square against this edge and the other in a position to secure an adjacent edge of the piece of glass being prepared. Repeat the operation of cutting and breaking off the waste.

In a similar manner, secure the opposite edges. First, measure carefully for the desired width or length at two points near each end of an edge already formed, and mark in each measurement by a short line—1/4″ is sufficient—made with the glass cutter. Connect these points by the edge of the blade of a carpenter's square or wooden straight-edge against which the glass cutter is run as before.

97. Setting a Pane of Glass in a New Frame. Place the pane of glass in the frame and very gently fasten it in position with three-cornered pieces of tin (glazier's points) used by glaziers, which may be secured when purchasing putty. Lay a triangular piece of tin flat on the glass as it rests in the frame on a bench or table top. With a finger or thumb, press one corner of this tin into the frame near a corner of the pane of glass. With the end of the putty-knife blade resting on the pane of glass as the knife is held in the right hand, or with a square-edged chisel, very carefully drive the point about 3/16″ into the wood by letting the edge of the putty-knife or chisel blade gently strike the point three or four times.

Likewise, insert other points, locating them so as to have one come near the corner of the frame on each edge of the pane, and others placed to make the distance between consecutive tins about 8″ or 10″. In case of a small pane, at least one point should be placed near the middle of each edge of the pane.

If a pane is being set in a vertical frame, as in a window sash in a window frame, care must be taken to hold it firmly in position with the left hand while the right hand is used to drive the points into the frame. Care must always be taken to have the pane well seated; that is, firmly resting against the frame on which the flat surface of the pane rests.

98. Applying the Putty. In order to seal the pane in the frame, making the joint waterproof, putty is pressed into the corner between the pane and the frame. Putty as it comes from the stock receptacle, may need to be mixed with a little boiled linseed oil to soften it. The oil should be mixed thoroly with the putty. Unless the putty is quite dry, the oil need not be added to it, as kneading it in the hands will make it soft.

In applying putty, one should practice the following method: (1) After having beaten and kneaded the putty to an even consistency, cut off a small amount and form it roughly into the shape of a ball. (2) Put this putty into the palm of the left hand and hold the putty knife in the right. Set the frame to be puttied on an easel or on some similar device so that the glass slants away from the operator. (3) Now, with the left hand preceding the right hand, and with the putty knife in position against the glass, feed the putty with the thumb and the first two fingers of the left hand from its position in the palm of the hand and under the corner of the putty knife. Move both hands slowly from right to left, feeding enough putty under the knife to fill the triangular opening formed between the knife and the wood and the glass. (4) When one complete stroke is made, go back and fill in any imperfect spaces, and also clean off any surplus putty which may be left. A little practice is necessary before a perfect job is made with the first stroke. Care should be taken not to allow the putty to get smeared on the glass more than is necessary. The putty should not be high enough to show above the wood on opposite side of the glass.

If a broken pane of glass is being replaced or the opening in an old frame is being filled, care must be taken to clean thoroly the corner into which the pane fits of all dirt, especially old putty. Use broken panes of glass as far as possible in re-glazing windows.

The projects in glazing should consist both of replacing an old pane or panes of glass, and setting the glass in a new frame. After the putty is thoroly dry and hard, it should be painted with the frame in which it is set.

99. Screening. Every farm home should be screened as a protection against the house fly, rightly called the typhoid fly. Screens for doors and windows of standard sizes can be bought in stock from most lumber dealers. One who is handy with tools can easily construct screens.

During the winter months, the screens should be removed from the windows and doors and stored away in a dry place. During spare time, they should be cleaned and painted. Paint especially prepared for this purpose is obtainable at most paint stores. Painting the screens keeps them from rusting and will increase their life many years.

PART II

Cement and Concrete

CHAPTER XI

History of Cement

100. Preliminary. The fact that concrete is now being used so universally, both on the farm and in the city, makes it desirable, if not necessary, that every one should study its possibilities and learn at least the first principles of correct concrete construction. There are too many poor jobs of concrete work, the failure of which is due to lack of knowledge on the part of the man doing the work. Concrete, when properly made, has too many good qualities to be condemned merely because of lack of information and judgment on the part of the man who uses it.

The main reasons concrete is being used to such a great extent are:

a) It is permanent.

b) It is more nearly fireproof than any other building material.

c) It is rat-proof.

d) It is attractive.

e) It is sanitary.

f) With the aid of steel, it can be used for most any purpose in building.

g) It can be used with success by the average farmer with less special training than is required with other available materials.

h) It is economical.

101. Pre-historic Uses of Concrete. Altho we now find concrete being used in nearly all types of construction work, it is only of recent years that the cement industry has been developed. Some form of cement was used thousands of years ago. The ruins of Babylon and Nineveh show traces of it, as does the Pantheon of Rome. It is said that the pre-historic people of America—the Aztecs and Toltecs—used a cement mortar that has been so durable that the mortar joints are projecting where the adjacent stones have been worn away by the weathering action during the ages.

There is little evidence of the use of cement during the intervening period from three or four thousand years ago up to the beginning of the nineteenth century. During this period, the art of making cement seems to have been lost and the builders of the Middle Ages had to resort to the use of lime and silt mortars, which were not very durable, as evidenced by the ruins of this age.

102. Re-discovery of Cement. The re-discovery of the method of manufacture of hydraulic cement, a cement that will set or harden under water, was made by John Smeaton, an English engineer, in 1756. He discovered that limestone containing clay, when burned and then ground until very fine, produced a material which would not only set under water, but also resist the action of water. This we call natural cement. The manufacture of this natural cement on a commercial basis is credited to Joseph Parker, who established a factory in 1796 and called his product Roman Cement. Other factories were established in Europe about the same time.

103. Natural Cement in America. In 1818, Canvass White established a factory at Fayetteville, New York, for manufacturing natural cement on a commercial basis. Other plants sprang up along the canals in New York state; also in Ohio, and a plant was established near Louisville, Kentucky. The output for a number of years was very small—about 25,000 barrels per year. After the Civil War, during the reconstruction period, an impetus was given to the cement industry, and the production of natural cement reached its maximum in 1899, when 10,000,000 barrels were produced. Since then, the production of cement from natural stone as found in the quarries has been on the decline. At the present time practically all cement used in America is artificial cement, or Portland cement.

104. Portland Cement. The process of making artificial cement, or Portland cement, was discovered by Joseph Aspdin, an Englishman, in 1829. The cement was given its name because it resembles the Portland rocks near Leeds, England. In the United States it was first manufactured in 1870 at Copley, Pennsylvania. Its use has increased so rapidly that now the output amounts to about 100,000,000 barrels per year. Portland cement manufacturing plants can now be found thruout the country. Wherever there is an abundance of suitable limestone and shale, or clay, and a supply of fuel and labor, a cement plant can be successfully operated. Portland cement is different from natural cement, in that the materials of which it is made are carefully proportioned and artificially mixed. The essential components of Portland cement are silica, aluminum and lime, with small quantities of other materials. The silica and aluminum are in the clay. The material is first ground, then mixed in proportion of three parts of limestone to one of clay; it is then burned to a clinker and re-ground to proper fineness. While there are a great many brands of Portland cement on the market, the composition is practically constant and the buyer can feel safe in buying any recognized brand.

CHAPTER XII

Properties and Uses of Cement

105. Properties. The properties of cement with which every builder is most concerned are those of strength and permanence. The requirements ordinarily mentioned are proper fineness, proper setting qualities, purity, strength in tension, and soundness. A cement that is fresh, free from lumps, properly packed and stored, is nearly always first-class.

106. Mortar. Mortar is a mixture of (1) cement or hydrated lime, or both, (2) sand, and (3) water. It is a plastic mass, the water content being varied with its use. Lime mortars are little used at present because they set slowly, will not set under water, are not very strong, and will deteriorate, due to weathering action. A small amount of lime, 10 to 20 per cent, is usually added to cement mortar to make it work well with a trowel and to make it more adhesive.

107. Definition of Concrete. Concrete is often defined as an artificial stone. It is made by mixing cement with sand and gravel, or broken stone, and water; or, in other words, it is a mixture of (1) cement, (2) a fine aggregate, (3) a coarse aggregate, and (4) water. The addition of water causes the cement to undergo chemical changes forming new compounds that develop the property of crystallizing into a solid mass. The strength and durability of plain concrete (that is, concrete without reinforcing) varies with:

a) The quality and amount of cement used.

b) The kind, size and strength of aggregate.

c) Correctness of proportioning.

d) Method and thoroness of mixing.

e) The amount of water.

f) Method and care of placing.

g) Method of curing.

h) Age.

108. Aggregates. As ordinarily employed, the term ag-

FIG. 137. Gravel bank.

gregates includes not only gravel or stone—the coarse material used—but also the sand, or fine material, which is used with the cement to form either mortar or concrete. Fine aggregate is defined as any suitable material that will pass a No. 4 sieve or screen (having four meshes to the linear inch), and includes sand, stone screenings, crushed slag, etc. By coarse aggregate is meant any suitable material, such as crushed stone or gravel, that is retained on a No. 4 sieve. The maximum size of coarse aggregate depends on the class of structure for which the concrete is to be used.

The fact that the aggregates may seem to be of good quality and yet prove totally unsuitable (Fig. 137), shows that study and careful tests are necessary if the best results are to be obtained. The idea that the strength of concrete depends entirely upon the cement, and that only a superficial examination of aggregates is necessary, is altogether too prevalent. The man who recognizes the quality of his aggregates, who grades them properly, sees that they are washed if necessary, then mixes them in proportions determined by thoro testing, study or actual experience, is the one who will make the best concrete.

In the selection and use of sand, more precaution is necessary than for the coarser aggregate, due to the physical condition of sand and a wider variation in properties. A knowledge of these properties and of the method of analysis to determine the suitability of sand for use in mortar and concrete, may easily be applied to an analysis of the coarse aggregate.

109. Presence of Rotten or Soft Pebbles in the Gravel. In many cases, gravel from the old glaciers has been used, which have been so badly weathered that the pebbles can be crushed between the fingers. In other cases, small lumps of shale or sandstone are mistaken for gravel. These lumps are not strong at best, and, under the action of water, especially alternate wetting and drying, they go to pieces. No pebbles which can be scratched with a thumb nail, or crushed in the fingers, are suitable for concrete. If there are only a few of them in gravel which is otherwise good, they will not seriously weaken the concrete, but it is a good deal better not to use them at all, since a hard concrete cannot be made from soft materials.

110. Presence of Dirt in the Aggregate. Most gravels and sands contain some clay, but clay in amounts up to three per cent by weight is not especially harmful. More than three per cent is harmful. Where gravels contain organic matter of any kind, the concrete made from them is very likely to go to pieces, and they should not be used unless the dirt can be washed out. Clay may also be removed by washing. To test for amount of dirt, shake up four inches of sand or gravel in a quart fruit jar, three-fourths full of water, for four or five minutes. Then let it stand three hours. If there is more than 1/2″ of dirt on top of the material, it is too dirty to use without washing.

111. Vegetable Matter in Sand. A coating of vegetable matter on sand grains appears not only to prevent the cement from adhering, but to affect it chemically. Frequently, a quantity of vegetable matter so small that it cannot be detected by the eye, and only slightly disclosed in chemical tests, may prevent the mortar from reaching any appreciable strength, Concrete made with such sand usually hardens so slowly that the results are questionable and its use is prohibited. Other impurities, such as acids, alkalis or oils in the sand or mixing water, usually make trouble.

Where limestone is used in an aggregate, it is well to see that the pile of limestone is thoroly wet down before using. This is for two purposes—(1) to remove the coating of dust which would otherwise prevent the formation of a bond between the cement and the stone, and (2) to allow the stone to absorb water before the mixing process. Limestone will absorb a great deal of moisture, and, if mixed dry, it is liable to take up part of the water needed in the process of setting or crystallizing.

CHAPTER XIII

Proportions and Mixtures; Handling of Concrete

112. Proportions. The theory of proper proportions is to use just enough sand to fill the air spaces or voids in the coarse aggregate, and enough cement to fill the air spaces in the sand, and also to coat each particle and thus serve as a binder. The small contractor in actual practice rarely attempts to carry this out; in fact, he seldom accurately measures the materials that go into the job. He uses a little cement, some sand and gravel, and, under average conditions, may get fair results. It is no wonder, however, that we find sidewalks going to pieces, foundations of buildings cracking and disintegrating when the work is done in such a haphazard fashion.

To make a concrete that is strong as well as economical, it is essential that the materials be well graded from the larger to the smaller-sized particles so that the voids around the particles are reduced to a minimum. The absolute elimination of voids is an ideal condition which we should strive to obtain. However, the densest concrete is not always the strongest. In some cases, a rather porous mixture with a small amount of fine aggregate is stronger than another piece of concrete with a great deal of fine aggregate and a small amount of coarse material, although the latter mixture would be the denser of the two.

113. Requirements of Good Concrete. The proper proportions to use, under practical conditions, will depend on the use to which the concrete is to be put. The three properties which are most often required are: (1) Strength, as in bridges, buildings, etc.; (2) resistance to wear, as in concrete sidewalks and roads; (3) water-tightness, as in water tanks, silos, etc. The practical mixtures that are ordinarily used for different kinds of concrete work are as follows:

114. Standard Mixtures. Rich mixture of 1 part cement, 1-1/2 parts sand, and 3 parts broken stone, or gravel, commonly called a 1 : 1-1/2 : 3 mixture, is used for columns of reinforced concrete buildings, for thin water-tight walls where very dense, strong concrete is required, and under all similar conditions.

A good, standard mixture of 1 part cement, 2 parts sand, and 4 parts broken stone, commonly called 1 : 2 : 4 mixture, is used for reinforced concrete work of all kinds, for water tanks, thin walls, etc.

Medium mixture of 1 part cement, 2-1/2 parts sand, and 5 parts broken stone, commonly called 1 : 2-1/2 : 5 mixture, is used for all plain concrete, that is, concrete without reinforcing—for foundations, walls, floors, etc. When the walls are to be water-tight, a 1 : 2 : 4 mixture should be used instead.

Lean mixture of 1 part cement, 3 parts of sand, and 6 parts broken stone, commonly called 1 : 3 : 6 mixture, is used for very heavy mass concrete where the loads are wholly compressive. Still leaner mixtures are sometimes used for very heavy foundations and abutments, but are not recommended for general use.

115. Common Errors in Proportioning Concrete. A rather common error that is made by the inexperienced concrete worker is to assume that when mixing one cubic foot of cement, two cubic feet of sand, and four cubic feet of gravel, he will secure seven cubic feet of concrete. This is an entirely erroneous idea, as the sand would simply fill the voids in the coarse material, and the cement would fill the voids in the sand and coat the particles of sand and gravel or stone. Since the amount of cement and sand used is more than enough to fill the voids in the gravel, the resulting concrete will be slightly more than four cubic feet, about 4.25 under average conditions. The same error is often made when unscreened, bank-run materials are used. In attempting to secure the equivalent of a 1 : 2 : 4 mixture, the contractor will use one part of cement to six parts of bank-run material, when, in reality, he should use only about 4-1/4 cubic feet of bank-run material to one cubic foot of cement to get the equivalent of a 1 : 2 : 4 mixture. This is assuming that the bank-run material is of the correct proportion of one part of fine aggregate to two parts of coarse aggregate, which should be accurately determined by testing. The only safe method of using bank-run materials is to screen them before using. Then when the materials are used, the proportions can be definitely secured.

116. Determining Quantities for a Job. In determining the quantities of material for a job, one must remember that the volume of concrete is only a little greater than the volume of coarse aggregate; in fact, this is often taken as a basis for estimate of materials needed. For example, suppose it is required to make 54 cubic feet of concrete of a 1 : 2 : 4 mixture. It is assumed that 54 cubic feet of coarse aggregate, 27 cubic feet of sand, and 13-1/2 cubic feet, or 13-1/2 sacks of cement are required. Another rule which may be used for all standard proportions is to take the sum of the proportions and divide into the number 11; the quotient will be the number of barrels of cement required to make one cubic yard of concrete of the particular proportion. For example, $\frac{11}{1+2+4}$ = 1-4/7 barrels of cement, or 6-2/7 sacks (4 sacks to a barrel) for one cubic yard of concrete. Since 54 cubic feet, or 2 cubic yards, of concrete is required in the above job, it will take 2 x 6-2/7, or 12-4/7 sacks of cement, 25-1/7 cubic feet of sand, and 50-2/7 cubic feet of coarse aggregate. For a small job, the first method may be used, but with the larger job, the latter method, which is more accurate, should be adopted.

117. Requirements of Good Mixing. The requirements of good mixing are: (1) That every particle of sand and stone is coated with cement paste, (2) that the sand and stone are evenly distributed through the mass, and (3) that the whole mixture is of a uniform consistency. A poorly-mixed concrete may be known by its lack of uniformity in color and the separation of fine and coarse material. It is just as important to have materials thoroly and carefully mixed as to have them properly proportioned. It is considered so important by well-informed concrete contractors, that they require the materials to be mixed for a definite period of time, if mixed by machine method, or turned a definite number of times if mixed by hand. Up to a certain limit, it has been found that the strength of the concrete is directly proportional to the length of time it has been kept in the mixer. (In the specifications for the construction of some concrete work, the time of mixing is definitely stated.)

118. Hand-Mixing. A water-tight platform is the first requirement for successful hand-mixing. In mixing by hand, there is always a tendency to mix in small units, which is sometimes a mistaken idea. It is usually best to mix at least enough so that one sack of cement or one cubic foot can be taken as a unit because, if the sack is emptied and only a part of a sack is taken, the cement will fluff up and form more than one cubic foot.

119. Procedure in Hand-Mixing. In the actual process of mixing, it is usually best to spread the sand on the mixing

FIG. 138. Spreading cement on sand.

board, and on top of this spread the sack of cement (Fig. 138); then two men using square-pointed shovels turn this sand and cement over several times until the streaks of color are merged into a uniform shade throughout the entire mass. The coarse aggregate is then added (Fig. 138-*a*), and during the first turning, water is added by means of a hose or from a bucket (Fig. 139). Care must be observed to prevent washing the cement out of the mass. It is best to turn the materials several times (Fig. 139-*a*), adding a small amount of water

FIG. 138-*a*. Measuring coarse aggregate.

FIG. 139. Adding water to mixture.

each time until it reaches the proper consistency. The only objection to the hand method of mixing is that a great deal of labor is involved, and this, in some cases, reduces the quality of the concrete because of the fact that the materials are not mixed as thoroly as when mixed in a mixing machine.

FIG. 139-*a*. Turning the mixture.

FIG. 140. Batch mixer.

120. Machine-Mixing. There are two types of machine mixers in use—the batch mixer (Figs. 140 and 140-*a*) and the continuous mixer. The latter type is not as satisfactory as the batch mixer and is seldom used except on small jobs.

Better results can be obtained with the batch mixer, because a definite quantity of materials is added and thoroly mixed before any concrete is discharged from the mixer. By allowing the materials to remain in the mixer for a definite period of time, they are more completely mixed, and all parts are of uniform proportion. In the continuous mixer, the dry materials are fed automatically from a hopper into a mixing trough where water is added and where the entire mass is mixed and carried along by blades to the discharge end, where the concrete is discharged continuously

FIG. 140-*a*. Another batch mixer.

121. Consistency of Mixtures. The amount of water used in making concrete will depend on the use for which the concrete is intended. There are three consistencies ordinarily referred to in discussing concrete. They are generally called the "dry," "quaky" and "wet" mixtures. The dry mixture is of about the consistency of damp earth and is used where the concrete is tamped into place. The quaky mixture is so named because it is wet enough to quake when it is tamped. It is used in molded products requiring reinforcing, such as fence posts, beams, columns, etc. It is also used in sidewalks, floors and foundations. The wet mixture contains enough water to permit its flowing from the shovel or conveyors from elevators to various points in the construction of large buildings. There is a tendency on the part of some contractors to make the mixture very wet so as to make it flow more easily. This will cause the separation of the coarse materials from the finer and reduce the quality of the concrete. One main point to remember in connection with the proper consistency is that the materials must not be too dry nor too wet; either condition will cause the separation of the coarse material from the mortar.

122. Placing of Concrete. No time should elapse between the "mixing" and the "placing." One's judgment must be used in placing; the method adopted will depend on the particular job. The essential feature in placing is to prevent the separation of the stone from the mortar.

123. Three Methods of Placing Concrete.

1) A dry mixture of concrete is placed by thoro tamping or by pressure. The density and the final strength of a dry mixture will depend on the extent of tamping. This method of placing concrete is used in making concrete products that are not reinforced, such as blocks, bricks and jardinieres. The material must be carefully tamped as the mold is being filled, either by hand or by power machines.

2) A quaky mixture can be placed by agitation or slight tamping. This method is used in making reinforced products, such as posts, large tile and tanks; also for slab work, such as floors and sidewalks. Some forms are designed so they can be vibrated to settle the concrete into place.

3) A wet mixture is simply deposited into place, and requires no tamping. A spade or board should be used for

working large stones back from the forms and leveling the surface so that no large stones are left uncovered (Fig. 141). This mixture and method of placing is used in nearly all reinforced structures where the reinforcing is put in place before the concrete is poured. For large structures, special apparatus is used for elevating the material.

FIG. 141. Working stones away from surface.

124. Handling Concrete. There are three common ways of conveying the mixture:

a) It may be shoveled off the board directly into the work.

b) It may be shoveled into wheelbarrows and wheeled to position and dumped.

c) It may be elevated by buckets and hoisting apparatus.

Where the concrete is mixed by hand, it is usually transported by wheelbarrow (Fig. 142). For machine-mixed concrete where the work is of some magnitude, some flexible

FIG. 142. Moving concrete with wheelbarrow.

method of handling it is best, usually a tower with elevating equipment. Derricks and bucket elevators are also used. The one objection to the use of tower and chutes is the tendency, in order to secure easy flow, to use too much water, causing a separation of the fine and coarse aggregate.

CHAPTER XIV

FORMS FOR CONCRETE; CURING CONCRETE

125. Necessity of Forms. The plasticity of concrete, and the readiness with which the material can be adapted to all shapes and sizes of construction, which are two of the chief merits of the material, make necessary the use of forms in connection with it.

126. Importance of Form Construction. The design and construction of forms is one of the most serious problems of concrete work. As a rule, on small work, the expense of the forms is from one-fourth to one-half of the total cost of the work in place. Many people do not appreciate this fact and neglect the forms with the result that the finished work is of poor quality, or else the forms have cost too much. The shape, dimensions and finish of the work all depend on the forms, and it is not possible to do good concrete work without good forms.

127. Earth Forms. In foundation walls, where care has been observed in excavation and the earth stands up properly, it can be used. Earth can be used also in making well tops, etc., where the work can be fashioned out in the clay. The earth must be wet down thoroly to keep it from absorbing too much moisture from the concrete. A combination of wood and clay can be used. Molds of wet sand are used in ornamental work. Frequently, colored sands are used for this purpose, providing both the finished surface and color to the concrete.

128. Cast, Wrought or Galvanized Iron Forms. These are used where a smooth surface is desired without further treatment after removal of forms. In construction work, where the same type of form is used a great number of times, it is economy to have a material which will not go to pieces, warp, swell and crack, even tho the first cost may be

FIG. 143. Commercial post mold.

higher. Steel forms, if strongly built, will meet these conditions. Forms made of iron are more easily cleaned, and can be used a great number of times. Rusty iron is not good for forms; the concrete will stick badly. There are steel forms on the market for concrete posts (Fig. 143), water tanks, silos, etc.

129. Wood Forms. Wood forms are most common, and are used most for concrete work on the farm. The chief reason for this is that lumber can be obtained easily in small quantities, and there is always a certain amount of old lumber around every farm.

130. Requirements of a Good Form.

a) One that can be used a number of times.

b) One that is strong so it will not bulge or crack.

c) One that is tight and free from leaks.

d) One that is true and properly aligned.

e) One that is made of good material suited to its use.

Soft woods are better than hard because they (*a*) are cheaper, (*b*) do not crack so badly, (*c*) are an easier material to work. Spruce and yellow pine make good forms; the boards used should be sound and free from knot holes. Partly green lumber is better than either green or kiln-dried, because it will swell just enough to make tight joints without buckling. Dressed lumber has several advantages over undressed: (*a*) It makes truer work, (*b*) tighter joints, (*c*) smoother surfaces, (*d*) forms are easier removed, and (*e*) forms are easier cleaned.

131. Use of Old Lumber for Forms. Where old lumber is to be used, it should be sorted and listed so that new lumber can be ordered of proper sizes that will work in best. Care must be observed in the use of old lumber to see that it is strong enough to support the load put on it by the concrete. A great deal of expense can be avoided by taking advantage of old lumber.

132. Sharp Corners in Forms. Sharp corners should be avoided as much as possible in concrete work. It is best to bevel the corners by setting strips in the forms, especially on inside angles. This gives both greater strength and better finish to the work.

133. Removing Forms; Care of Forms. Forms should not be removed until the concrete is thoroly set. The time of setting varies with the wetness of the mixture, and with the weather. Concrete sets much faster in warm, dry weather than in cold or damp weather. On foundation walls or similar work, where the concrete is used in direct compression, the forms may be removed in a few days. Under floors or beams, which are subjected to bending, the forms should be left two weeks or longer.

Care of Forms:

Forms for concrete posts, etc., should be oiled with a heavy oil before they are used. As soon as they are removed, they should be thoroly cleaned with a stiff wire brush. Oiling metal forms or molds after using is better practice than to wait, as a coat of oil prevents rust. In removing wooden forms, care must be observed to avoid splitting boards. All boards should be cleaned, the nails pulled, and boards stacked to prevent warping.

Curing Concrete:

Proper curing of concrete is very essential to success. It must not be allowed to dry out too rapidly. If freshly made and exposed to the intense heat of the summer's sun, it must be protected. The drying out not only produces check cracks, but hinders the setting action of the concrete, making it weak. Floors and walks that are protected and kept moist for some days will harden into a very dense and almost dustless material, while those not adequately protected will wear rapidly and be dusty.

CHAPTER XV

Reinforcing Concrete; Cement-Working Tools

134. The Principle of Reinforcing. Plain concrete is strong in compression, but will not resist a very great load when in tension. Steel is a material that has a great tensile strength, as well as compressive strength, so, by combining the two, we have a resultant material which is strong in both tension and compression, and can be adapted to most any use.

The design of reinforced concrete structures is quite technical and has no place in a text of this character. For simple types of construction, such as reinforcing for a silo, water tank, retaining wall, fence posts and well tops, the student can refer to tables in hand-books, or use his best judgment, bearing in mind that the amount of reinforcing will vary from 3/4 to 1-1/2 per cent of the cross-section of the member being reinforced.

135. Compression and Tension in Beams. A consideration of the basic principles underlying simple reinforced concrete construction may be of interest. Consider a simple beam of uniform cross-section like a 2″ x 4″, supported at each end, with a load applied at the center (Fig. 144). It will be found that the upper part of the beam will be in compression, or tending to crush together, and the lower part will be tearing apart, or in tension. It will be noted that there is a plane perpendicular to the force applied and cutting the beam in half where there is neither tension nor compression. This is called the neutral plane or neutral axis.

Now, since the lower part of the beam is in tension, and

since concrete is weak in tension, it is apparent that to make the lower part of the beam as strong as the upper part, we must imbed some material in the beam that is high in tensile

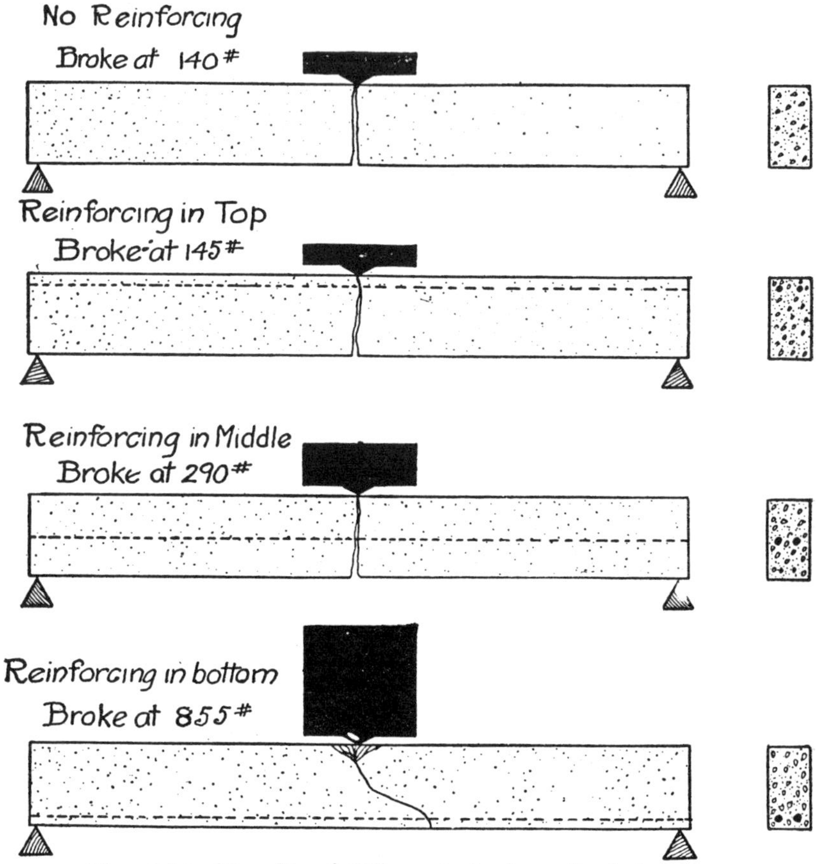

FIG. 144. Results of different placing of reinforcing.

strength. Steel is not only high in tensile strength, but its co-efficient of expansion is the same as that of concrete, so a strong bond between the two can be maintained. It must be kept in mind that the steel must be placed as far as possible from the neutral axis to be most effective. It must not be placed too near the surface of the concrete. It must be kept in mind, further, that in any reinforcing job, the steel must be placed where it will be under a tensile strain. Fig. 144 shows the relative strength of a concrete beam with reinforcing placed in various positions.

136. Kinds of Reinforcing. As to the kinds of reinforcing, probably square twisted steel rods, or the deformed bars, are best. Round rods are sometimes used, but they should be carefully anchored to give the best results. Some engineers specify either the twisted or the deformed rods, since a better bond is secured between the concrete and the steel with this type of reinforcing. Some contractors claim that a small amount of rust on the reinforcing is advantageous. A very small amount of rust may be of some value in forming a bond between the concrete and the steel. However, if the steel is left outside until it has become pitted with rust, the resultant piece of work would be weakened, as the bond between the steel and concrete would be a poor one.

137. Use of Scrap Iron for Reinforcing Concrete. It is thought by some that scrap iron will make good reinforcing. It is seldom true that as good a job can be secured by using scrap iron, old gas pipe, etc., as by using regular reinforcing steel. Gas pipe that is of value as pipe is expensive reinforcing material.

138. Tools for Concrete Work. Very inexpensive tools are required for concrete work; in fact, few tools that are not found on the average farm. For special work, special tools will be required, which may be secured from any good hardware supply house. A panel containing many of such special tools is shown in Fig. 145. The tools commonly used in farm concrete work and such as will be needed in the following projects are as follows:

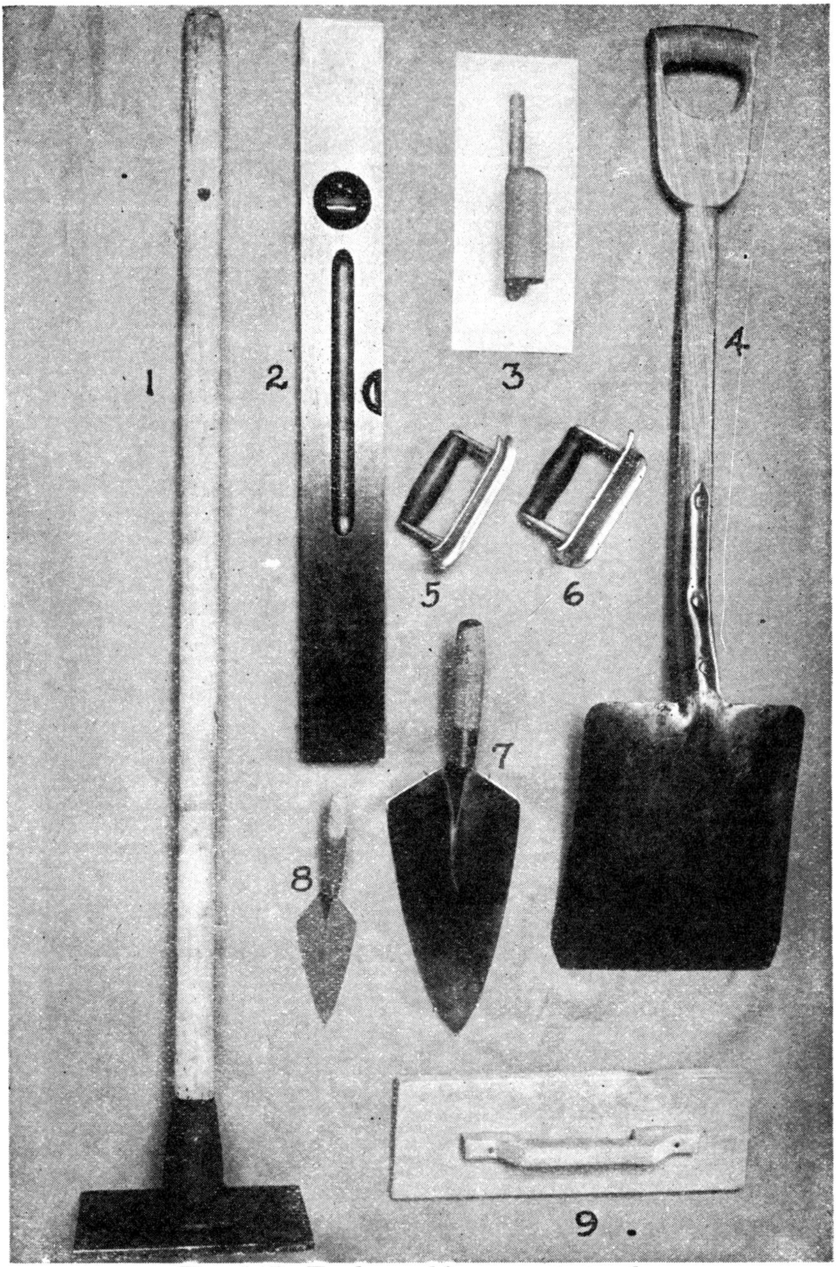

FIG. 145. Tools used in concrete work.

1, Tamper; 2, level; 3, finishing trowel; 4, shovel; 5, groover; 6, edger; 7 and 8, trowels; 9, hand float.

a) For screening aggregate—a moulder's riddle for small work, or a screen, as shown in Fig. 138.

b) For washing aggregate—a trough in which dirty aggregate can be freed from clay.

FIG. 145-*a*. Mixing concrete. Measuring boxes and other equipment.

c) For mixing and placing—a platform, as shown in Fig. 142; shovel, spade, hoe, tamper, striking board and wheelbarrow (Figs. 142, 145 and 147).

d) For measuring ingredients—a measuring box, as shown in Fig. 145-*a*.

e) For finishing—trowel, edger, groover, hand float, etc. (Fig. 145).

f) Water container—a barrel or, for large construction, a water tank, to which is attached a hose.

Tools for wood construction—carpenter's square, hammer, saws (rip and crosscut).

Note: To these tools there may be added a mixer, either hand or power, depending upon the extent of the work to be undertaken.

CHAPTER XVI

Projects in Concrete Construction

Project No. 1

139. Study of Concrete Construction and Concrete Materials (Figs. 146 and 146-*a*).

Requirements: To investigate as many types and classes of concrete work as are available and as time will permit.

FIG. 146. Defective concrete walk.

The following are suggested: Concrete tanks—one circular and one rectangular—sidewalks, feeding floor, foundation wall, retaining wall, fence posts, roads, tile, and block. These should be studied with the idea of noting the results obtained by use of poor materiais and poor workmanship, and the use of good materials and careful workmanship, and also to determine quantity of material needed for certain jobs. Make a written report on results obtained.

Tools Needed: Rule for taking dimensions.

Preliminary Instruction: Carefully read the preceding paragraphs. Keep in mind the general principles of concrete construction. Remember the requirements for

FIG. 146-*a*. An attractive walk.

well-made concrete, good aggregate, proper proportions, careful mixing and placing, and correct reinforcing.

Working Instructions:

a) Examine at least one of each of the different types of concrete work listed under requirements and report on the following:

1) General condition of the job.
2) If cracks are forming, to what are they due?
3) Where cracks have formed, note if there is a clear fracture, or, if the aggregate is pulled out of the mortar.
4) Was the coarse aggregate worked back from the form when placed?
5) Was a dry, quaky or a wet mixture used?

6) Does the job indicate that the forms were well made?
7) If the forms were not well made, what was wrong with them?
8) Why do poor foundations often cause cracks in concrete walls?
9) Examine the foundation and note if care was observed in its preparation.
10) Is the foundation well drained?
11) What is the effect of poor drainage under a foundation wall? Under a sidewalk? Under a road?
12) What precaution should be taken in constructing an earth-retaining wall?
13) If cracks have formed, were they due to lack of or insufficient reinforcement?
14) Where should reinforcing steel be placed in such a wall? Why?
15) Why should a wet or quaky mix be used where the concrete is reinforced?
16) Write a brief statement about each piece of work, giving your opinion as to what should be done to make a first-class job.

b) Examine concrete material, note the quality, etc.

1) Examine a sack of cement. See if it is free from lumps and is fresh.
2) Note the brand of cement examined.
3) Note the condition of the bag.
4) Why is it important to take care of the bags and not allow them to get wet?
5) Examine available sand. See if it is clean, free from clay, coal or other organic matter.

6) Test a small quantity of sand for clay by putting about 4″ or 5″ in a fruit jar, adding water and shaking until clay is in solution. Set aside and let clay settle on top of the sand. Determine the per cent of clay present.
7) What per cent of clay is allowable in average concrete work?
8) Examine available gravel or broken stone. See if it is free from clay, organic matter or soft particles.
9) Can you scratch the stone with your thumb nail?
10) What would the effect be to use soft stone in making concrete?
11) Is the coating of fine dust ordinarily found on limestone detrimental in making concrete?
12) Examine some bank-run sand and gravel as in Nos. 5 and 8.
13) Why is it poor practice to use ordinary bank-run material for making concrete?
14) Suppose it is required that a piece of concrete work be made of bank-run material that has 50 per cent as much sand as gravel, and that it is to be equivalent in strength to a 1 : 2 : 4 mixture where the sand and gravel are graded. How much would be required for each sack of cement?

c) *Problems:*

Assume a 1 : 2 : 4 mixture and determine the amount of materials needed; also cost:

1) To make a circular tank 6′ 0″ inside diameter at the top and 5′ 4″ diameter at the bottom, and 2′ 0″ deep. The wall of the tank to be 4″ thick at the

top and 8″ thick at the bottom, the bottom of tank to be 5″ thick.

2) To make a rectangular tank with the same capacity as No. 1, to have same thickness, walls and bottom, and to be 4′ 0″ across inside at the top.

3) To make a sidewalk 40′ long, 3′ wide, and 4″ thick.

FIG. 147. Making block.

4) To make six concrete fence posts. Assume 20 cents a post for steel.

140. **Molded Concrete** (Figs. 147 and 147-*a*).

Project No. 2

Requirements: To make tile of different sizes, block, flower boxes, and other pieces of concrete work requiring a dry mixture.

Tools Needed: Shovels, bucket, measuring box, screen, mixing platform, trowels, and suitable molds.

Material Needed: Cement, sand and water.

Preliminary Instructions: The principles outlined in the discussion on selection of sand must be kept in mind. Only the best sand should be used. In the kind of work outlined in this project, a relatively dry mixture must be used, one about as wet as damp earth when plowed; with such a mixture the molds may be removed immediately. Good results cannot be obtained if the materials are either too wet or too dry. The

FIG. 147-*a*. Making flower box.

product will stand up due to the adhesiveness of the concrete, and it must be allowed to set thoroly before handling. Careful measurement of materials is an essential requirement of all concrete work.

Working Instructions:

1) Use a 1 : 3 mixture; that is, one part of cement and three parts of sand, for the various jobs outlined. Where coarse aggregate is available, the block may be made of a 1 : 2 : 4 mixture with a 1 : 2 face.
2) After measuring the sand, spread it out in a thin layer on a water-tight platform; then spread the cement on top of the sand and mix together dry, continuing the turning until the color is uniform and without streaks. Water is then added slowly from a sprinkling can or by

a hose, the mixing being continued until all parts of the mass are of the same color and wetness.

3) Carefully clean the molds and apply a thin film of oil after using, so they will be ready for the next job. See that they are absolutely clean before placing any concrete.

4) Tile, block, etc., are made by thoroly tamping or pressing the concrete in the molds to be used. Any dry mixture must be thoroly tamped to make dense concrete.

5) Extreme care must be observed in removing the molds to avoid cracking the product or causing it to get out of true shape. Tapping the mold slightly will often prevent failures.

6) After the product has set for twenty-four hours, sprinkle it carefully with water, repeating this frequently for ten days. It should not be used for one month or more. Where such products are made on a commercial scale, they are often cured in a steam kiln.

7) Write a report on each product made. Give the general method of procedure and why. Carefully determine cost of materials in each.

Project No. 3

141. Sidewalk and Floors (Figs. 148 and 148-*a*).

Requirements: To prepare foundation, construct forms to proper grade and position, and construct sidewalk and floors of various kinds requiring a quaky mixture.

Tools Needed: Shovels, buckets, measuring box, screen, mixing platform, trowels, edger, groover and float. Woodworking tools suitable for constructing forms.

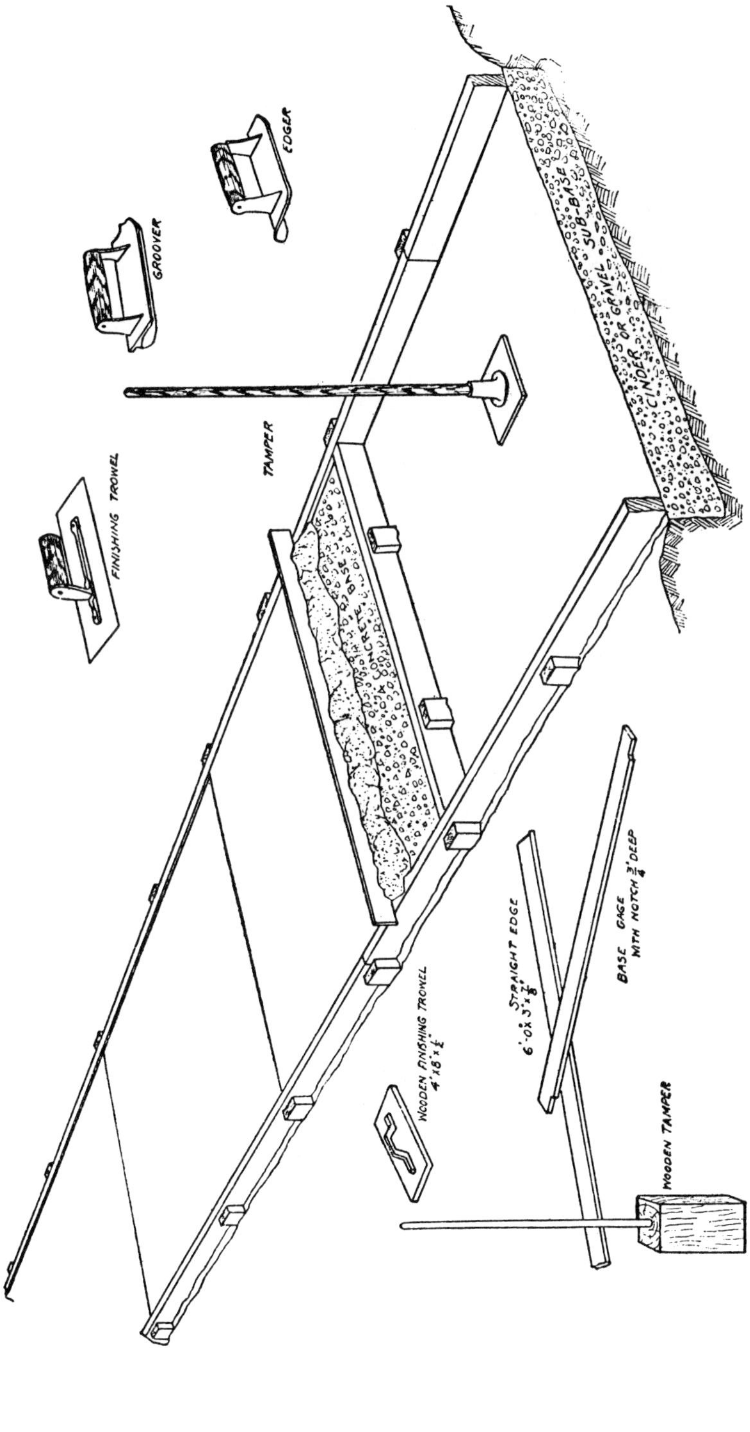

FIG. 148. Sidewalk construction.

Materials Needed: Enough cement, sand and gravel or broken stone, and water to complete the job. For a 1 : 2 : 4 mixture, 1 sack of cement, 2 cubic feet of sand and 4 cubic feet of gravel should make 4-1/4 cubic feet of

FIG. 148-*a*. Boys constructing sidewalk.

concrete, or 13 square feet of walk or floor 4 inches thick. Material for forms must also be provided—2 x 4's with suitable stakes are very satisfactory.

Preliminary Instructions: The general principles of proper proportioning, mixing and placing should be carried out in constructing sidewalks the same as in any other type of concrete construction. In work of this class, a quaky mixture should be adopted. A walk should not be made by putting down coarse material and pouring over it a cement-sand mortar. Because of the close resemblance between other types of floor constructions, such as feeding floors, barnyard pavements, basement floors, garage floors, etc., and concrete walks, only a detailed description of the construction of one type will be given. The location and drainage of any walk or floor must be considered.

Working Instructions:

1) In laying out a walk, the first consideration is its location with reference to buildings and the road. If it is to be located with reference to a certain building, either parallel or at a right angle, it should be definitely located by careful measurement. Stake out the position of the walk and draw a tight string so that the surface may be properly leveled to a uniform grade. This surface should be thoroly tamped to prevent any settling after the walk has been placed.

   Under certain conditions, where there is a tendency for water to collect under a walk, cinders or gravel may be used as a sub-base. Ordinarily, the concrete will be placed directly on the well-tamped soil.

2) Make the forms of 2″ lumber, either 4″ or 5″ wide, depending on thickness to which walk will be made; 4″ is satisfactory for most conditions. Place the forms carefully to grade, and fill in with earth and tamp any low places before placing any concrete. Proper and careful alignment of the forms is the most important feature to insure a good-looking job. Definite measurements must be taken to locate carefully the position of the forms. A level should be used in order to see that the forms are properly leveled.

To support the forms, drive stakes every 3′ or 4′. It is considered good practice to put in alternate sections of the walk, and, after this has set, remove the end form and fill in the section not built. For short pieces of walk, however, this is unnecessary. If it is desired to give the walk a slight slope to one side, this can be done by use of a level and straight-edge, placing one of the 2 x 4's lower than the other—1/4″ to 1′ is a good side slope for a walk, and will cause it to shed the water very quickly. To make such a slope on a walk to be 4′ wide, the form in the direction of the slope will be set 1″ lower than the upper one.

3) For a one-course walk, nothing leaner than a 1 : 2 : 4 mixture should be used; that is, one part of cement to two parts of sand and four parts of broken stone. Both sand and gravel, or broken stone, should be clean and free from clay or other foreign material. If bank-run materials are used, careful screening to get the proper proportions is necessary.

4) After measuring the sand required for one batch, spread it out in a thin layer on a water-tight platform; then spread the cement on top of the sand and mix together dry, continually turning until the color is uniform and mixed together without streaks. The cement and sand is then spread out and the coarse material placed on top. It is then again mixed and water is added until it is of a quaky or jelly-like consistency. Such a mixture can be quickly spread about in the forms and easily leveled with a strike-board resting

upon the top of the forms. Avoid using too dry a mixture for floor construction.

5) The concrete may be shoveled directly from the mixing board into the form, or handled by means of a wheelbarrow.

6) Level the material off and tamp it enough to force the coarse material in from the surface, and bring enough cement-sand mortar to the surface to make a smooth finish. Slight tamping is also done to remove any air or water bubbles from the material. A spade or board should be pushed in along the side of the form so that all coarse material will be worked back from the edge of the walk.

7 If the walk is to be 50′ or more in length, an expansion joint should be placed approximately every 50′. This expansion joint can be provided by putting in a board 1/2″ thick at intervals of 50′, which should be removed after the concrete has properly set, and the groove filled with heavy asphalt or Tarvia. To leave the board in place is worse than no expansion joint. This practice is sometimes followed.

8) If the material has been mixed to the right consistency, the surface can usually be given its final finish within one-half hour after placing. The first part of the finishing should be done with a wood float, merely to level off the surface and make a smooth job. If it is desired to make a very smooth surface, continue the finishing by using a steel trowel. The troweling process tends to bring an additional amount of cement and

fine sand to the surface, making it very slick. Ordinarily, this practice is not desirable.

The edges of the walk must be finished with the edger to give a rounded corner. To line the walk off into sections, use a straight-edge and groover. This must be done before the concrete has begun to set because it is sometimes necessary to force coarse material farther below the surface to make a good groove. Lay off the walk so that the length of the sections will be about one and one-half times the width; that is, a walk 2′

FIG. 149. Form for double step.

wide should be divided into sections 3′ long, or a walk 3′ wide into sections 4-1/2′ long.

9) If the walk is built where it is exposed to extreme drying from the sun, it is well to protect it until it has set. The protection may be in the form of moist sand or a tarpaulin of some sort. The hot sun and dry winds will tend to remove the moisture from the concrete and prevent it from hardening. Sprinkle the surface for a week or ten days, after which the walk may be put into use.

142. Constructing a Doorstep (Figs. 149 and 149-*a*).

Requirements: To prepare foundation, construct the form and place the concrete for a step and platform at some door, or a step at the curb, walk or driveway entrance to the house. A 1 : 2 : 4 mixture should be used for such a job.

Tools Needed: Same as in Secs. 140 and 141.

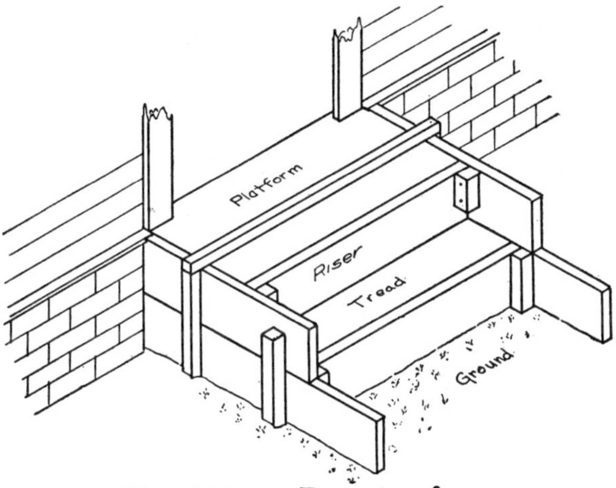

FIG. 149-*a*. Doorstep form.

Material Needed: Enough cement, sand or gravel or crushed stone, and water to complete the job, using a 1 : 2 : 4 mixture. A sufficient quantity of fence boards and 2 x 4's to construct the form. Boards 1-1/2″ thick are preferred to light ones.

Preliminary Instructions: In constructing each piece of concrete work, the requirements of good concrete must be ever kept before you. In a job of this kind, the construction of the forms deserves a great deal of attention. If a carriage step or small step at curb is to be built, it will require little foundation; the ground should be leveled and well tamped. For a doorstep, a sub-base should be provided, and if it is a large one, the central portion may be tamped full of clay to serve as a filler; in this case, not less than 6″ of concrete should surround the filler.

Working Instructions:

1) Follow general instructions given for concrete construction. Carefully prepare the form for the step to secure correct dimensions as planned—the proper area of platform, the correct width of tread and the correct height of riser. It is suggested that the riser be 8″ high and the tread 10″ wide; then stock 8″ boards can be used as the part of form for riser. Have each part of form properly braced so there is no danger of its bulging.

2) For a solid step, a 1 : 2-1/2 : 5 mixture is adequate. If the step is to be made from one level to another without backing, and is to be reinforced, a 1 : 2 : 4 mixture should be used; in fact, for small jobs, such a mixture is best.

3) Carefully mix the concrete to a quaky consistency as outlined in Sec. 141. Place the material in the form and tamp it lightly, working the coarse aggregate back from the surface to secure a smooth finish.

4) The finishing coat of one part cement to two parts sand for the platform and the treads should be placed immediately after the surfaces have been leveled off. Where it is not desired to give an extremely smooth finish, enough fine material can be worked to the surface by troweling, and this can be leveled off. The risers and sides of the steps can be finished only after

the form has been removed. Forty-eight hours should elapse for the ordinary job to allow for setting. To finish the risers and sides of steps, remove all marks made by forms by the use of a stiff brush. If care has been observed in working the coarse material back from the form and no air pockets have been formed,

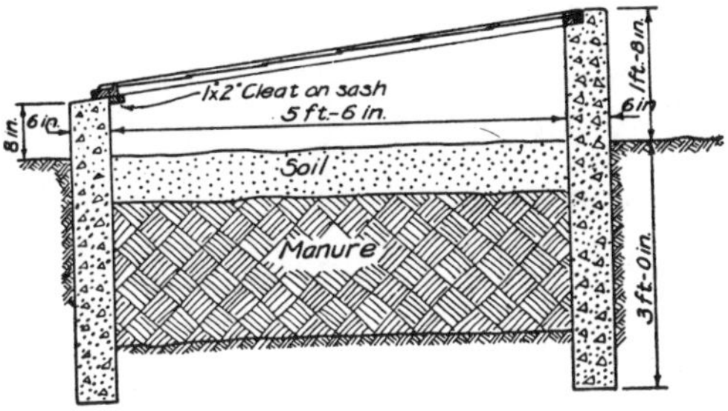

FIG. 150. Section thru hot-bed.

this method of finishing is sufficient. If the wall is left quite rough on removal of the forms, they should be wet down and a cement mortar of the same proportions as used on the treads should be applied with a brush. Keep the step moistened for a week or ten days until ready for use.

143. Hot-bed, Foundation Wall, or a Similar Type of Construction (Figs. 150, 151, 152).

Requirements: To build a form such as needed for the walls of a hot-bed or the foundation for a small building. Determine the quantity of material required. Prepare and place the concrete, remove the form in due time, and finish the job. A mixture of wet consistency should be used.

Tools Needed: Same as in Secs. 140 and 141.

Materials Needed: Enough cement, sand and gravel or

crushed stone to complete the job, using a 1 : 2 : 4 mixture, a sufficient quantity of boards, and 2 x 4's to make and brace the form, and pieces of wire with which to fasten it together.

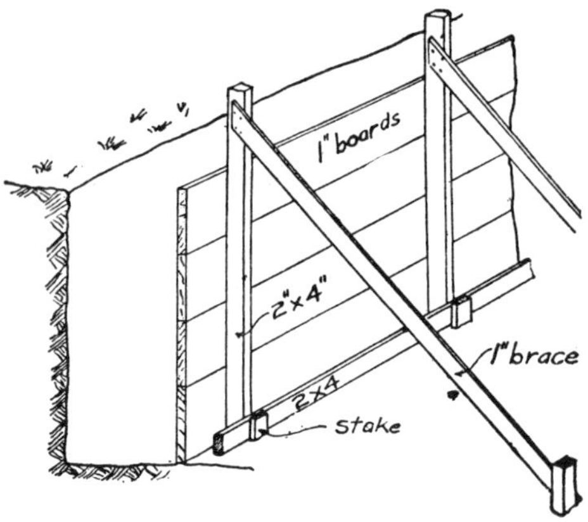

FIG. 151. Foundation wall form.

Preliminary Instructions: Concrete is the best material available for foundation wall construction. The super - structure may be built of some other material, but usually concrete will be used for the foundation. The particular location of hot-bed or foundation wall should be definitely decided so the work will not be held back at the beginning of work period. To lay out a rectangular foundation, one should be careful to have all intersections of walls exactly 90 degrees. This can be easily checked by the "3, 4, 5" method. This rule is applied by measuring along one wall a distance from the corner equal to 3 feet; then measure from the same point along the other wall a distance of 4 feet; then, if the two lines form an exact right angle, the distance between the ends of the 3- and 4-foot lines will

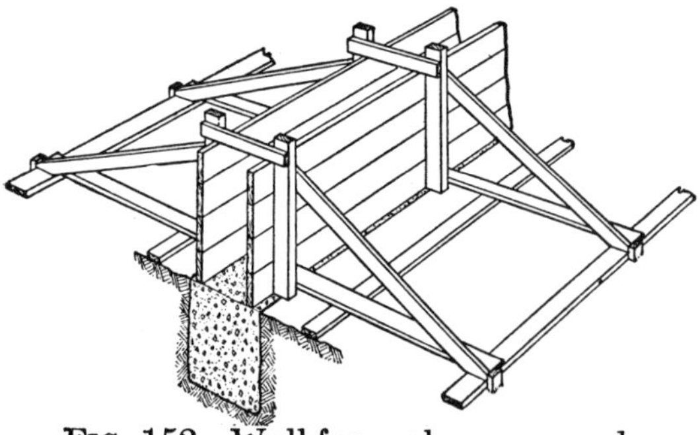

FIG. 152. Wall form above ground.

be exactly 5 feet. For convenience and accuracy, any multiple of 3, 4 and 5 may be used.

Working Instructions:

1) Carefully excavate all soil to proper depth. If the soil is firm, it may be used as the outside form up to the surface, above which a double form will be necessary. For all kinds of foundation walls, it is always essential that the footing be wider than the wall proper, and that it be carried deep enough to be below the frost line. If double forms are necessary, due to the soil caving it will have to be excavated to a greater width.
2) Construct the form with care, duplicating the inside and outside wall dimensions as desired. See that corners are square, walls are well braced, vertical, and carefully aligned. If walls are to be more than six feet high, tie wires should be used in addition to the supporting braces (Fig. 152). If this precaution is not followed, a bulged wall is likely to be the result. The inner form on a hot-bed or other small piece of concrete work, may be supported by braces on the inside, running from one wall to the opposite one.
3) For thin walls up to six inches, a 1 : 2 : 4 mixture should be used. Walls more than eight inches thick may be made of a 1 : 2-1/2 : 5 mixture.
4) For a job of this kind, the concrete may be mixed to a slightly wet consistency. Care must be exercised to avoid the separation of the coarse material from the fine, which is possible in a wet mixture. Shovel the concrete into form and force the coarse aggregate back from the surface of the wall by means of a spade or a

thin board. When the job is a fairly large one, do not mix less than the amount produced when a sack of cement is taken as a unit. It is desirable to complete the job without interruption after it is started. In case it is necessary that the work be discontinued for a period, see that the surface of the dry concrete is cleaned and thoroly wet down before fresh concrete is poured.

5) To insure against cracks in a concrete wall, a few reinforcing rods bent at right angles and placed at succeeding heights of 12 to 18 inches in the corners, will be invaluable. Reinforcing placed around openings is also recommended

6) The forms on a wall of more than six feet in height should stay on several days. The forms on walls only two or three feet high may be removed in forty-eight hours. As to finishing the surface of the wall, follow instructions given under this heading in Sec. 142.

Note: When a wooden superstructure is to be built on a concrete foundation, it is advisable to set some bolts in the concrete at intervals of every five or six feet, to which the sills may be fastened.

144. Constructing Fence Post (Fig. 153).

Requirements: To construct line fence posts and corner and end posts requiring quaky or wet mixtures and reinforcing.

Tools Needed: Shovels, buckets, measuring box, screen, mixing platform, straight-edge, flat trowels and suitable forms or molds, or woodworking tools suitable for constructing same.

Materials Needed: Cement, sand, gravel or broken stone and reinforcing steel. For line posts, provide 1/4″ to 3/4″ stone; and corner and end posts, 1/4″ x 1-1/4″ stone.

Preliminary Instructions: There is nothing that adds more to the appearance and usefulness of a fence than a good

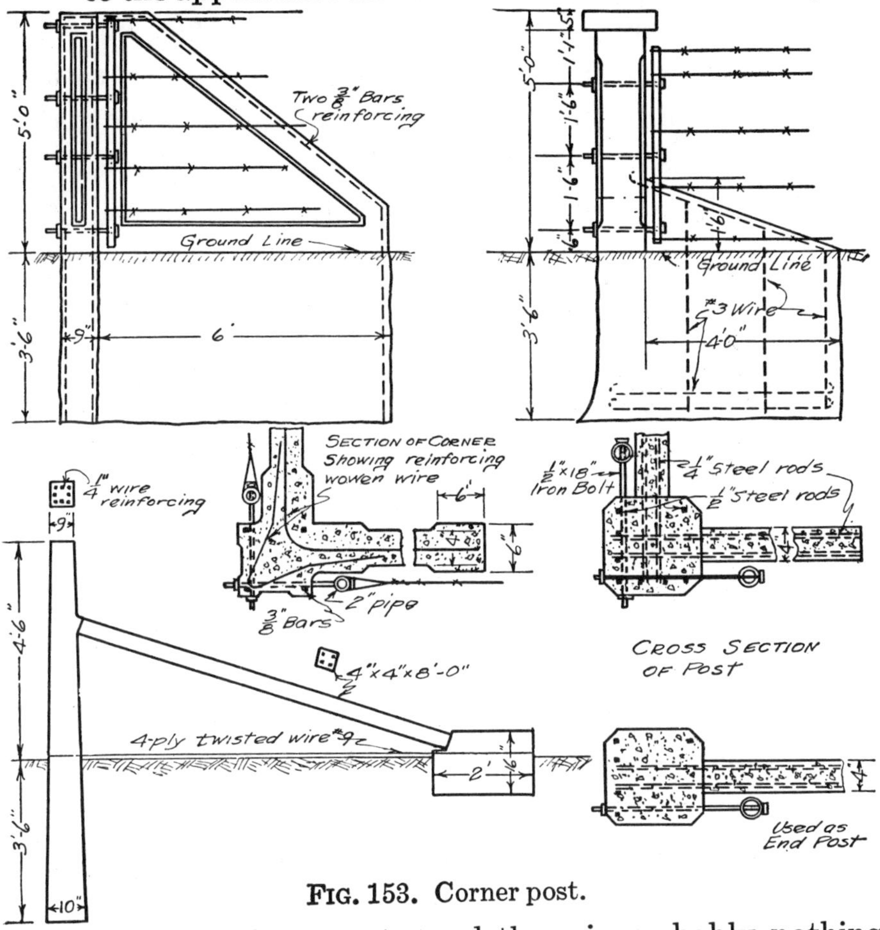

FIG. 153. Corner post.

line of uniform posts, and there is probably nothing that adds more to the appearance of a farm lay-out than a good, serviceable fence. A good fence is a real necessity on every farm.

Many of the early concrete posts were failures because

they were not properly made. People tried to make posts without knowing the first principles of correct construction. Posts were made of poor material, lean mixtures, and incorrectly reinforced. To make good, uniform posts, provide well-made forms. There are a lot of good patented forms on the market, but home-made forms are just about as good. A very satisfactory form for posts is outlined under woodworking projects, Sec. 79 and Fig. 136.

The chief difference between the construction of line posts, and corner and end posts is that the corner and end posts are usually made right in place, as shown in Fig. 153. The hole is excavated, the form built over it, and the steel tied in place, and the concrete then poured. The method of constructing line posts will be definitely outlined.

Working Instructions:

1) Place forms so they will be level. Clean them with a brush, and apply a thin film of oil before placing concrete.
2) For corner and end posts, a 1 : 2 : 4 mixture may be used. For line posts, use a 1 : 2 : 2-1/2 mixture, the stone not to be larger than 3/4″. Where materials are not screened, use one part of cement to three parts of sand and pebbles for line posts.
3) Mix the materials to a quaky consistency and fill the form half-full of material. Tamp until the material is free of water and air bubbles.
4) Press two 1/4″ twisted steel rods into the concrete so that they will be within 1/2″ of the corners of the post.

Then fill the form full of the mixture, tamp it lightly, and smooth off the surface. Press two more rods in place at each corner about 1/2″ under the surface; then smooth the surface to proper finish.

5) Leave the posts in the molds at least forty-eight hours under most conditions. If the weather is extremely dry and hot, they may be removed earlier. To take out the post, turn down the hinged end of the form, lift the dividing boards between the posts, then grasp the post and slide it on the bottom of form by a pulling motion; after it is loosened, it may be lifted out. Handle the posts with care when green as they are liable to be broken.

6) Set the post on end in sand to cure. Sprinkle daily in dry weather for a week. Do not use until the posts are one month old.

145. Constructing a Circular Stock Tank (Figs. 154, 154-*a* and 155).

Requirements: To construct form according to plan, prepare foundation and construct a circular stock tank to be provided with inlet pipe with float control and outlet. Plumbing work is outlined in Sec. 351 under head of "Plumbing."

Tools Needed: Same as in preceding projects.

Materials Needed: Enough cement, sand and gravel, or crushed rock, to construct tank of a 1 : 2 : 4 mixture according to plan. Enough heavy hog wire 30″ high to extend around tank and lap 30″, and enough to extend twice across the bottom and up the sides. For a tank

6′ inside diameter, it will require about four rods of fence.

Preliminary Instructions: A stock tank is a needed piece of equipment on every farm. It should be carefully located with reference to lots for convenience; in fact, it

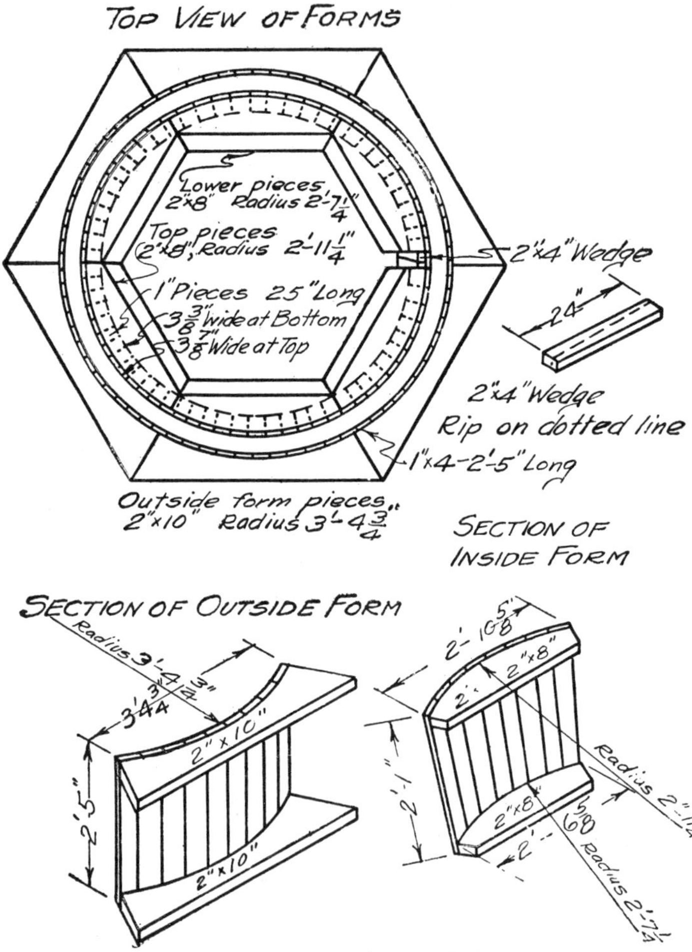

FIG. 154. Circular tank forms.

may be placed between two lots or where four lots corner. A drainage outlet must be provided which must be given consideration when the tank is located. Extreme care must be observed in mixing, placing and reinforcing to insure a strong water-tight construction.

Working Instructions:

1) Like every other piece of concrete work, the water tank must be constructed on a solid foundation. The soil should be firmly tamped before the form is set in place. In the preparation of the foundation, the proper placing of the outlet and inlet pipes must be given consideration, since both should be brought thru the bottom of the tank. For a large tank, it is well to excavate and form a sub-base of cinders or gravel.

2) The form for a circular tank is the most difficult part of the tank to build. However, by carefully studying the plan, one should experience little trouble. It will be noted on plan that both the inside and outside forms are made in six sections. This makes the length of each section equal to one-half the diameter of the tank. If the inside diameter of the tank is to be 6′, the outer length of section for inside form will be 3′, less the thickness of boards used. The inner length of outside section will be equal to one-

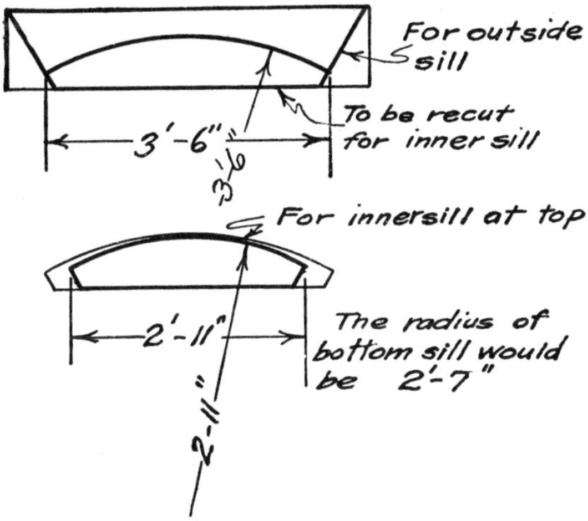

FIG. 154-*a*. Detail of sill for circular form.

half the diameter of tank plus the thickness of wall and thickness of boards used. If the wall is to be 5″ thick at the top and boards 1″ thick are to be used, then the sections would be 3′ 6″ long at the inner length. Since the outside surface of the wall of the tank is vertical, both sills for the outside form will be cut the same. The inner surface should be given a slope of 2″ to the foot, or, for a tank 2′ deep, the bottom sill for the inner form will be 4″ shorter than the top one. The sills for this form are best cut from a 2″ x 10″ or 2″ x 12″ timber when a jig or band saw is available, making it possible to get both the inner and outer sills from the same piece, as shown in Fig. 154-*a*. After sills are cut, the boards must be carefully fitted to make a tight wall. The boards for the inner section are made 5″ shorter than those for the outer section to allow for thickness of floor. After these sections are completed, they are assembled in place and can be fastened together by strips across ends.

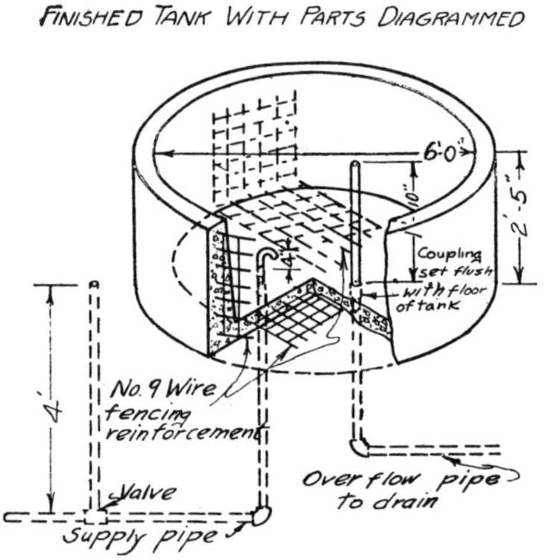

FIG. 155. Circular tank complete.

3) For concrete construction such as this, never use a mixture leaner than 1 : 2 : 4. For small tanks, a 1 : 2: 3 mixture is better.

4) Follow method of mixing and placing as outlined in Secs. 141 and 143, with the exception of the following:

Set the outer form in place and put in floor first. Spread about 3″ of concrete on floor; then put two or three strips of the hog wire fence across the floor and extend it up the sides. Place balance of concrete for floor and tamp in place. Put a strip of hog wire in place for wall reinforcing, lap the ends, and wire to it the strips that were placed across the floor. Then place inner form in position, carefully center it, and fasten in place with boards nailed across the top. Pour the rest of concrete, keeping the reinforcing near the center of wall. It is desirable to provide a concrete box in the center of the tank to provide protection for the inlet pipe and automatic float. A form for this box should be constructed, set in place and the concrete poured as the tank is being completed. For the outlet pipe, a drain with a 1-1/2″ coupling should be set in a low place in the floor. A short piece of pipe screwed into the coupling and extending to a height that it is desired the water should stand, will act as an overflow.

5) Remove the forms from the tank in about forty-eight hours, and, after wetting it thoroly, apply a cement paint to the entire surface. Allow this coating to set, then wet down again, after which the tank may be filled with water. It should not be put into use for a week or ten days, as the green concrete can easily be broken by stock.

CHAPTER XVII

Supplementary Concrete Projects

146. Constructing Garden or Lawn Roller (Figs. 156, 157).

Requirements: To make a garden or lawn roller, as illustrated, complete with handle for pulling or pushing it.

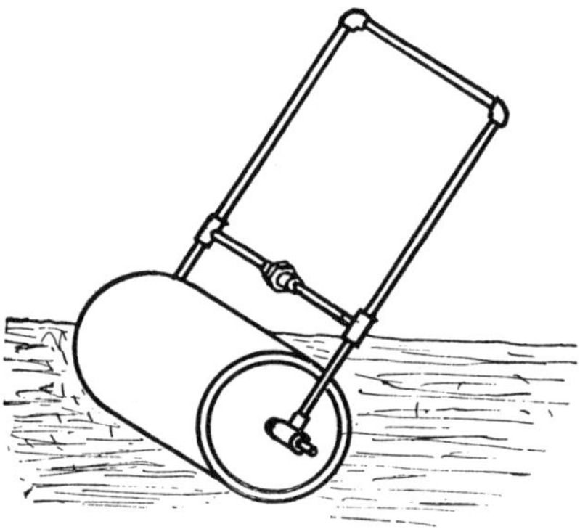

FIG. 156. Garden roller.

Instructions:

1) Secure a length of drain tile of size desired. If drain tile is not available, an old carbide can or other cylindrical can may be used.
2) Secure lengths of 1/2″ pipe and fittings for axle and handle.
3) Construct a platform on which to make the roller.
4) Lay out a circle on platform slightly larger than tile.
5) Bore a hole in platform, the diameter being equal to outside diameter of pipe for axle.
6) Make cross-frame of two 1″ x 4″ pieces.

7) Center and bore hole in cross-frame as has been done with platform. Nail blocks on ends of cross pieces to hold in place when assembled.
8) Place tile on platform and center axle in place with cross-frame. Nail blocks on platform to hold tile in place.

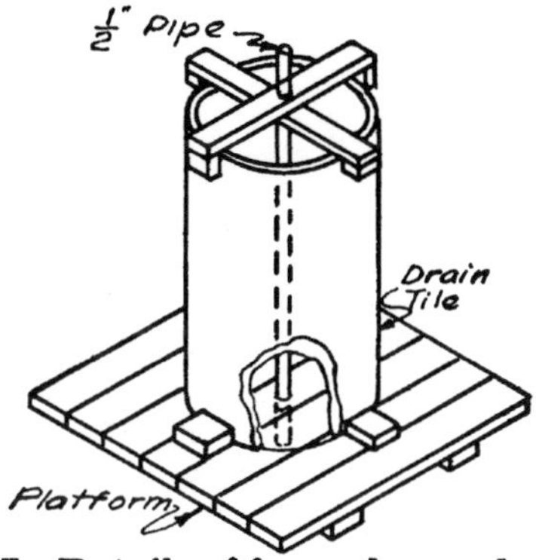

FIG. 157. Details of forms for garden roller.

9) Axle should extend out of the tile at least two inches.
10) Mix concrete 1 : 2-1/2 : 4 proportion to a quaky consistency.
11) Place concrete in tile around axle. Leave in place for a week or more before using.
12) For handle, assemble pipe and fittings, as illustrated in plumbing project. This makes a very good elementary pipe-fitting exercise. See Sec. 334.

147. A Hog Trough (Fig. 158).

Requirements: To construct form, mix and place concrete, and properly reinforce a trough that will be suitable for feeding slops to hogs.

Instructions:

1) Construct form as illustrated. The inner part of form may be made of heavy clay if it is desired to make the bottom of trough with a curved surface.

2) Provide reinforcing. If the trough is to be more than 4′ in length, 1/4″ rods should be used in addition to the wire netting.
3) Use a 1 : 2 : 3 proportion, and mix to a wet consistency.
4) Place concrete and reinforcing.

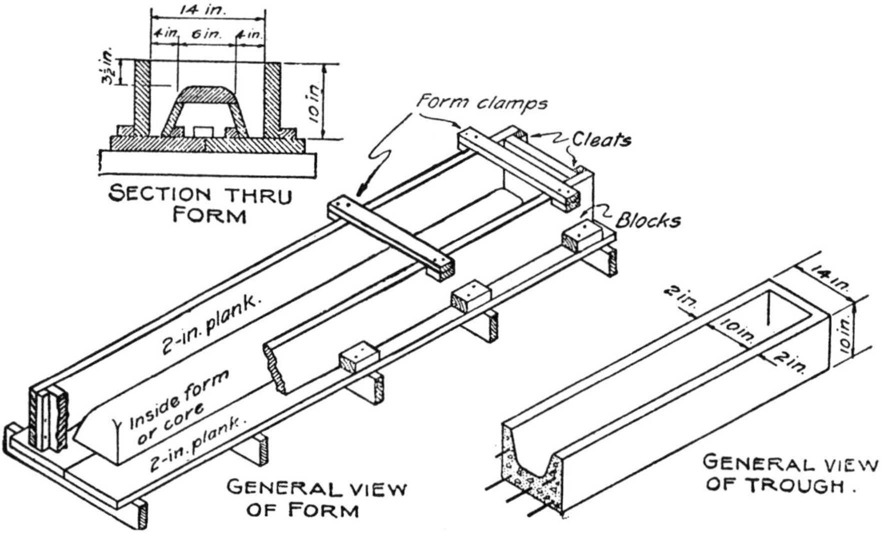

FIG. 158. Hog trough.

148. Engine or Machine Foundation (Fig. 159).

Requirements: The requirements of this job will depend on the particular machine. A machine subject to a great deal of vibration should have a heavy foundation. The proper-sized foundation can best be determined by the maker of the machine. The structural details would be about the same for all machines.

Instructions:

1) Excavate and prepare footing for foundation.
2) Construct form according to plan.
3) Provide bolts to fasten machine to base.
4) Provide a template to locate bolts in base.

5) Provide pieces of 1″ gas pipe for bolts.
6) Mix concrete of 1 : 2-1/2 : 5 proportions to a quaky consistency.

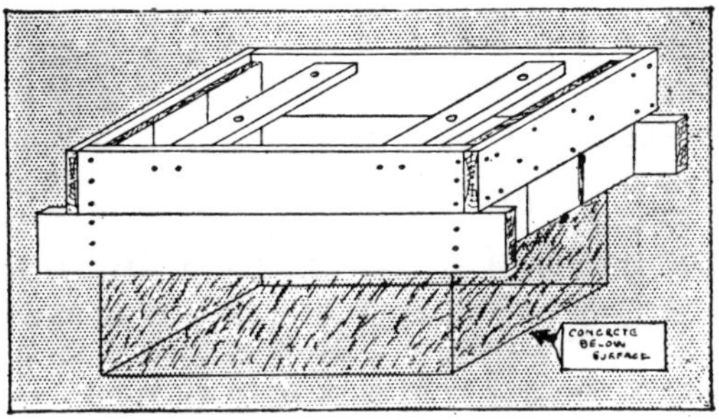

FIG. 159. Machine foundation.

7) Place concrete in form.
8) When form is practically full, set pieces of gas pipe with bolts approximately in place.

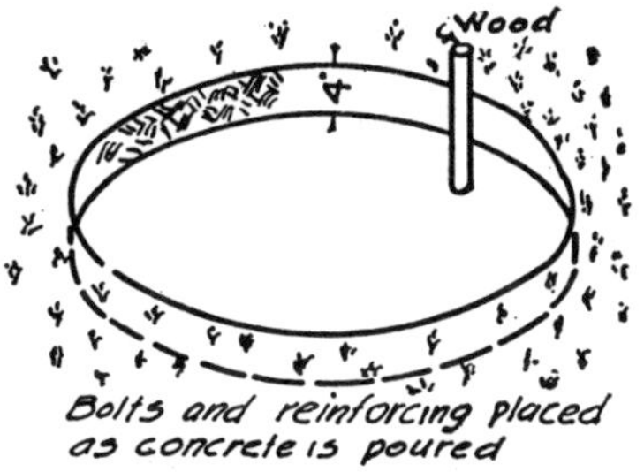

FIG. 160. Earth form for cistern or well top.

9) Fill forms, finish surface, and adjust bolts into correct position by aid of the template.
10) When initial set has been taken, remove template and trowel to a smooth level finish.
11) Remove form after several days and finish surface.
12) Bolt machine in place.

149. Cistern or Shallow Well Top (Fig. 160).

Requirements: To make a circular top for a well or cistern.

Instructions:

1) Describe a circle the exact size of top desired on a smooth level place on the ground.
2) Carefully excavate inside of the circle to a depth of 4″.
3) Cut out a cylindrical wood block and locate where pump pipe will pass through.
4) Provide four bolts to fasten pump to top.
5) Cut two pieces of hog wire for reinforcing across top, and two pieces of large, smooth wire for the edge.
6) Mix concrete of 1 : 2 : 3 proportion to a quaky consistency.
7) Sprinkle form so it will not absorb water from concrete.
8) Place concrete in bottom half of form.
9) Place reinforcing and set bolts in place.
10) Fill form with concrete.
11) Build up concrete where pump is to stand.
12) Finish surface with slight slope toward one side so water will drain off.
13) Sprinkle top from day to day. Remove at the end of a week or ten days.

150. Manure Pit and Cistern (Fig. 161).

Requirements: To excavate for manure pit and cisterr, construct form, and place the concrete and reinforcing where needed.

Note: Refer to project in Sec. 143.

Instructions:

1) Excavate for both pit and cistern, and prepare foundation.
2) Construct outside form if needed.

3) Construct inside form for pit in place.
4) Provide tile from pit to cistern.
5) Arrange reinforcing for cistern. Heavy hog wire may be used instead of rods.
6) Construct inner form for cistern.

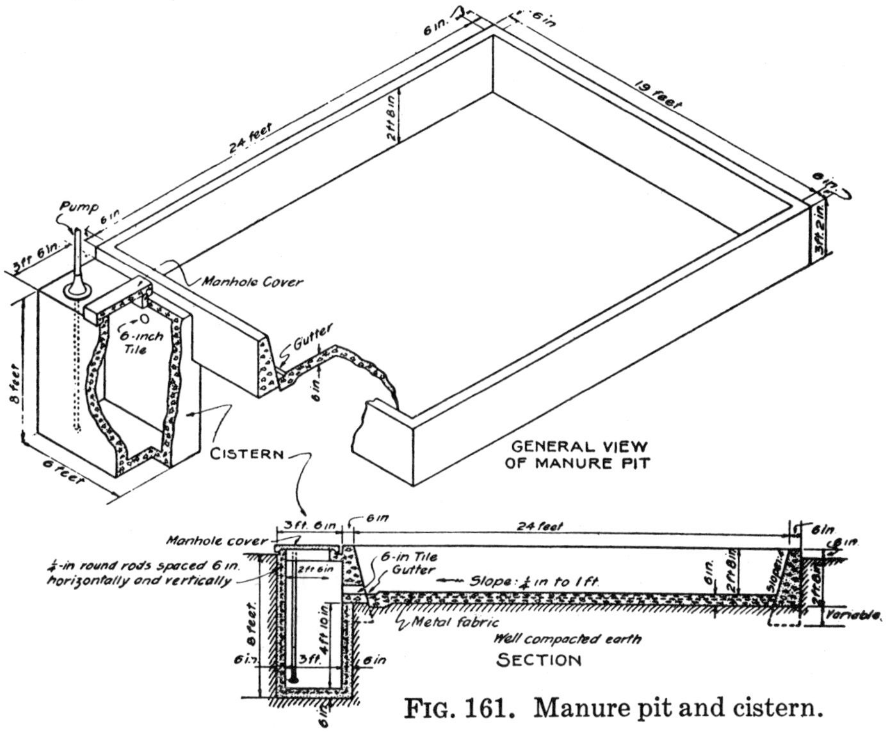

FIG. 161. Manure pit and cistern.

7) Use 1 : 2 : 4 proportion and mix concrete to a wet consistency.
8) Place concrete in walls.
9) Remove wall forms.
10) Place concrete in floor.
11) Construct form for cistern top, providing place for pump, also for manhole cover.
12) Place concrete for top with reinforcing, and also for manhole cover.

13) Remove form from cistern thru manhole.

14) Remove form from manhole top.

151. Feeding Floor (Fig. 162).

Requirements: To prepare foundations, construct forms and place concrete for feeding floor for ten hogs. It takes 12 to 15 square feet of space per hog.

Note: Refer to Sec. 141.

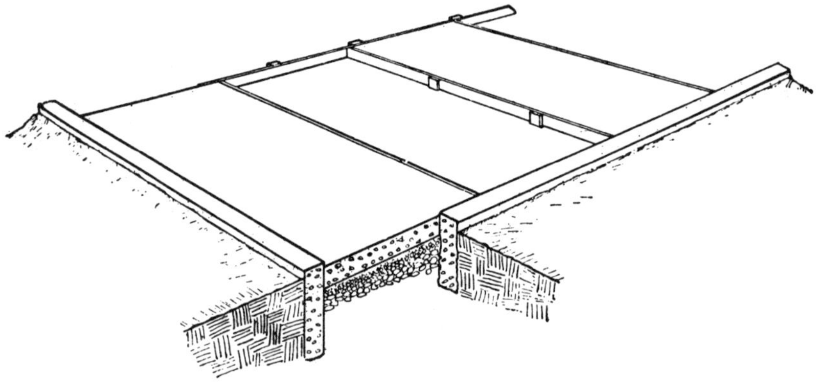

FIG. 162. Feeding floor.

Instructions:

1) Prepare foundation by leveling the spot where floor is to be built. Remove all vegetable matter and have soil thoroly tamped.
2) Construct form to grade so that floor will be at least 4″ thick. Have a slope of 1/4″ to 1′ in one direction.
3) Mix concrete of 1 : 2 : 4 proportion to a wet consistency.
4) Place concrete in floor; complete one section at a time.
5) Remove forms.
6) Excavate for curb around floor.
7) Construct form for curb.
8) Place concrete in curb.
9) Remove curb form.

152. Constructing a Scale Pit (Fig. 163).

Requirements: To excavate for scale pit, construct form, and place the concrete.

Note: Refer to project under Sec. 143.

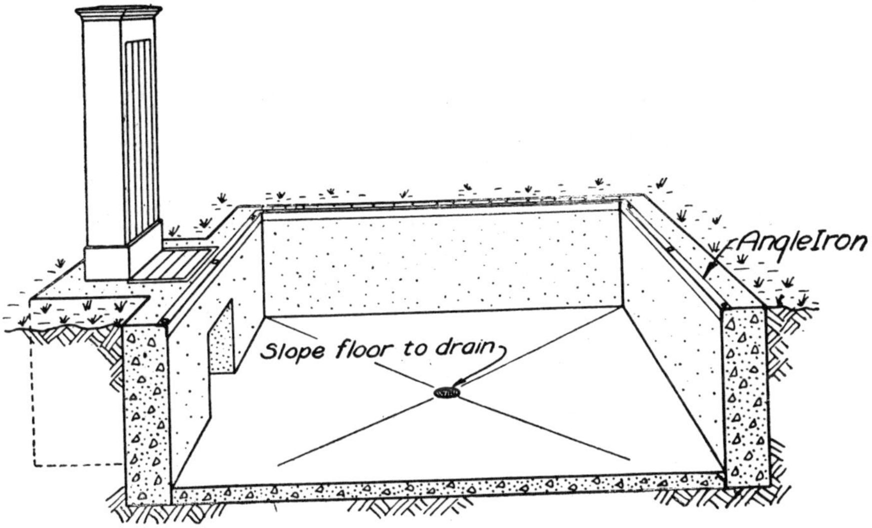

FIG. 163. Scale pit.

Instructions:

1) Excavate pit to dimensions to be determined from size of scale.
2) Provide drain for center of pit.
3) Construct outside form if needed.
4) Construct inner form so wall will be at least 6″ thick.
5) Use 1 : 2 : 4 proportion and mix to a wet consistency.
6) Place concrete in wall.
7) Provide bolts at top of wall to fasten angle iron.
8) Remove forms from wall.
9) Place concrete in floor with slope toward center drain.

153. Vault for Privy (Fig. 164).

Requirements: To construct a sanitary vault for privy with partition as illustrated in plan. As many sections can be made as desired. This is a dry type of vault, dry earth or ashes being used to absorb liquids.

Instructions:

1) Prepare footing for vault so its lower level will be no lower than the surface of the ground.
2) Construct form in place.
3) Provide pieces of wire for reinforcing to insure against shrinkage cracks.
4) Mix concrete of 1 : 2 : 3 proportion to a wet consistency.
5) Place floor and wall of vault as one unit.
6) Remove inner form after twenty-four to forty-eight hours, and paint up any holes with 1 : 2 cement-sand mortar.
7) Paint inner surface with a cement wash.
8) Remove outer form after several days.
9) Finish outer surface.

154. Milk-Cooling Tank (Fig. 165).

Requirements: To excavate, construct form and place concrete and reinforcing for a milk-cooling tank to be 2′ 6″ wide, 20″ deep, length as needed, bottom 8″ lower than floor of milk room. The bottom to be corrugated to allow free circulation of water with drainage outlet.

Note: Refer to Sec. 143.

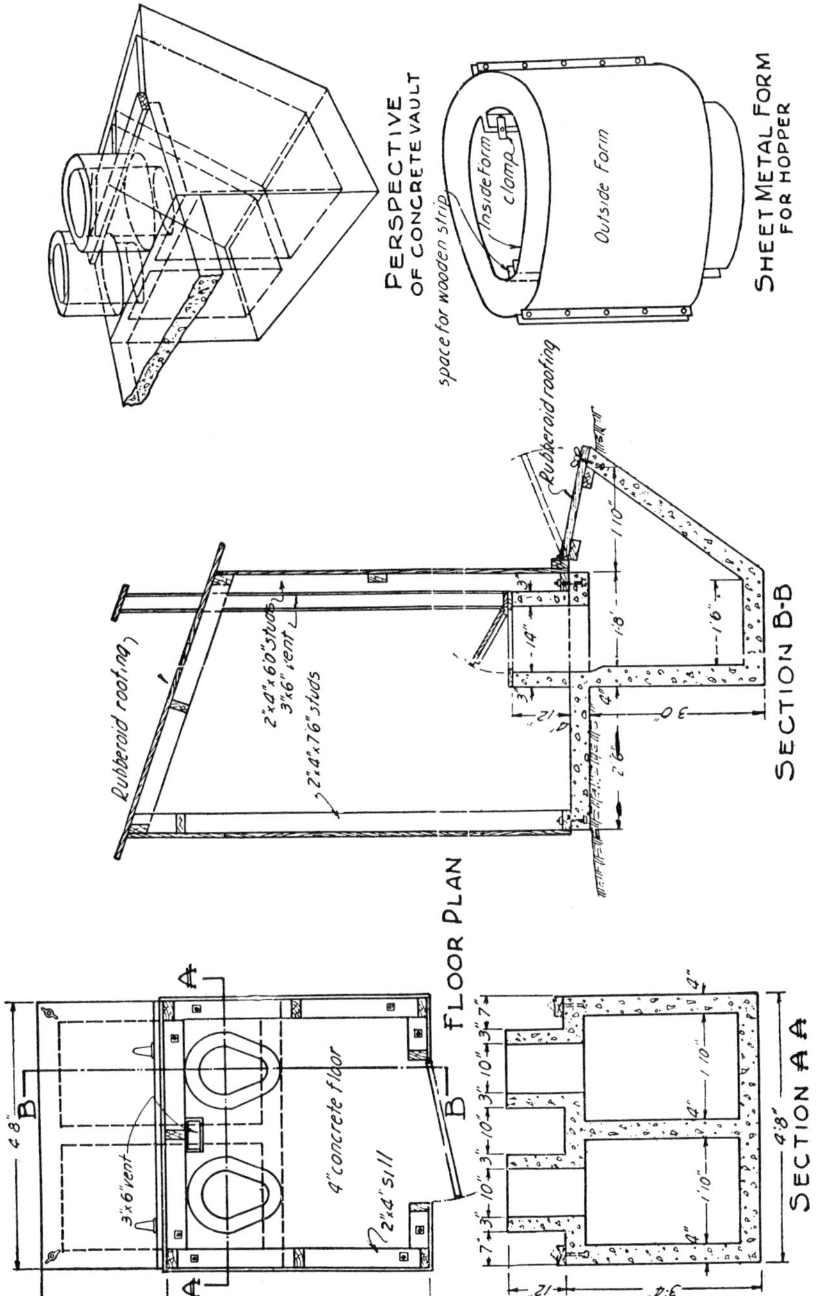

FIG. 164. Plan of sanitary privy.

Instructions:

1) Excavate to a depth of 14″ below floor level.
2) Construct outside form in place.
3) Construct inner form, to be put in place after floor is made, so wall will be 4″ thick.
4) Provide reinforcing material, either rods or heavy hog wire.
5) Put drain in place so coupling will be at surface of low place in floor.
6) As a protection to top of inner wall, provide a 4″ channel iron with 3/8″ by 6″ anchor bolts threaded into it, as illustrated.
7) Mix concrete of 1 : 2 : 4 proportion to a quaky consistency.
8) Place concrete in floor to a depth of 6″ with reinforcing in place.
9) Form corrugations in bottom of tank sloping toward outlet.
10) Adjust inner form in place, with reinforcing extending up from floor and entirely around wall of tank.
11) Place concrete in walls of tank.
12) Firmly seat the channel iron with anchor bolts on inner wall, hammering it into place with a wood maul.
13) Remove inner form at the end of twenty-four to forty-eight hours, and finish surface with a cement wash. If there are any holes, use a 1 : 2 cement-sand mortar to fill them.
14) Remove outside form after several days, and finish surface v:ith a stiff brush.

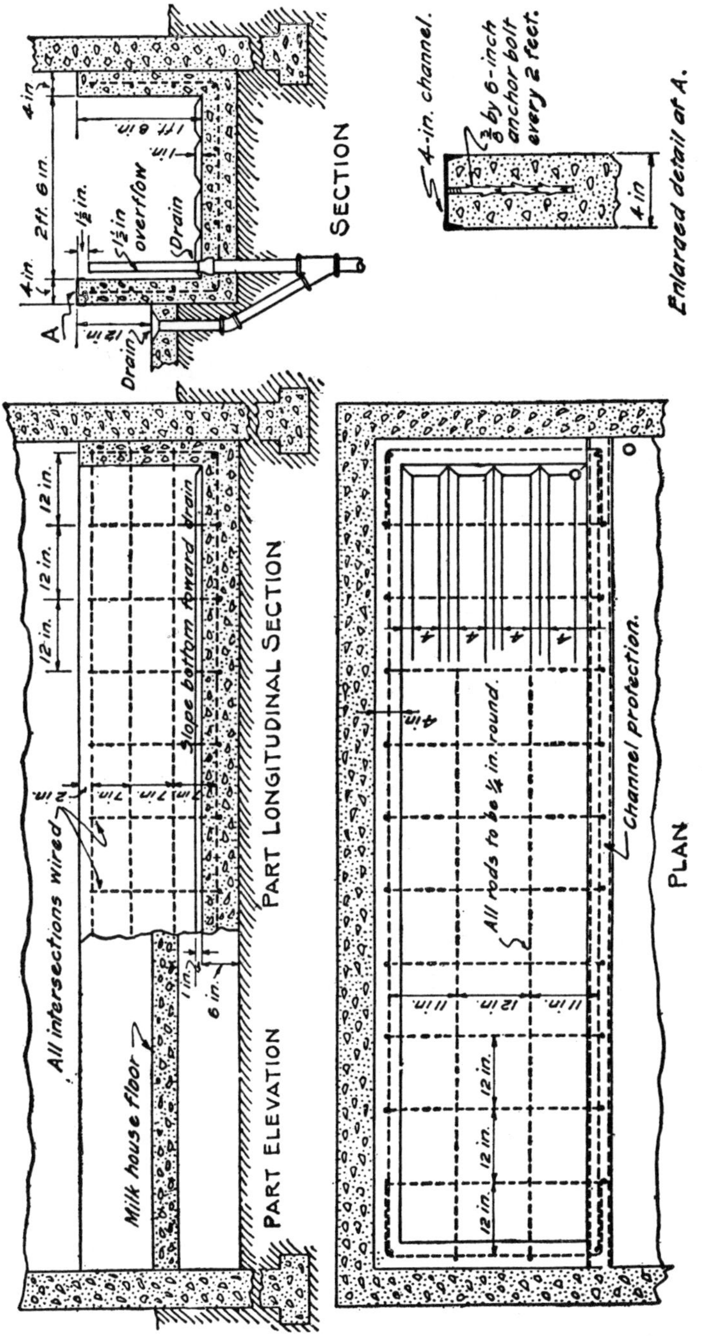

FIG. 165. Milk-cooling tank.

155. A Rectangular Water Tank (Figs. 166, 167, 167-*a*).

Requirements: To construct form according to plan, prepare foundation and construct a rectangular water tank, to be provided with inlet pipe with float control and outlet pipe.

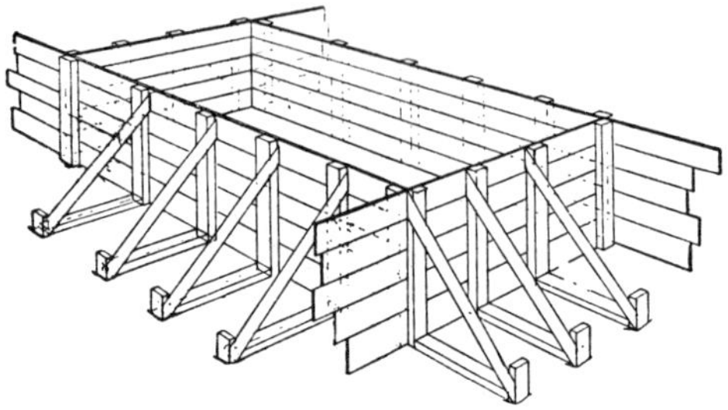

FIG. 166. Outside form for rectangular water tank.

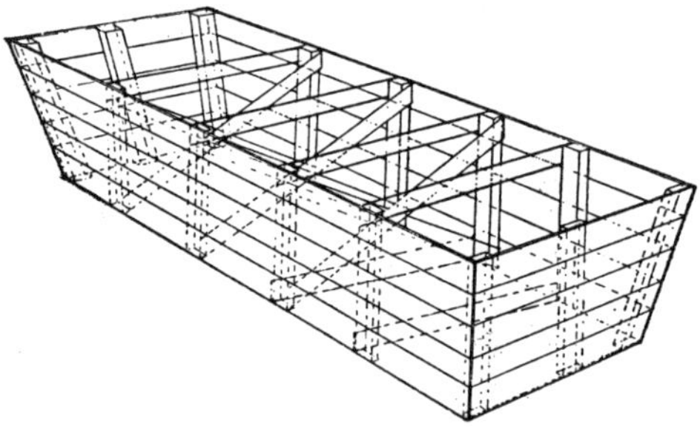

FIG. 167. Inside form for rectangular water tank.

Note: This project is quite similar to that described in Sec. 145, with exception of shape.

Instructions:

1) Prepare foundation. Set inlet and outlet pipes in place.
2) Construct outside form in place 38″ high (Fig. 166).
3) Construct inner form ready for use so that tank will be 2-1/2′ deep with 6″ floor, and 5″ wall at top and 10″ wall at the bottom.
4) Construct form for float box.

5) Mix concrete and place floor of tank with reinforcing. Use 1 : 2 : 4 mixture.
6) Set inner form in place.
7) Place form for float box.
8) Put wall reinforcing in place. Use at least four twisted 1/4″ rods 3′ long, bent at right angle at corner, in addition to hog wire.
9) Place balance of concrete.
10) Remove forms after concrete is thoroly set.
11) Finish surfaces.

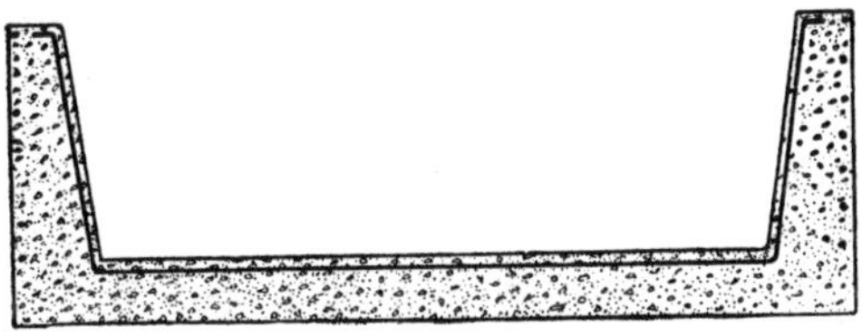

FIG. 167-*a*. Cross-section of finished tank.

156. Potato and Fruit Storage Cellar (Figs. 168, 169).

Requirements: To excavate, construct forms, and place concrete and reinforcing for storage cellar as illustrated.

Note: Refer to project under Sec. 145.

Instructions:

1) Lay out, excavate and prepare foundation for storage cellar according to plan.
2) Construct end forms in place.
3) Construct inner side form in place. The sills supporting top section of inner form to be divided into three parts, the length of each part to be equal to one-half the width of cellar.
4) Provide wedges at bottom of form support to make the form easily removed.

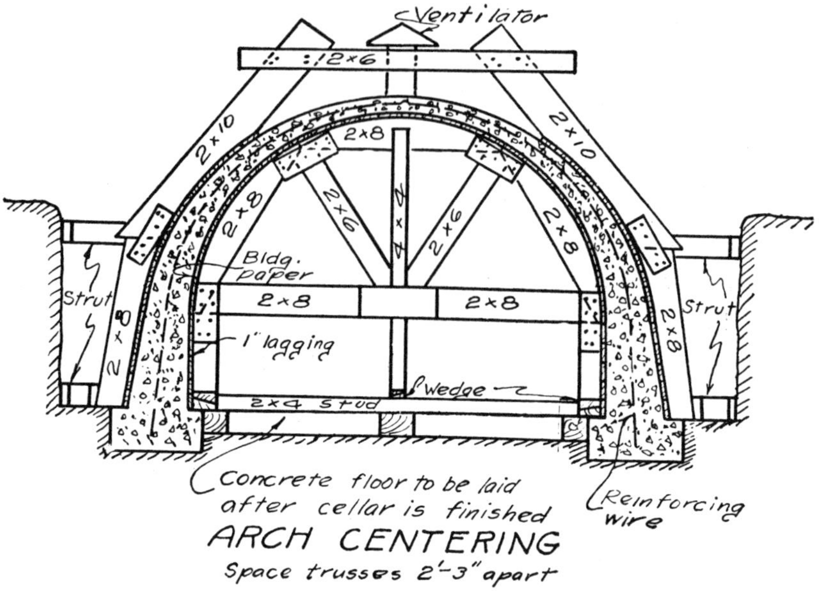

FIG. 168. Fruit storage cellar.

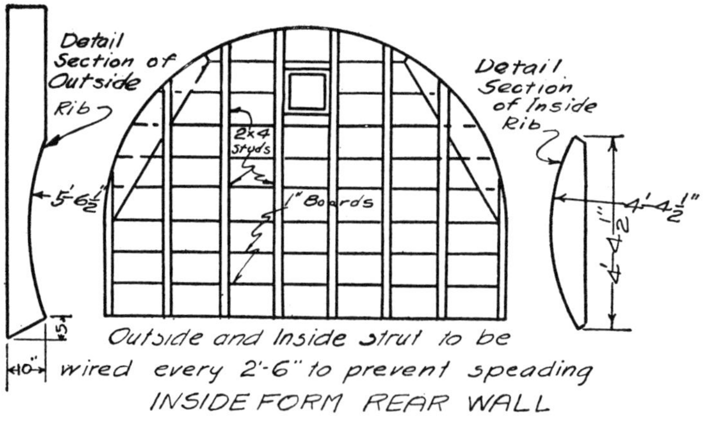

FIG. 169. Inside form of fruit storage cellar.

5) Construct outer side form so wall will be 10″ thick at bottom of arch and 6″ thick at top. When excavation is carefully done, the outer form will be required only above the ground surface. Be very careful in bracing both the inner and outer forms to get best results.

6) Mix concrete 1 : 2 : 4 proportion to a wet consistency, except for the top of arch, which should be to a quaky consistency.
7) Place concrete in lower side wall.
8) Place heavy hog wire from lower walls over arch to insure against shrinkage cracks.
9) Place concrete over arch.
10) Keep concrete from being exposed to extreme heat of sun and moisten each day.
11) Remove forms after a period of about one week.
12) Finish job by smoothing off rough places with a brush and by plastering where necessary.

157. Hog Wallow (Fig. 170).

Requirements: To excavate for hog wallow suitable for 20 or 30 hogs weighing 200 pounds each. To construct form and provide overflow drain and inlet pipe similar to drain and inlet for tank described in Sec. 145. To reinforce floor and side walls of wallow with wire mesh.

Note: Refer to project under Sec. 145.

Instructions:

1) Excavate and prepare foundation for wallow.
2) Place inlet and overflow pipes.
3) Construct inner form ready for use.
4) Construct form for box to protect inlet and overflow pipes.
5) Use a 1 : 2 : 4 proportion and mix concrete to a quaky consistency.
6) Place floor about 4″ thick.
7) Put reinforcing in place across the floor and extending up the wall, as illustrated in cross-section.

8) Place balance of concrete in floor.
9) Put forms in place.
10) Place concrete in walls.
11) Remove forms and finish job.

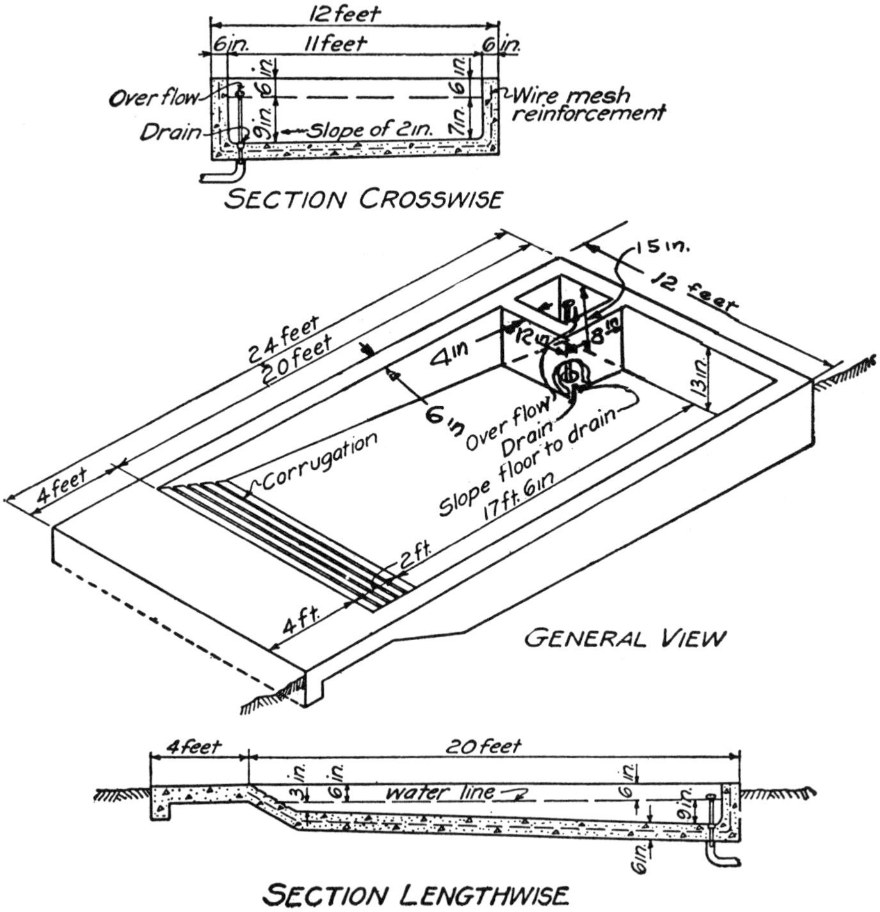

FIG. 170. Hog wallow.

158. Dipping Vat for Hogs (Fig. 171).

Requirements: To excavate for dipping vat, to construct the forms according to plan, and to place the concrete and reinforcing.

Note: Refer to project under Sec. 143.

Instructions:

1) Excavate main part of vat first, which is 8′ 6″ long and 2′ 10″ wide. With a 5″ wall, this gives 2′ in the clear.
2) Excavate sloping incline for outlet, this to be 8′ long and same width as body of tank.

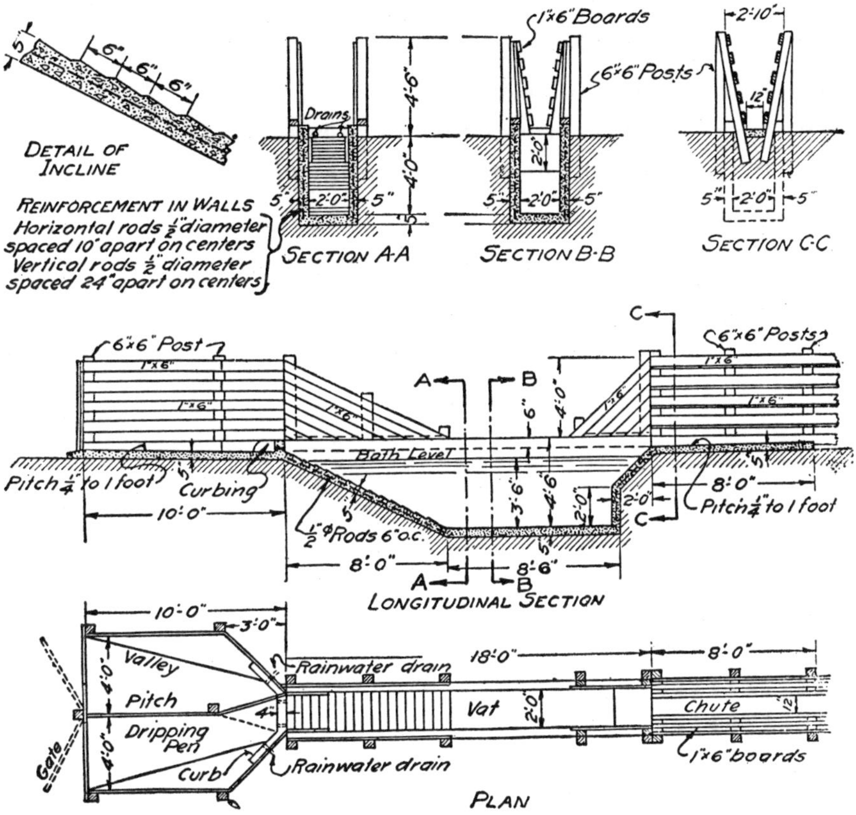

FIG. 171. Dipping vat for hogs.

3) Excavate sloping "step-off" incline; this to have 2′ drop and be 2′ long.
4) Construct an inner form so that floor and walls will be at least 5″ thick.

5) Outside form should be unnecessary if care is observed in excavation.
6) Construct form for curb and floor of dripping pen.
7) Provide reinforcing to insure against cracks. Heavy hog wire is sufficient.
8) Use a 1 : 2 : 4 mixture and mix to a quaky consistency.
9) Place concrete in floor first with reinforcing in place.
10) Put in inner forms.
11) Place concrete in walls.
12) Form treads on incline before concrete sets.
13) Place concrete floor and curb in dripping pens.
14) Remove forms.
15) Coat surface with cement wash to insure water-tightness.

PART III

BLACKSMITHING

CHAPTER XVIII

MANUFACTURE OF IRON AND STEEL

159. Preliminary. There is quite as great need on the farm and in the house for a knowledge of metalwork and facilities to carry it on as for woodwork and cement work. The house-owner and home-maker is more independent if he can do the ordinary things about the home premises which demand the use of metalworking tools for the simpler constructions and repairs.

Under the general head metalwork, we shall consider, under separate parts, the following special branches of metalwork: Forging, Sheet-metalwork, and Farm Machinery Repair and Adjustment.

Under the sub-heads given above, the first will deal chiefly with steel, wrought iron or cast iron, while under the second, tin, zinc or lead, or sheet iron, will be the material handled.

160. Iron Ore. The commercial varieties of iron are pig iron, wrought iron and steel. Iron is found in the ground in natural deposits as "ore," which consists of metal imbedded in mineral and extraneous matter of no value. If the ore contains 50 per cent or more of metal, it is called "rich." It cannot be worked commercially with profit if it contains less than 30 per cent of metal. The valuable ores are oxides, hydrates or carbonates of iron. Ores appearing as sulphides are poor, as it is difficult to remove the sulphur. However, weathering ore—allowing it to stand in the open—will change sulphides to sulphates, which are largely dissolved out by rain.

One of the richest ores is magnetite, or black ore, which, when pure, contains 72.4 per cent iron and 27.6 per cent oxygen. Hematite, or red ore, when pure, contains 70 per cent iron and 30 per cent oxygen.

161. Pig Iron is made by crushing ore to uniform size and heating it in a blast furnace until it can be drawn off at the bottom in a molten condition. The blast furnace is a long, vertical cylindrical shaft which is fed from the top with ore, fuel or flux. Air under pressure is introduced at the bottom for purposes of combustion. The metal when molten is drawn off at the bottom, usually twice during twenty-four hours, and run into sand molds or iron chilled molds to form "pigs" of cast iron. Cast iron has 4 or 5 per cent of impurities such as carbon, sulphur, phosphorus, manganese and silicon. The amount of carbon present determines whether the iron is gray or white. If the greater part of the carbon is free as graphite, the iron is known as gray. If the greater amount of carbon present is combined, the iron is known as white. White iron, or iron with low combined carbon, is soft.

162. Wrought Iron is pure carbonless iron produced in a pasty condition. It is the converse of cast iron, as it is fairly tenacious and extremely ductile. When heated, it can be welded better than any other iron or steel. When heated to full red and quenched in water, it will not harden.

Wrought iron may be produced from iron ore in one operation, but this is costly, as the yield is low. Commercially, it is produced by indirect methods, by purification of pig iron, removing impurities by oxidation. This can be done in an open hearth or reverberating furnace, the methods being known as the open-hearth and Bessemer processes, respectively.

163. The Open-Hearth Process oxidizes the impurities of the pig iron by means of adding iron ore to a bath of molten pig iron. The fuel is, therefore, in contact with the metal, and the oxygen of the blast combined with the impurities are eliminated as oxides. This is a comparatively slow process of refinement, taking from seven to twelve hours to complete. Its advantages are a fine quality of iron produced and a large amount of material which can be handled at one time.

164. The Bessemer Process also is an oxidizing one, but the metal and fuel are not in contact. The oxygen is furnished by means of a large volume of compressed air blown thru a bath of molten pig iron. The oxygen combines with the carbon to evolve as gases while it combines with other impurities to form slag. The process requires but a few minutes—from twelve to twenty.

165. Steel. It is practically impossible to define steel accurately. It is an alloy of iron and carbon, but as alloys of iron and carbon include cast iron, this definition is not a technical one. Ordinary steel may be said to be iron containing from 0.1 to 2.0 per cent of carbon in combined form which has been subjected to complete fusion and poured into an ingot or mold for the production of forgeable metal. Such a metal—steel—has the composition of wrought iron, but it has been produced in a steel-melting furnace.

166. Tempering Steel. The greater the amount of carbon in steel, the harder it is, but the more ductile. The amount of carbon in steel practically determines the purpose for which steel may be used. Steel is hardened when heated to redness and quenched in water or oil.

When steel is heated and allowed to cool, naturally, it softens. It is upon this fact that tempering, which is the process of getting the proper combination of hardness and ductibility, is based. As the hot steel cools, surface oxides are formed which range from faint yellow thru straw, full yellow, brown, purple and full blue to dark blue. The lightest of these colors indicates the highest degree of hardness.

Machine and Tool Repairs

Under this heading is considered such work as one may be called upon to do in constructing tools and machines made of iron or steel, and which does not require the heating of the metal. For the most part, such work will be done with hand tools, as hammer, chisels, files, drills, taps, dies, rivets, etc. Work which requires the careful shaping or fitting of cold metal will need to be done in a machine shop and is not considered here.

Tools and Equipment

For general use about the premises, a small out-building or room should be equipped with the following:

One wooden bench made of well-braced 2″ x 4″ uprights and stringers covered with plank and fitted with a spring screw vise, or machinist's vise.

One hand forge and anvil, with the common forge tools.

One grindstone, hand- or foot-power type, about 24″ in diameter and 3-1/2″ thick.

One bench hand emery grinder and oilstone.

In the room should be stored:

Wooden horses, wooden and metal blocks, skids, a block and tackle, and, possibly, a chain block, crowbars, pinch bars, rollers and pieces of iron pipe, rope and rope lashings with ends tied or wound, and jacks of the adjustable top and simple and heavy erecting types. The bench tools should consist of a simple equipment, some of which can be made and others purchased, such as:

Machinist's hammers with ball, straight and cross peens, each weighing from 1 to 1-3/4 pounds.

Hand hack-saw and blades.

Center and prick punch.

Machinist's chisels, principally the flat or cape chisels.

Files, handled, of the rough and middle-cut grades principally, and both single- and double-cut in flat, round, half-round, square and triangular shapes. The total number need not exceed 12.

Drills in sizes ranging from 1/16″ to 3/4″ graded to sixteenths.

One drilling ratchet and one breast drill.

A variety of wrenches, including a good pipe wrench, monkey, alligator and a variety of single-end and solid or closed wrenches such as those included in a first-class automobile tool kit. A variety of socket wrenches will also be found very handy.

Two or three sizes of outside and inside calipers and dividers.

One scriber.

One surface gage.

One surface plate, about 2′ square.

One 2′ rule, carpenter's folding.

One 6″ and one 12″ steel scale.

One 6″ screwdriver, one 12″ screwdriver.

A variety of machine screws, bolts and nuts, washers, rivets and cotter pins.

One small set of taps for cutting machine thread.

One small set of dies for cutting machine thread.

One pair 6″ end pliers.

One pair 6″ side pliers.

One 4″ spirit level.

One carpenter's level.

One plumb bob.

One gasoline blow-forge.

Such supplies as the following should be accessible:

Waste, cotton wick, emery, emery cloth, lard and machine oil, and cup grease.

It will be well to keep in stock a small supply of bar strap and sheet iron.

FIG. 172. Arrangement of forge and tools, showing position of blacksmith at the forge.

CHAPTER XIX

Equipment for Blacksmithing; Fundamental Processes

167. Use of the Forge on the Farm. The village blacksmith shop has always been a place of both first and last resort in helping to solve the many construction problems of a community. Likewise, the blacksmith's forge on the farm may be made the means of developing and repairing many tools and machines. The farmer who would save both time and expense may very well, therefore, be familiar with the work of the blacksmith.

It is suggested that the forge be a part of the equipment of the farm shop and occupy one end of a room, along one side of which may be placed the metalworking bench, thus bringing the vise near the anvil. It is frequently desirable to grasp a hot piece of metal in the vise when it is taken from the forge.

168. The Forge and Anvil. The forge which will be as serviceable as any on the farm, is one of the hand-operated fan, or bellows, type (Fig. 172). In front of it should be placed the anvil at easy-turning distance from the forge (Fig. 172). It may be mounted on the end of a heavy hardwood block or piece of the trunk of a tree, or it may be mounted upon a concrete pillar, to which it should be lagged. The height of the face of the anvil from the floor should be approximately 30″. It should weigh from 150 to 200 pounds.

169. Blacksmith's Tools. In addition to the forge and anvil, the following general equipment of tools should be at hand:

One each 1 to 3-pound cross-peen, straight-peen and ball-peen hammer.
One sledge, 5 to 10 pounds.
One pair of flat-jawed tongs for general work.
One pair of hollow-bit tongs for holding rod stock.
One pair of anvil or pick-up tongs for holding short pieces of heavy work while upsetting.
One bell tong for flat or scroll work.
One short-piece tong.
One handled top and bottom swage.
One handled top and bottom fuller.
One handled punch.
One handled flatter.
One handled hardie or hot chisel.
One heading tool.
One hardie for anvil.

Figs. 173 and 174 show photographs of a number of these tools. Tools other than those listed above and ordinarily included in a blacksmithing kit, are listed under the head of "Farm Machinery."

Of these, the most essential are:

Carpenter's square.
Calipers.
Dividers.
Scriber.
Folding steel rule.
Tire measurer.
Vise (solid box blacksmith).
Cold chisels, one on handle in shape of hammer.

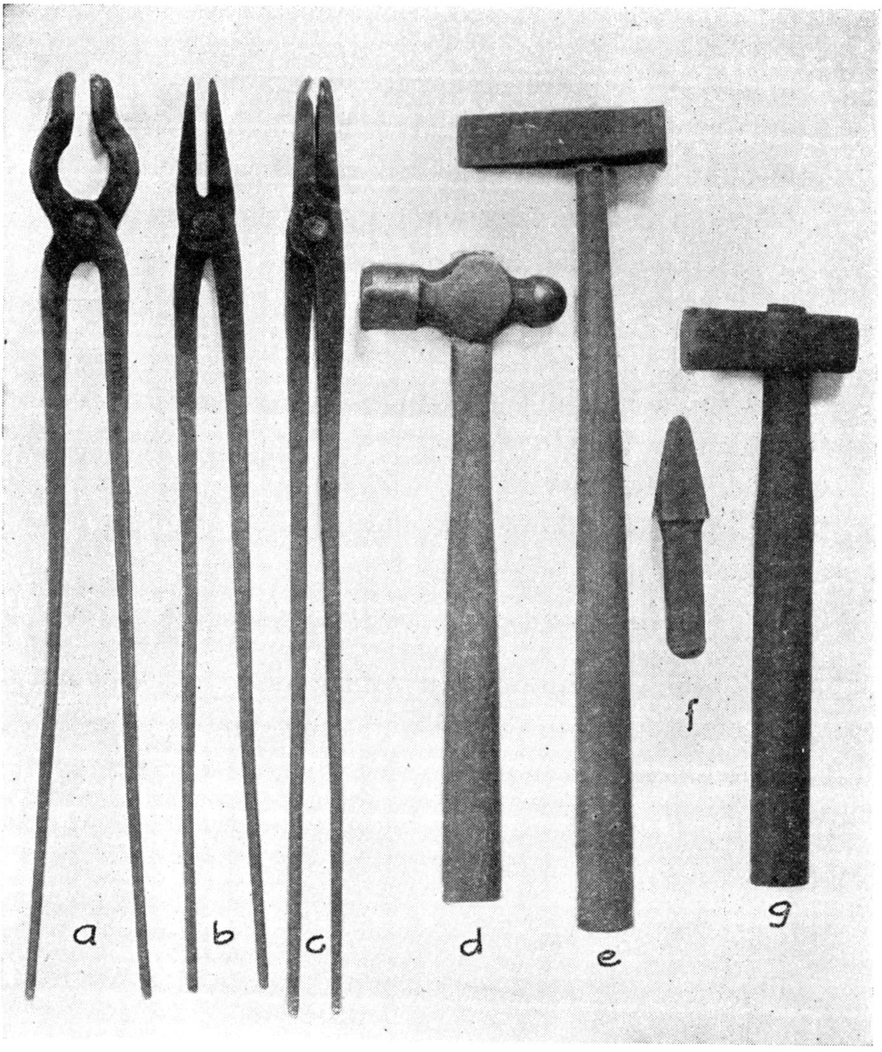

FIG. 173. Forge tools: *a*, hollow-bit tongs; *b*, flat-jawed tongs; *c*, pick-up tongs; *d*, ball-peen hammer; *e*, handled chisel; *f*, hardie for anvil; *g*, chisel.

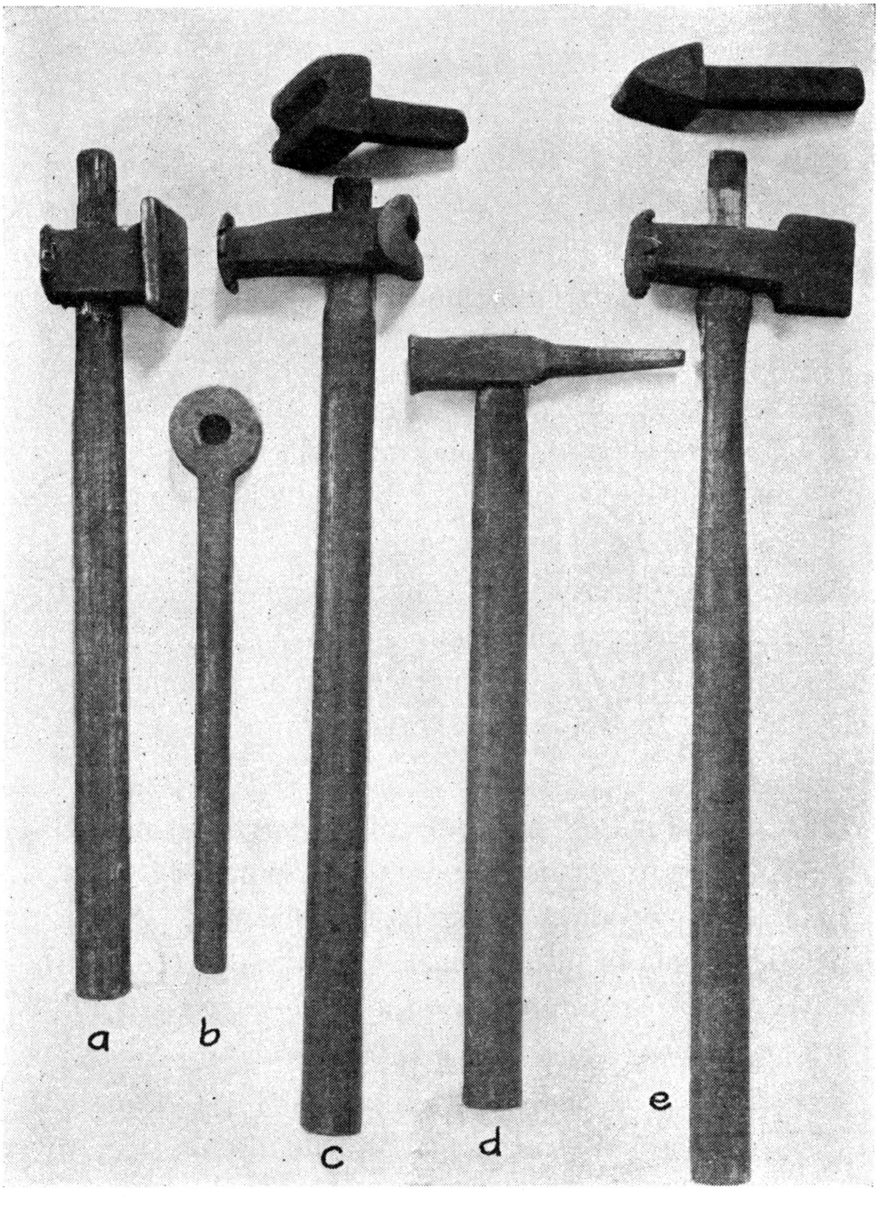

FIG. 174. Forge tools: *a*, flatter; *b*, heading tool; *c*, swages; *d*, handled punch; *e*, fullers.

170. Supplies for Forge Work. It is well to carry in stock a small supply of wrought iron and steel in the following sizes:

3/8″ rods.
5/8″ rods.
1/4″ x 5/8″ bars.
1/4″ x 1″ bars.

(*Note:* Also material for buggy tires, bolts and rivets.)

171. Use of Wrought Iron. Wrought iron will be used chiefly. It can be worked either hot or cold. When worked cold, it becomes denser, harder, more elastic and brittle, but can be brought to its original condition by heating to red and cooling slowly.

The ordinary processes of tool construction are described in the instructions for projects. For ordinary work, a "red" heat is given the stock. When pieces are to be joined to form one solid piece by welding, however, the stock is brought to a "white" heat.

172. The Fire. The blacksmith's forge is a pan with a grate at the bottom which admits the air pumped for the purpose of creating a draft. The pan, or fire pot, contains the coal. This must be bituminous, or soft, coal of the very best quality. It is very important that it be free from sulphur and phosphorus.

To build the fire, remove all clinkers, slate, stone and other foreign material. Push the coal and coke to one side to expose the grate, tuyere, or wind box. Upon this, place a few shavings, some straw or paper, and cover with a little kindling as the match is applied.

Use a very light blast at first. As the fire burns, add green coal. When the fire gets strong, surround it with a ring of green, dampened coal, except toward the front, which should be kept open for the insertion of the iron to be heated and used to hold the iron while being heated, and for the tools. These should be kept in a horizontal position. As the work proceeds and the fire extends into the ring of green coal, it may be dampened to hold the fire to a limited area. Green coal may be added at the rear and the sides, but the fire should not be disturbed by poking it. As it burns from underneath, cinders should be raked out to keep the fire clear, and the coal should be gently patted down with a small shovel. Continuing this process will keep a clean, well-confined and fresh fire. Fig. 175 shows a cross-section thru the fire-pot.

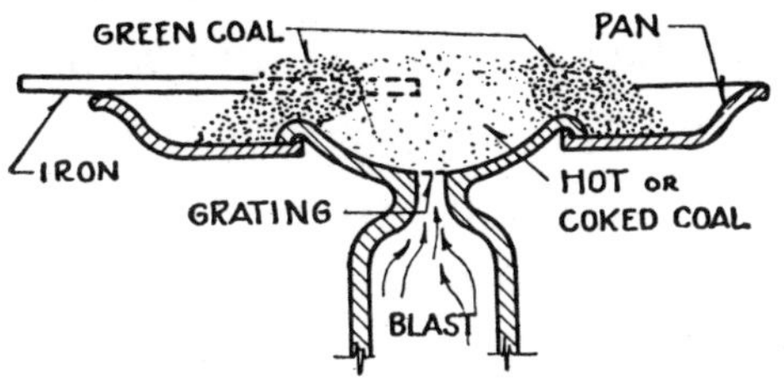

FIG. 175. Cross-section of forge.

As iron heats in the fire, the following shades of color will appear, indicating the proper condition of the iron for certain classes of work:

a) Dark blood red (block heat).

b) Dark red, low red (finishing heat).

c) Full red.

d) Bright or light red (scaling heat).

e) Yellow heat.

f) Light yellow heat (good forging heat).

g) White heat or welding heat (beyond this, iron will burn).

173. Welding. Upon continued heating of wrought iron or mild steel, the temperature increases, the metal becomes increasingly soft, and, if another piece equally soft is touched to the first, the two will stick; light tapping will complete the weld. The greater the range of temperature thru which the metal remains pasty, the more easily may it be welded. The greatest trouble in welding is in heating the metal properly. The fire must be clean and bright; otherwise, small pieces of cinder, etc., will stick to the metal. The heating must be slow enough to get the metal heated thru. Have all tools in place before taking a piece of metal from the fire. Hold the tongs on metal so that pieces can be easily placed in position without difficulty. When "stuck," first tap the thin parts of the pieces to be welded, as these cool first and most rapidly.

Do not have an oxidizing fire in welding; that is, not too much oxygen going thru fire.

In the welding process, the oxide formed is really a flux. In welding, steel will burn before the oxide becomes white hot; hence, a flux is used made of sand and borax; this is put in at yellow heat and protects the surfaces to be welded, preventing the forming of oxide. The oxide melts at a much lower heat when combined with the flux. This is the principal object of using a flux. Sal ammoniac seems to clean the surface, so a flux is sometimes made of one part sal ammoniac and four parts borax.

The following typical welds should be familiar:

a) Fagot or pile.
b) Scarfed.
c) Lap (flat).
d) Lap (round).
e) Ring (round stock).
f) Chain-making.
g) Butt.
h) Jump.
i) Split.
j) Angle.
k) "T" (round stock).

CHAPTER XX

Projects in Blacksmithing

Problem No. 1: Drawing and Bending of Iron.

Projects Suggested for this Group:

a) Staple (Fig. 176).
b) Gate hooks (Fig. 177).
c) Hay hook (Fig. 178).
d) Eyebolt (Fig. 179).
e) Stove poker (Fig. 180).

174. Tools to Be Used. The tools needed to make projects in this group, aside from the forge and anvil, are a blacksmith's hammer (light) and a pair of flat-jawed or hollow bit tongs.

175. Maintaining the Fire. Every operation at the forge requires the maintenance of a good fire, the heating of iron to the proper temperature, and the proper handling of the blacksmith's tools to accomplish satisfactory results. Before beginning work on this project, read carefully the instructions on preparing the fire (Sec. 172). While work is progressing, green coal should be added from time to time, but always on the rim or edge of the fire, not on the live fire. The fire should be prevented from running into the green coal farther than desired by occasionally dripping water on the inside edge of the rim of green coal. This coal should be kept well packed down, thus forming a wall around the fire to be kept confined to the grate only. As the coal in the fire is consumed, remove clinkers and draw in fresh coal from the rim.

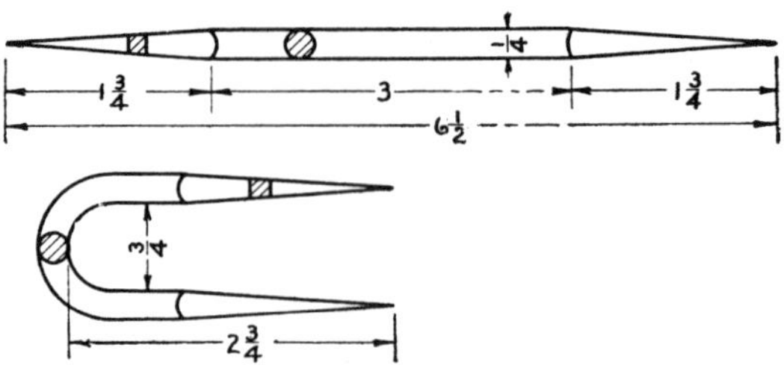

FIG. 176. Staple.

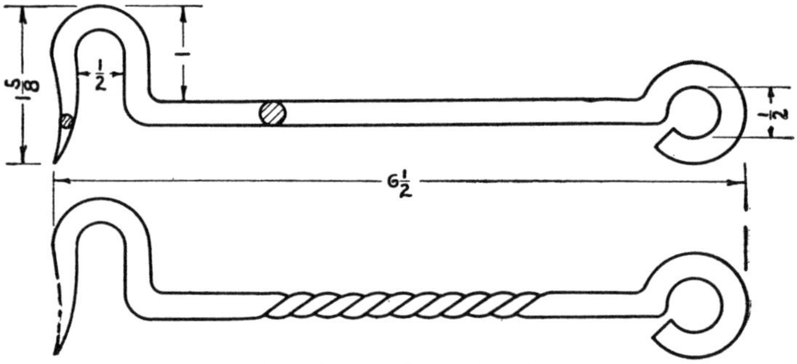

FIG. 177. Gate hook.

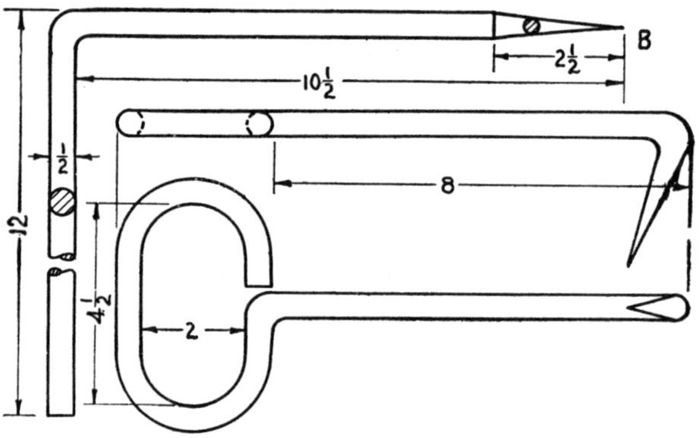

FIG. 178. Hay hook.

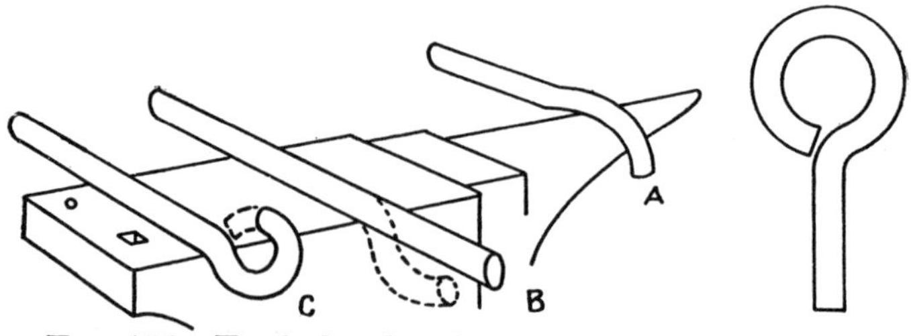

FIG. 179. Eyebolt, showing steps in construction.

The operator must at all times keep his tools in good order and near at hand. The hammer to be used may well be laid in position on the anvil (Fig. 172) to be grasped by the right

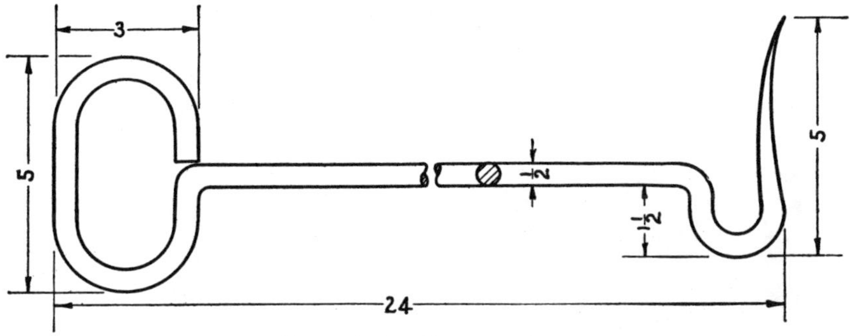

FIG. 180. Stove poker.

hand immediately when the iron taken from the forge reaches the anvil. The tongs may be laid on the top of the forge at

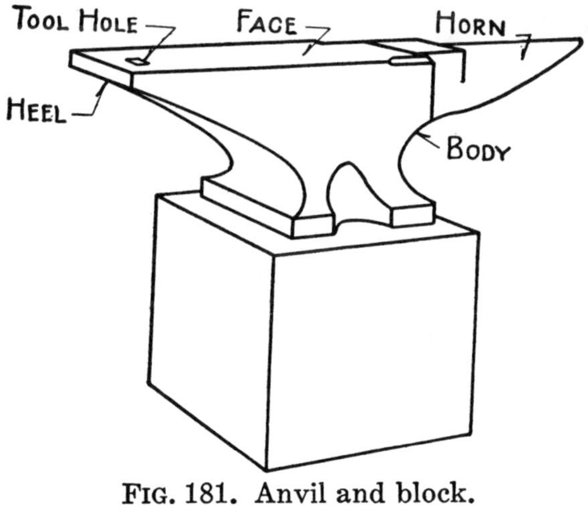

FIG. 181. Anvil and block.

the left side of the fire, so that they may be handled by the left hand in removing the iron from the fire.

Working Instructions for the Gate Hook:

Stock: One piece of 1/4″ round wrought iron 10″ long.

176. Bending Iron. Place one end of the rod in the

tongs held in the left hand, with which place the opposite end of the rod in the front and at the base of the fire in a horizontal position. Heat this end of the rod for 3″ to a light yellow or lemon color.

Withdraw the iron with tongs in the left hand and place on anvil with the heated end projecting over the horn 2-1/2″. Fig. 181 shows anvil with parts named. Grasp the hammer well toward the end of the handle with the right hand. Raise the hammer above the iron and strike it a light blow just beyond the point where it is in contact with the edge of the anvil (Fig. 182). Continue this process until the iron assumes the form shown in solid lines at the right in Fig. 183. This form should be made without reheating the iron.

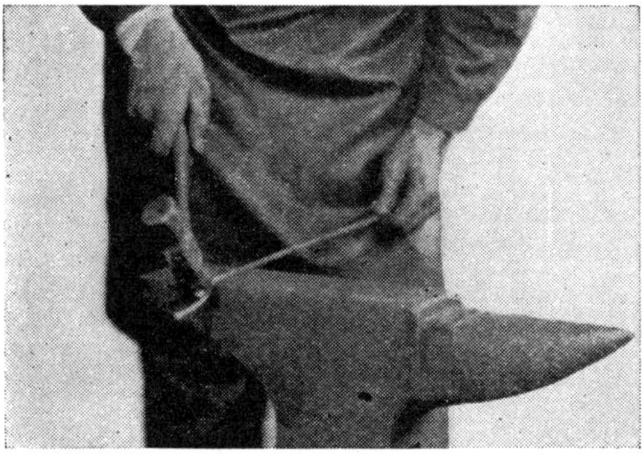

FIG. 182. Method of bending iron.

Reheat the same end of the iron, again to lemon color.

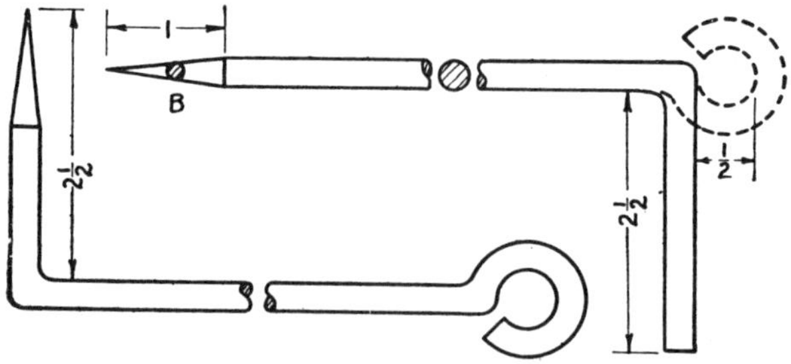

FIG. 183. Steps in making gate hook.

Grasp as before with the tongs, but with the iron turned over in the tongs so that the part made at a right angle with the rod in the first operation is upward. Place on the horn of the anvil, as shown in Fig. 184, and, by striking the end at an angle with the hammer, shape this end to a complete circle centrally located on the end of the rod. The dotted lines at the right end of the rod (Fig. 183) show this finished shape. The hole in the ring should be 1/2″ in diameter. It can be made the right size and circular by forming it over the end of the horn (Fig. 184).

177. Drawing Iron. Heat the opposite end of the rod to lemon color, and form 1″ of it to a cone (*B*, Fig. 183). The

FIG. 184. Making the eye on gate hook.

cone is formed by resting the heated end of the rod at the angle of the cone on the face of the anvil and gradually rolling it from side to side while the hammer strikes the iron lightly a repeated number of blows. This end of the rod is to form the hook.

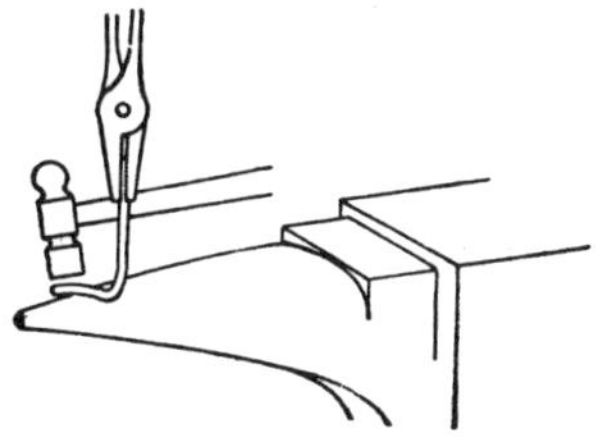

FIG. 185. Forming the point on gate hook.

Reheat the hook end of the rod for 3″ to lemon color and bend it over the horn of the anvil to form a 2-1/2″ right-angle shoulder. This operation is the same as the first one described in forming the ring end of the hook.

Now, grasp the tongs, as shown in Fig. 185, and proceed as in forming the ring of the hook to bend the hook end in the middle of the 2-1/2″ portion of the L-shaped end to a half-circle (Fig. 177). Bend the point of the cone outward slightly over the end of the horn of the anvil. Lay the hook flat on the face of the anvil and straighten with a few light blows of the hammer.

If it is desired to have the hook twisted in the center (Fig. 177), heat the central portion of the hook to a light yellow color, grasp the hook end with the tongs, place the ring end in the vise, and twist or turn in one direction until the desired number of twists are formed and until the hook and the ring are in the same plane.

Each of the projects in this group is made so nearly the same as the gate hook, that they require no special instructions. The handle both for the hay hook and the stove poker is formed of two half-circles joined by straight portions of the handle. A little care on the part of the operator after making the gate hook will enable him to make either of these handles. The iron may need to be heated a few more times, but this will not be serious unless the number of heatings is sufficient to weaken it or unless the temperature approaches that for welding heat and the iron is burnt in consequence. It is always desirable to heat iron as few times as possible to secure the desired shape and form in order not to weaken the metal or burn it, as well as to save as much time as possible in the work.

Problem No. 2: Upsetting and Punching.

Projects Suggested for this Group:

a) Open-end wrench (Fig. 186).
b) Punched screw clevis (Fig. 187).
c) Machine bolt (Fig. 188).
d) Log hook (Fig. 189).

178. Tools Needed for Upsetting and Punching. The same tools as those named for the group of projects in Prob-

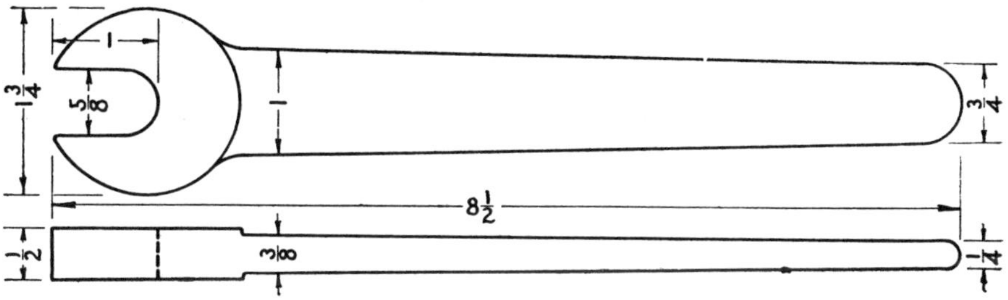

FIG. 186. Open-end wrench.

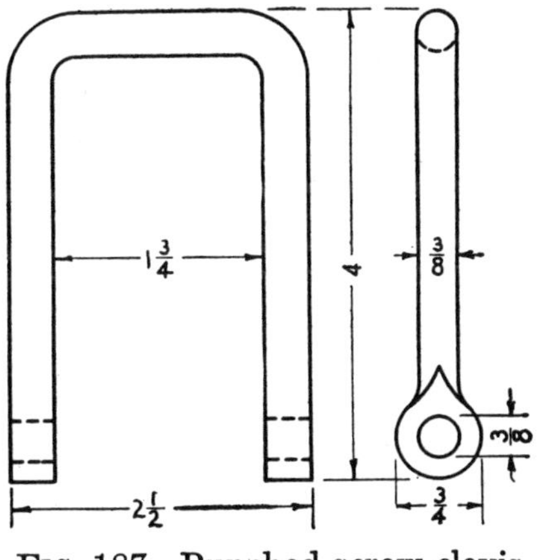

FIG. 187. Punched screw clevis.

lem 1 will be required in this group, and in addition, the upsetting tool and punch.

179. Upsetting and Punching. It is frequently necessary to enlarge some portion of a piece of iron. This is done by upsetting. To upset stock, heat it at the point to be enlarged, place it on end on the anvil, and pound it on the other end with a hammer. Repeat this process for each reheating until the stock is of the desired size where it is to be upset.

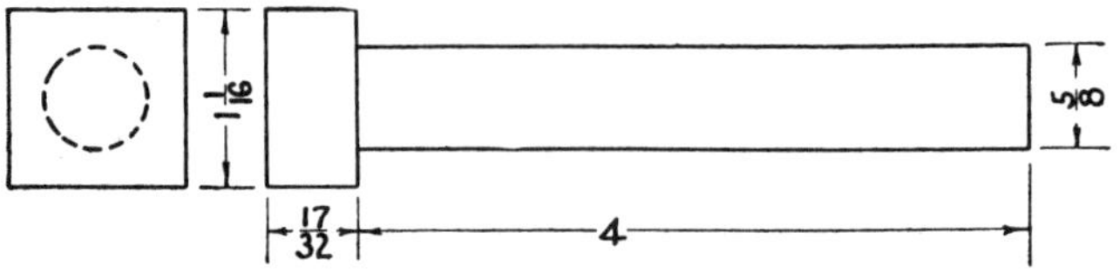

FIG. 188. Machine bolt.

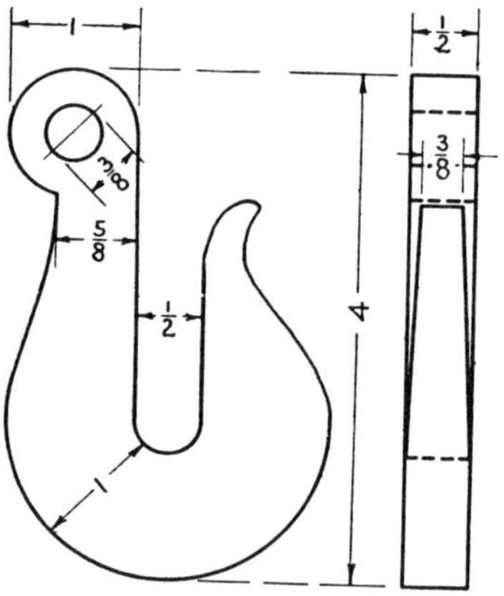

FIG. 189. Log hook.

At times, to make a hole thru a piece of iron with forge tools, it is only necessary to drive a punch thru it when hot. At other times, the stock will need to be bent around to lap back on itself, when it must be welded as described in the next group in this section, or the hole will have to be drilled.

180. Working Instructions for the Punched Screw Clevis. One piece of 1/2″ wrought iron 12″ long will be used for this project.

1) Heat one end of the iron to light red and bend 1-1/4″ of

it to right angles with the rod over the back edge of the anvil (Fig. 190).

2) Reheat the same end to lemon color, place on the face of the anvil with bent end upwards and upset by pounding on this upturned end with quick, sharp blows of the hammer. Roughly shape to approximate circular form by working the cylindrical surface on the surface of the anvil and over its corner. Reheat and continue to upset and shape until thickness of flattened end is approximately 3/8″.

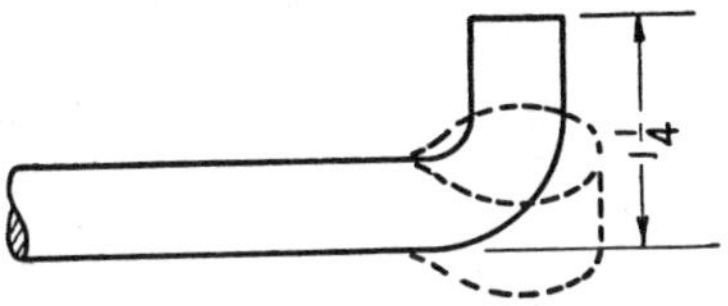

FIG. 190. Upsetting for clevis.

3) Reheat to welding, or white, heat, using extreme care not to burn the iron. Remove the iron from the forge the moment it becomes white. Place it quickly on the face of the anvil in former position for upsetting, and strike quickly with the hammer two or three times. Finish flat surfaces with the flatter (Fig. 191). Turn the iron on edge over the corner of the anvil, and strike quick, sharp blows to form circle. If the iron is at welding heat and the work with the hammer is done quickly, the iron will weld or become a solid mass. Any seams which may have formed in the upsetting process will be obliterated. Fig. 192 shows the finished end. In a similar manner, as described up to this point, forge the other end of the rod.

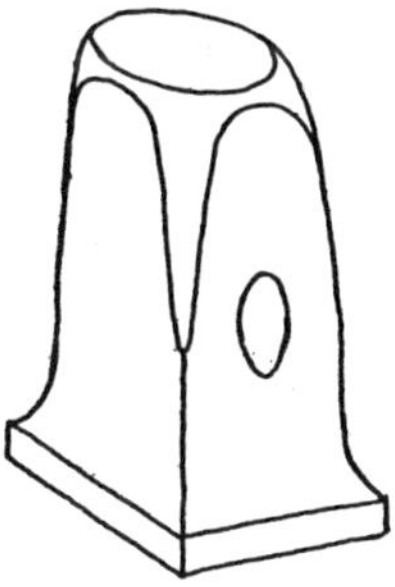

FIG. 191. A flatter.

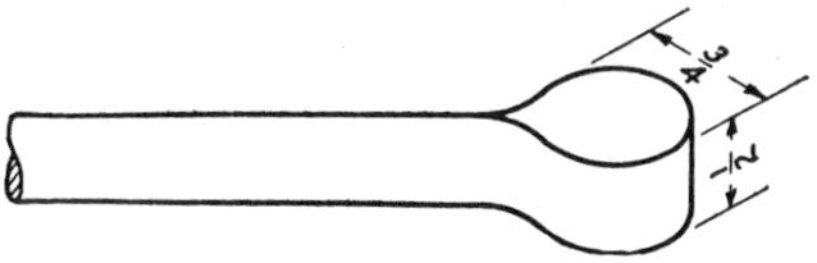

FIG. 192. Appearance of finished job of upsetting.

4) Reheat each end separately to yellow color, mark center with prick-punch and punch 1/4″ hole one-half way thru iron on this prick-punched mark with punch, shown in Fig. 193. Reverse the stock, place the end over the hardie hole, and drive the punch thru from the other side. Reheat the stock, if necessary, and drive the punch thru from each side to enlarge the hole to 3/8″ (Fig. 194).

FIG. 193. Handled punch.

5) Punch a hole in the other end in a similar manner (Fig. 195).

6) Heat the stock in the center for a space of 3″, and bend it over the horn of the anvil to the shape shown in Fig. 196. The central portion of the curved end of the clevis should be straight.

7) By laying the clevis on the face of the anvil with the punched ends hanging over the edge of the anvil, and striking

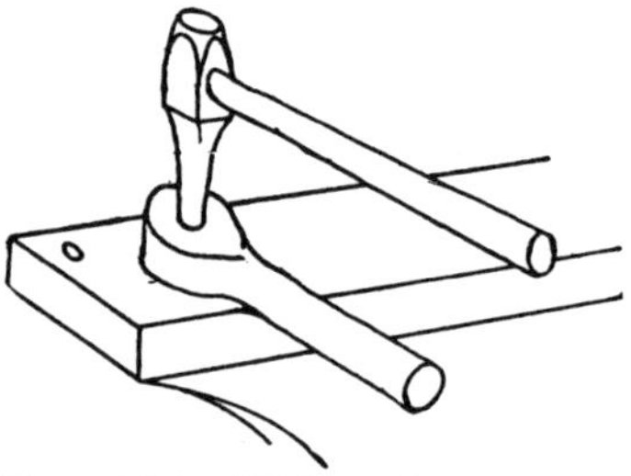

FIG. 194. Using the punch.

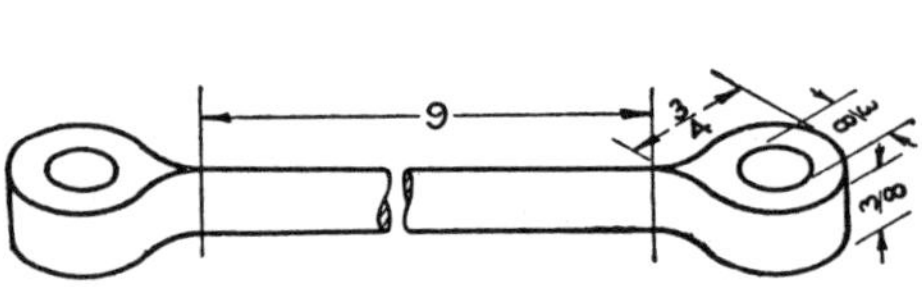

FIG. 195. Clevis ready to be bent into shape.

the two legs of the clevis with light hammer blows, it may be straightened. The two punched holes must be in line. Fig. 187 shows the finished clevis.

Supplementary Instructions:

181. Open-End Wrench. Heat 4″ of one end of 1-1/2″ x 7/16″ soft steel to lemon color, and draw it out to shape and dimensions shown at *A*, Fig. 197. Mark the stock 1-1/2″ from the point where the forging of the handle was begun, as shown by the dotted line (*A*, Fig. 197). Cut the stock off on the anvil hardie (Fig. 198), or with the handled hardie (Fig. 173), cutting, first, from one side and, then, from the other, and, finally, breaking off over the edge of the anvil by striking the stock not to be used a sharp blow with the hammer just beyond the anvil edge.

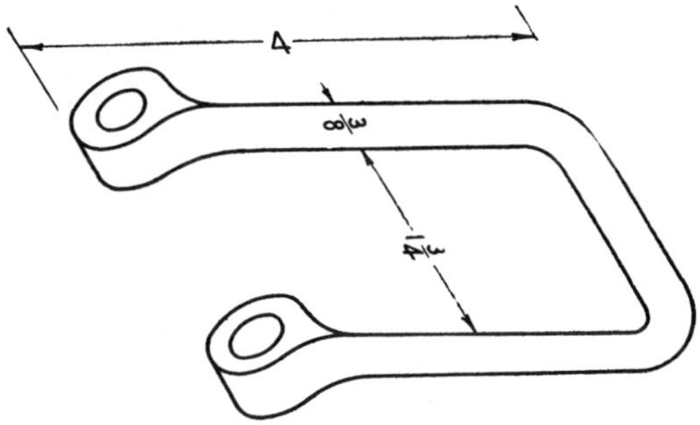

FIG. 196. Completed clevis.

Heat the stock to lemon color and forge to shape, as shown in *B*, Fig. 197. The wrench end should be rounded up, keeping stock to original thickness, by first forming an octagon, then a sixteen-sided figure, and, finally, a circle. This work should be done over the corner of the anvil and by moving the edge being formed into different positions as the hammer strikes the iron. Reheat the metal and punch a hole 1/2″ out of center toward the wrench end and expand

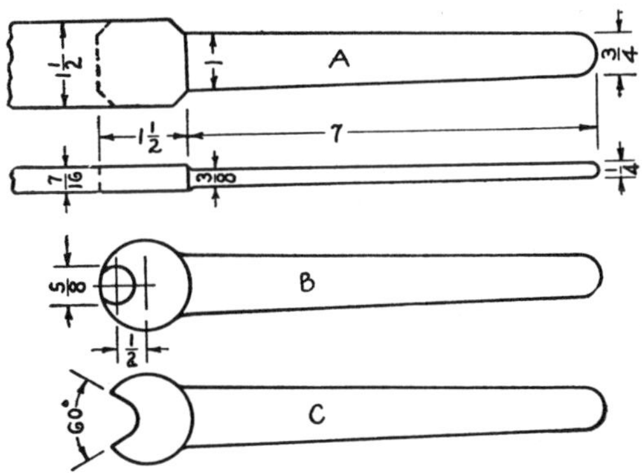

FIG. 197. Steps in making wrench.

it until it is 5/8″ in diameter (*B*, Fig. 197). Cut the end out with a hot chisel or handled hardie to 60 degrees, keeping same centrally located, as shown at *C*, Fig. 197. Reheat and forge to shape and dimensions, shown in Fig. 186. This should be done by holding the wrench edgewise on the face of the anvil with the handle held downward at an angle and striking the wrench end an angle blow on the end of each prong of this end, finally flattening the inside of jaws and their surface on the heel end of the anvil. Smooth up with flatter.

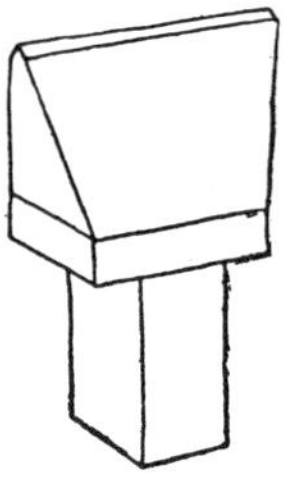

FIG. 198. Hardie for anvil.

The wrench should be hardened to make it serviceable. Heat it to lemon color and plunge it in water for a few moments. This cools the outer surface. When the metal is

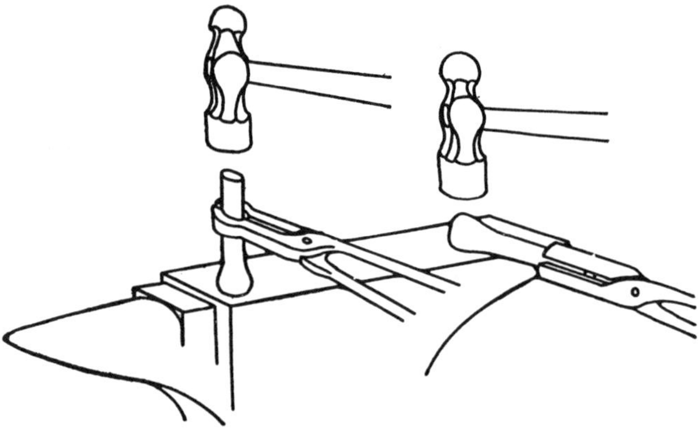

FIG. 199. Upsetting and shaping bolt.

withdrawn from the water, the heat of the center will draw out toward the surface. While still quite warm, put in water to completely cool.

182. Bolt Head. The construction of the square bolt head involves upsetting (Fig. 199). Care must be taken not to upset too far, however. When the approximate dimensions given in Fig. 200 have been secured, heat the upset end to lemon color and place the bolt thru the hole in the heading tool (Fig. 200-*a*) and into the hardie hole in the anvil, as shown in Fig. 200-*b*. Proceed to upset the head and to keep it circular in form by occasionally removing it from the heading tool, and, by rolling it in the tongs on the face of the anvil (Fig. 199), hammer the head into a true cylindrical form. When the diameter of this cylinder is slightly less than the distance between

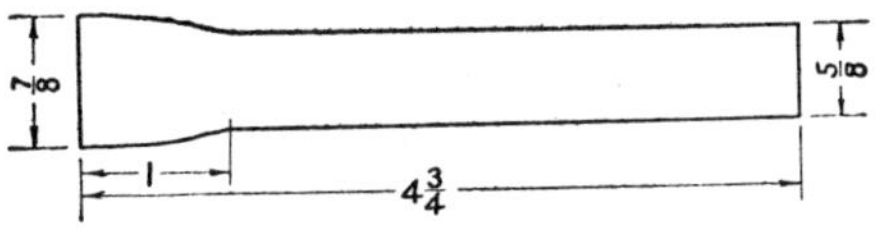

FIG. 200. The upsetting completed.

FIG. 200-*a*. Heading tool.

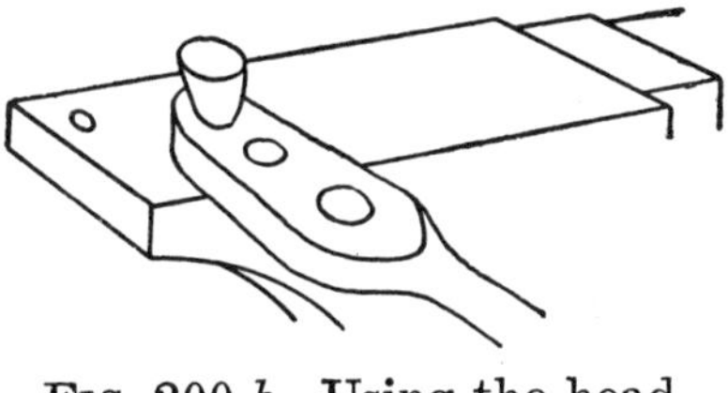

FIG. 200-*b*. Using the heading tool.

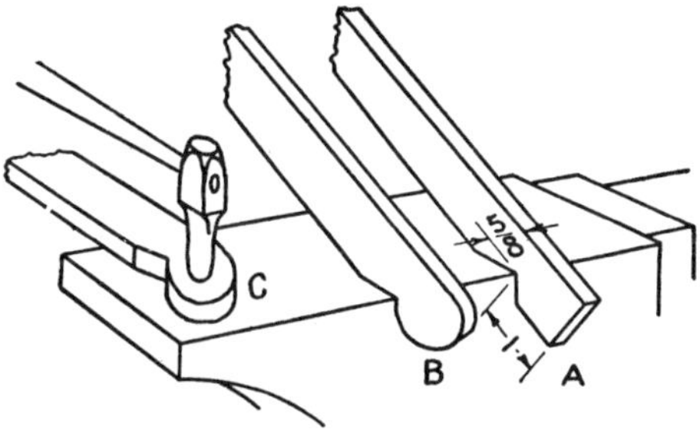

FIG. 201. Steps in making log hook.

corners of the finished head, reheat the stock on the head end to lemon color and forge the square head (Fig. 188).

183. Log Hook. Heat 2″ of one end of 1/2″ x 1″ wrought iron stock 5-1/2″ long to a yellow glow; place over outside edge of anvil with 1″ overhanging, and forge to shape, shown in *A*, Fig. 201. Reheat and forge to shape, shown in *B*, Fig.

201. Reheat and punch hole, as shown in *C*, Fig. 201. Round corners of hole over horn of anvil to shape, shown at *C*, Fig. 202.

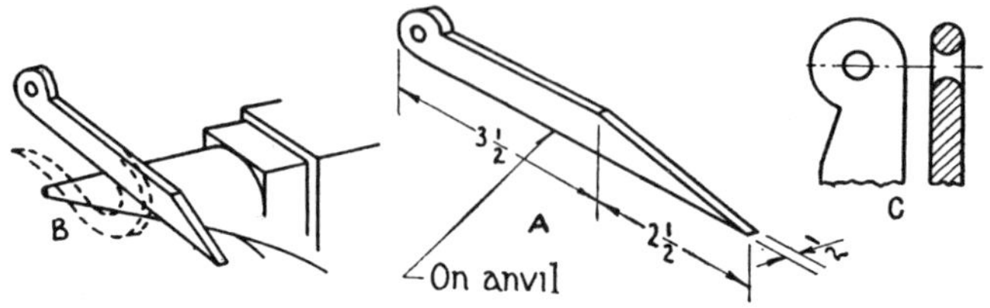

FIG. 202. Further operations in construction of log hook.

Heat the other end and taper to shape and dimensions, shown in *A*, Fig. 202. Bend the point slightly over horn of anvil. Reheat center of stock and form over horn of anvil, as

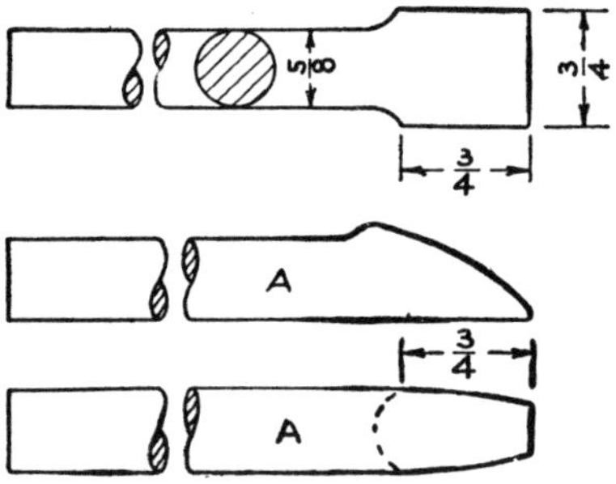

FIG. 203. Two-piece weld.

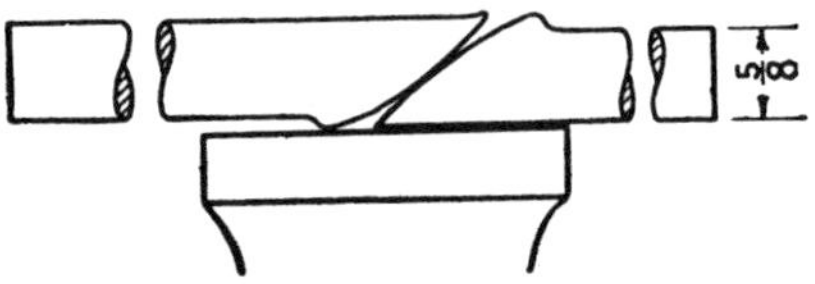

FIG. 204. Position of pieces when welding.

shown by dotted lines at *B*, Fig. 202. Finish to dimensions given in Fig. 189.

Problem No. 3: The Process of Welding.

Projects Suggested:

a) Two-piece weld (Figs. 203 and 204).

b) "T"-weld (Fig. 205).

c) Welded clevis (Fig. 206).

d) Wagon wrench (Fig. 207).

184. Preparation for Welding. The same tools as those named for the previous grcups, in addition to which the

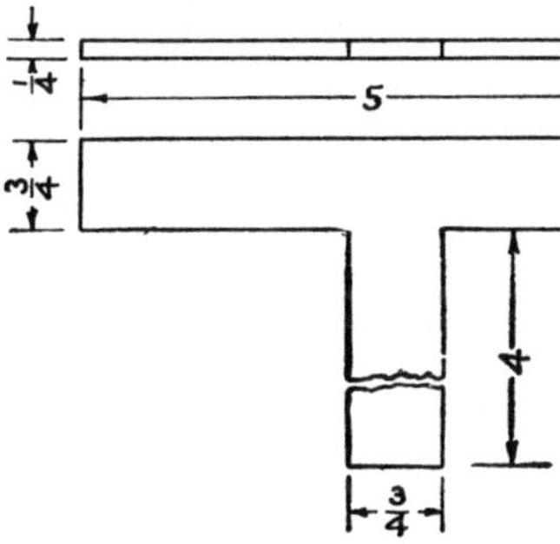

FIG. 205. "T"-weld.

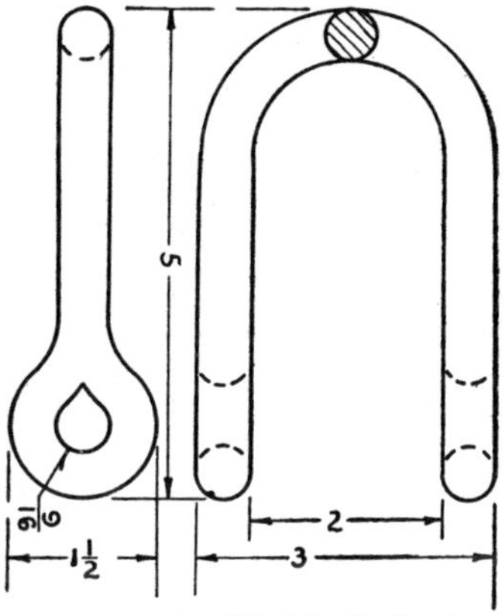

FIG. 206. Welded clevis.

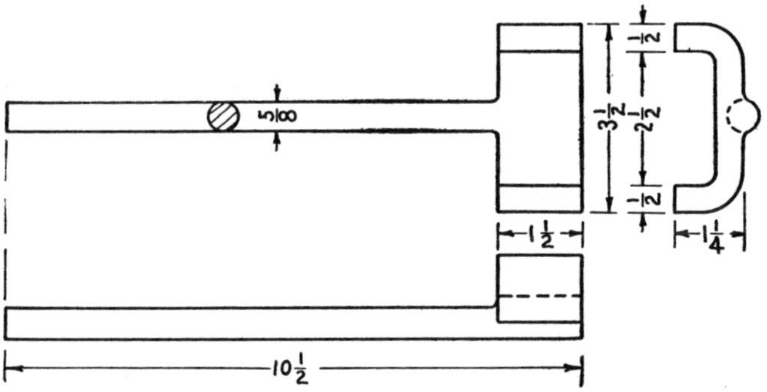

FIG. 207. Wagon wrench.

operator should have available the hardie and two pairs of flat-jawed and two pairs of hollow bit tongs. Some of the work in this group should be done by two people working together at the forge; hence, the desirability of two pairs of tongs. The top and bottom swage, the flatter and the top fuller will be needed for some projects.

While it is true that the punched screw clevis required a welding heat, the exercise of welding on it was comparatively simple. Welding is probably the most difficult forge work. It requires a perfectly clean fire, exactly the proper temperature of heated metal, and both accurate and rapid manipulation of tools. The end weld is one of the simplest of all the welds. It should be practiced until it can be made upon first trial, when other welds will be accomplished with comparatively little difficulty.

It is necessary always to have the two pieces of metal to be welded first hammered into the proper shape. Both must then be given the welding heat at the same time, taken out of the fire together, quickly placed one on the other, and then immediately hammered with light, quick blows, while the stock is changed in position on the anvil to permit the hammer to strike all portions which must be joined.

Just before taking the iron from the fire, it is well to put some kind of flux on each of the surfaces to be placed together. Sal ammoniac or rosin is generally used.

Working Instructions for Two-Piece Weld:

Stock: Two pieces of wrought iron or soft steel, each about 5/8″ in diameter and 4″ long.

185. Preparing the Scarfs. Heat one end of each piece of stock to lemon color and upset it to 3/4″ from the end. This is done by setting the stock on end on the face of the vise and pounding the end to be upset (Fig. 208), then rounding the enlarged part of the stock on the face of the anvil (Fig. 199).

Reheat each piece of stock to lemon color and scarf the up-set end to shape, shown at *A*, Fig. 203. Each scarf should be one and one-half times the diameter of the stock.

186. Making the Weld. Place scarfed surfaces of each piece of stock down in the fire and heat to white or welding heat. Grasp one piece with the hollow-bit tongs in the left hand, and the other with the flat-jawed tongs in the right hand. Take both pieces from the fire, quickly turn the one held by the right hand as it is moving toward the anvil, so as to place it quickly on the anvil under the scarf of the piece held with the left-hand tongs, as shown in Fig. 204. Instantly drop the right-hand tongs and pick up the hammer which should be lying near at hand. Strike quick, sharp blows on the ends to be welded, at the same time turning the pieces with the left-hand tongs. Continue until the two pieces are thoroly joined, then until the diameter is reduced to that of the original stock and the surfaces of the stock at the weld are smooth.

FIG. 208. Upsetting for two-piece weld.

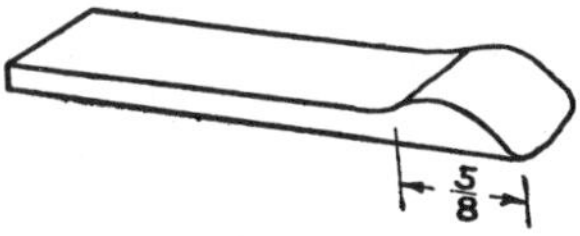

FIG. 209. One member of the "T"-weld.

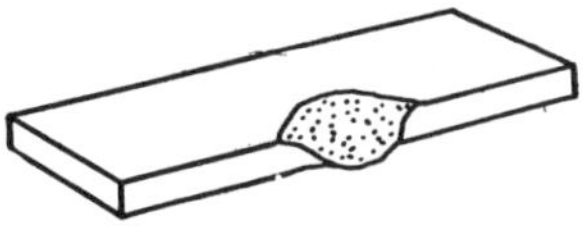

FIG. 210. The second member shaped for welding.

Supplementary Instructions: To form and weld the parts of the other projects listed in this group, a few special instructions are needed beyond those given for the two-piece weld.

187. "T"-Weld. The center of one piece and the end of the other must be upset, as shown in Fig. 209. Fig. 210 and Fig. 211 show how these pieces must be swaged to form the welded joint. A difference of 1/8″ between the thickness of

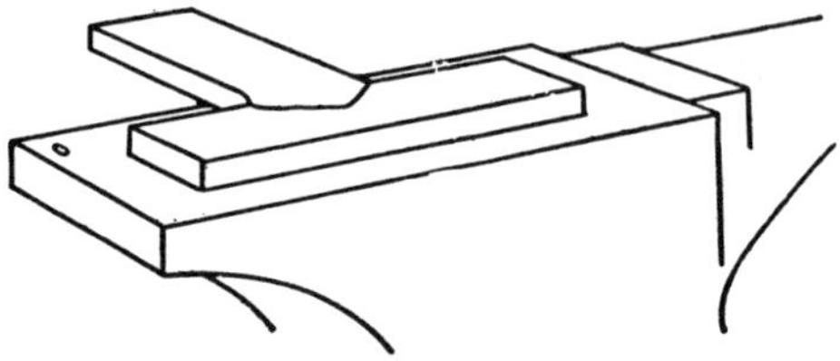

FIG. 211. Position of weld on anvil.

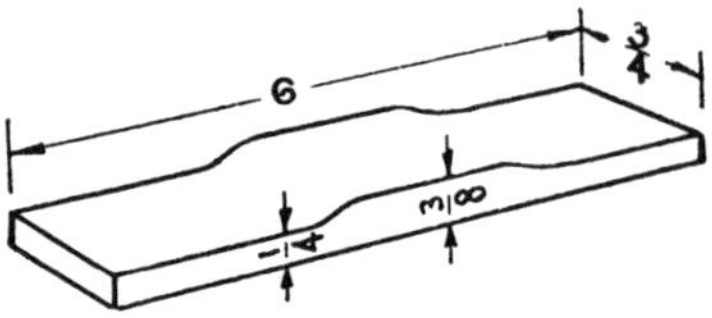

FIG. 212. Effects upon piece of iron from upsetting.

stock and the upset portions of stock will be sufficient to form the welded joint to the thickness of stock, as shown in Fig. 211.

188. Wagon Wrench. The preliminary steps of heating and upsetting the two pieces of stock for this project are similar to those already described. A little more difficulty may be experienced because of the dimensions of the stock and the lengths of the upset portions of same. When

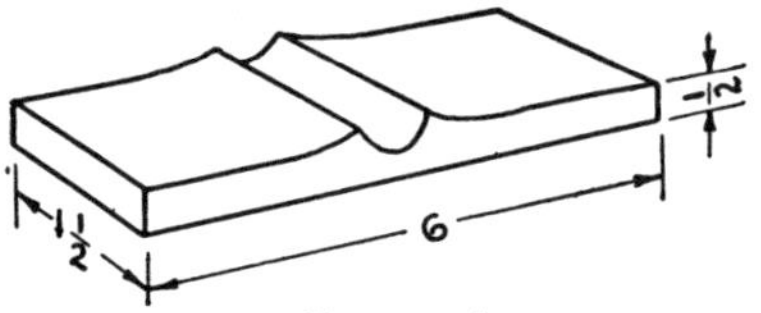

FIG. 213. Preparing wagon wrench for welding.

the rectangular stock is fully upset, it must be laid flat on the face of the anvil and pounded on the upper surface near each end to flatten the lower surface (Fig. 212). This will make the additional thickness of the upset portion of the stock offset on the top surface. Heat this part of the stock and make a groove 1/4″ deep with a 5/8″ fuller (Fig. 213).

The remaining exercises involved in making this project should be clear by a study of Figs. 214, 215 and 207. Mark the points where the bends are to be made on the rectangular stock of the wagon wrench with prick-punch or hardie before heating to make either bend over the edge of the anvil.

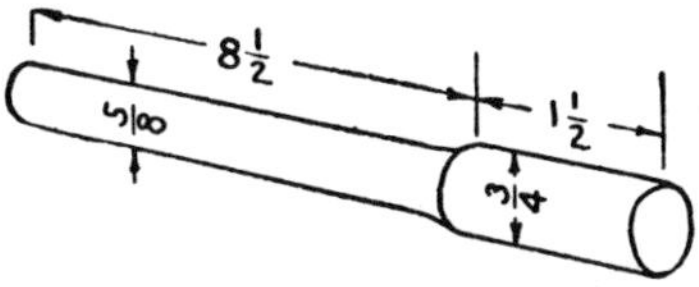

FIG. 214. The handle of the wrench prepared.

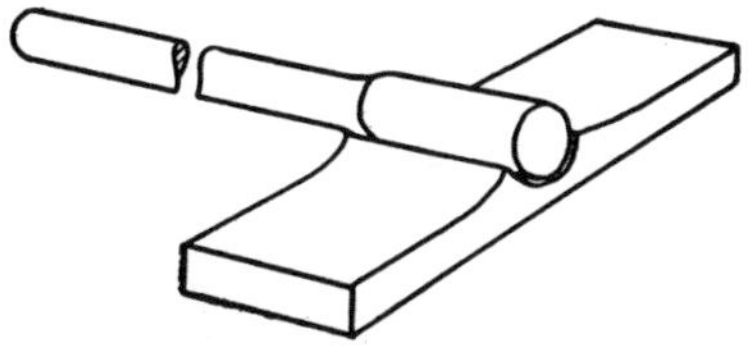

FIG. 215. The pieces ready for welding.

189. Welded Clevis. The drawings for this project show in detail the succeeding steps in forming one end of the clevis. The offset at *C*, Fig. 216, should be made by striking light blows just over the edge of the anvil with the peen

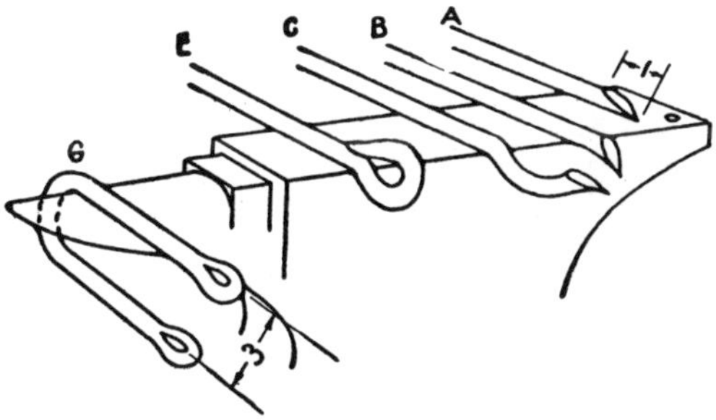

FIG. 216. Operations in making welded clevis.

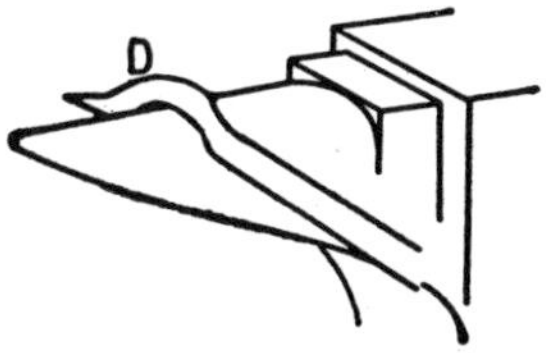

FIG. 217. Bending iron for welded clevis.

of the hammer 1-1/2″ from the end of the stock. The form shown at *E*, Fig. 216, is made over the end of the horn of the anvil, as shown at *D*, Fig. 217. When the ring for the end is nearly completed, the stock should be reversed on the horn, placed over the end and rounded up carefully with the hammer, leaving the joint to be welded in perfect condition. One end of the clevis should be welded before the other is formed. Before taking the welding

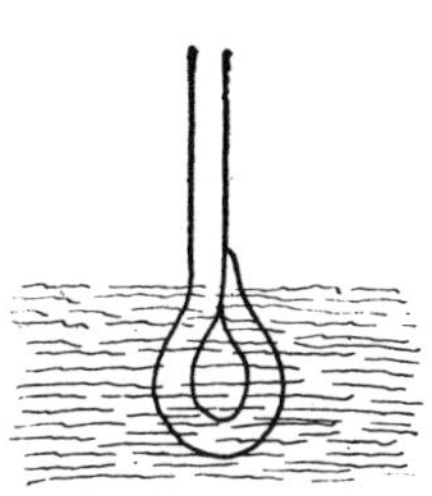

FIG. 218. Dipping iron in water preparatory to welding.

heat, dip the end to be welded in water, as shown in Fig. 218, and then, when the heat is completed, make the weld over the edge of the anvil, as shown at *E*, Fig. 216. Reheat and drive a 5/8″ punch in each eye from each side (Fig. 219). Finish over end of horn (Fig. 220).

FIG. 219. Punching the clevis.

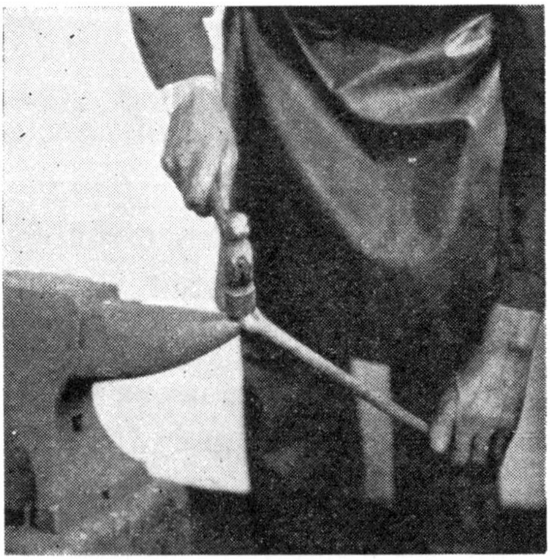

FIG. 220. Finishing eye of clevis.

Problem No. 4: Welding and Tempering Steel.

Suggested Projects:

a) Butcher-knife (Fig. 221).

b) Punches (Fig. 222).

c) Cold chisel (Fig. 223).

d) Sharpening cultivator shovel (Fig. 224).

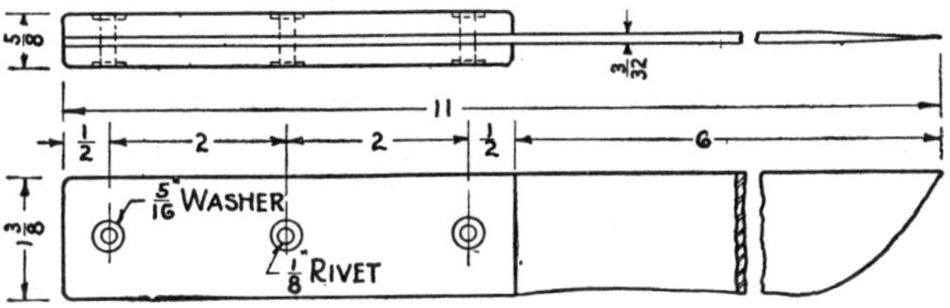

FIG. 221. Butcher knife.

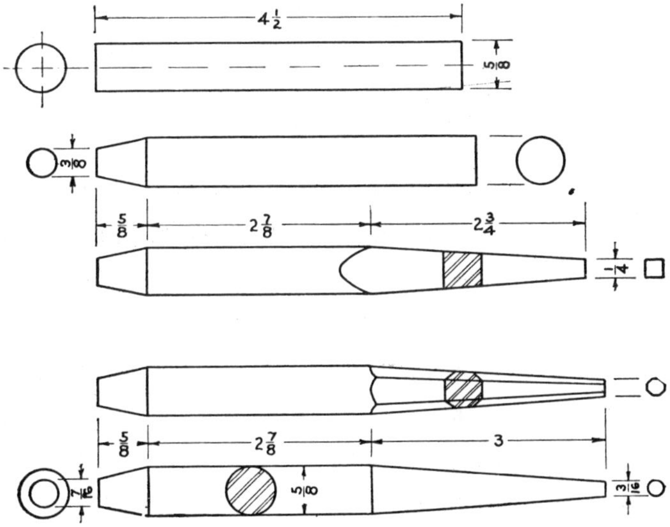

FIG. 222. Punches.

190. Forging Steel. Tools needed are those required for ordinary work at the forge, including flatter and swage.

The forging of tools which are not of unusual shape demands only the use of simple exercises in forging. The new exercise is that of tempering.

191. Working Instructions for Cold Chisel.

Stock: One piece 3/4″, six- or eight-sided tool steel, 7-1/2″ long.

1) Heat 1″ of one end of stock to lemon glow and round to

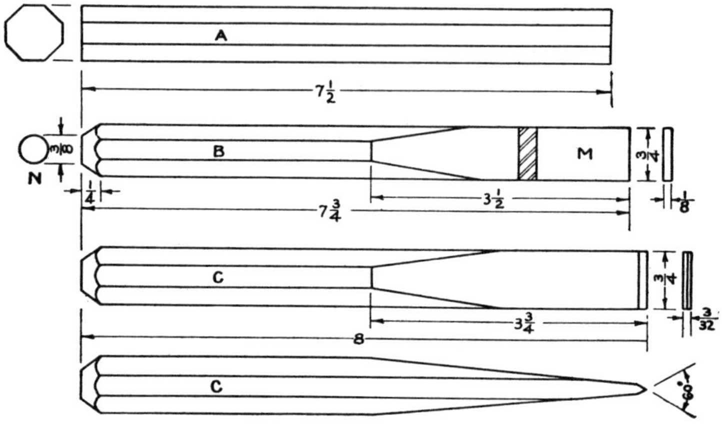

FIG. 223. Cold chisels.

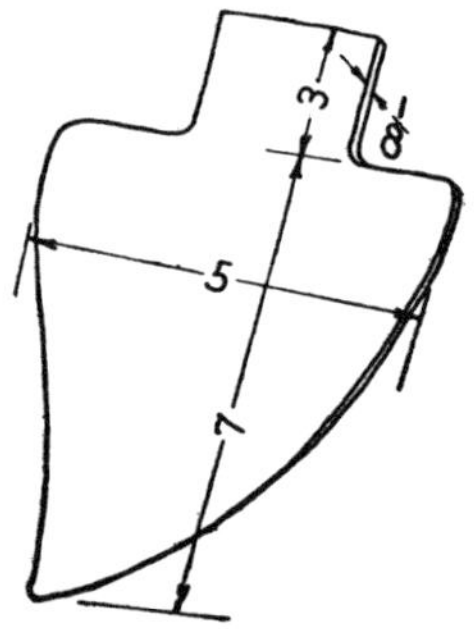

FIG. 224. Cultivator shovel.

cone shape, leaving 3/8″ flat on end in form of circle. Keep circular flat end centered on axis of stock (*N*, Fig. 223).

2) Heat 3″ of opposite end of stock to lemon glow. Forge to shape and dimensions, as shown at *M*, Fig. 223. Care must be taken to keep taper uniform on both sides and to keep width of stock unchanged.

3) Reheat chisel end of stock to bright red and smooth with hand hammer, and, if necessary, finally with flatter.

4) Heat entire stock to dull red, plunge each end for entire length of forged part in water for a few moments. Remove stock from water and allow color to run to light blue at ex-

treme end, then plunge in water to harden completely. It may be well to temper each end separately.

5) Grind chisel end of tool to a cutting edge, with ground surfaces making angle of about 60 degrees. If the flattened surfaces forming the chisel end and the conical end are rough, grind them smooth. All grinding should be done on an emery wheel if available; otherwise, on a grindstone. Keep the tool from overheating and, possibly, burning if it is ground on an emery wheel running dry, by frequently plunging tool in water.

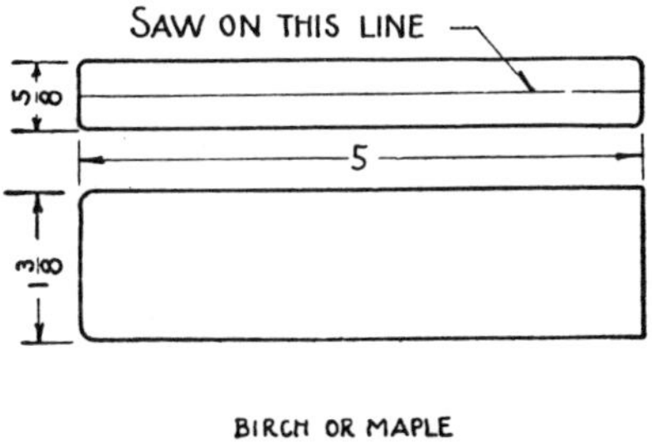

FIG. 225. Handle for butcher knife.

192. The Butcher-Knife. The butcher-knife is made from 1/16″ or 3/32″ tool steel, forged thin on one edge to form cutting edge of knife. The handle should be made in two halves, or, better, in one piece (Fig. 225), to be cut in halves. The two halves of the handle should be held in place on knife-blade when holes are drilled thru both knife-blade and handle. Soft-steel rivets placed in each hole can be riveted down on each side of the handle over a rivet washer, to fasten the knife-blade and handle securely together. The knife-blade is tempered by heating to dull red, plunging in water, or, better, oil, and almost instantly withdrawing and allowing a light blue color to draw to edge. The knife-blade can then be ground for use.

193. A Cultivator Shovel. This is sharpened by heating, forging and tempering in the general manner described for the cold chisel or the butcher-knife.

More difficulty may be experienced, however, in forging to shape. Fig. 226 suggests the position of the cultivator shovel on the face of the anvil. Position, as shown at *A*, is the one taken after first heating when point of shovel is drawn to a

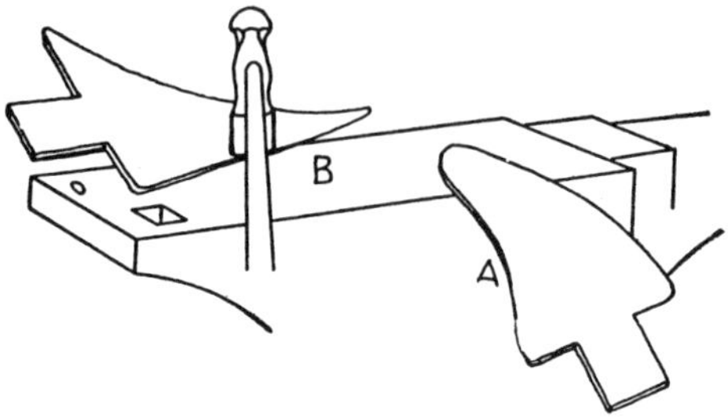

FIG. 226. Steps in sharpening cultivator shovel.

sharp point by quick blows of the hammer. Position, as shown at *B*, is the one taken after a second heating when the side of the shovel is drawn to an edge. Care must be taken to keep the surface of the shovel free from hammer marks.

CHAPTER XXI

SUPPLEMENTARY PROJECTS IN BLACKSMITHING

194. Directions for Making Wagon-Box Stake-Irons (Figs. 227 and 228).

1) Secure 1/4″ strap band iron of proper width, or use as substitute old wagon-wheel tire.

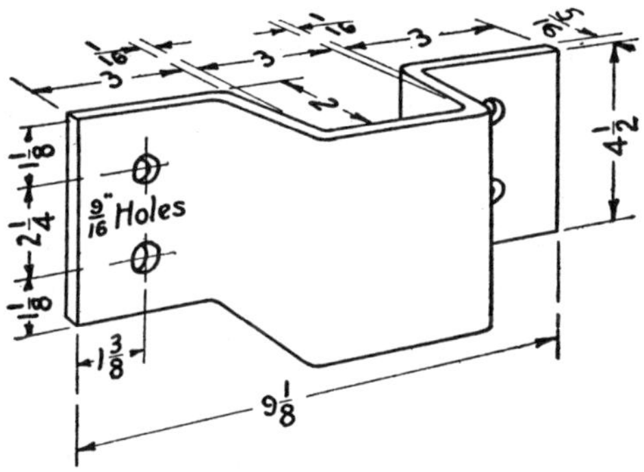

FIG. 227. Wagon-box stake-iron.

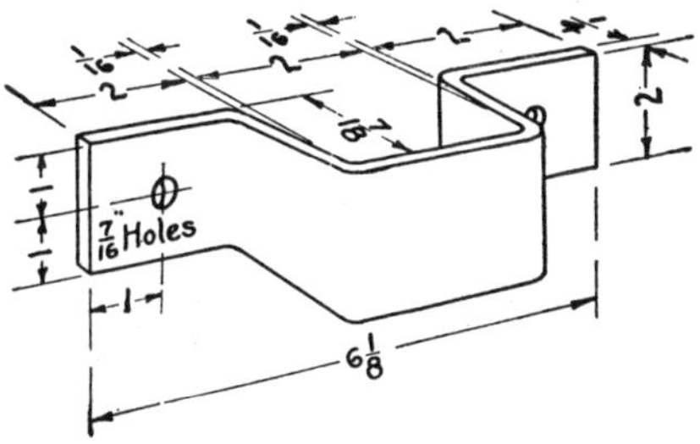

FIG. 228. A lighter stake-iron.

2) Cut to length as per dimensions with cold chisel or over anvil hardie.

3) Heat in center portion and make inside bends over corner of anvil

4) Heat between center and end, and make each outside bend over corner of anvil.

5) Prick-punch for center of holes, and drill or punch, heating metal in latter case.

6) Straighten on surface of anvil with hammer and flatter.

195. Making a Ring (Fig. 229).

1) Cut calculated length from band or rod iron.

2) Heat one end to light red and draw out, as shown in *A*, Fig. 230.

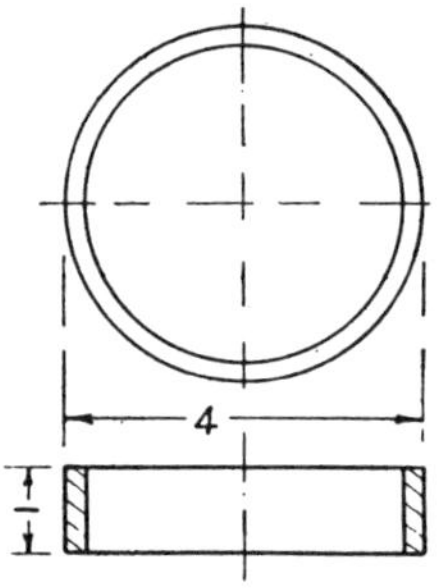

FIG. 229. A ring constructed from rectangular stock.

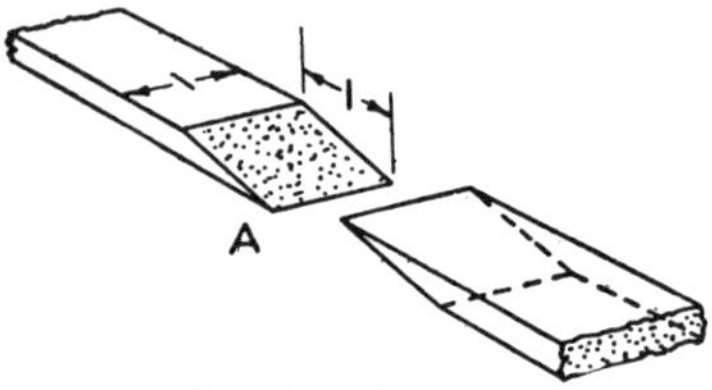

FIG. 230. Ends of metal prepared for welding.

3) Repeat operation on second end, making drawn-out taper on reverse side.

4) Reheat entire rod to light red and round over horn; bring ends together on face of anvil (*B*, Fig. 231), ready for welding heat.

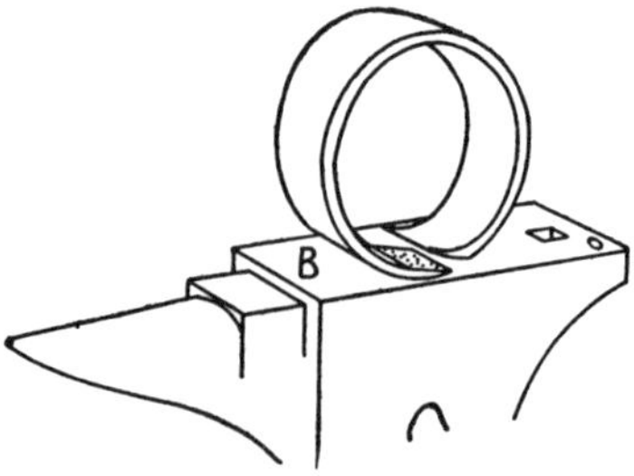

FIG. 231. The ring shaped for welding.

5) Heat ends of ring to welding temperature, and weld over horn of anvil.

6) Reheat welded part to light red and smooth up over horn and on face of anvil.

196. Constructing a Chain (Fig. 232).

1) Cut to link lengths 1/4″ round, soft steel or wrought iron.

2) Heat and swage ends of link, forming same roughly, as

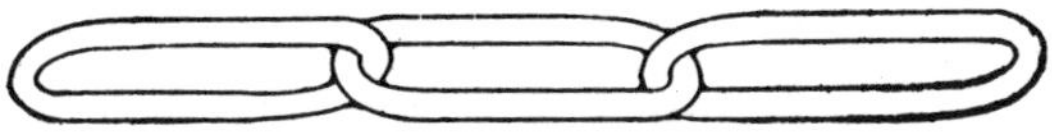

FIG. 232. Chain links.

shown in perspective in *A*, Fig. 233, and *B*, Fig. 234.

3) Put link into last one welded, heat and form carefully on face of anvil (*C*, Fig. 235), ready to weld.

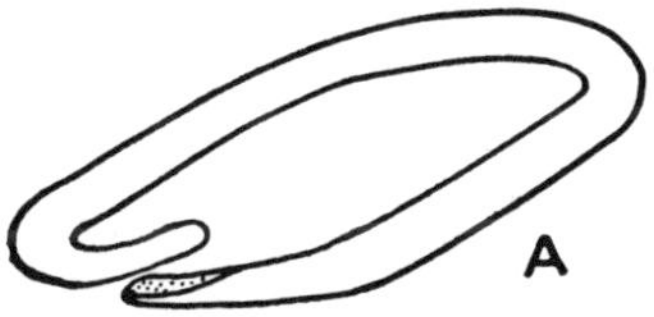

FIG. 233. Preparing the weld.

FIG. 234. Link ready for welding.

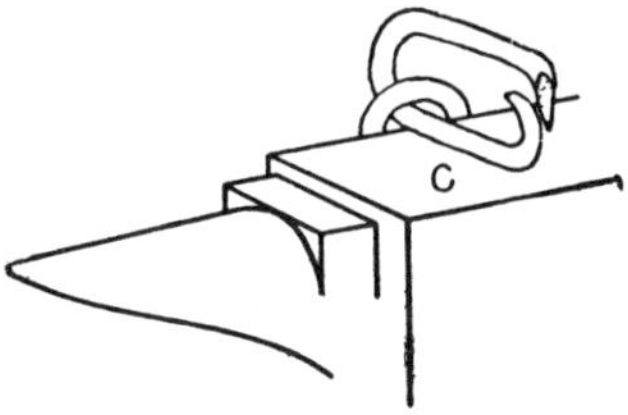

FIG. 235. Link inserted in chain.

4) Heat to welding heat, weld on face of anvil, and smooth over end of horn.

197. Making Ice Tongs (Fig. 236).

1) Cut to estimated length two pieces 3/8″ x 3/4″ rectangular rod.

2) Heat one end and form handle.

3) Heat center and flatten, and form portion for joint.

4) Heat remaining portion of hook end, form over horn of

anvil to semi-circular shape, and forge end over corner of anvil to shape of blunt-pointed spur.

5) Heat flattened portion to light red and punch for 3/8″ bolt.

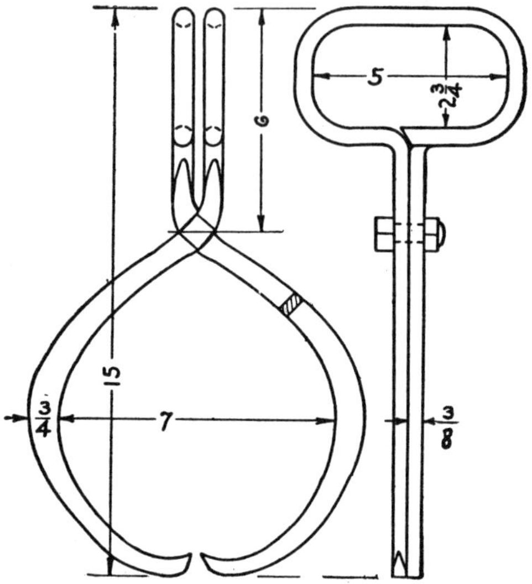

FIG. 236. Ice tongs.

6) Straighten and smooth on face and horn of anvil.

7) Insert bolt and burr-end over nut.

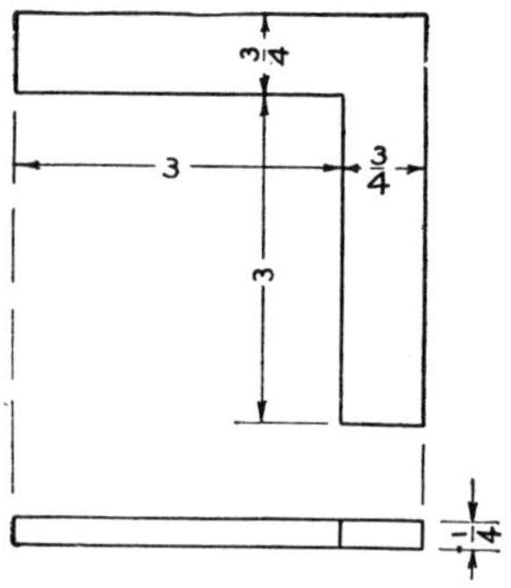

FIG. 237. Right-angle weld.

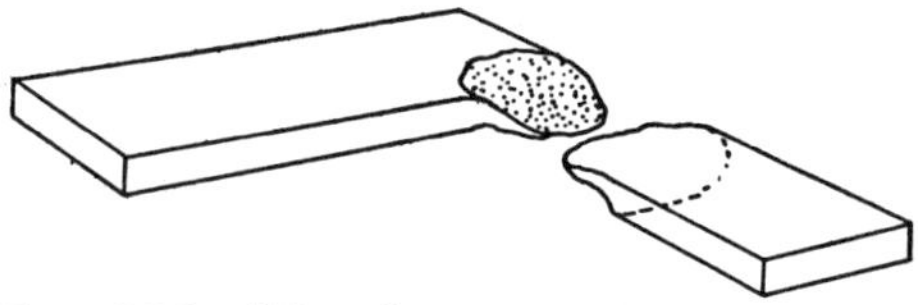

FIG. 238. Metal prepared for welding.

198. A Right-Angle Weld (Fig. 237).

1) Heat both pieces 1-1/2″ on one end to lemon color. Upset 1/8″ thicker than rest of stock 3/4″ in length.

2) Scarf both pieces, using peen of hammer (Fig. 238).

3) Heat both pieces, scarfs down, to welding temperature (white heat). Lay together and weld with quick, hard blows.

4) Finish to perfect right angle. Round inside corner and keep outside corner square (Fig. 237).

199. Forge Tongs (Fig. 239).

1) Heat one end of stock, 18″ x 3/4″ x 3/8″, to lemon color.

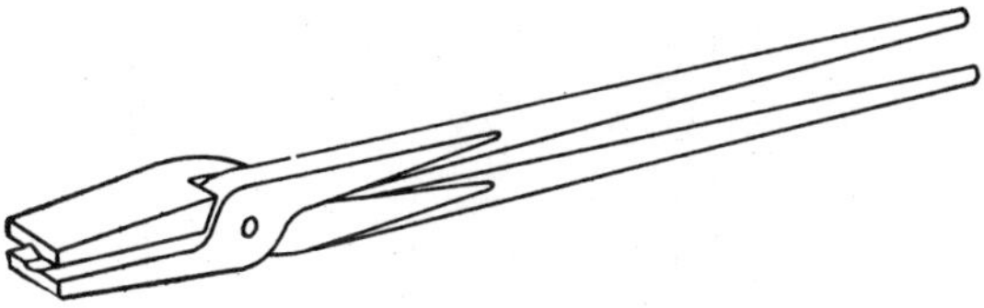

FIG. 239. Forge tongs.

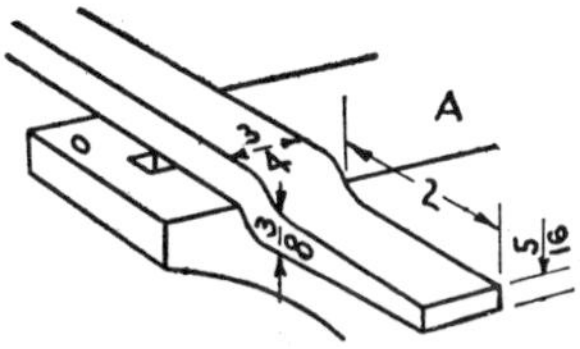

FIG. 240. Bending iron for forge tongs.

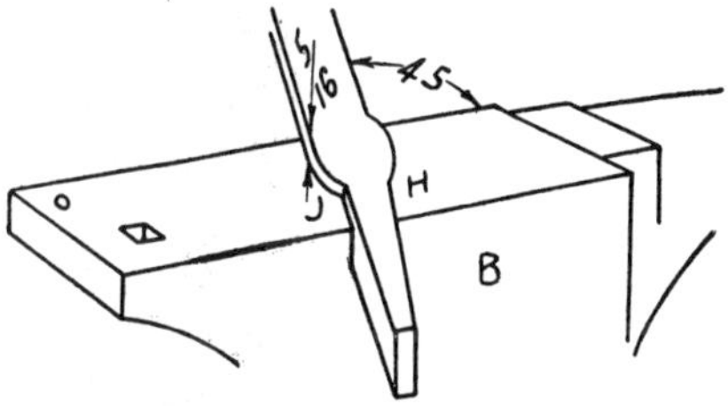

FIG. 241. Shaping the joint of forge tongs.

2) Lay flatwise over round corner right angle to anvil, forge jaw 2″ long, 3/4″ wide, and taper from 3/8″ to 5/16″ to dimensions, as in *A*, Fig. 240.

3) Reheat to lemon color. Place on anvil at an angle of 45 degrees, as in *B*, Fig. 241; finish to 7/8″ wide by 5/16″ thick. Place stock edgewise and use fullers (Fig. 242) as shown in Fig. 243, to secure shape, as at *H* and *J*, Fig. 241.

4) Reheat to lemon color. Place over anvil 7/8″ from shoulder, jaw down, as in *C*, Fig. 242; strike at *D*, forging shank to *E*, Fig. 244.

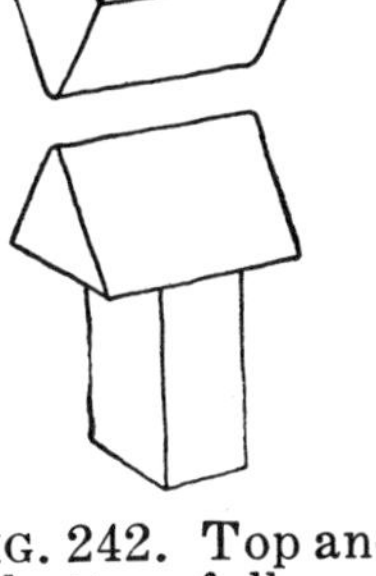

FIG. 242. Top and bottom fullers.

5) Heat other end of forging to lemon color. Forge to 5/16″ round to form the handle; cut to 18″ over all.

6) Reheat the jaw to lemon color. Put 1/4″ fuller lengthwise on inside of jaw and fuller 1/8″ deep (*F*, Fig. 245).

FIG. 243. Using the fullers.

7) Reheat eye at *G*, Fig. 245, to lemon color. Punch 5/16″ hole for rivet in center of eye.

8) Repeat operations for other half.

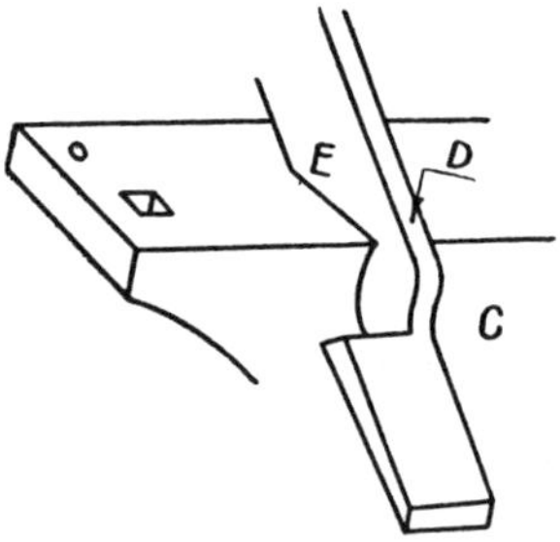

FIG. 244. Another step in construction of tongs.

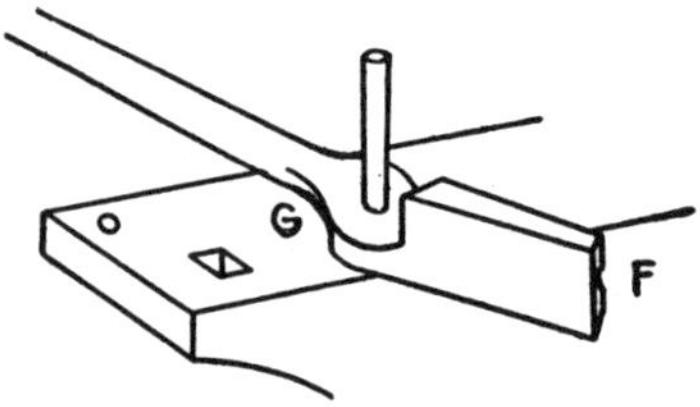

FIG. 245. Punching for rivet.

9) Heat one end of piece cut from handle to lemon color. Cut off 1″ for rivet. Reheat and insert rivet and rivet with hammer (Fig. 239).

Tongs for special uses are shown in Fig. 246. Bottom and top swages (Fig. 247) may be used to finish handles, as at *A*, *B*, *C* and *D*, Fig. 246.

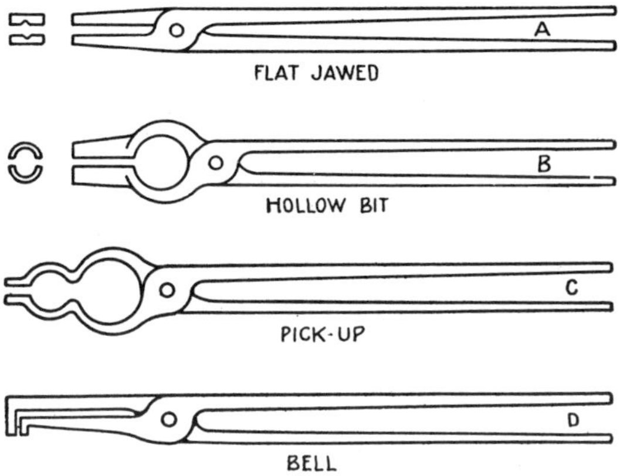

FIG. 246. Several types of tongs used in forge shop.

200. Repointing Cultivator Shovel (Fig. 248).

1) Mark new stock for lines *A* and *B* under shears (Fig. 249).

2) Heat to bright red. Cut on lines *C* with hot chisel (Fig. 249).

3) Reheat to bright red; scarf inside edges (*C*) to dimensions in drawing.

4) Heat old shovel to bright red. Straighten shovel.

5) Reheat shovel, place borax on back side of section to be welded; leave it there until dissolved.

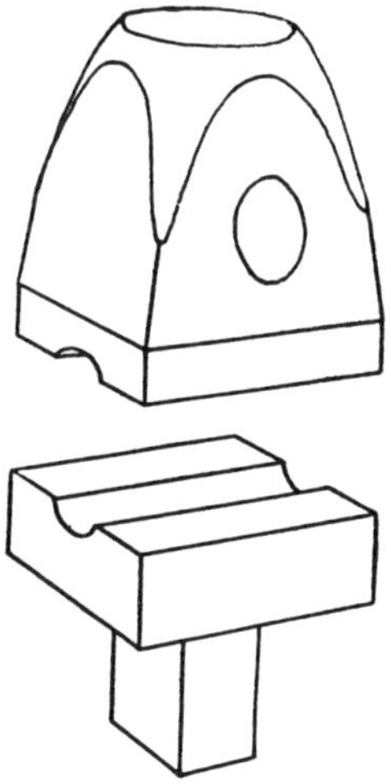

FIG. 247. Top and bottom swages.

6) Place new point on shovel (Fig. 250), allowing it to project 1/2″ beyond old point.

7) Rake coke (good supply) in fire hole, place shovel on it, add more coke on top of shovel, then spread a shovelful of wet coal on top of this. Heat slowly to welding temperature.

8) Remove to anvil and strike series of blows all over new point.

9) Reheat other side to welding temperature.

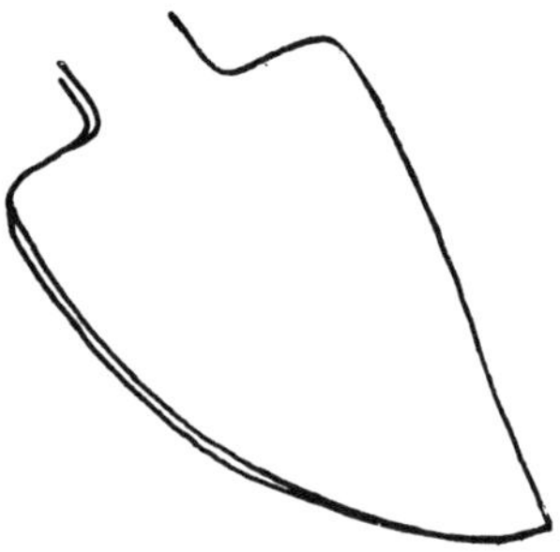

FIG. 248. Cultivator shovel.

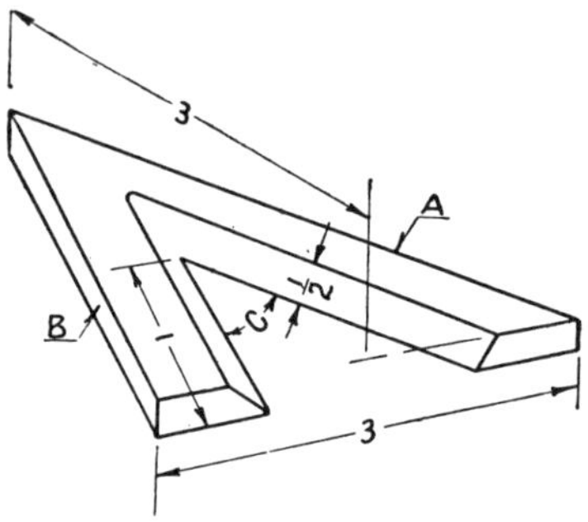

FIG. 249. New piece of stock for cultivator shovel.

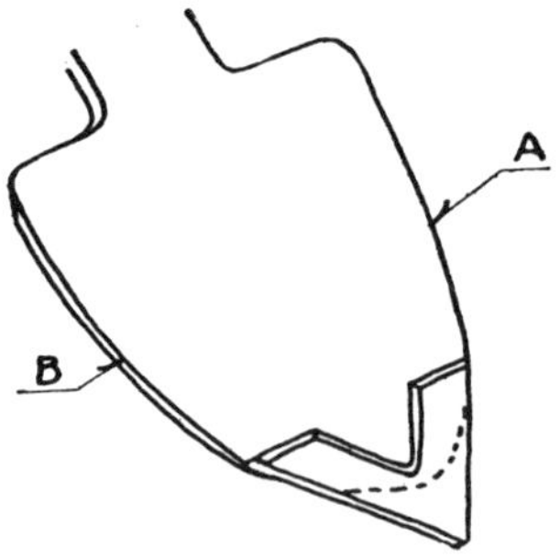

FIG. 250. Correct placing of new points.

10) Remove to anvil and weld this side onto point.

11) Reheat to lemon color, hammer on edges at *B*, Fig. 250, until sharp. Grind off irregular edges.

12) Reheat to bright red. Bend shovel over horn to shape as at the beginning (Fig. 248).

13) Draw color to straw and plunge in water to harden.

201. Sharpening Plowshare (Fig. 251).

1) Place share on floor and mark around outside lines with chalk.

2) Heat 4″ of share, starting at *A*, Fig. 251, to a bright red.

3) Place on anvil, as shown in Fig. 252, and forge to sharp edge.

4) Reheat 3″ or 4″ at a time, and forge to sharp edge until share is finished from *A* to *B*, Fig. 251.

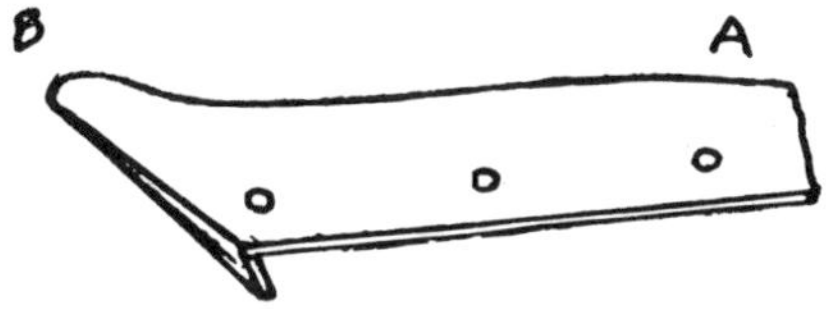

FIG. 251. Old plowshare.

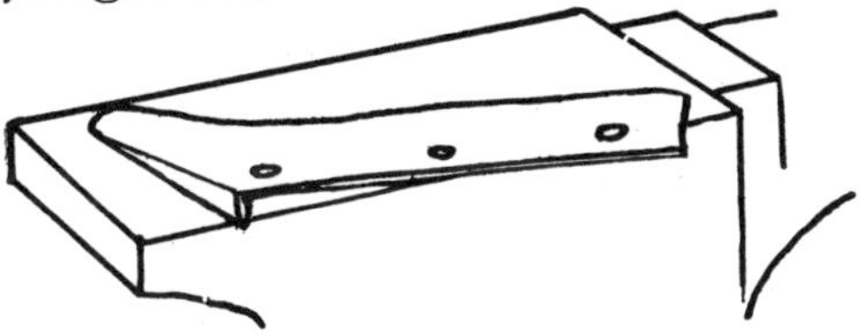

FIG. 252. Position of plowshare on anvil when sharpening.

5) Heat point to bright red, place on anvil and forge to sharp point.

6) Grind off irregularities.

7) Reheat point and set share so it will have correct suction and landside, which are 1/8″ and 1/4″, respectively.

FIG. 253. Piece of steel for new point.

FIG. 254. Steel for point shaped for welding.

8) Reheat to bright red and case-carbonize with potash.

9) Share should fit as nearly as possible to outline on floor.

202. Pointing Plowshare (Figs. 253 to 256).

1) Heat 3″ of new stock on one end to lemon color.

2) Scarf end, as shown at *A*, Fig. 253.

3) Heat other end to lemon color. Scarf and split, as shown at *B*, Fig. 253.

4) Heat center of stock to lemon color. Bend into shape of V, as in Fig. 254, having bottom, or split, side 1″ longer than top side.

5) Heat old share (Fig. 255) to red heat.

6) Place on anvil and apply borax on both sides of share.

7) Heat new point to red heat.

8) Place new point on share, as in Fig. 256. Reheat to

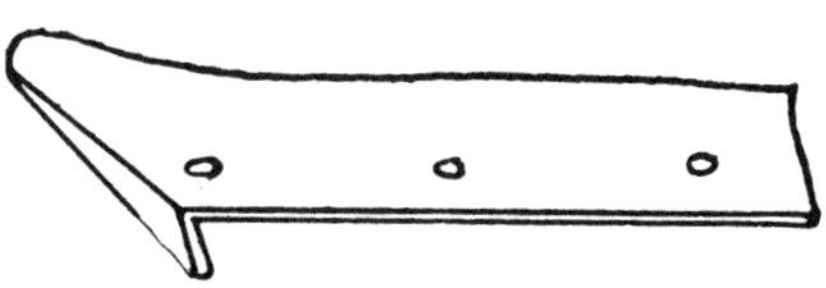

FIG. 255. Plowshare to be re-pointed.

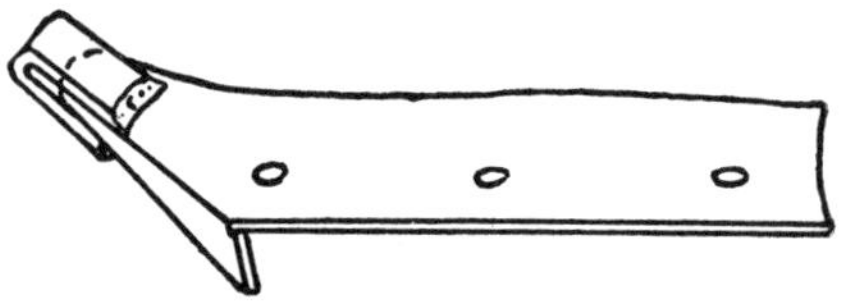

FIG. 256. The point in place for welding.

welding heat. Apply a little borax to share while it is heating.

9) Remove to anvil and strike a few blows until point is welded. Reheat to welding temperature. Continue to weld on both sides until finished. Cut surplus stock off sides and grind.

10) Reheat as much of share as possible and set to have correct suction and landside, which are 1/8″ and 1/4″, respectively.

11) Reheat to bright red and case-carbonize with potash.

203. Shortening Buggy Tire Without Cutting (Fig. 257).

1) Heat several inches of tire, holding same in vertical position, to light red.

2) Bend heated portion inward over horn of anvil (*A*).

3) With aid of helper, grasp tire either side of bent portion with flat-jawed tongs over and against rough surface of horse-

shoeing rasp (Fig. 258); place crosswise over surface of anvil, and hammer.

4) Repeat operation No. 3 until stock is upset sufficiently to shorten tire.

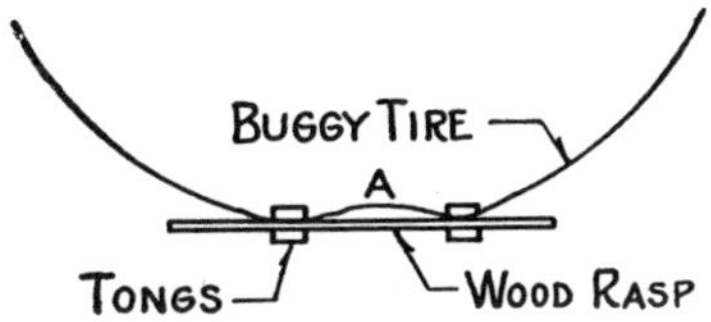

FIG. 257. Shortening buggy tire.

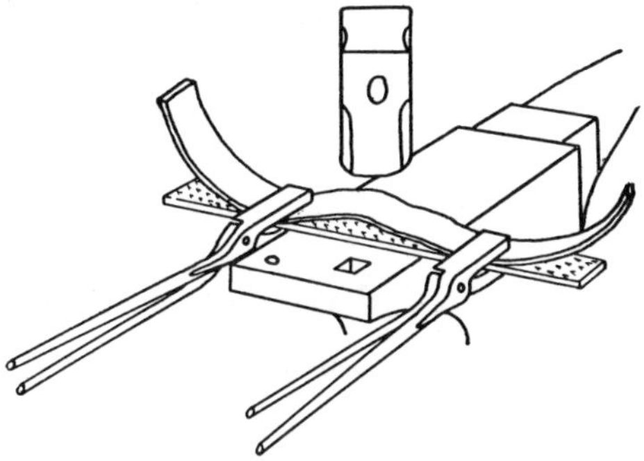

FIG. 258. Details of method of shortening tire.

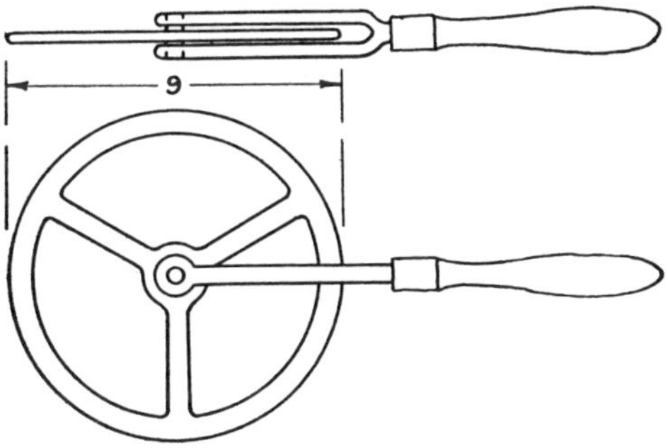

FIG. 259. Tire-measuring tool.

5) Measure outside of felly and inside of tire with tire-measuring tool (Fig. 259). Tire measurement should be about 1/4″ less than felly measurement.

6) Heat tire to red, one-half way around. Slip tire over felly, and shrink on by immediately running in water. If tire is too short, it will "dish" wheel too much. Wheel should be dished (out of true plane) not more than 1″.

PART IV

SHEET-METALWORK

CHAPTER XXII

TOOLS AND SUPPLIES; FUNDAMENTAL PROCESSES

204. Need for Sheet-Metalwork on the Farm. There are many opportunities about the farm for sheet-metal repairs and construction, especially in tinwork. Kitchen utensils, the equipment of the dairy and creamery, farm machines, water and sanitary systems, and roofs and gutters on buildings, all furnish problems in sheet-metalwork.

The chief operation in sheet-metalwork, aside from calculating sizes and cutting the metal, is that of fastening, which may be divided into three classes, viz., soldering, brazing and riveting. Welding is not included, as it seldom is used in working sheet metal, and, besides, it is considered under the heading of Forge Work.

205. The Process of Soldering. Soldering is the process of joining two pieces of metal by means of a more fusible metal or metallic alloy. The metal, or alloy, called solder, should be selected with the following considerations in mind: (1) Its strength should be as great, or greater, than that of either of the pieces of metal it joins; (2) its color should be as nearly as possible that of the joined metals, and (3) its fusing point should be considerably lower than that of either of them.

206. Classes of Solder. Solder is classed as soft or hard, depending upon the degree of fusibility, and, to some extent, upon the class of metals to be joined by it. Soft solder, sometimes called white or tin solder, is made of soft, readily fused metals or alloys. Such metals as tin, lead-tin and alloys of tin, lead and bismuth are usually used. A good formula for the composition of soft solder is: Lead, 207 parts; tin, 118 parts. To weaken the solder increase the number of parts of tin. Increasing the number of parts of lead will strengthen the solder. The solder may be prepared in a graphite crucible at a low temperature by mixing with an iron rod and then running into iron molds.

207. **Soldering Fluxes** are substances used to remove the oxide which forms on the surface of a metal. They are melted and run on the metal where the soldered joint is to be formed. The fluxes generally used are powdered rosin or a solution of chloride of zinc, used alone or combined with sal ammoniac.

A soldering fluid is a liquid flux and may be prepared by mixing 27 parts neutral zinc chloride, 11 parts sal ammoniac, and 62 parts of water; or 1 part sugar of milk, 1 part glycerine and 8 parts of water.

A very common liquid is prepared by dissolving in an earthenware vessel small pieces of scrap zinc in commercial muriatic acid. Dissolve one piece at a time to prevent too rapid generation of heat, which might break the jar. Finally secure a saturated solution by adding more zinc than will dissolve. For use in soldering, the solution should be diluted with the addition of its own bulk of water, mixed and filtered. The addition of a few drops of liquid ammonia will increase the activity of the flux, which should be kept in a wide-mouthed bottle and applied to the joint to be soldered, just before the soldering operation begins, by means of a stick or brush. This flux may be used on almost any metal except aluminum, zinc or galvanized iron.

FIG. 261. Equipment for soldering.

The Soldering Process. Certain metals require special solders and fluxes. For most purposes, however, the solder and fluxes described are serviceable.

The best of tools and materials, however, will not secure good results unless used in the hands of a good workman. To solder successfully the metals to be joined must be fitted accurately and cleaned thoroly, either by some means of mechanical cleaning, such as scraping or grinding, or by removal of dirt and grease with acid.

It is dangerous to use the latter, however, as it may injure the metal surfaces, besides its possible injurious effects upon the workman.

When the metal is clean, apply the flux to all surfaces which will come in contact, join these as planned and run the soldering iron over or against the joint.

208. The Soldering-Iron, which is made of copper, must be "tinned" to serve as a solder carrier. Fig. 261 shows the shape of a soldering-iron. The end is kept filed to form well defined edges and a point. When thoroly clean, heat and rub on solder, then wipe with a cloth, a piece of felt serving the purpose very well.

To use the soldering-iron heat it in a clean fire, using a gasoline torch, a blacksmith's forge, or a tinsmith's gas forge, and place it against a bar of solder, when a little will adhere to the soldering-iron.

Another method of using the soldering-iron is to provide an open-mouthed bottle of chloride of zinc fluxing solution and when the iron is heated, dip the point of it into the solution to clean it. Then place the iron against the bar of solder, and if properly heated a little solder will adhere to it. This is the customary method of tinsmiths. Fig. 261 shows an open-mouthed bottle of the fluxing solution, together with a can of cleaning material, a block of sal ammoniac and a wiping rag. The Bunsen burner shown in this picture is frequently used to heat the tinner's iron when gas is available.

The iron is now run on the joint and the solder which the iron holds will fill the joint, cool, and effect a union of the two pieces of metal. The bar of solder is used to hold the tin in position. In case a long joint is to be made, the iron may be run slowly against the metal with the bar of solder held against the iron. The solder will thus melt, run down and off the iron and fill the joint. Care must be taken not to flood the joint by using too much solder. While an iron may be run over a joint several times, it is advisable to run it over but once. Superfluous solder and the extended use

FIG. 262. A clean joint.

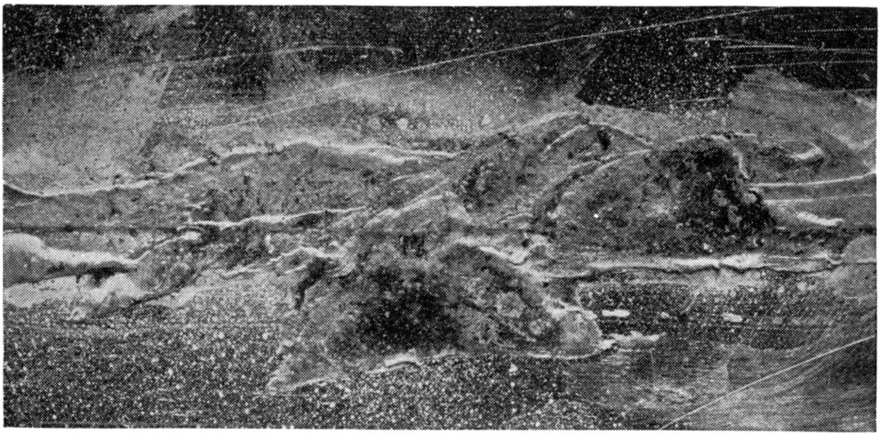

FIG. 262-*a*. A joint where too much solder has been used.

of the soldering-iron are signs of a poor workman. When the soldering-iron is run over the joint many times, the solder will flow out on the surfaces of the metal near the joint, resulting in a "smeared" joint. Fig 262 shows a soldered joint on which no superfluous solder has been used; Fig. 262-*a* shows one which has been smeared with too much solder.

CHAPTER XXIII

PROJECTS IN SHEET-METALWORK

Problem No. 1:

Making a Lap Joint as Used on Tin Roof.

209. Stock and Tools for Lap Joint. The stock needed is two strips of medium weight, clean new tin, each about 10″ long and 3″ wide.

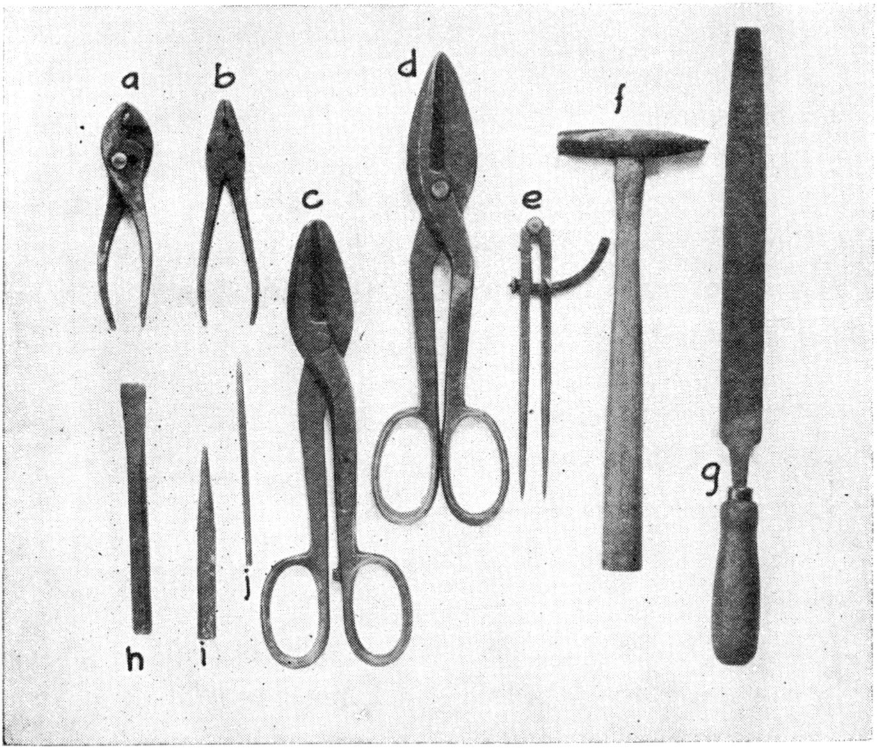

FIG. 263. Tools for sheet-metalwork: *a*, cutting pliers; *b*, flat-jaw pliers; *c*, straight snips; *d*, curved snips; *e*, compass; *f*, tinner's hammer; *g*, flat file; *h*, cold chisel; *i*, punch; *j*, scratch awl.

A limited number of sheet-metalworking tools suitable for ordinary work on the farm is necessary. The equipment may consist of:

1 gasoline soldering torch,
1 soldering iron,
1 pair straight snips,
1 pair curved snips,
1 tinner's hammer,
1 wooden mallet,
1 carpenter's square,
1 pair cutting pliers,
1 pair dividers,
1 punch,
1 scratch awl,
1 bar solder,
1 piece sal ammoniac,
1 bottle cleaning solution,

and tools shown in Fig. 263.

210. Working Instructions for Lap Joint. On one long edge of one piece of tin, scribe a mark ½″ from the edge

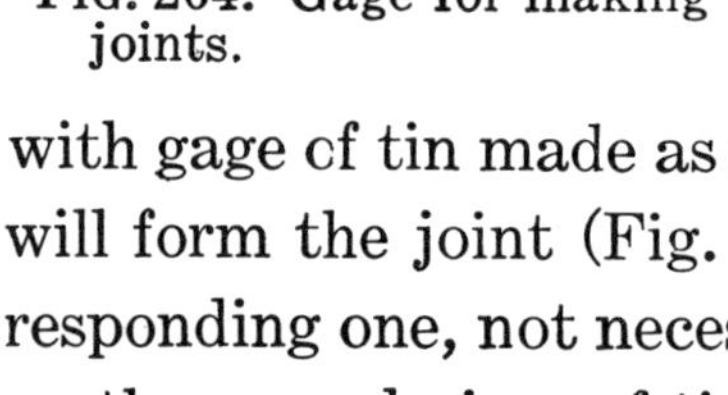

Fig. 264. Gage for making joints.

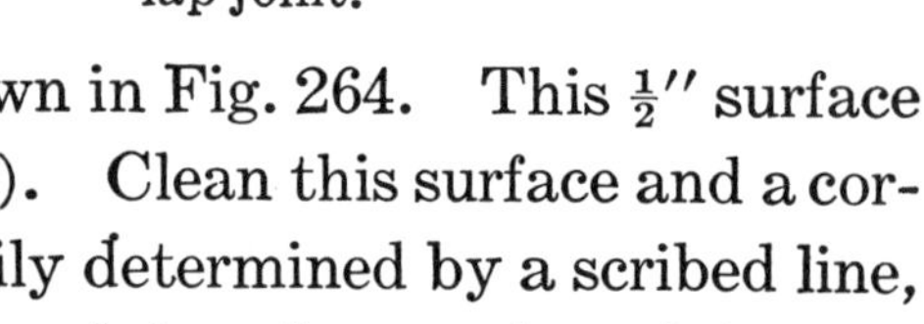

Fig. 265. Position of pieces for lap joint.

with gage of tin made as shown in Fig. 264. This ½″ surface will form the joint (Fig. 265). Clean this surface and a corresponding one, not necessarily determined by a scribed line, on the second piece of tin, by wiping clean and applying the flux. Place the two pieces of tin together flat on a board so that the surface of one piece of tin laps over on the surface of the other, the edge of the first coinciding with the scribed line on the second. The two pieces of tin now lap ½″.

Grasp a short piece of wood about the size of a screw-driver handle with a square or beveled end in the left hand, and with it press the two pieces of tin together (Fig. 266). This may also be done by using the bar of solder in place of the stick. With the right hand, grasp the handle of the hot, well-tinned soldering-iron, wipe the iron on a cloth or piece of felt conveniently placed on the bench or table on which you are working, touch this iron to a piece of solder and immediately run the end of one of the four "flats" of the iron on the joint (Fig. 267) and near edge of the lap. The holding-stick or bar of solder must be kept near the part of the joint being soldered. It must be moved from point to point as the iron is moved along the joint. The heat of the iron should heat the joint sufficiently to run the solder on the iron between the lapped surfaces of the two pieces of tin. As the iron moves from one point to another the heated surfaces will cool, forming a soldered joint. The iron must be touched against the solder frequently to renew the supply of solder on the iron. When the joint has been formed,

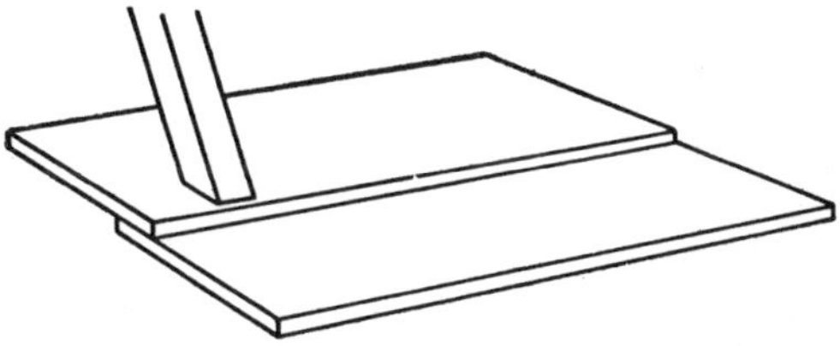

FIG. 266. Holding two pieces of tin for soldering.

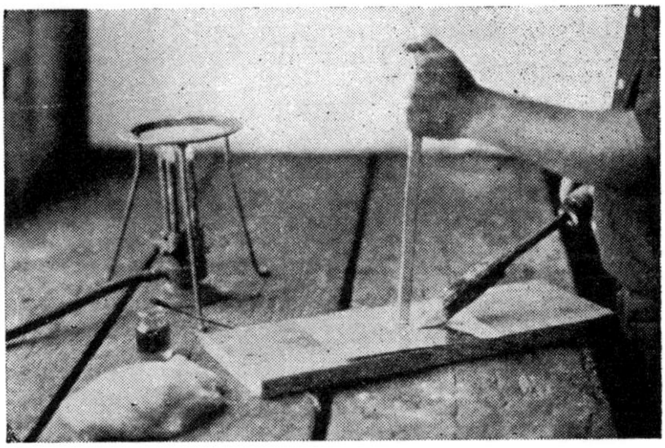

FIG. 267. Running solder.

run the iron slowly the entire length of the joint with one stroke, to make a smooth finish.

This exercise should be repeated, if necessary, until a perfect joint can be made with a few strokes of the soldering-iron.

FIG. 267-*a*. Correct position of soldering iron.

Problem No. 2: To Patch a Tin Receptacle (Figs. 268 and 269).

Stock—Any tin receptacle with a hole in it.

Tools—Those used for Problem No. 1.

211. Preparation for Patching. Perhaps one of the most general uses of the soldering-iron in the home is for patching

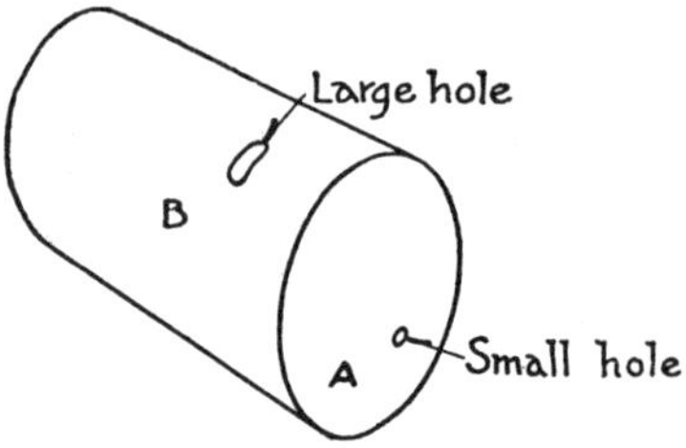

FIG. 268. Patching small hole.

FIG. 269. Patching large hole.

tin utensils. Such work may be listed under two heads, viz., small-hole patching, where an additional piece of tin is unnecessary, and large-hole patching, requiring a piece of tin to cover the hole.

In the first case, the hole is first closed as far as possible by pounding the tin around it with a mallet over a surface as nearly the shape of the tin surrounding the hole as possible.

The tin is then cleaned by scraping if very dirty, or by the use of a little muriatic acid, which may be put onto the surface of the tin with a stiff feather. The flux is then applied and solder run into the hole with the soldering-iron used as in soldering a seam (*A*, Fig. 268).

If the hole is too large to be closed with solder, a patch must be applied and soldered on. *B*, Fig. 268, shows the hole, and Fig. 269 shows it patched.

212. Completing the Patch.

1) Secure a receptacle with a cracked seam or a small hole

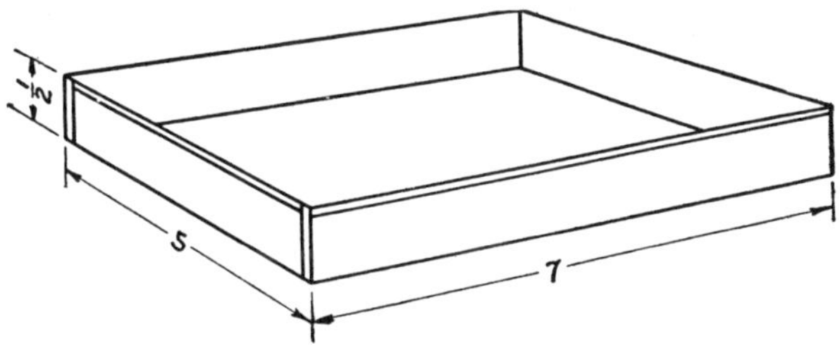

FIG. 270. Shallow watering pan.

and with a large hole 1/2″ or more in diameter. Prepare the small hole (*A*, Fig. 268) for soldering, as described in Sec. 210, and solder, as described there.

2) Trim the large hole (*B*, Fig. 268) with a pair of tinner's snips (Fig. 263), either straight or curved, depending upon the shape of the hole and the tin, whether flat or curved.

3) Cut a piece of tin from an old can or a piece of sheet tin the shape of the hole, but enough larger than the hole to provide for a 1/4″ or 3/8″ lap all around the hole. Clean the tin on the receptacle, and that of the patch also; apply the fluxing material and solder, as described in Sec. 210.

Problem No. 3: To Construct a Shallow Watering Pan for a Chicken Coop (Fig. 270).

Other Projects Suggested for this Group:

Any low, straight-sided tin dish not requiring a wired edge.

Stock—Tin of medium weight cut to size and the same as, or similar to, pattern shown in Fig. 271.

Tools—Those used for Problem No. 1, Sec. 209, and a wooden mallet and ruler, or carpenter's square. It will be necessary, also, to have a sharp-edged piece of hard wood or a straight-edged piece of iron as long or a little longer than the longest edge of the pan.

213. Strengthening the Edge. Ordinarily, it is desirable to strengthen the upper edge of a tin receptacle by

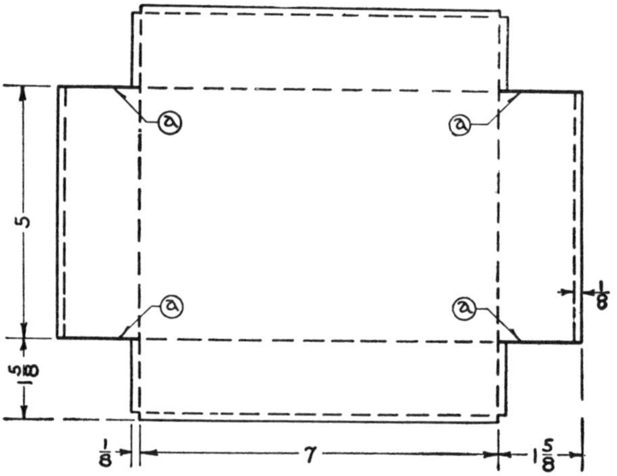

FIG. 271. Tin cut to shape for watering pan.

running a wire around this edge under the tin which is rolled over the wire, as in the case of a tin drinking cup or a funnel (Fig. 278).

This portion of the receptacle may be strengthened, but not so well, by folding a small portion of the upper edge over and pounding it down against the surface of the tin (Fig. 272).

214. Laying Out and Cutting Tin to Shape. With carpenter's square, or with try-square and rule, lay out rectangle, 10-1/4″ x 8-1/4″. Inside of this rectangle, scribe lines with scratch awl and straight-edge (leg of carpenter's square), 1-5/8″ from and parallel to outside edges of this rectangle. Scribe lines in the corners for portion to be cut out. Turn the piece of tin over and scribe lines 1/8″ inside the rectangle and parallel to the outside edges.

With straight snips, cut out the corners, as shown in the drawing (Fig. 271); also cut to the corners of the inside rectangle, formed by the first lines scribed, on the lines marked heavy on the drawing and lettered *a*.

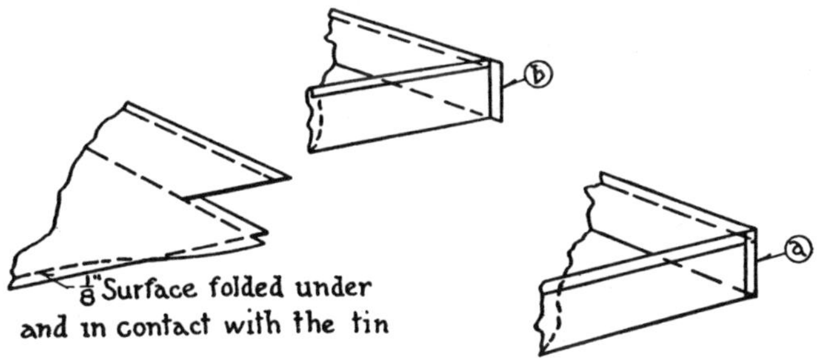

FIG. 272. Details of soldering watering pan.

215. Folding. Over the edge of the piece of hard wood or straight-edged piece of iron, fold with a mallet the 1/8″ of tin between the outside edges and the lines scribed 1/8″ from same. These surfaces must be folded toward the surface of the tin on which the lines were scribed 1/8″ from the outside edges. Fig. 272 shows the folding operation. Pound these surfaces down until they are in contact with the sheet of tin to form the strengthened edges of the pan (Fig. 270).

In like manner, but in the opposite direction, fold over the corner of the piece of hard wood or straight-edged piece of iron the 1-5/8″ surfaces to form right angles with the sheet of tin and to make the vertical surfaces on the edges of the pan (Figs. 271 and 272).

Carefully fold the corner laps, lettered *b*, Fig. 272, to come in contact with the long, or 7″, edge of the pan (Fig. 271).

Place each corner of the pan over a square corner of a hard piece of wood and square up and smooth with the mallet.

Solder the inside of each corner of the pan between the end and side edges, and also the edge of the corner lap (*a*, Fig. 272). Apply fluxing material and use soldering-iron, as described in Sec. 209.

Problem No. 4: To Construct a Receptacle Requiring the Assembly of Heavy Pieces of Tin or of Galvanized Iron.

Projects Suggested for this Group:

a) Watering trough (Fig. 273).

b) Flower box (Figs. 274, 274-*a*, 274-*b*).

c) Drip pan (Fig. 275, 275-*a*).

Stock for watering trough: 2 pieces heavy tin, 12″ x 5″; 1 piece heavy tin, 26″ x 12″.

Note: Galvanized iron may be substituted.

Tools—A full set of sheet-metalworker's hand tools (Fig. 263).

216. Constructing Watering Trough. Mark and cut the ends of the piece of metal to form the trough, as shown in Fig. 273. Fold the ends up on lines shown dotted in the figure, and then turn the piece of metal over, laying it along the corners of a square-edged timber on the center line shown as the long dotted line in the drawing (Fig. 276). Bend the metal down over the timber until the surfaces on either side of the line are in contact with the surfaces of the timber, thus forming the trough.

Lay out lines on one surface of each end piece of the trougn,

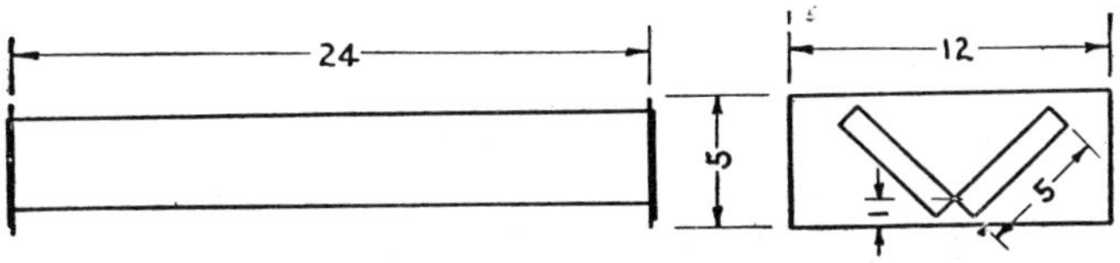

FIG. 273. Watering trough.

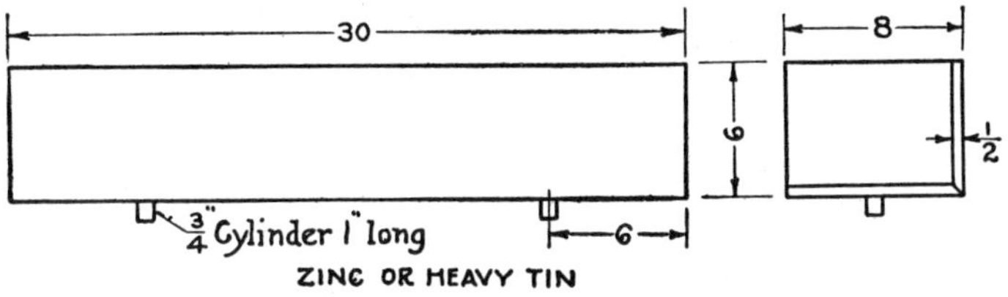

FIG. 274. Flower box.

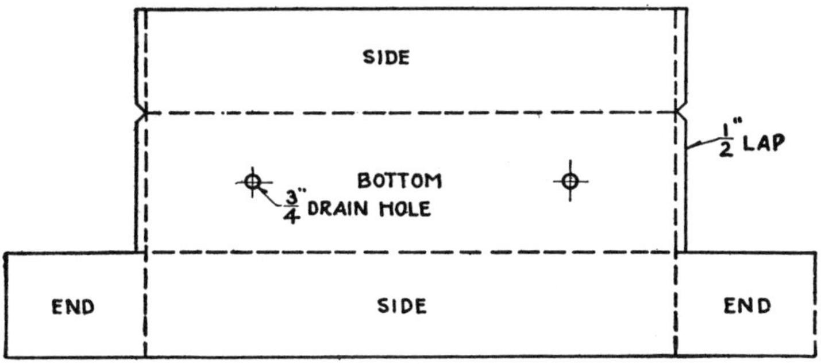

FIG. 274-*a*. Details of flower box.

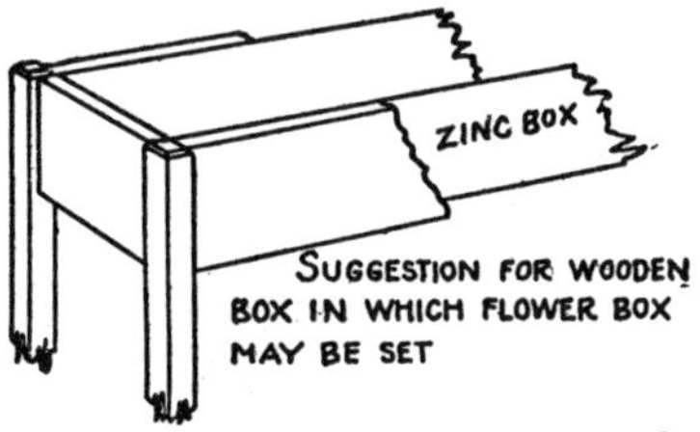

FIG. 274-*b*. Perspective of flower box.

to form slits into which the folded ends of the trough piece may be inserted that it may hang on the ends (Fig. 277).

Lay each end piece of tin with the lined surface up, flat on a smooth, hard board. With a sharp cold chisel and hammer or mallet, cut along each scribed line.

Carefully insert the end laps of the trough into the slits in the end pieces of the trough from the side on which the cold chisel cut, and gently pound into shape with a mallet over the

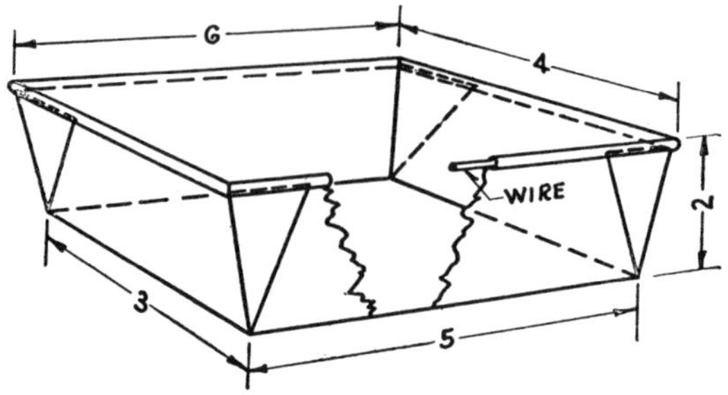

FIG. 275. Drip pan.

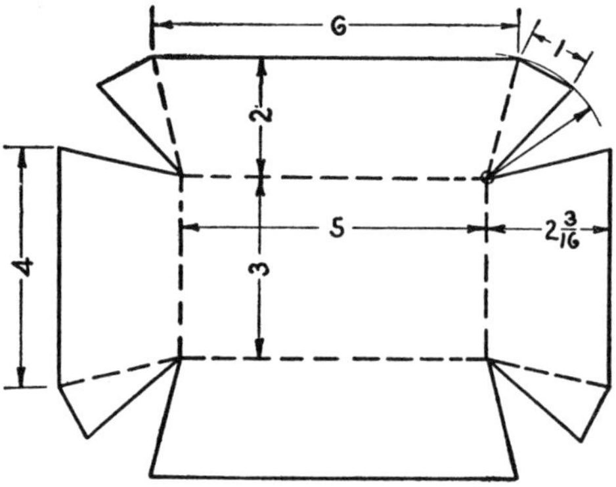

FIG. 275-*a*. Layout for drip pan.

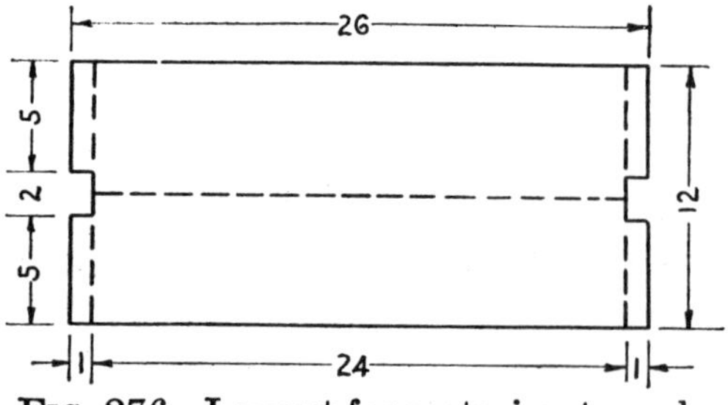

FIG. 276. Layout for watering trough.

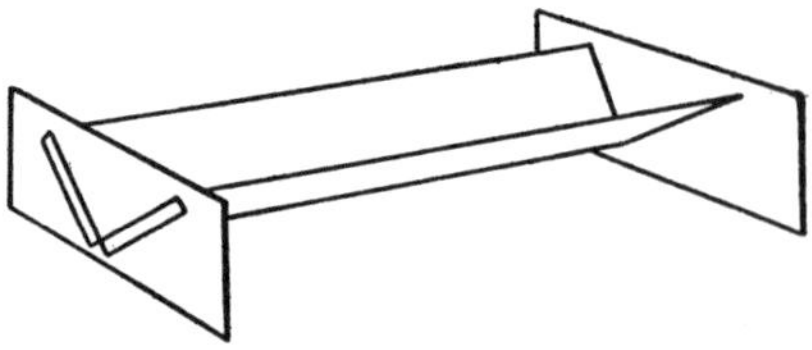

FIG. 277. Completed trough.

corner of a board. Solder all these joints and run solder in the intersection between end pieces and trough near bottom of trough, where the end laps on trough were not cut, to make trough water-tight.

Problem No. 5: Making a Cylindrical Receptacle with Handle and Reinforced Edge.

Suggested Projects:

a) Drinking cup (Fig. 278).

b) Small pail (Fig. 279).

c) Cylindrical pan (Fig. 280).

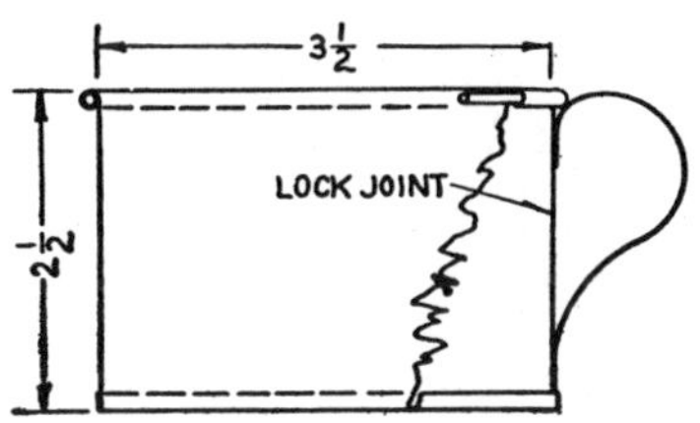

FIG. 278. Drinking cup.

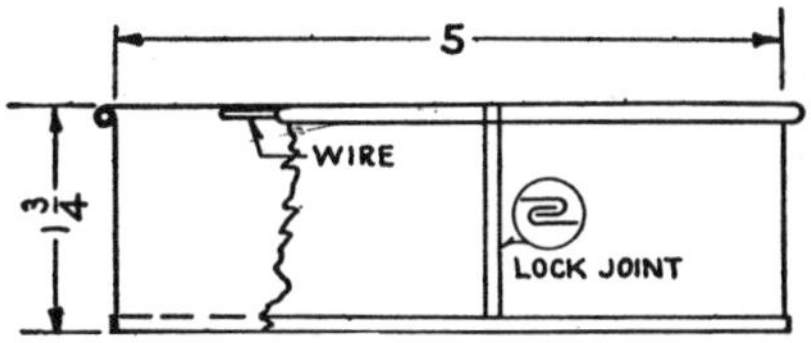

FIG. 280. Cylindrical pan.

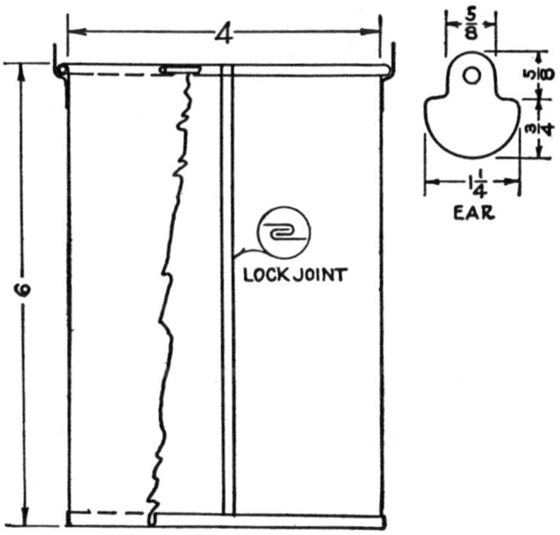

FIG. 279. Small pail.

Stock for drinking cup—1 piece circular tin, 3-3/4″ diameter; 1 piece rectangular tin, 11-1/4″ x 2-3/4″; 1 piece rectangular tin, 5″ x 1-1/2″.

Tools—A full set of sheet-metalworker's hand tools.

217. Methods of Inserting Wire. The customary method of strengthening the upper edge of a tin receptacle is to roll the edge of the tin over a piece of wire in what is known as a wiring machine. The wire may be inserted by hand, as described below, altho with less likelikood of securing a perfect job.

218. Shaping Bottom. Pare the end of a round piece of stove wood with a draw-knife to a diameter of 3-1/2″.

Sandpaper the surface smooth and saw the end off square (Fig. 280-*a*).

Place the stove wood in a vise with the cylindrical end up. Over this place the circular bottom for the cup so that the

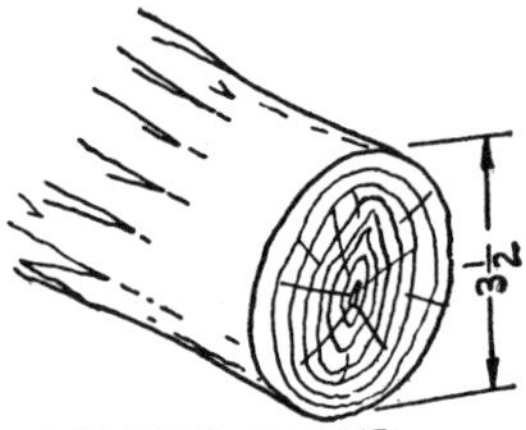

FIG. 280-*a*. Piece of wood for shaping iron.

FIG. 281. Sheet-metal shaped on wood form.

1/8″ surface to be folded projects evenly around the piece of wood (Fig. 281). Hold the tin with the left hand and gently pound the edge of it down around the piece of wood with a mallet. It may be necessary to snip the edge of the tin in a few places to prevent it from buckling. The bending must be done carefully. When the edge is finally bent over in contact with the cylindrical surface of the wood, pound the folded portion firmly against the wood until it fits like a cap (Fig. 281). The tin may now be pried off.

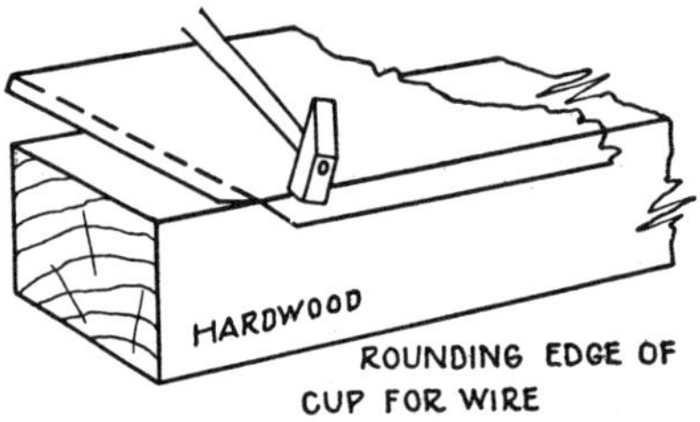

FIG. 282. Bending sheet-metal over piece of wood.

219. Inserting Wire in the Edge. Over a slightly-rounded corner of a piece of hard wood, pound the 1/4″ surface for the wire to strengthen the upper edge of the cup (Fig. 282). When this has been done, place the proper length of 1/16″ wire in the rounded corner turned upward as the tin lies flat on the bench, fasten the bent edge of tin over the wire at each end with a pair of pliers, then carefully pound the remaining portion of the bent edge over the wire until it lies smooth and hugs the wire the entire length (Fig. 283). Fig. 284 shows the process of folding a wire in the edge of a piece of tin.

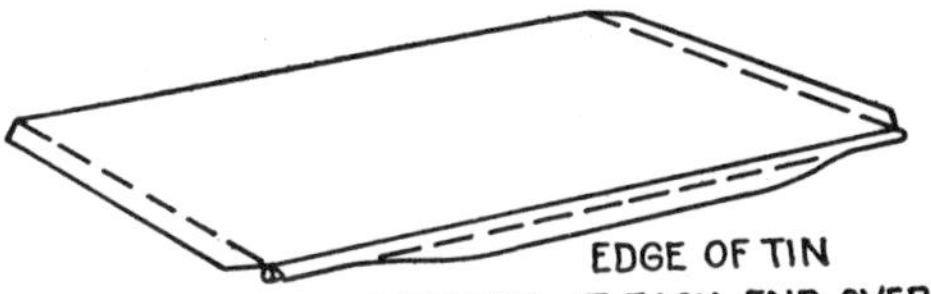

FIG. 283. Inserting wire.

Fold the end laps of the pattern in opposite directions to form the lock joint seam for the cup, as shown in insert, Fig. 279. Roll the entire surface over the cylindrical end of the piece of wood used to form the bottom of the cup, having the wire on the outside; lock the joint, pound down with the mallet and, at the same time, slip the cylindrical surface from the wood.

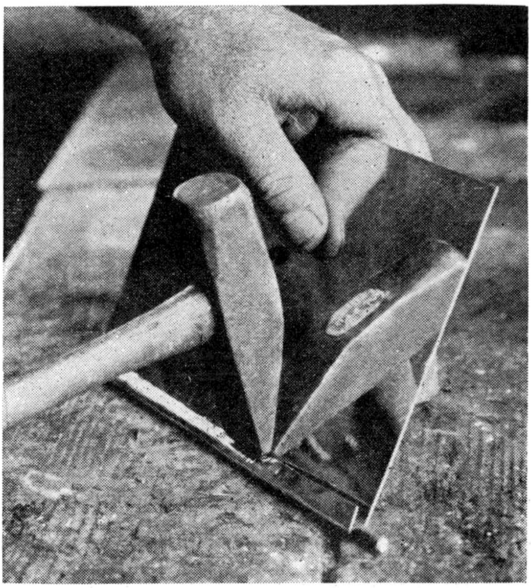

FIG. 284. Folding metal over wire.

Solder the inside and outside of the lock seam, slip the body of the cup into the bottom, and solder around the bottom edge. The cup is now complete except for the handle.

220. Handle for Drinking Cup. Fold the two 1/8″ outside edges of the strip for the handle (Fig. 285) as in the case of the upper edge of the watering pan (Problem 3). With the folded edges on the inside, form the handle, as shown in the drawing for the drinking cup (Fig. 278), and solder both

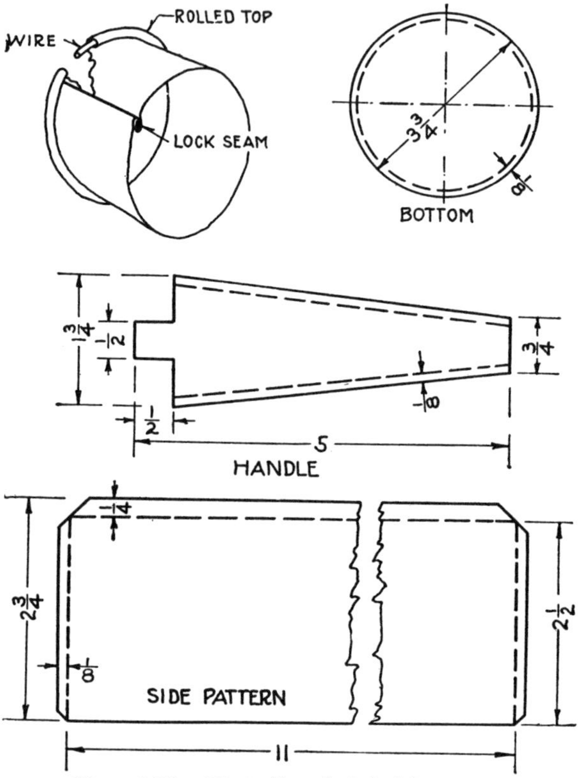

FIG. 285. Details of drinking cup.

ends to the cup—one against the wire and the other against the bottom seam—over the lock seam of the cup. First, gently pound the ends firmly in contact with the cup over the seam. This may be done by putting the cup over the end of a cylindrical stick, such as a tool handle.

Problem No. 6: To Make a Conical Dish.

Suggested Projects:

a) Funnel (Fig. 286).

b) Flaring pan (Fig. 287).

c) Flaring pail (Fig. 288).

d) Cream dipper (Fig. 289).

Stock for the funnel—1 piece of tin, 12″ x 6″; 1 piece of tin, 5″ x 4″.

Tools—A full set of sheet-metalworker's hand tools.

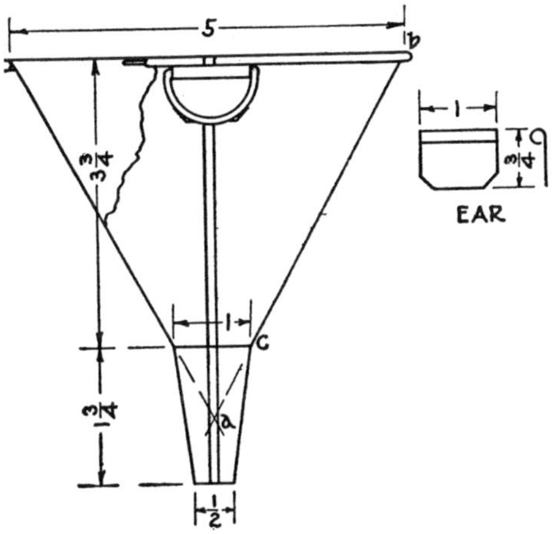

FIG. 286. Funnel.

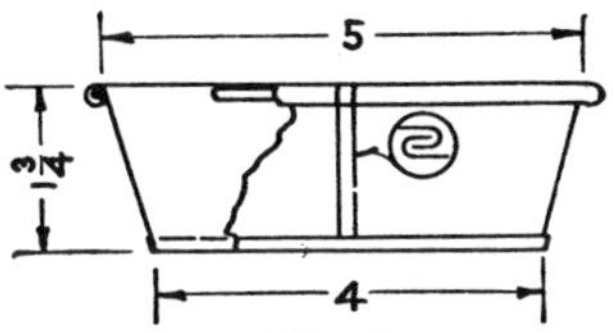

FIG. 287. Flaring pan.

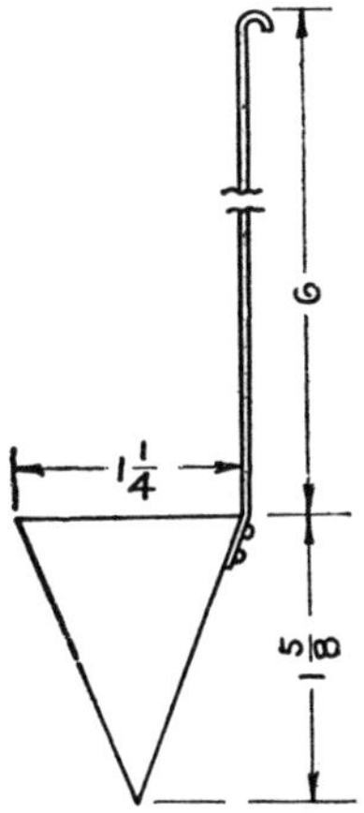

FIG. 289. Cream dipper.

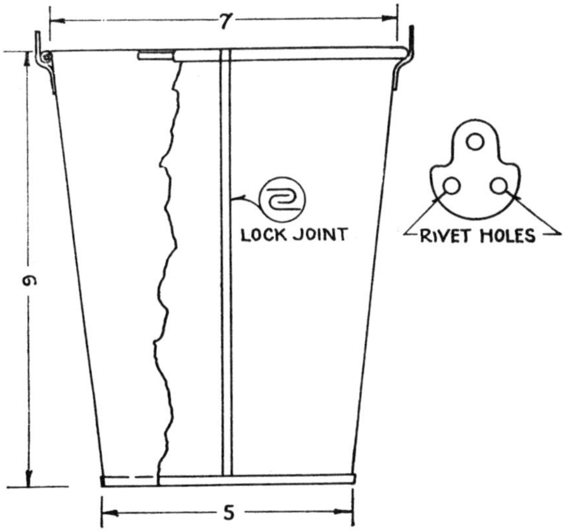

FIG. 288. Flaring pail.

221. Laying Out Conical Shapes. The pattern for a cone or for a frustum of a cone is made by describing an arc of a circle with a compass or a pair of dividers, the distance between the points being the slant height of the cone and the length of the outside arc being circumference of the base of the cone.

222. Construction of Funnel. Lay out the pattern for each of the two parts of the funnel (Fig. 290), producing the side lines of front view to locate the apex of each cone part, in order to secure the radius to strike the proper arcs (Fig. 290).

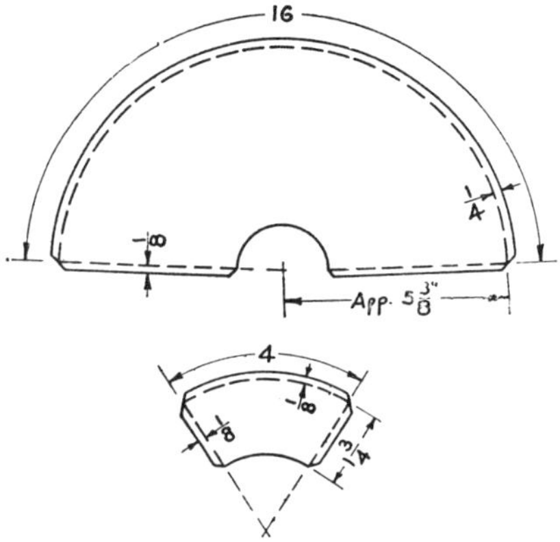

FIG. 290. Metal cut for funnel.

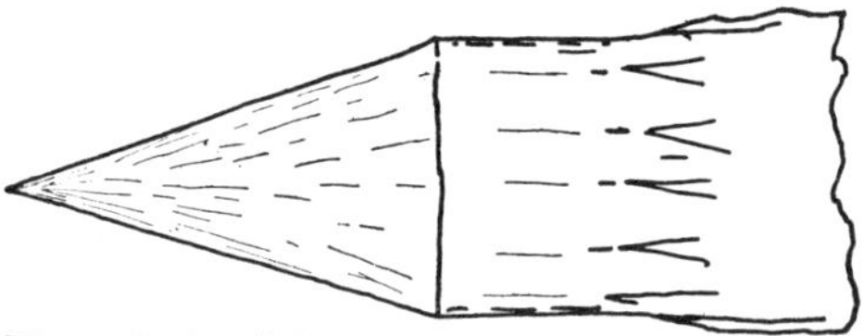

FIG. 291. Piece of wood for shaping funnel.

As in the case of the cylindrical part of the cup, insert a 1/16″ wire in the space marked 1/4″ on the outside of the large pattern, and fold in opposite directions the laps for the lock seam joints. Carefully form each portion of the funnel over a cylindrical piece of stove wood tapered on one end to a cone (Fig. 291). Lock and solder the joint for each part, slip the upper part into the lower, first spreading out the upper opening of the lower part over the surface of the cone-shaped piece of wood, and solder the two parts together. The ear may be made as shown in Fig. 286, and a small piece of wire formed to slip into it to form a hanger. The ear may be soldered on or fastened with rivets.

CHAPTER XXIV

SUPPLEMENTARY PROJECTS IN SHEET-METALWORK

223. Cylindrical Receptacle (Fig. 292).

1) Lay out pattern for bottom, leaving 1/8″ for fold.

2) Lay out pattern for body of receptacle, leaving 1/8″ lap on each end for lock joint.

3) Solder lock joint of body of pattern.

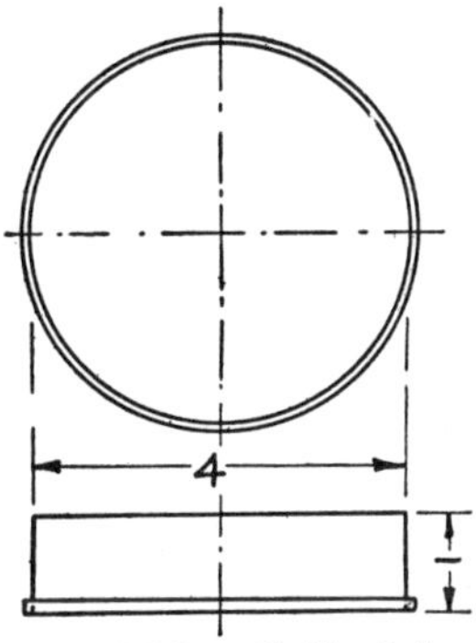

FIG. 292. Cylindrical receptacle.

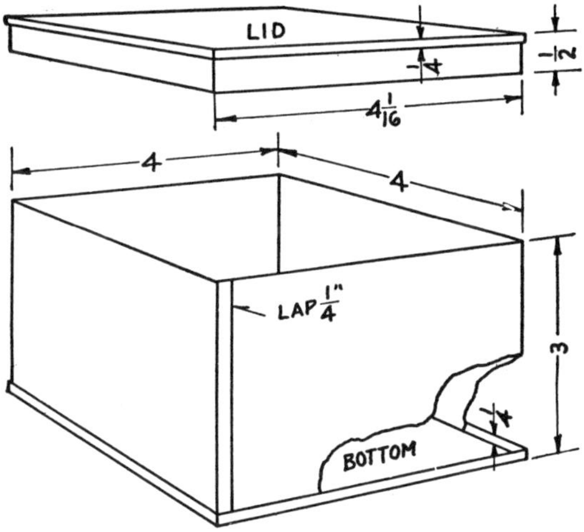

FIG. 293. Cubical box with lid.

4) Place bottom in position on body of receptacle and solder in place. (See instructions for Problem No. 5.)

224. Cubical Box with Lid (Fig. 293).

1) Lay out pattern for body of box—a rectangle 3″ wide and 12-1/4″ long. The 1/4″ added to the 12″ is to provide a lap which should be formed on one corner.

2) Lay out pattern for bottom of box—a square 4-1/4″ on a side. The 1/4″ added to the 4″ is to provide two 1/8″ laps—one on each side of the square.

3) Solder seam on box after it is folded into shape of square.

4) Fold edges and corner laps on bottom, place in position on box. and solder in place, including corner laps.

5) Construct cover for box by following description for making the body of box.

225. Stovepipe Collar (Fig. 294).

1) Lay out pattern for cylindrical part of collar, allowing 3/8″ for lap to be riveted. Rivet joint.

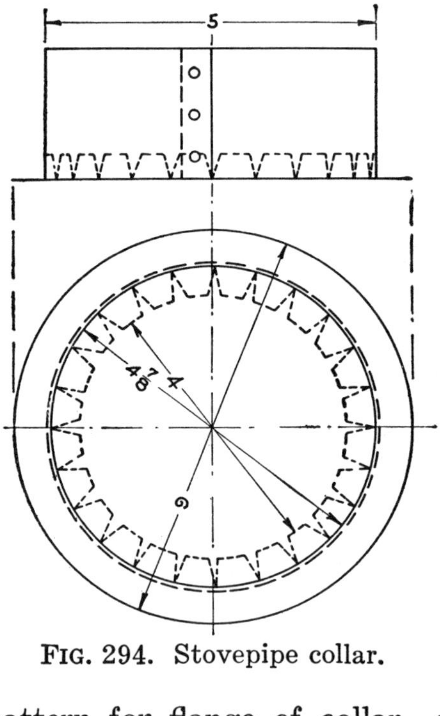

FIG. 294. Stovepipe collar.

2) Lay out pattern for flange of collar—a ring, outside diameter, 6″, and inside diameter, 4″. Scribe a 4-7/8″ circle on this ring. Clip several narrow notches on inside of ring limited by the scribed circle.

3) Fold notched part of ring into cylindrical part of collar and pound in contact with same over cylindrical stock.

4) Solder or rivet two parts of collar together.

226. Conductor Elbows (Fig. 295).

1) Lay out each section of elbow, as shown at *A*. Divide the end view (circle) into twelve parts, each point to be regarded as the end of a line on the cylindrical section drawn

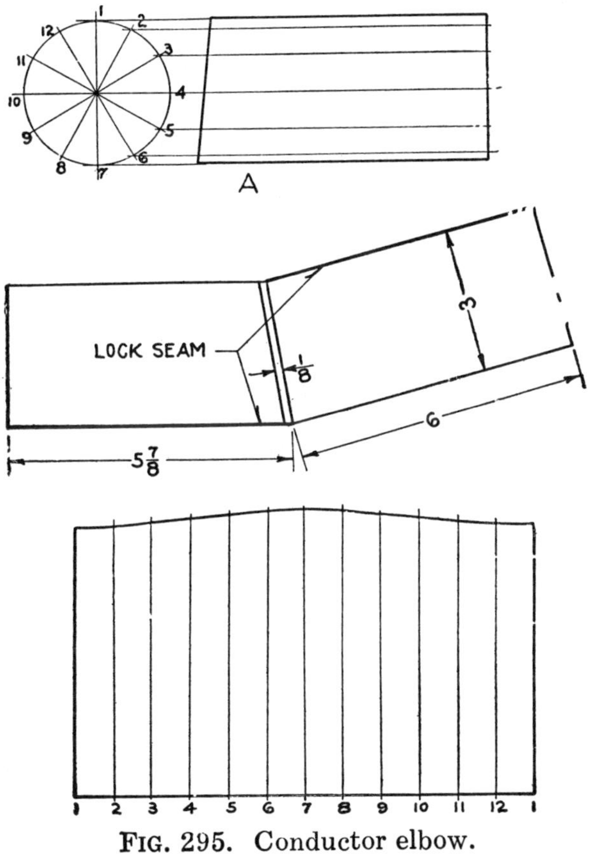

FIG. 295. Conductor elbow.

opposite the point. Space the length of the section of the pattern into twelve parts, and lay off on line thru each point the length of same line in drawing *A*.

2) Form lock seams, as indicated, and allow for flange for joint between sections.

3) Form each section and solder seams. Place the parts of

elbow together and solder. Note that seams of sections are placed on opposite sides of elbow.

227. Roof Ridge Flange (Fig. 296).

1) Lay out cylindrical pattern (Fig. 297). Determine length of lines, as in pattern for conductor (Fig. 295).

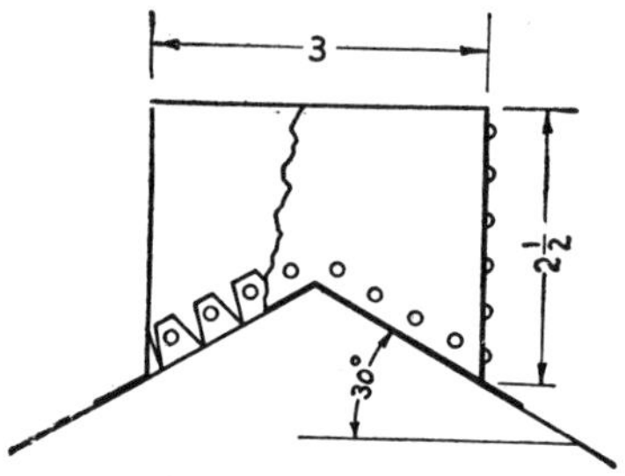

FIG. 296. Roof ridge flange.

2) Lay out pattern for flange, notch and punch holes for rivets, unless solder alone is to be used to fasten it to cylinder.

3) Fit cylinder and flange together, bending flange to proper

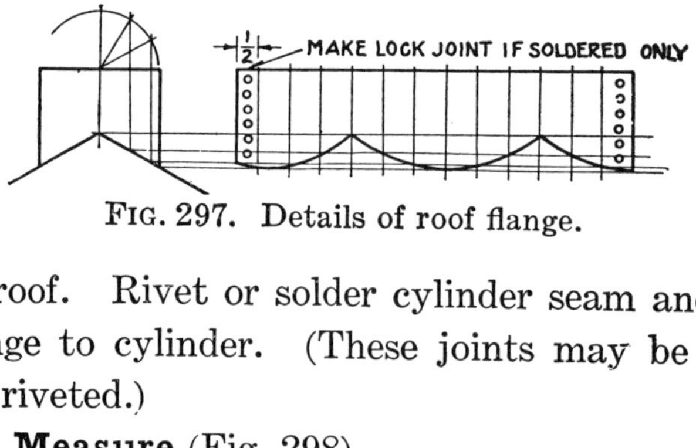

FIG. 297. Details of roof flange.

angle for roof. Rivet or solder cylinder seam and rivet or solder flange to cylinder. (These joints may be both soldered and riveted.)

228. A Measure (Fig. 298).

1) Lay out pattern for bottom, as in Problem 5. Fold over edge.

2) Lay out pattern for body, as in Problem 6, for upper portion of funnel. Solder lock seam.

3) Lay out pattern for rim of measure, regarding it as a cone

with apex (*a*, Fig. 299). (See pattern, Fig. 290.) Note radii distances lettered similarly in Figs. 298 and 299. Begin at *b* (Fig. 299) and measure the distance *hb* six times in each direction. This will locate points *g* and *g*. Draw lines *ag* and *ag*, and extend both to *d*. Also extend *ab* to *c*. To secure the arc thru *c* (Fig. 299), connect points *c* and *d* and erect perpendicular to this line at center point *e* to intersect line *ac* at *f*. Use *f* as a center and draw arc *dcd*. Angles between radii *ad* and *ac*, *ac* and *ad*, reading from left to right in Fig. 299, are equal.

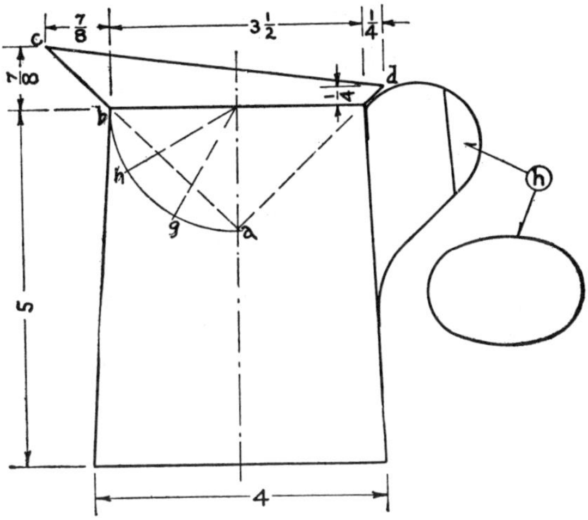

FIG. 298. A measure.

4) Make short and narrow V-cuts with snips in lap surface on lower edge of pattern for rim. Bend this lap to fit into top of body of measure. Bend end laps. form rim and solder to top of measure body after soldering rim-seam at *d*.

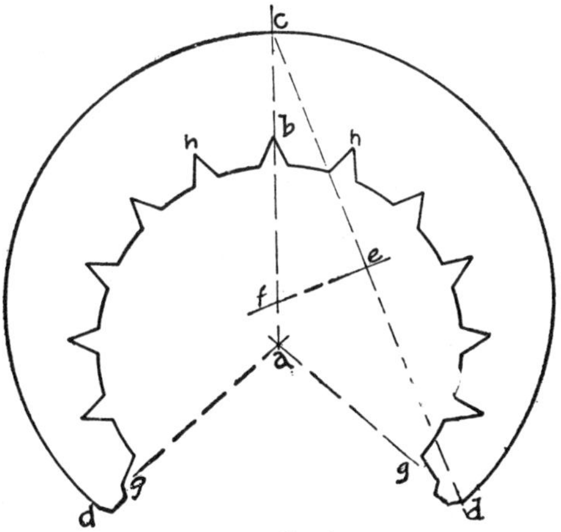

FIG. 299. Details for measure.

5) Place bottom in position on body, pound firmly in contact with body over end of cylindrical stick and solder seam.

6) Lay out handle, as in Problem 5; form and solder in piece of tin *h* cut to fit. Solder on handle over seam of body.

229. Three-Piece Elbow (Fig. 300).

1) Lay out pattern for each part of elbow, first making full-

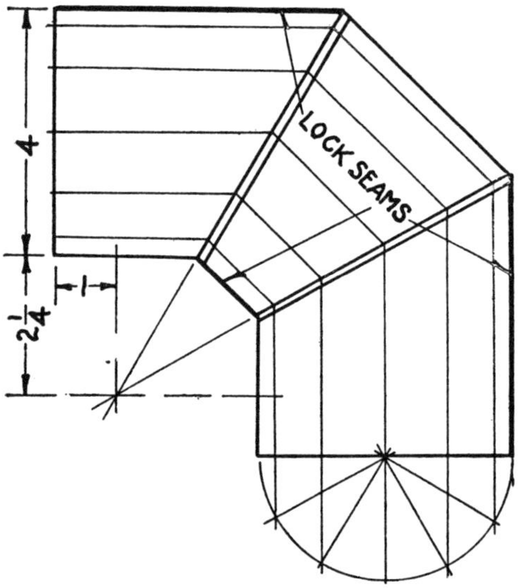

FIG. 300. Three-piece elbow.

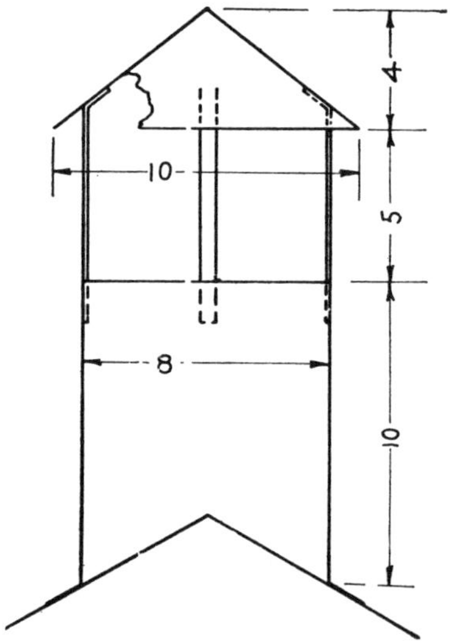

FIG. 301. Roof cap and ventilator.

sized bench drawing. Use methods given in cases of conductor elbow (Sec. 226) and roof ridge flange (Sec. 227). Allow laps for lock lap joint on each section of elbow. Allow 3/32″ lap on each end of central section of pipe to fit over, and solder onto, end sections.

2) Solder lock joint on each section and solder sections together.

230. Roof Cap and Ventilator (Fig. 301).

1) Lay out and construct 8″ cylinder, as in case of roof ridge flange (Sec. 227).

2) Lay out and construct conical cap for ventilator, as for

funnel (Problem 6). (Seam should be riveted for ventilator of size given.)

3) Fasten conical and cylindrical parts of ventilator together with four strips of 1/2″ band iron or heavy tin. Ends should be riveted.

231. Gutter Miter (Fig. 302).

1) Lay out pattern for each part of gutter. This will be a

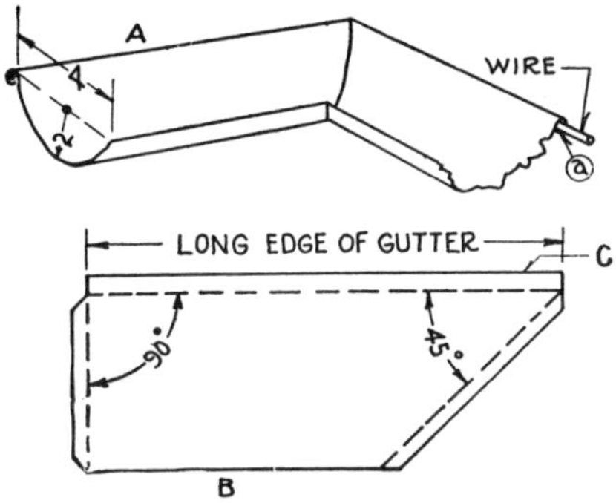

FIG. 302.

rectangle, length the long edge of the gutter and width one-half the circumference of a 2″ circle, plus 1/2″ to roll over heavy wire on outside edge (*A*, Fig. 302). Cut one end of pattern square and other edge at 45 degrees (*C*, Fig. 302). Leave lap on square end to fold, and solder against end of gutter. Leave joint lap on end cut at 45 degrees.

2) Fold edge of gutter over wire. Form gutter (*A*, Fig. 302).

3) Solder end of gutter in position.

PART V

Farm Machinery Repair and Adjustment

CHAPTER XXV

Farm Machinery as an Economic Factor

232. Farm Machinery and National Progress. It is not the purpose of this section to furnish information on each type of machine used on the farm, but to present a few general statements, followed by outlined studies of a few machines and their uses, and a few definite problems of repair and adjustment. For a more complete discussion, the reader is referred to the list of books and bulletins given below.

Farm Machinery and Farm Motors. By Davidson and Chase. Orange Judd Co.
Agricultural Engineering. By Davidson. Webb Publishing Co.
Equipment for the Farm and Farmstead. By Ramsower. Ginn & Co.
Farm Machinery. By Wirt. John Wiley & Sons.
Bulletins from the U. S. Department of Agriculture and State Agricultural Experiment Stations.

The greatest growth in agricultural development is marked by the use of modern machinery. We find the plow substituted for the crooked stick; the binder, reaper and mower substituted for the cradle and scythe; the threshing machine substituted for the flail, and steam and gas power for man and horse power. Every country that is backward in the use of these modern farm machines, is backward also in every other phase of its development. The most striking difference between the American farmer and the Chinese farmer, or the American farmer of today and the American farmer of fifty years ago, is a difference mainly of equipment and the efficient use of that equipment.

The effect of the use of modern machinery on our people is many fold. It has really made possible our high stage of development. In fact, the development of any country is measured by its ability to produce an adequate food supply. It has been only a few years ago that people of this country thot that starvation was staring them in the face. That was in times of peace. It has been estimated that in 1800, 97 per cent of the people of the United States lived on farms, and many of them felt the bite of hunger.

Our farm population decreased slowly until 1850 from 97 per cent to 90 per cent. This was during a period of a half-century. There was no marked development of farm machinery during this period, and our development along other lines was equally retarded. It was the imaginative minds of such men as John Deere, who gave us the first steel plow in 1837; McCormick, who gave us the binder in 1834, and Pitts, who gave us the threshing machine in 1837, that made a start for modern farm machinery. Few of these machines were built before 1850, but after this period, when factories were established and the number of machines built began to increase, the production of food on a much larger scale was made possible, and during the next fifty-year period the population decreased from 90 per cent to about 40 per cent on the farm, or a little over one-third of the total population was on farms.

We can easily imagine the condition that we would be in at the present time if 97 per cent of our people were on the farms without modern equipment. We would be one of the most backward people of the world. We would not have any of the things which go toward making life pleasant and the farm a good place on which to live.

The use of more and better farm equipment has changed the mental attitude of the farmer, it has increased the wages of the farm laborer, it has decreased the necessary labor of women in the field and home, it has increased the production per capita many fold, decreased the cost of production, and improved the quality of products produced.

An abundance of food has made possible our cities, our industries, the arts and sciences, our very civilization. It has made America the greatest nation of the world. These things are made possible because one farmer is capable of producing enough food for three families instead of just his own. Many farmers at the present time are producing even more than this, and doing it with a minimum of labor.

233. Latest Machinery Most Economical. (Fig. 303.) Agricultural production is quite similar to factory production. We find in the factory certain machines for certain particular operations. For example, when we go into a cotton mill, we find a carding machine for making the cotton suitable for use on the spindle. The same thing is true on the farm; we find certain equipment for preparing the soil, special types of seeding machinery for planting, and special equipment for harvesting. The tendency has been too great on the part of many farmers to try to get along without buying the latest improved machines. The farmer can no more get the best results without the latest modern machines than can the manufacturer.

The difference between modern cotton-mill operations and the hand-power method of former days is quite comparable to the modern farmer as compared with the farmer of seventy-five years ago. Production in both cases requires machinery, and without machinery of the right kind and properly taken care of, neither will be successful. The effect of machinery on

FIG. 303. Motor cultivator, two-row.

production per capita is very marked. In those sections where poor equipment is used, the people simply exist and seldom are in a position to improve their living conditions.

The following data collected several years ago illustrates the effect of machinery on the production per capita:

234. Influence of Farm Machinery on Income.

INFLUENCE OF FARM MACHINERY ON INCOME*

State	*Annual Income of Each Worker*	*Value of Farm Implements for Each Farm*
Florida	$119.72	$ 30.43
Alabama	143.98	33.40
Iowa	611.11	196.55
North Dakota	755.62	238.84

The use of machinery and modern equipment has not only brought about a greater production per capita, but has also

*From Circular 21, Bureau of Plant Industry, United States Department of Agriculture.

influenced our agricultural conditions along almost every line.

235. The Problem of Farm Power. The farm power problem is one that is being given much more attention at the present time than ever before. To show the tendency toward mechanical power, the census of 1914 shows that the power from horses and mules is equal to 14,230,000 H. P.,

FIG. 303-*a*. Two-row cultivator with team.

while the power from mechanical sources is equal to 9, 675,-000 H. P. This vast amount of power is more than that used by all other industries combined. The investment is also much larger than that invested in other forms of power in the United States.

236. Wasting Power and Machinery on the Farm. Some of the greatest losses and wastes on the farm are due to the use of inadequate machines, poor operators, and to lack of care of the machinery. All three of these factors should have the serious attention of every farmer at the present time. Every machine should be adequate for the use for which it is intended. It is very easy to get a machine that

FIG. 304. Checking up machinery for repairs.

is too small or too large to be efficient for a particular use. A great many tractor failures have been due to either the tractor's being too large or too small for a particular farm operation. To use a tractor of 20 to 30 H. P. to drive a pump requiring only 2 H. P. is a mistake often made. It is also as poor economy to operate a single-row corn planter when a two-row planter might be used equally well. In selecting a piece of equipment of any sort, the following points should be kept in mind:

1) It should be the most satisfactory for the particular work at hand.

2) It should be easy to operate with least danger.

3) It should be efficient.

4) It should be capable of easy adjustment.

FIG. 304-*a*. Unprotected machinery.

5) It should be designed so all parts are accessible and easily replaced.

6) It should be well built of good material to resist breakage and wear.

7) It should not cost too much.

Wasting Machinery Thru Ignorance.

The lack of knowledge on the part of the operator has been the cause of many failures with modern machines. This is especially true of power machinery. There have probably been more tractor failures due to this one thing than all other causes combined. Many machines are bought and taken into the field and operated until some trouble develops. It is then found that a wearing part was without lubricant or was not properly adjusted. Every machine should be carefully studied before it is used. An instruction book should be secured with each machine, and it should be studied as a text. With a thoro knowledge of the working parts of a machine, there is little danger of accident, and the best results are assured.

The lack of knowledge of a machine usually results in lack of care and lack of adjustment. It goes without saying that the man who leaves his binder outside to rust and decay does not appreciate its fine points. The same is true of the tractor. If the farm machines were given the attention they deserve, they would be cared for as machinery is cared for in the factory and as the sewing machine is cared for in the home.

Many machines are being run that should be undergoing repairs. The farm machine, as a general rule, is allowed to get in a run-down condition and is not repaired until absolutely necessary, and often such repairs must be made when the machine is in the field and when the work should be in progress. We cannot expect the best results from machines that have been neglected, that have been left in the fields for months, or, if under shelter, are not examined until the day before they are to be used. The farmer would be greatly shocked to see a sewing machine left on the porch for a week at a time where the rain and sun would affect it. Yet, many farmers allow the binders with their delicate tying mechanism to stay out in the weather for months. These machines depreciate in value, become rusty, and are weakened, and there is a loss of time when they fail to give service after they are taken into the field; also, a loss in production.

237. Three Considerations—Housing, Repairing, and Painting. The proper care of machinery might be classified under three heads—(1) housing, (2) repairing, (3) painting. In the housing of farm equipment, we do not have to provide an expensive building. The implements are not affected by cold weather. In sections where the dust is bad, the walls and roofs of the buildings should be made tight enough to prevent its entrance. It has been estimated that the value of machinery on the average farm at the present time is about $1,000. For such an amount of machinery, the farmer can well spend $400 or $500 for a good machinery house. Plans for such a shed can be secured from the U. S. Department of Agriculture or nearly every state agricultural college.

In the repairing of farm equipment, the farmer should be systematic. If the machines are examined on completing a job, and there is not time to repair them at that time, each part should be labeled so that parts can be ordered, and at a later date they can be replaced. The time to repair equipment is not when a machine is needed in the field, but during the time when the machines are in the machinery shed.

In regard to painting, it is well to repaint all wooden parts of farm implements, as it not only increases the life of the implements, but improves their appearance, and where a machine is sold after it has been in use a number of years, the cost of the addition of paint is repaid many fold. Quite often, where the farmer looks after his equipment properly, he will find that discarded machines can be repaired at slight expense and be made to give as good service as a new machine. There are many farmers who discard a machine after it has seen three or four years' service, when it really needs only a few slight repairs. Such machines can often be found standing in fence corners and are used to supply bolts, etc., about the farm.

CHAPTER XXVI

Tools and Materials for Machinery Repair

238. Necessity for Good Tools. Every man who farms will find use for a good kit of tools. In fact, suitable tools will often give an inspiration to do repair jobs that would not be attempted when inadequate tools are provided. Many of

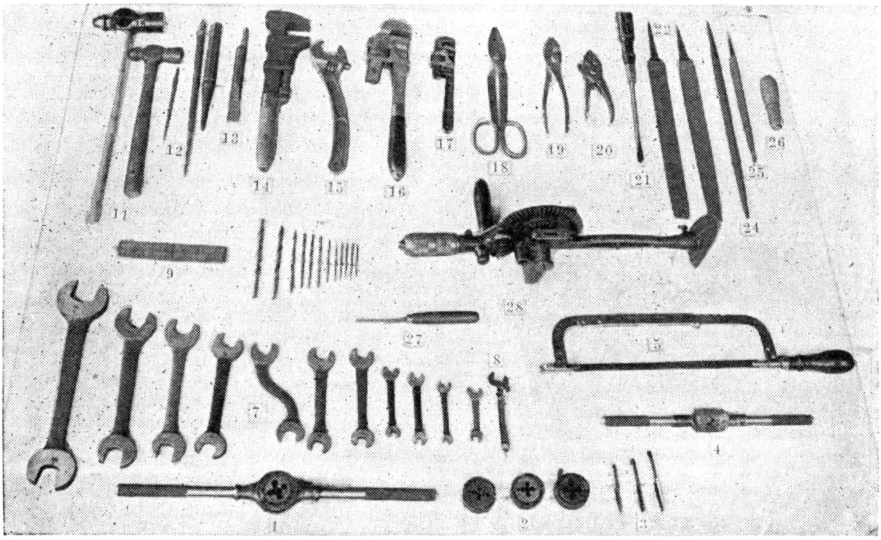

Fig. 305. Principal tools needed in implement repair:

1. Die-stock.
2. Dies.
3. Tap.
4. Stock.
5. Hack-saw.
7. End wrenches.
8. Crescent wrench.
9. Rule.
10. Drill bits.
11. Hammers.
12. Punches.
13. Cold chisel.
14. Monkey wrench.
15. Crescent wrench.
16. Stillson wrench.
17. Trimo wrench.
18. Tin snips.
19. Pliers.
20. Cutting pliers.
21. Screw-driver.
22. Flat files.
24. Round file.
25. Triangular file.
26. File handle.
27. Knife.
28. Breast drill.

the tools described in the sections on woodworking and metal-working are needed for machine repair and adjustment. There are a few not included in either of these lists that will be mentioned here. All the tools of this group are used without a forge. In fact, the great majority of machinery repair jobs on the farm are "cold jobs" that are made in the field or in the machinery shed. Fig. 305 shows a photograph of the tools which are most likely to be useful in making these repairs.

239. Wrenches. Wrenches for turning nuts and screws are made in various shapes and sizes suited for different uses. They are classed as (1) movable-jaw wrenches adjustable for turning different-sized nuts, the monkey wrench and the crescent wrench being common examples, and (2) fixed-jaw wrenches (the distance between jaws being fixed), the straight-end wrench, the *S* wrench and the alligator wrench being examples. The alligator type can be used on different-sized nuts, but is not as satisfactory as either the fixed or adjustable type.

Socket wrenches with *T*-shaped handle are designed for use where the nut cannot be reached with an ordinary wrench. Socket wrenches can be secured in a set of different sizes with a ratchet handle.

Pipe wrenches are made for gripping pipes or cylindrical rods.

In the use of wrenches, one should always be careful to select a wrench that will fit the particular nut snugly. If an adjustable wrench is used, screw the jaw down on the nut tight before attempting to screw it. Always remember to exert force on the handle toward the adjustable jaw.

240. Vise. A bench vise such as described in section on metalwork is well suited for machinery repair.

241. Hammers. A ball-peen machine hammer and a light-weight riveting hammer are needed for many repair jobs.

242. Chisels. The flat chisel, usually referred to as a cold chisel, is useful for cutting rivets or old bolts. Other special-shaped chisels are useful for cutting key ways and oil grooves.

243. Files. There is a number of types of files designed for different uses. Files are used either for smoothing down pieces of work or for sharpening tools such as saws and tools with cutting edges like hoes. Files can be secured of all degrees of coarseness from the rasp used by the horseshoer to the very smooth-cut file used for finishing hard metals. A rasp, one or two flat files, one or two triangular, and several round files should be provided for general repair work.

244. Screw-drivers. Several screw-drivers of different sizes are needed. Keep sides of point of the screw-driver filed parallel to prevent injury to slot in screw.

245. Pliers. Cutting pliers as well as holding pliers are needed. Do not use a pair of pliers where a wrench should be used, or for cutting extremely hard wire when a file will give best results.

246. Hack-Saw. The hack-saw is very useful for cutting pipes, bolts or other pieces of soft metal. It may also be used for cutting slots in screw heads or for similar work.

247. Drills. The most common drills are the breast, post and ratchet drills. The breast and ratchet drills are best suited for general repair work since they can be used at any place without taking a machine apart. The breast drill is designed for small holes, while the ratchet can be used for making holes of almost any size.

248. Stock Taps and Dies. Taps and dies are useful for cutting threads on bolts and for threading nuts. Pipe taps and dies are not to be used for bolt work. Machine screw taps can be used for tapping for screws when desired.

249. Materials Needed. For machinery repair, it is essential that there be kept on hand an assorted lot of machine, carriage and stove bolts with nuts and washers; an assorted lot of copper and soft iron rivets; an assorted lot of screws of different kinds and sizes; an assorted lot of cotter keys and pieces of iron rods of different diameters; pipe and pieces of strap iron for general use.

CHAPTER XXVII

How to Study Farm Machinery

250. Three Methods of Approach. Three classes of projects can be worked out to meet the need of the student when studying farm machinery. The first class can hardly be termed projects, but exercises or studies of various types of farm implements and power machines. In taking up these exercises, students will be expected to obtain a general knowledge of all kinds of machinery and make a careful study of those machines used on the home farms. They will be expected to secure booklets describing particular machines under discussion; these booklets may be obtained from manufacturers or from local dealers. The machines are studied on the implement dealer's floor, in farm-machinery sheds, or in the school shop. Most of this work would be done during the time of year when the weather will not allow outdoor work.

The second type of project is the study of the machine while operating under actual farming conditions, the student being given a chance to make adjustment as well as actually operating the machine. A study of the cost of doing the job is carried out in this connection. It may be preparing the the seed bed, planting the grain, or harvesting. Each step is studied, the work is actually done, the time required for it and the cost noted.

The third type of project is a study of the care, adjustment and repair of machinery. Not only can this problem be studied by visiting various farms and studying conditions, but actual repairs can be made. Many machines are left in the shed without checking up repairs at the end of the season's work. Such machines can be inspected, parts ordered and repairs made. Gas engines can be overhauled, tractors gone over and put in first-class shape. The instruction books furnished by manufacturers are an excellent source of information for this work.

A few general exercises and projects such as suggested above will follow, with additional ones briefly outlined. It is suggested that a machinery laboratory manual* be available for student reference for additional subject-matter, it being impossible to cover the subject in this section.

251. Tillage Machinery.

Requirements: To make a careful study and make a complete report on each of the chief tillage machines, including a walking plow, a sulky, a gang and a tractor plow; a peg-tooth, spring, and disc harrow; a disc and a shovel riding cultivator; and a smooth and a corrugated roller.

Tools Needed: Monkey wrench, screw-driver, rule and pair of pliers.

Preliminary Instruction: The importance of a careful study of all types of farm machines is well justified by the part machinery plays in farm production. The lack of knowledge and lack of care of many machines on the farm with the resulting losses should be an example for every boy in his preparation for future farm work. The study of tillage machinery is just as important as the study of the tractor and other power machines, altho it may not be so interesting.

*Valuable suggestions can be obtained from *Farm Machinery* by Wirt, John Wiley & Sons, New York.

Working Instructions: After being assigned a group of machines, the student will read carefully description in text references assigned by instructor. In addition, he should secure catalogs and booklets describing such machines. Next, from a catalog cut out, with a pair of scissors, an illustration of each of the machines being studied. Paste the illustration on a blank sheet of paper. Then, while going over the machine being studied, label all the principal parts. As a report, with the illustration give a statement of the function of each part, its construction and adjustment. These facts may be determined from reference text, from catalogs, from discussion in classroom, by examination, removing parts and taking measurements, or from the instructor in the laboratory.

252. Study of Seeding Machinery.

Requirements: To make a careful study of the different types of seeding machines that the particular type of farming demands, including a study of grain drills, corn planters, cotton planters, broadcast seeders, pea and bean planters and drills. To make a test of the accuracy of planting of the machine studied and calibrate it to plant a definite amount, and make a report.

Tools and Materials Needed: Monkey wrench, screw-driver, rule, pair of pliers, scales for weighing, seed for testing, and paper bags or other containers.

Preliminary Instruction: The accuracy of planting determines to a great extent the final yield of the crop. So every one should know how to test a planter, drill or other seeding device. One should not only know how, but should actually make a test before using the machine in the field.

Working Instructions: Follow instructions under exercise in Sec. 251, and, in addition, the machine may be tested as outlined in Secs. 277 and 279.

253. Study of Fertilizer Drills, Manure and Straw Spreaders.

Requirements: To make a careful study of different types of fertilizer and limestone drills, including the agitator, force-feed and end-gate type. To study manure spreaders and straw spreaders; also straw-spreading attachments for manure spreaders.

Tools Needed: Same as in Sec. 251.

Preliminary Instruction: Keeping up the fertility of the soil is one of the greatest problems of a permanent agriculture. The use of fertilizer drills, manure spreaders and straw-spreaders for distributing materials on the soil greatly facilitates this work.

Working Instruction: Follow instruction in Sec. 251.

254. Study of Haying Machinery.

Requirements: To make a careful study of the various classes of haying machinery—the mower, rakes of different types, tedders, loaders, stackers, presses and other haying machinery such as is used in the community.

Tools Needed: Same as in Sec. 251.

Preliminary Instruction: The hay crop is one of the most valuable of the American farmer. By many it is given little consideration; much hay is lost due to lack of care in handling. Modern machinery has made it possible to handle the hay crop with a minimum amount of labor.

Working Instruction: Follow instruction in Sec. 251.

255. Harvesting Machinery.

Requirements: To make a careful study of grain-harvesting machinery, corn binders, grain binders, shocking attachments, push binders, headers, combines and such harvesting machinery as is used in the immediate neighborhood.

Tools Needed: Same as in Sec. 251.

Preliminary Instruction: The modern harvesting machinery on the farm plays a similar part in production to the automatic machines in the factory. They make possible greater production per capita, allowing more people to enter other lines of endeavor. The cost of production where modern harvesting machinery is used is a great deal less than where harvesting is done by hand method.

Working Instruction: Follow instruction as outlined under Sec. 251.

256. Study of Power-Driven Machines.

Requirements: To make a careful study of power-driven machines used on the farm, such as grain separators, silage cutters, feed grinders, corn shellers, limestone grinders, cane mills and other machines in that section.

Preliminary Instruction: With the advent of the stationary engine and the tractor on the farm, power-driven machines in greater numbers will be used each year. Many farmers are already buying small threshing outfits where formerly the grain was threshed by a large threshing outfit. Such practices make for greater efficiency and better products. The grain can be threshed when in the best condition, and the corn cut for silage when at the proper maturity if the farmer has his own equipment. A careful knowledge of such equipment is necessary for its efficient use.

Working Instruction: Same as in Sec. 251.

257. Study of Gas Engines, Tractors and Trucks.

Requirements: To become thoroly familiar with at least one type of gas engines, one type of tractors and one type of trucks.

Preliminary Instruction: There is more power used on the farm than in all other industries combined. The total horse power has been estimated to be more than 25,000,000. More than one-half of this is mechanical power. Altho the farmer is one of the greatest power users, it is only within recent years that he has paid any attention to this phase of his farm problem. Every farmer should become familiar with the construction of an internal-combustion engine.

Working Instruction: Follow instruction as outlined in Sec. 251. Pay especial attention when studying a stationary engine to its general construction, the ignition system, system of carburation, method of cooling, oiling devices, type of governor, and determine for what type of work the engine is best suited. In addition, for tractors and trucks, note how the power goes from engine to drive wheels, the clutch, transmission, differential and drive shaft and observe the lever control. Note the wheel construction, fenders for protection, seat, arrangement of fuel tanks, etc.

CHAPTER XXVIII

Projects in Farm Machinery Operation

258. Conditions for Carrying Out Projects. While this series of projects can be carried on at the same time with the study of machinery, they are better adapted for home projects and can be carried on as outside assignments under actual farm conditions along with production projects, such

Fig. 306. Plowing with horse-drawn riding plow.

as growing five acres of corn, an acre of potatoes, etc. It is not essential that the particular projects that are outlined be followed; the chief thing in mind should be to study the machinery that is being operated on the farm with the idea of, first, becoming familiar with the general method of doing the job; second, determining if the method used is the best or most efficient, and, third, determining how much it costs. For those students who do not live on farms, this work can be done by visiting a farm when a particular operation is being carried on.

259. Preparation of Land for Planting. (Figs. 306 and 306-*a*.)

Requirements: To operate horse-drawn and tractor-drawn implements in the preparation of a seed bed. To become familiar with all the details of operation, determine cost

FIG. 306-*a*. Disking with tractor power.

of preparing land for planting by the two methods, and compare the results obtained.

Tools and Equipment Needed: Implements and power available for the particular job.

Preliminary Instruction: A well-prepared seed bed is essential to a good crop, and the work done at the least expense means the greatest income to the operator.

Working Instructions:

1) Each student should harness team and hitch to plow; should lay out a field under supervision of instructor or farmer, and plow at least one acre of ground, noting time required to do the job. The team should then be hitched to harrow, and field harrowed, noting time required. Make all adjustment necessary to make the plow operate effectively and with the least draft.
2) Each student should get tractor ready for field work, make proper hitch to plow and carry out work of plowing as outlined in previous paragraph. Proper adjustment for proper depth and adjustment to avoid side draft should be made. Note time required to plow and harrow one acre.
3) Considering cost and depreciation of the two outfits and all other expense entailed, calculate cost of doing the work by the two methods. In report, compare quality of work done by two outfits.

260. Planting Corn. (Fig. 307.)

Requirements: To operate a corn planter. To select proper plates for particular corn. To make all adjustments necessary to have planter drop and cover effectively. Determine cost of planting corn per acre.

Equipment Needed: Planter complete and team.

Preliminary Instruction: Careful grading and selection of seed corn is as important for good results as proper seed, preparation and careful planting.

Working Instruction:

1) Select proper plates for planting and test them out upon going into the field.

2) Drive in stake, attach check wire and unreel it from the drum the first trip across the field. Place stake at opposite side of field so it will be directly behind the planter tongue after it has been turned into position, and draw check wire up to proper tightness as directed by instructor.
3) Place check wire in trip, set the openers in position,

FIG. 307. Planting corn.

lower marker in place and drive across the field. Note if planter is dropping.
4) Observe extreme care to make a straight row the first time across the field. After turning into position, change stake and draw check wire up to proper tightness. Follow marker track with tongue directly above it for second trip across field, and continue as outlined above.

261. Drilling Grain. (Fig. 308.)

Requirements: To operate a drill in drilling grain. To set seeding devices for a definite rate of seeding, and drill a definite area, determining the cost of the operation.

Tools Needed: Drill and team.

Preliminary Instruction: Same general instruction with reference to selecting seed corn also applies to small grain. In general, it should be remembered to plant *across* the slope instead of *along* the slope. This is to check erosion and avoid starting a small gully by washing at the wheel tracks.

FIG. 308. Drilling grain.

Working Instruction:

1) Adjust feeding device for a definite rate of seeding. It is best to do this by test rather than to be guided by dial.
2) After drill is driven in position, lower the furrow openers into ground.
3) Drive across field, noting that the openers do not clog and that the seed is passing down into the soil.

4) On all following trips, be careful to note where the last track was made in order that no ground will be missed or gone over twice.

262. Harvesting Corn for Silage. (Fig. 309.)

Requirements: To assist in harvesting corn and putting it into the silo. To operate each machine for a period long enough to become familiar with each detail of the work. To determine the cost of each operation in harvesting the corn from the field to putting it into the silo as silage.

FIG. 309. Cutting silage.

Equipment Needed: Corn binder, wagons, silage cutter, teams and engine for power.

Preliminary Instruction: Due to the fact that corn as silage is so highly palatable and nutritious, practical, successful dairymen and cattle feeders have silos. When corn is put into the form of silage, practically none of it is wasted.

Working Instruction:

1) Operate binder in cutting the corn.

2) Note the rate of cutting and estimate the number of acres cut per hour and cost of cutting per ton.
3) Compare cost of cutting by machine and cutting by hand.
4) Haul a load of corn from field to silage cutter.
5) Determine the cost of hauling per ton.
6) Operate silage cutter.
7) Note special safety devices on cutter.

FIG. 310. Harvesting grain with tractor power.

8) Note the rate of cutting in loads and in tons per day.
9) Note the type of engine used to drive cutter.
10) Determine the cost of operating engine.
11) Note the method of elevating the silage into the silo.
12) Assist in packing the silage in the silo.
13) Note the total number in the crew on the various types of work.
14) Determine the total cost of getting the silage into the silo.
15) Determine the capacity of the silo.
16) Determine the cost per ton in getting the corn from the field into the silo as silage.

263. Harvesting Grain. (Fig. 310.)

Requirements: To assist in the various operations of harvesting grain, from cutting with a binder and shocker through threshing. To determine the cost as far as possible for each operation, to be able finally to determine cost of producing a bushel of wheat or a bushel of corn.

Equipment Needed: Binder, teams or tractor, wagon, and threshing outfit.

Preliminary Instruction: It is just as essential that the farmer know how much it costs to grow a bushel of grain as that the manufacturer know how much it costs to mill 100 pounds of flour. The harvest season on the farm is a season when labor is in demand. It is essential that the grain be cut when at the proper stage of ripeness and threshed when properly cured. For these reasons it is important that some study be made of the processes of harvesting grain.

Working Instruction:

1) Get binder ready for cutting, with a satisfactory hitch and properly adjusted and lubricated.
2) Operate binder and note the rate of cutting.
3) Learn to shock the grain properly so it will not fall down or blow over.
4) Note the number of men required behind the binder.
5) Determine the cost of cutting and shocking per acre.
6) Later, when grain is ready for threshing, load grain on rack and haul to threshing outfit.
7) Pitch grain from rack onto threshing feed table.
8) Note each operation that takes place in the threshing machine, from the time the grain bundles are on the feed table until the grain is weighed.

9) Determine amount of grain produced per acre.
10) Make a summary of the cost of each operation in producing an acre of wheat, the total cost per acre, and the cost per bushel.

264. Harvesting Hay Crops. (Fig. 311.)

Requirements: To assist in the various operations of harvesting hay from cutting to baling. To determine the cost of each operation as accurately as possible, and, finally, to determine cost of producing a ton of hay.

FIG. 311. Using a hay loader.

Equipment Needed: Mower, rakes, loaders, balers and power.

Preliminary Instruction: Hay is a crop that has to be made while the sun shines. It must be cut at the right time, and cured to the right degree before it can be stacked, stored or baled. Handling of the hay depends much on the weather. The condition of the crop must also be considered. The proper time to cut alfalfa and other hay crops will be taken up in the study of crops.

Working Instructions:

1) See that mower is properly oiled and that the sickle is sharp. A steady team is essential to the best success in mowing.
2) Lay out land for cutting, size and shape depending on area to be mowed.
3) If ground is rough, adjust cutter bar so it will not cut into the ground.
4) Locate stumps or other obstructions in the field. This is to avoid accident.
5) Drive at a uniform speed. It is the slowing down which causes clogging in heavy grass.
6) Observe care in judging width of swath; cut a full width, but do not leave any uncut.
7) When a side-delivery rake is used, follow in same direction as with mower.
8) Ordinarily, rake after dew is off and before leaves have dried to a point where they shatter.
9) With a dump rake, practice care in dumping so the rick or wind-row of hay will be reasonably straight. This makes loading easier.
10) The loader is best used when the hay has been raked with a side-delivery. Hook the loader on back of wagon and drive straddle of the rick.
11) Keep one man on the wagon to distribute hay on load, and another to drive.
12) If slings and carrier are to be used in unloading, put on three or four slings to the load.
13) If fork and carrier are to be used, put on one sling at bottom of load to clean off the rack in unloading.

14) If hay is baled, carry out each operation in this work, feeding the hay, putting in dividing block, placing wires, tying, etc.
15) Determine as accurately as possible cost of harvesting hay by the ton.

265. Operating Household Equipment. (Fig. 312.)

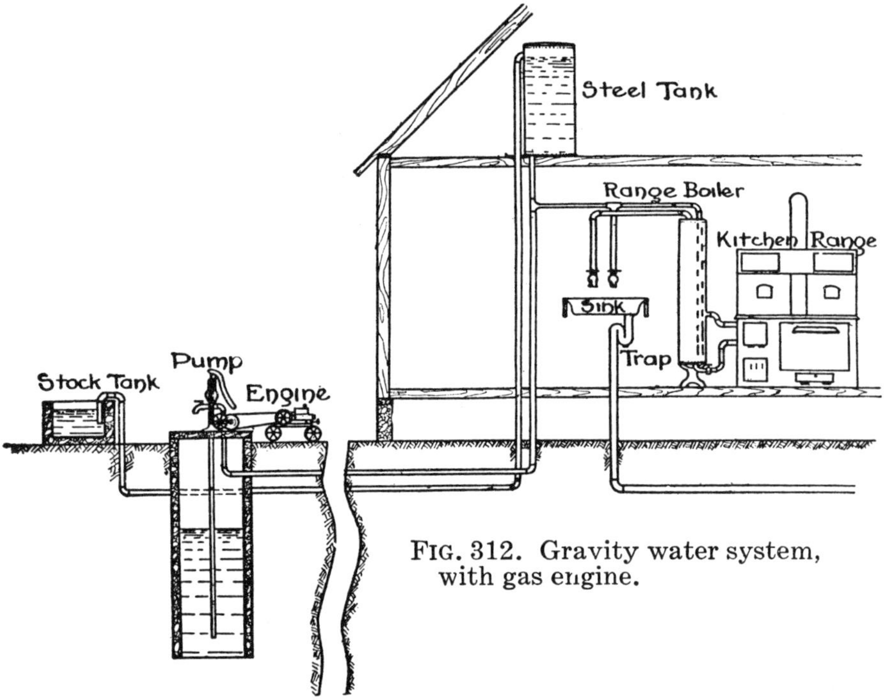

FIG. 312. Gravity water system, with gas engine.

Requirements: To operate each of the various machines about the household under the supervision of some one thoroly familiar with their use. To make a report on value of equipment in the home from the standpoint of time- and labor-saving.

Equipment Needed: The equipment for this project can be found in any modern farmhouse. It is simply a matter of the instructor or students obtaining permission to use equipment in the home as a laboratory.

Preliminary Instruction: So many farm homes are now being equipped with modern lighting, heating and water systems and sewage-disposal plants, that it is essential that every farm boy, and girl as well, become acquainted with the use of this equipment. The best way to become acquainted with its use is to use it. Follow instructions furnished by manufacturers.

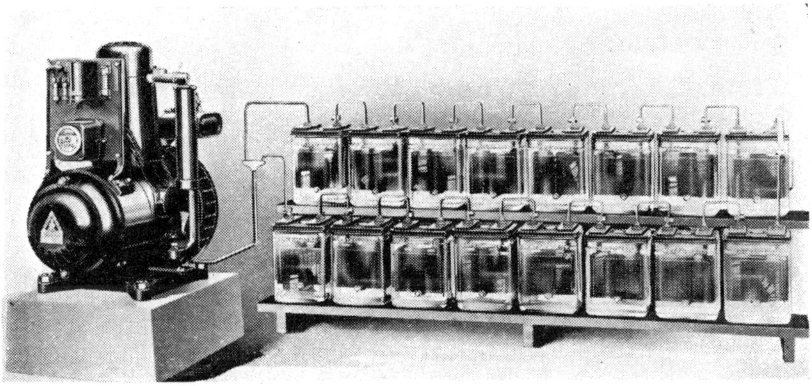

FIG. 312-*a* Farm lighting plant with storage battery.

Working Instruction:

1) Lubricate plant, put in fuel and fill radiator.
2) Start electric plant.
3) Turn lights off, and on.
4) Stop plant.
5) Turn lights on so they use power from storage battery.
6) Charge storage battery, note rate of charging.
7) Stop plant; note automatic stopping device.
8) Operate acetylene light plant.
9) Remove water and sludge from plant.
10) Put in a charge of carbide and fresh water.
11) Operate Blau gas plant.
12) Disconnect and replace a container of Blau gas.
13) Operate gasoline plant.

14) Fill tank with gasoline.
15) Crank up pressure motor or pump air into tank.
16) Fire a furnace and clean out all ashes and clinkers.
17) Note use of special devices for controlling draft and temperature.
18) Start and operate different water systems.
19) Note the difference in amount of work required when water is carried in and when it is pumped by machinery.
20) Study washing equipment.
21) Note difference in amount of time required to do the washing when a power washing machine is used and when a scrub board is used.

266. Gas Tractor Operation. (Fig. 313.)

Requirements: To become thoroly familiar with the method of operation of as many types of tractors as possible.

Tools and Materials Needed: Set of tools secured with tractor. Fuel, oil and extra spark plugs.

Preliminary Instructions: In operating and handling a tractor, one should be very careful to avoid breaking any parts. *Always be sure—then go ahead.* Do not attempt to start a tractor for the first time unless under the direction of *some one who knows.* Remember, that there is more danger in starting a tractor than in starting a small stationary engine, on account of danger of personal injury and of damage to the tractor and buildings. Remember, also, that you are handling an expensive machine when operating a tractor.

Working Instructions:

A. Getting tractor ready and starting it.

1) See that the tractor is completely lubricated.

2) See that the clutch works freely.
3) If brakes are provided, see that they are released.
4) Study the manipulation of the various controlling levers.

FIG. 313. Plowing with a tractor.

5) See that the gears are not in mesh.
6) See that the clutch is not engaged.
7) Turn on gasoline.
8) Open needle valve on carburetor.
9) *Retard the spark.*

10) Trip the impulse starter, if any.

11) Prime the motor with gasoline if weather is cold.

12) Crank the motor.

B. Tractor operation.

1) To start the tractor forward or reverse, (*a*) see that the pulley wheel is not revolving; (*b*) see that clutch is not engaged; (*c*) shift gears slowly—if they do not mesh, engage the clutch slightly, then disengage it—continue the process until gears mesh; (*d*) engage clutch and the tractor should run.

2) To stop tractor, (*a*) disengage clutch; (*b*) apply brake if necessary; (*c*) shift gears to neutral position.

3) Take tractor outside and practice starting and stopping. (*a*) Run forward a few yards in low, then stop; (*b*) reverse, run backward a few yards, then stop; (*c*) run forward a few yards in high, then stop; (*d*) turn the tractor around, as in plowing, and note the space required to turn it in.

4) Examine the tractor carefully and see that it is in perfect condition. Clean off dust or dirt.

5) Drive tractor back into building under supervision of some one who has had experience.

C. If possible, make study of a tractor while plowing in the field, and obtain the following information:

1) Number of plow bottoms.

2) Size and type of plow.

3) Length of furrows.

4) Width of furrows.

5) Depth of furrows.

6) Time required to plow a furrow.

7) Time required for turning.

8) Kind and condition of soil.
9) Acres plowed per hour.
10) Acres plowed per ten-hour day.
11) Fuel used and cost per ten-hour day.
12) Fuel cost per acre.
13) Lubricant used and cost per ten-hour day.
14) Lubricant cost per acre.
15) Labor cost per ten-hour day.
16) Labor cost per acre.
17) Depreciation cost per acre.
18) Interest on investment per acre.
19) Repair cost per acre.
20) Total cost per acre.

Assume the following condition with reference to a one-man outfit—operator cost, 50 cents per hour; 10 per cent depreciation on original cost of outfit; interest on investment at 6 per cent; cost of repairs, 4 per cent; all three charged to 100 days' service.

D. Write a report on this exercise, giving the information outlined under *A*, *B* and *C* and also:

1) Name of tractor.
2) Where manufactured.
3) Rated brake H. P. and drawbar H. P.
4) Number of cylinders in motor.
5) Arrangement of cylinders.
6) Make and type of carburetor.
7) Make and type of magneto.
8) System of lubrication.
9) Method of cooling.
10) Describe the clutch and transmission system.

CHAPTER XXIX

PROJECTS IN FARM MACHINERY REPAIR

267. The Proper Time for Checking Up Needed Repairs. The repair and adjustment of machinery is best carried on during the winter months when the weather is not suitable for outdoor work. Especially is this true of the repairs; the final adjustment must often be done after the machine is taken into the field.

It is best to go over a machine carefully when the work is finished for the season and tag all broken or worn parts. By so doing, the work of putting the machine in condition for field use is much easier. One is always more familiar with the condition of the machine just after using it than nearly a year later when it is being taken into the field the first time for the season. When worn and broken parts are not tagged the year before, a careful inspection is very essential. This part of the work should be done some weeks before the actual repair work is to be done and a longer time before the machine is needed in the field. This will give a chance to order parts needed, which often cannot be obtained from the local dealer. This work is best done in the school shop where there are plenty of tools and material. Many students can bring old implements in from the home farm for overhauling. Gas engines can be cleaned up, valves ground, and new piston rings put in place, the cutter bar on the mower can be straightened and the sickle sharpened, and other jobs can be done, a few of which are outlined merely to suggest the possibilities along this line. Such work is of immediate value in putting the machinery in repair, and the practice is of untold value to every student who later is to farm for himself.

The projects in this chapter are arranged in six groups according to the general type of machine. Additional minor groups might be added, but these are the machines in which all farmers are interested: First, tillage machinery; second,

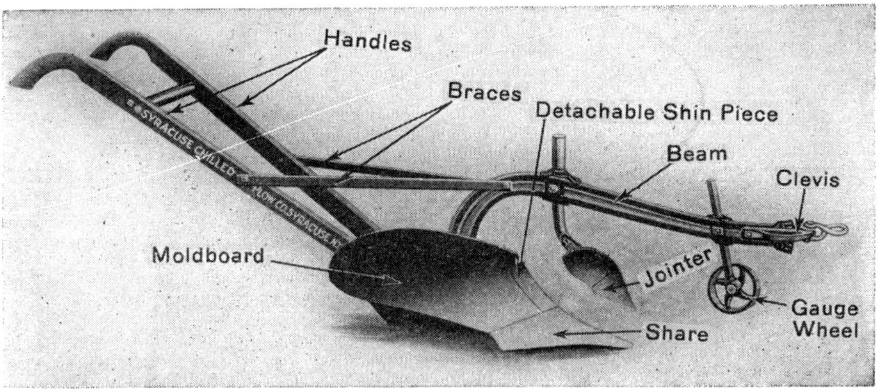

FIG. 314. Walking plow.

planting machinery; third, fertilizer distributors; fourth, harvesting machinery; fifth, belt-driven machinery; sixth, stationary engines and tractors. Projects in the repair of only one or two machines in each group are outlined.

268. Repair and Adjustment of Tillage Machinery. (Fig. 314.)

Requirements: To repair and adjust ready for field use the chief tillage machines, including plows, harrows, rollers and cultivators.

Tools Needed: It is well to have access to a complete set of shop tools. The exact number of tools required will be determined by the repairs needed.

Preliminary Instruction: The plow is the principal implement in the preparation of the seed bed. Because it is simple, it is often neglected and used very inefficiently. Plows not cared for are hard to operate, and a poor job of work is the result. The same principle holds true to a greater or less extent with all other tillage machinery.

269. Repairing a Walking Plow. (Fig. 315.)

1) Share—Badly-worn cast-iron shares must be renewed;

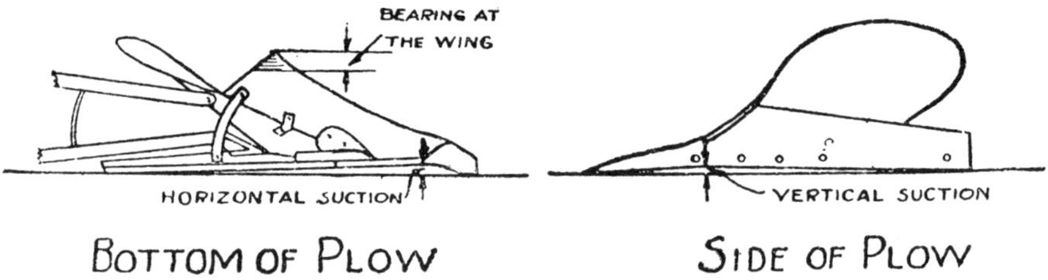

FIG. 315. Detail showing horizontal and vertical suction.

steel shares may be sharpened. Provide bearing at wing of 3/4″ for 10″ bottom to 1-1/4″ for 16″ bottom, and vertical suction of 1/8″ and horizontal suction of 1/8″ to 1/4″, as shown in figure.

2) Landside—If heel is detachable and worn, renew entire landside.

3) Moldboard—See that moldboard is well bolted to frog. If badly worn, renew.

4) Bracing—Tighten all bolts and brace rods.

5) Handles—See that handles are tight and rigid thruout.

6) Beam—See that beam is bolted tightly to the frog. If a steel beam, be sure it is not sprung.

7) Jointer—Renew or sharpen the jointer. Bolt tightly to beam.

8) Gauge Wheel—Renew bearings if badly worn. Bolt standard rigidly to the beam. Adjust to proper height.

270. Walking Plow Adjustment.

1) Depth of Furrow—Raise or lower clevis hitch vertically. For variable soil conditions, regulate by changing wheel gauge.
2) Width of Furrow—Change the clevis hitch in a horizontal position. Position of beam may be adjusted on some plows. It is usually changed to accommodate a different number of horses.
3) Handles—Change height to suit operator.
4) Jointer—Set so its point is just above the point of the share, slightly to the landside of the shin and 1-1/2″ to 2″ deep into the soil.
5) Hitch—Plow runs best when hitched to form a straight line from a point on moldboard 2″ from shin thru the hitch at beam clevis to a point midway between the tug rings at harness. A proper hitch means easy operation and less draft for the team.

271. Sulky and Gang Plows. (Fig. 316.)

1) Wheel Bearings—If worn, put in new bearings when possible. Clean thoroly, repack with heavy grease and make adjustments.
2) Frame Beam and Frog—Tighten all bolts. Straighten any part of frame that is twisted.
3) Levers—Tighten all connections, take up lost motion, straighten levers, replace new springs.
4) Share—Sharpen or replace with new share.
5) Landside—Renew entire landside if badly worn. Renew heel when provided.
6) Rolling Coulter—Clean bearings and oil. Tighten standard rigidly to frame.

272. Adjusting Sulky or Gang Plow.

1) Depth—Change depth by lowering bottom in the frame.

2) Width of Cut—Change hitch on frame, change landing of furrow wheel.

3) Jointer—Adjust as on a walking plow.

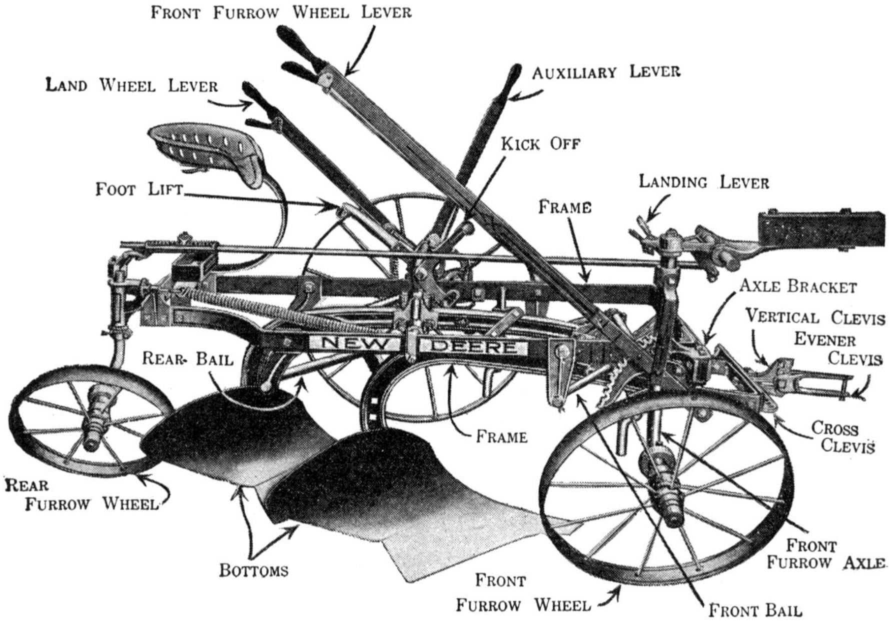

FIG. 316. Gang plow.

4) Rolling Coulter—If used with a jointer, set ahead of it. If used without jointer, adjust to the position of jointer when it is used alone and about one-half the depth of furrow, depending on the soil.

5) Wheels—Adjust land wheel to run straight to the front. Give the front and rear furrow wheels a slight lead from the land. Set rear wheel 1″ to 2″ outside of landside of plow.

6) Hitch—Point of hitch can be changed to take more or less land; and so the load is carried by wheels.

273. Repair of Peg-Toothed Harrow. (Fig. 317.)

1) Frames—Straighten all bent parts and tighten bolts.
2) Teeth—Adjust to uniform depth. Re-sharpen worn teeth, and renew lost ones.
3) Levers—Straighten all levers, renew worn parts and tighten connections

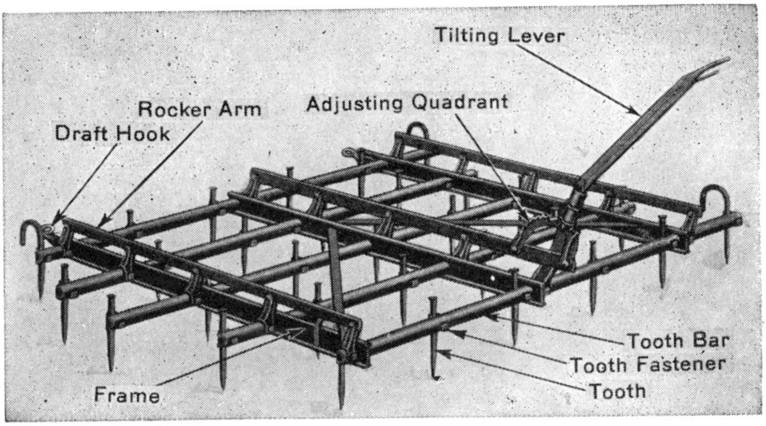

FIG. 317. Peg-toothed harrow.

4) Draft Connections—Renew if badly worn. Straighten if bent.

274. Repairing a Disc Harrow. (Figs. 318 and 318-*a*.)

1) Frame—See that all bolts are tight and all braces are straight and rigid.
2) Bearings—Clean out bearings by washing with kerosene. Replace if worn, pack grease cups and see that grease gets to bearings.
3) Discs—Sharpen discs on regular sharpener or on emery.
4) Gang Bolts—See that gang bolts are straight and the discs are tight on bolts so they will not wobble.
5) Bumpers—Adjust so they carry end thrust.

6) Scrapers—Replace if badly worn. See that they come in contact with disc without causing undue friction.
7) Snubbing Blocks—Adjust so gangs run level.
8) Levers—Straighten bent levers. Replace worn parts.
9) Draft Connection—If worn, renew.

Adjustment—Change angle of disc to increase or de-

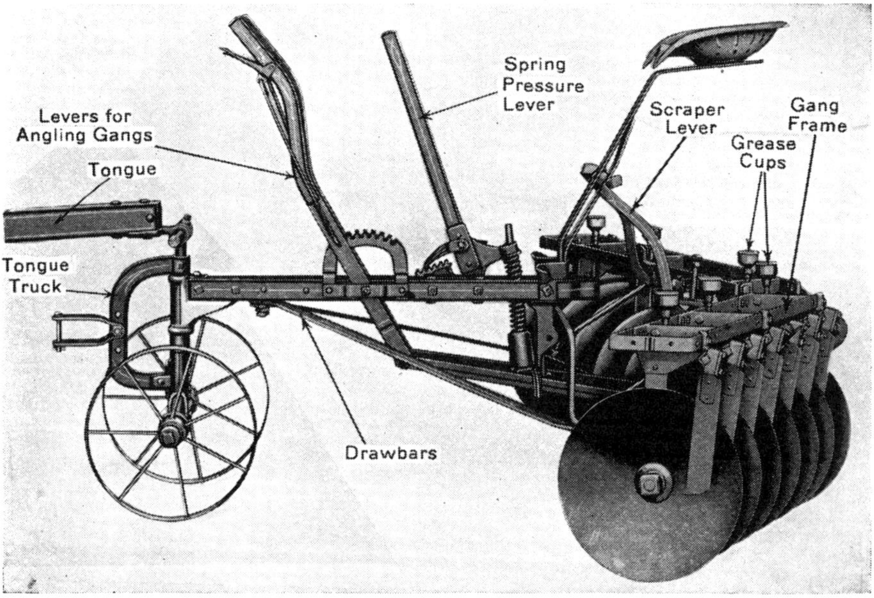

FIG. 318. Disc harrow.

crease amount of suction. Weighting is sometimes resorted to in hard ground to increase the depth.

275. Repair and Adjustment of Planting Machinery.

Requirements: To repair and adjust ready for field use planting machinery such as used in the particular locality. A corn planter and drill are outlined.

Preliminary Instruction: Every planting machine should be in first-class repair when taken into the field, to avoid a poor stand due to its poor condition.

276. Repairing a Grain Drill. (Fig. 319.)

1) Grain Feeds—Clean out old grain and dirt. Examine grain feed cup or fluted cylinder, and grain cells. Renew badly-worn or broken parts. Examine method of changing rate of seeding.

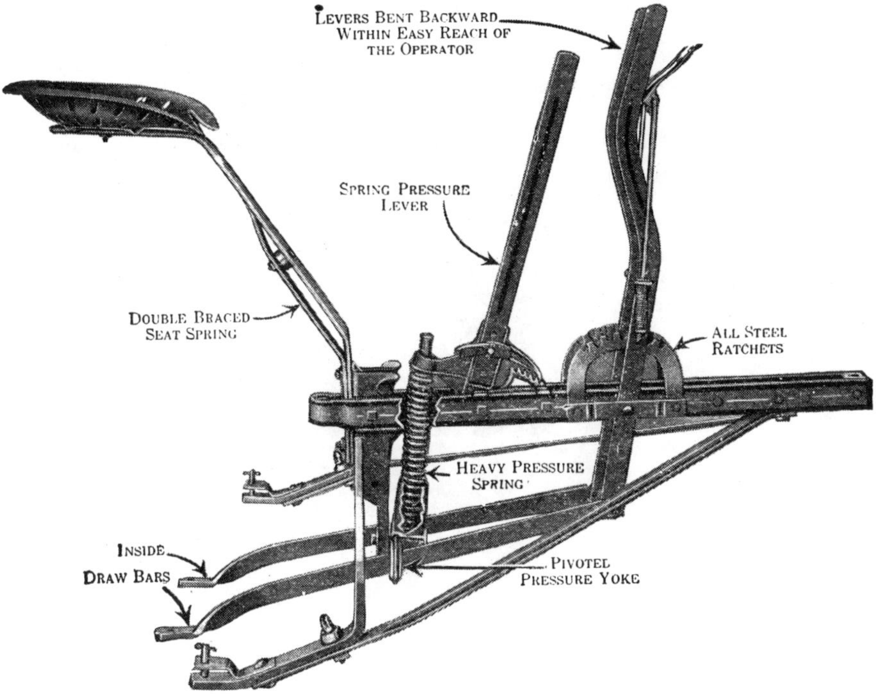

Fig. 318-*a*. Details of construction of disc harrow.

2) Chains, Drive Shaft and Gears—Trace power from wheels thru chains, shaft and gears to feeding device. See that there is no lost motion due to loose, broken or worn parts.

3) Openers—Sharpen opener if dull. If disc opener, examine the bearings and replace if badly worn. See that they are properly lubricated. Adjust springs so enough pressure is on openers.

4) Seed Tubes—Test seed tubes to see that they do not clog easily.

5) Wheels—If wheels are of wood and are dried out so that the tire is loose on the rim, they should be soaked in water until swelled tight. The pawls in the hub are an important part of wheels to give positive drive. See that the pawls engage and start the seeding device as soon as the wheels turn.

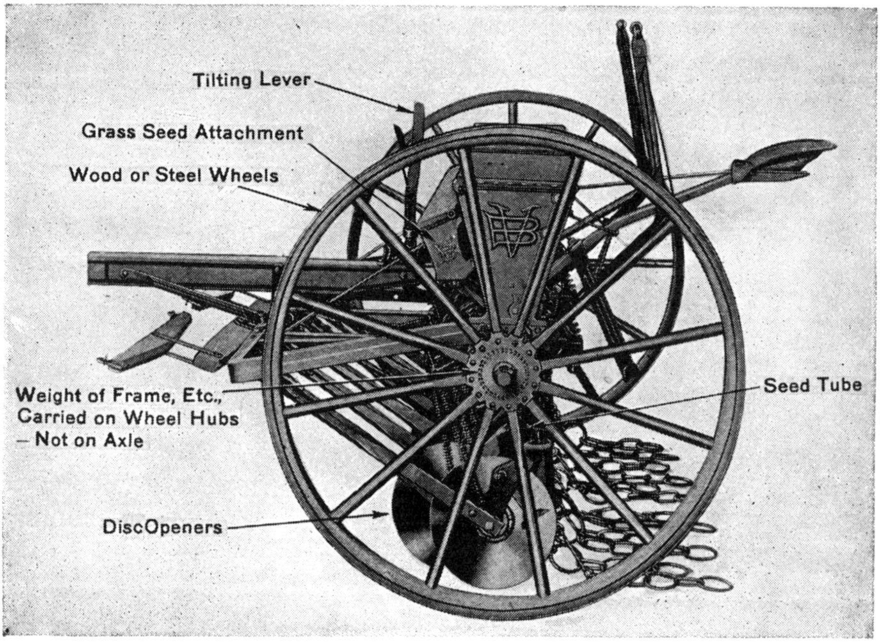

FIG. 319. Grain drill.

6) Frame and Levers—See that all bolts are drawn up tight and the frame is rigid. Examine levers and see that they are straight and function properly.

7) Attachments—See that attachments such as surveying device and devices for setting rate of seeding are tight. Check their accuracy if they are to be depended upon.

8) Miscellaneous—See that all covering devices, hitch, braces, etc., are in place and properly adjusted.

277. Adjusting a Grain Drill. Calibration—The principal adjustment on a grain drill is the one for accuracy of planting when the indicator is set at different positions on the scale. The adjustment is accomplished by calibrating the machine. The drill must be calibrated for each kind of grain. The method is as follows:

Set the drill on stands or saw horses so that the wheels clear the ground. Put the grain in the hopper, place the indicator for certain rate of seeding per acre, put paper bags under each of the spouts, throw in the clutch and you are ready to begin. Turn the drive wheel thru 100 revolutions. Weigh the seed caught under each spout. By measuring the circumference of drive wheel in feet and multiplying by 100, the number of turns, the distance traveled is found. Multiply this by the width of seeded strip in feet and the area is obtained. Knowing the area and the total pounds of seed drilled, the rate of drilling is easily obtained. By comparing the rate from test with the actual setting of indicator, the accuracy of the machine is determined. By making several tests at different settings of indicator, the proper adjustment for a certain rate of planting can be established. Unless a drill is carefully tested, the rate of planting is not definitely known, due to the inaccuracy of the indicating device.

278. Repairing Corn Planter. (Fig. 320.)

1) Seed Box and Plates—See that a full set of plates is available and suitable for planting seed at hand. Examine the parts in bottom of seed box and the plates to see that they are not worn. Renew parts as needed.

2) Sprockets, Chains, Gears and Clutch—Trace the power from wheels thru axle, chain, sprockets, drive shaft and clutch to the plate. See that there is no lost motion due to loose, worn or broken parts.

3) Openers—See 3 under Drills.

FIG. 320. Corn planter.

4) Valves—Examine valves in feed shank and see that they function properly when the drive wheels are turned.

5) Frame and Levers—See 6 under Drills.

6) Check Wire and Trip—See that the check wire is free from kinks and in good condition. See that the trip works.

7) Miscellaneous—Examine marker, hitch, etc., and see that they are in good condition.

279. Adjustment of Corn Planter.

1) Depth—Adjust for proper depth by setting the tongue; also, by means of the lever, just in front of the seat.
2) Width—The width of rows can be adjusted by shifting the boxes and shoes as a unit on the frame. Shift the position of the wheels on the axle and move the wheel scrapers accordingly.
3) The Drop—the drop is changed by moving the lever to point indicating two, three or four grains per hill.
4) Drilling—Most planters can be adjusted to drill by opening the valves and holding the trip back. A lever is often provided so that the change to drilling can be made from the seat.
5) Accuracy—Proper plates should be selected for the particular seed and the accuracy of drop tested before the planter is taken into the field. If the plates are of the type where one kernel is selected at a time, try out several by taking some kernels of corn and fitting them into the spaces. If they do not fit—are too tight or too loose—try other plates until one is found that fits fairly well. Place this plate in position in box, partially fill it with the corn to be planted, place the planter on a stand or saw horses, and you are ready for test. Set the lever to position of number of grains to be dropped at each hill. Trip clutch and turn drive wheel; catch the grains as they drop out at each hill and count them. Trip for 100 hills; if lever is set for three grains, it should test at least 90 per cent accuracy. Out of 100 hills, if there are 60 threes, 30 twos, 8 ones and 2 fours, a plate should be selected with slightly larger openings. The correct selection of

plate is very important from a standpoint of accuracy in planting. The careful grading of seed and proper selection of plate are big factors in securing a good test.

280. Repair and Adjustment of Fertilizer Distributers.

Requirements: To repair and adjust ready for field use the principal fertilizer distributers, including manure spreader, straw spreader, fertilizer and lime drills (Fig. 321).

Preliminary Instruction: The manure spreader is a machine that is found on most farms where there is stock. Straw spreaders, fertilizers and limestone drills are becoming more common thruout the country.

281. Repairing Manure Spreader. (Fig. 321.)

1) Box and Apron—Tighten all bolts in box so that it is rigid. Examine apron for broken places or damaged chain. Replace broken or worn parts. See that the rollers that carry the apron turn easily and offer little resistance.
2) Frame—Tighten all loose parts on the frame of spreader and renew all broken parts.
3) Beater—See that bearings are in first-class condition. Tighten the bars and see that the teeth are straight and firmly in place. Replace all broken teeth.
4) Driving Mechanism—Examine carefully the drive chains, gears and sprockets that transmit the power from the drive wheel to the beater and to the apron. Weak parts should be replaced. Adjust chains to proper tightness. See that all bolts are drawn up tight.
5) Wheels—Take off drive wheels and examine the pawls. Examine bearings on rear axle and on trucks.

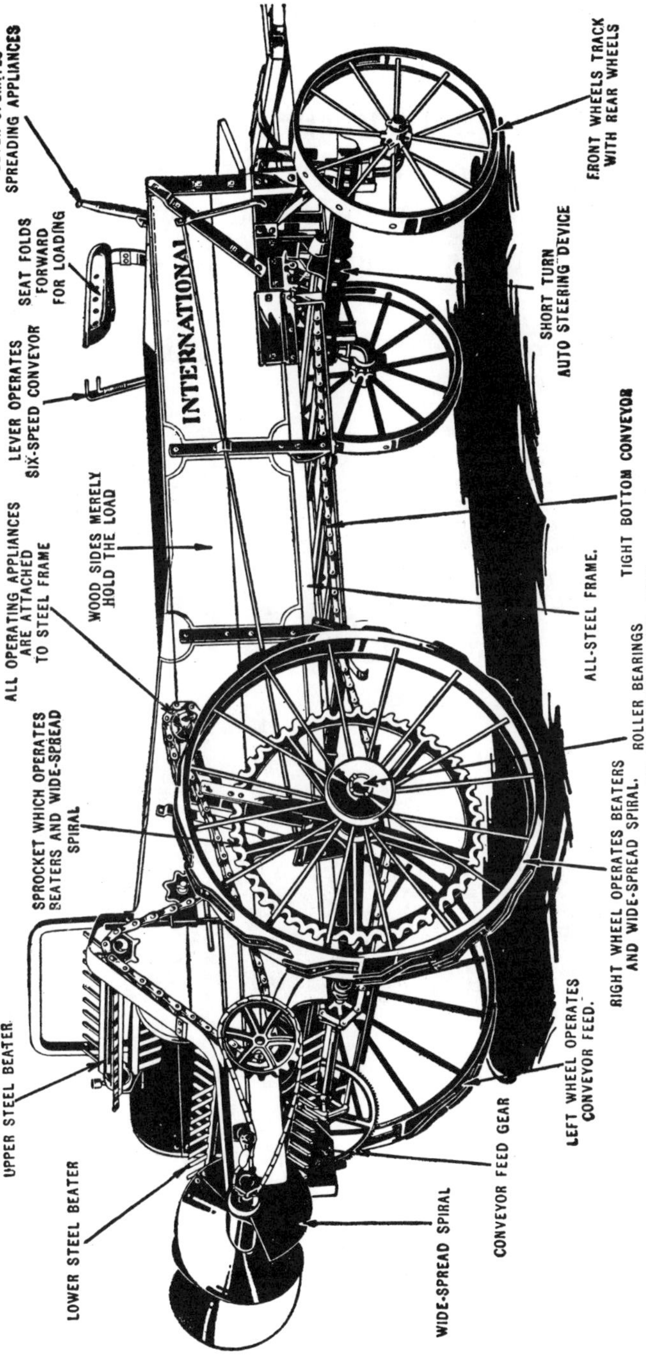

FIG. 321. Manure spreader.

6) Miscellaneous—Straighten levers and connecting rods. Tighten all nuts and put in new bolts where needed.

282. Repairing and Adjusting Straw Spreader. (Fig. 322.) Most straw spreaders are either an attachment for a manure spreader or an attachment for a wagon.

1) Tighten all chains by adjusting idlers, and renew worn links.
2) See that sprockets are centered on wagon wheel.

FIG. 322. Straw spreader.

3) Go over entire feeder, tighten bolts and renew broken parts.
4) Straighten levers and see that they work easily.
5) Follow instructions of manufacturer in making adjustment.

283. Repairing a Lime and Fertilizer Sower.

1) See that feeding device is free from old lime or fertilizer and rust.
2) Renew badly-worn gears, sprockets or chains.
3) See that adjusting levers work properly.
4) Examine wheels and axles.
5) Repair box or hopper if needed.
6) Renew feeding device if badly worn or broken.

284. Repair and Adjustment of Harvesting Machinery.

Requirements: To repair and adjust a mower, a binder and other harvesting machines such as are used locally. The mower and binder are outlined, as they represent the two most common harvesting machines thruout the country. The tools needed are the same as in previous projects.

Preliminary Instructions: To avoid loss at harvest time, all equipment should be in a first-class condition. Harvest season is a time when delay may mean a great loss. So every farmer should realize the importance of having such equipment ready. The best time to inspect harvest machinery is just at the end of the harvest season rather than the beginning. If the inspection has been properly carried out and parts ordered to take the place of broken and worn ones, the work of repair will be very simple.

285. Repairing a Mower. (Fig. 323.) Place the machine where there is plenty of room and where all sides are accessible.

Working Instructions:

1) Align Cutter Bar—Block tongue to normal position of

running with inside shoe just floating. Test alignment by stretching a string from center of pitman bracing thru center of knife head bracing to outer side of cutter bar. If properly aligned, the outside end of knife will lead string by 1″ for five-foot bars and 1-3/8″ to 1-1/2″ for

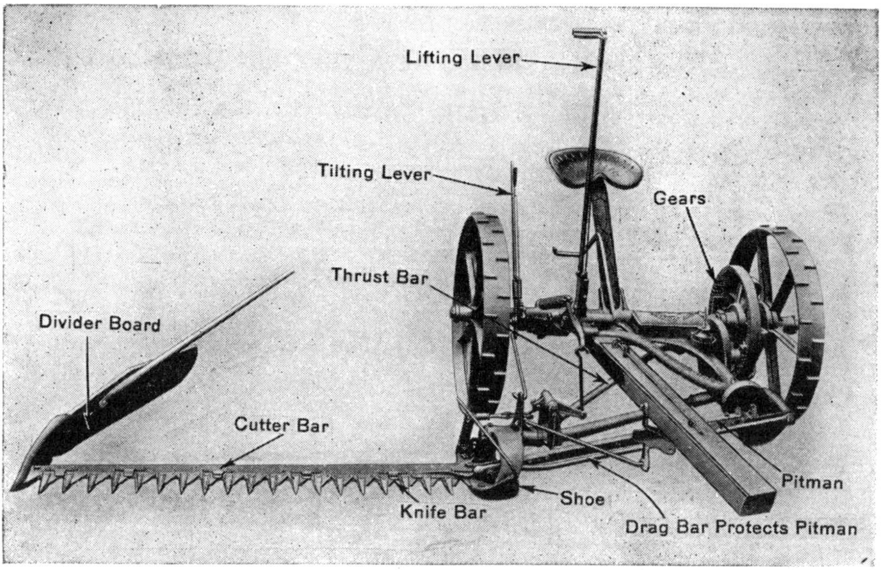

FIG. 323. Mower.

six-foot bars. If not properly aligned, examine machine for special provision for alignment and make proper adjustment.

2) Aligning Guards—Remove blade and sight along guards, or use a straight-edge to detect the ones that are high and the ones that are low. Drive guards that are out of alignment back into place by a sharp blow with a hammer.

3) Adjusting Cutter-Bar Clips—Examine knife bar to see that it is straight; then put it in place. The knife should have little play, and the clips should fit snugly. Adjust

all clips by tapping each with hammer until it begins to tighten; then loosen it, and begin on the next. When all are adjusted, tighten them.

4) Putting on New Guards—Bolt new guards in place where old ones are damaged. If the new guard brings the ledger plate too high, remedy this by putting pieces of tin between the guard and the bar.

5) Shoes—Examine both the outside and inside shoes on cutter bar. If parts are badly worn, replace them. See that they are adjusted for proper height.

6) Knife Sections—Broken or badly-worn knife sections can be easily removed by placing the vertical edge of bar on an anvil or heavy piece of iron, with a square, straight corner. Strike the back of the section with a hammer, making it cut the rivet off. Use soft steel rivets of proper size for putting on new sections. Test the knife to see that sections center properly. The sections are properly centered if each is directly under a guard when the pitman is at either end of its stroke. Examine to see if a centering device is provided on machine. When steel pitmans are used, they are usually made adjustable for length. This makes centering easy.

7) Pitman—Adjust both the knife head and wrist pin bearing to secure the least amount of lost motion.

8) Gears—If badly worn, make adjustment so they will work properly where possible. If gears are badly worn, replace with new ones.

9) Bearings—Examine all bearings for wear. Free them of all grit, dirt and vegetable matter. Lubricate all parts with new oil.

10) Drive Wheels—Take up all end play by adjustable collar or washers. Examine pawls for wear. Some are reversible, making possible longer use. Renew springs if weak.
11) Miscellaneous—Tighten all nuts, straighten levers, and see that all bolts, cotter keys, etc., are in place. Replace worn parts where needed.

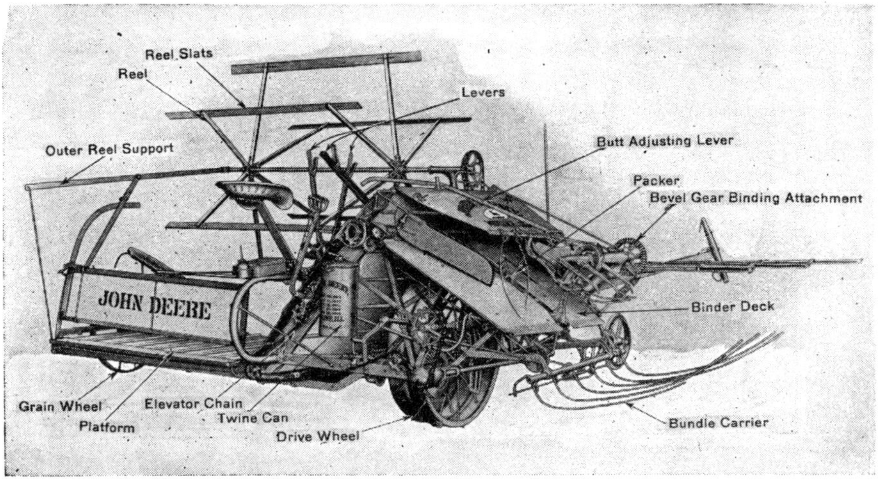

FIG. 324. Grain binder.

286. Repairing and Adjusting a Binder. (Fig.324.) Practically all the suggestions for the mower also apply to the binder with the following additions:

1) Canvases—See that all rollers work easily, are in good repair, and are properly aligned. Anything wrong with the rollers will cause trouble with the canvases. Test the frame of the machine (either by means of a square or by measuring the diagonals) to see that the canvases are properly squared to it. If canvases are not squared, trouble will result. Replace all broken slats and straps on canvases with new ones.

2) Chains and Sprockets—Replace badly-worn or broken sprockets. See that they are aligned by sighting along the face. Adjust chain tightener so there will not be too much play.
3) Reel—Renew slats if broken. Examine bearings. If they are badly worn, renew them. Take up all lost motion in reel levers.
4) Gears and Bearings—Examine all gears for wear, and if badly worn, replace with new ones. Adjust to mesh where possible. Renew bearings where badly worn.
5) Binder Attachment—The binding attachment is the most complicated device on the binder. Replace all broken or badly-worn parts. See that the tying device is timed to work properly in tying bundles. Use instructions for particular machine furnished by manufacturer.

287. Belt-Driven Machinery.

Requirements: To repair and adjust at least one belt-driven machine. It may be a threshing machine as outlined, or another type of machine. The feed mills, silage cutters and corn shellers, all come in this class. The tools needed are the same as in previous projects.

Preliminary Instruction: A separator that has not been carefully overhauled will cause loss of time and waste of grain. This is a job that should be done some weeks before the threshing season is on, in order that if there is need of any parts, they can be secured and installed without causing a delay. The same general principles as outlined for overhauling a separator apply to other belt-driven machines. It is always a good idea to study carefully the instruction books furnished by the manufacturer before beginning to repair or adjust any part of a belt-driven machine. The points suggested here under working instruction can then be carried out with a much greater degree of intelligence.

288. Repairing a Grain Separator. (Fig. 325.)

Working Instruction:

1) Cylinder—Renew all badly-worn, bent or otherwise damaged teeth. Tighten all loose teeth, and see that the cylinder is firmly keyed to the shaft. If cylinder bearings are worn, they can be made to fit snugly by removing shims. If the bearings are badly worn, they should be re-babbitted or new bushings put in. (See instructions on babbitting at end of this exercise.) Examine the shafts for rough spots. If necessary, smooth them up with a fine file and emery cloth. After the cylinder shaft and bearing are in first-class condition, the cylinder should be carefully balanced before the bearings are adjusted. This is necessary when a number of new teeth have been added. To balance the cylinder, provide two saw horses or other suitable stands to support the ends of the cylinder shaft. Level up the supports and place on them pieces of smooth steel, on which the cylinder is to rest. Place the cylinder on supports and allow it to revolve. Mark the top of cylinder where it came to rest and roll it over again. If it comes to rest in the same position as before, it will indicate that the opposite side is heavy. Provision is made on some cylinders to counterbalance this by driving slugs of lead into the holes in the ends of cylinder. Where no provision is made, new teeth can be put in on the opposite side, or wedges can be driven in under

the center band. When cylinder is put back in place, adjust to the bearings so there is no lost motion. It should make a snug fit, but should not bind. Avoid too much end play. The thickness of wrapping paper at each end of cylinder will be sufficient.

2) Concaves—Replace badly-worn concave teeth. Be careful to avoid breaking the concave bars. Adjust the concaves so the teeth are centered as far as the cylinder teeth are concerned. If the concave and cylinder teeth come closer together than 1/8″, cracking of grain is liable to result. Teeth that are out of line or bent should be brought back into place by the use of a hammer. Inspect the device for raising and lowering the concaves. If badly worn, put in new parts.

3) Separating Grates—See that all bolts are tight and there is no loss motion. Straighten all bent rods or bars. See that all parts work without undue friction.

4) Feeding Attachment—Inspect the frame for looseness, badly-worn or split parts. Tighten all bolts and screws. Tighten the carrier chain; see that slats or canvas is in good repair. Examine band cutter knife; replace it if it is broken or badly worn. See that all bolts are tight and bearings are in good condition on retarder and shaking feed bottom.

4) Beaters and Apron—See that there is no play or lost motion in the beater. If the blades are wood, replace those that are split or badly worn. See that there are no rough surfaces on the blades. See that apron or check board works freely.

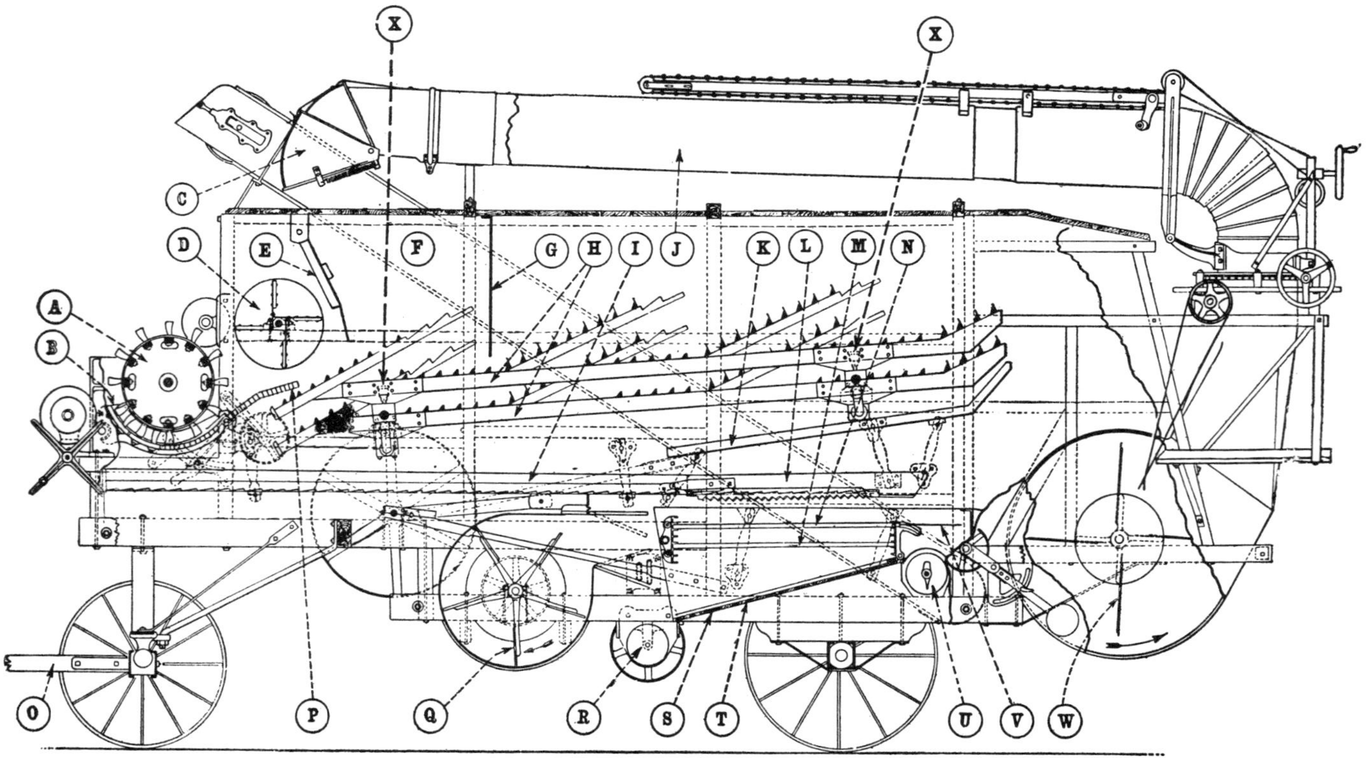

FIG. 325. Sketch of grain separator.

A—Cylinder; *B*—Concaves; *C*—Wind-stacker hood; *D*—Beater; *E*—Check apron; *F*—Elevator; *G*—Check apron; *H*—Straw-racks; *I*—Grain pan; *J*—Straw chute; *K*—Return pan; *L*—Chaffer; *M*—Adjustable sieve; *N*—Shoe chaffer; *O*—Tongue; *P*—Grate; *Q*—Fan; *R*—Grain auger; *S*—Screen door; *T*—Weed screen; *U*—Tailings auger; *V*—Tail rake; *W*—Wind-stacker fan; *X*—Grease cups for straw-rack boxes

5) Racks—Inspect the racks for broken slats. See that the bearings are tight. Replace or adjust worn links and pitmans.
6) Conveyor—See that all parts are tight to avoid wasting grain. Renew metal if it is badly rusted.
7) Screens—See that frames are in good shape. If screens are damaged, renew them. Examine the shoe to see that the castings that carry the screens are in good condition and fastened to the shoe. See that bearings and pitmans are in good shape.
8) Fan—Inspect the fan housing, the bearings and the blades. Replace worn parts where needed.
9) Grain Augers and Elevators—Examine the auger troughs and elevator housing, and all bearings. Replace badly-worn parts. See that the chain is in good condition; also, that the chain tightener is in good working order.
10) Stacker—See that fan, fan housing and bearings are in first-class shape.
11) See that all adjustments are made to insure efficient operation.

Note: Bushing can usually be secured to take care of badly-worn bearings on power-driven machines, but in some cases, babbitting must be resorted to. The following on babbitting will be of interest under such conditions:

289. Babbitting Machine Bearing Boxes. Machine bearings become loose with wear. If the bearings are made in two parts in the form of a split box, adjustments may be made to tighten the bearing until it is practically worn out. If the bearing is in one piece in the form of a solid box, little, if anything, can be done when it is worn to tighten it except to reline or refill it. The process of repairing a bearing by pouring in new metal is called babbitting.

Babbitt is a soft metal consisting of one part of copper, two parts antimony and twenty-two parts tin, melted together. Some of the cheaper grades of babbitt contain some lead and, sometimes, a little zinc.

290. Babbitting a Solid Bearing. Chip or melt out all of the old babbitt and clean out the retaining holes. Warm the box to prevent the babbitt cooling too rapidly when it is poured. This may be done by holding the bearing in the fire or by placing a hot iron against it. Clean the shaft and place it in line in the bearing, first wrapping one thickness of writing paper about the shaft just the length of the bearing, and fastening it by winding twine about it in a spiral shape. The paper will prevent too tight a bearing, and the space occupied by the twine will form oil grooves. Close up the bearing at each end by placing a heavy cardboard over the shaft at each end and puttying up the holes or filling them with soft clay. Reserve the oil hole to pour in the babbitt, or, if it is too small, drive a wooden plug into it clear to the shaft and form a funnel-shaped opening at one end of the bearing with clay.

Heat the babbitt in an iron ladle until it burns or chars a stick, and gently pour it, if necessary, by means of a funnel, thru the hole reserved for the purpose, first making a few vent holes thru the end protections with a wire. When the babbitt is set, and before it thoroly cools, remove the end protections, the plug that fills the oil hole and the shaft. Wipe out the hole formed by the shaft to remove the burned twine and any foreign matter, and the bearing will be ready for use when the babbitt is cold.

291. Babbitting a Split-Box Bearing. Place the shaft in the lower part of the box which forms the bearing and block it in position. Place liners on the box to touch the shaft the full length, first cutting two or three notches on the liner next to the shaft thru which the babbitt can run from the upper half of the box to the lower. Bolt the top part of the box in position, stop the ends and pour the babbitt. When the babbitt is set, drive a cold chisel between the boxes to break the babbitt formed in the notches of the liner, bevel the edges of the babbitt next to the shaft, and cut oil grooves in the babbitt of each half of the box with a diamond point or round nose chisel. These grooves should cross on the oil hole and run to the ends of the box to form carriers for oil.

A split box may also be babbitted by pouring the babbitt on the shaft when placed in the lower half of the box only. When the babbitt reaches the level of the top of the half box, place the liners in position, then the upper half of the box, and pour it full.

292. Scraping a Babbitted Bearing. With the split bearing, it is nearly always necessary to fit the bearing to the shaft by scraping. This is done by coating the surface of the shaft with lampblack and oil, or Prussian blue, and adjusting it in the bearing; then revolve the shaft. Open the bearing and note if it formed a good contact with the shaft; if it only touched the shaft at spots, scraping is necessary. Scrape the high places in bearing with regular bearing scrapers or with a triangular file that has been ground for this purpose, until practically the entire surface of bearing is in contact with shaft.

293. Repair and Adjustment of a Motor. (Fig. 326.)

Requirements: To repair and adjust a gasoline engine, either a simple type or a tractor, truck or automobile engine. The tools needed are the same as in previous projects.

Preliminary Instructions: The gas engine is the most common type of mechanical motive power on the farm. Every boy needs to know how to make the simple repairs and adjustments, because the gas engine that is not in good adjustment will waste fuel, will develop only a fraction of its power, and will waste the time of the operator. First become thoroly familiar with the engine before trying to repair it. Study it carefully, analyze its troubles before trying to remedy them. In the work of dismantling and putting an engine in shape for operating, the workman must observe extreme care to avoid breaking or marring any part of the machine. Do not use pliers where a wrench should be used, nor a screw-driver where a cold chisel is best suited. Be careful not to tear or destroy the packing. Do not screw the coupling on fuel line too tight, as the threads are liable to be stripped. Clean all parts as they are removed. Place small parts, as nuts and screws, in a box provided for that purpose. Where timing gears are removed, see that they are marked so they will be meshed properly when re-assembled. Secure instruction book on engine as furnished by manufacturer.

294. Overhauling an Engine. The method of procedure will vary slightly with different engines, but the following steps will indicate the general procedure:

1) Disconnect the wiring.

2) Remove the magneto.
3) Remove the igniter block or spark plug.
4) Remove the cylinder head.
5) Scrape the carbon from the face of the cylinder head.

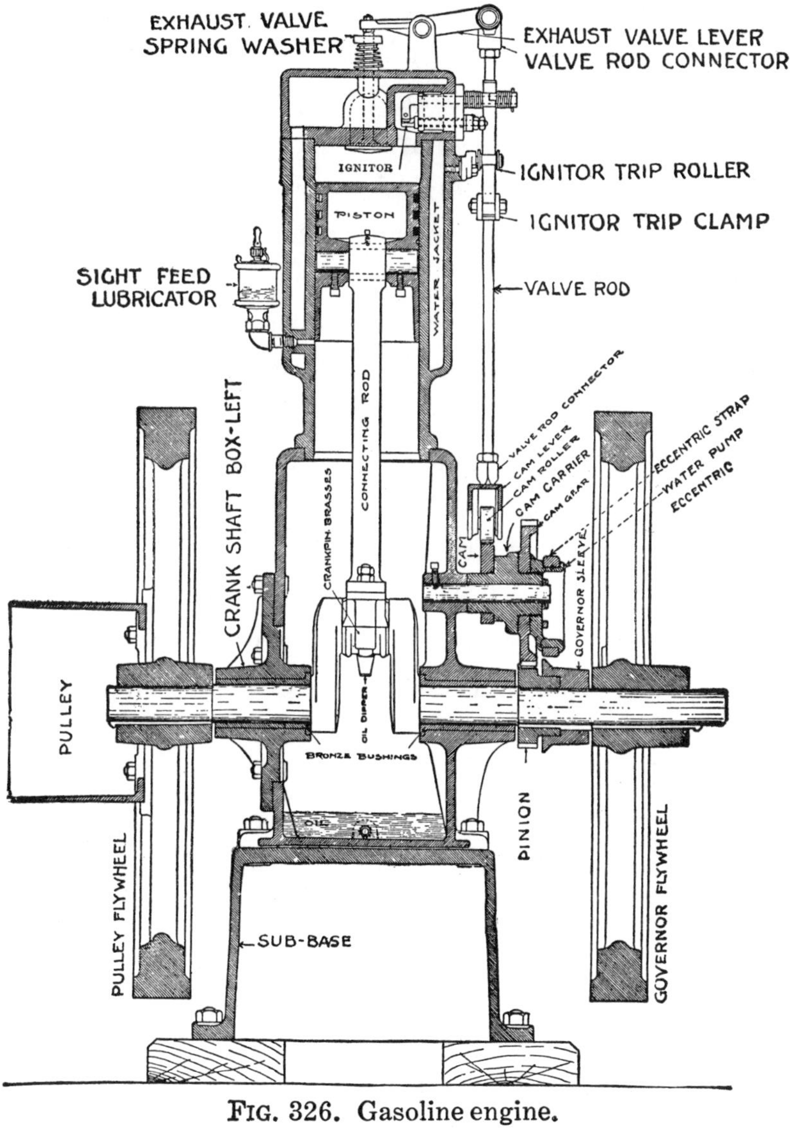

FIG. 326. Gasoline engine.

6) Remove the valves and free them from all carbon.
7) Note the valve seats to see if they are free from carbon and not pitted.
8) If valves are in poor condition, they should be ground as follows: (*a*) Apply a little coarse valve-grinding compound to the valve seat, put the valve in place and grind it by inserting the point of the screw-driver in the slot, or use a valve-grinding tool, and grind by revolving back and forth about one-fourth turn, exerting a little pressure. Lift the valve occasionally to reseat it. Continue the process until the rough surface on the valve is removed. (*b*) Apply a little fine valve-grinding compound to the valve seat and repeat the process as outlined under (*a*). Continue process of grinding until the valves are all seated. (*c*) Clean the valve and valve seat to prevent any compound from entering the cylinder.
9) Disconnect the connecting rod from the crank shaft, and remove the piston from cylinder. (*a*) Clean all carbon from the piston. (*b*) Examine all piston rings; note if any are stuck or broken. (*c*) If necessary to put on new rings, use three or four thin pieces of tin with which to slip on the rings. Rings are very brittle and must be handled with care.
10) Note the wall of the cylinder to see that it is not scored.
11) Remove all oiling devices and see that oil or grease passes thru to the points lubricated.
12) Examine crank-shaft bearings.
13) Remove governor. Examine the spring.
14) Remove push rods and lever.
15) Examine cam shaft and gears.

16) Disconnect pipe line from carburetor to fuel tank. See that it is not clogged.
17) Remove carburetor or mixing valve and examine the following points: (*a*) Type of air valve, if any; (*b*) how the gas is drawn to carburetor; (*c*) how it is controlled at the carburetor; (*d*) screw out the needle valve and note its condition.
18) Clean out any dirt or other material that may be collected in the cooling system.
19) Reassemble the engine in the reverse order in which it was dismantled.
20) Adjust the engine by timing the valves and the ignition and setting the governor for rated speed.

General Questions to Answer in Report on this Exercise:

1) Does the engine have high- or low-tension ignition?
2) Draw a diagram of the wiring.
3) Why is insulation provided on the wire?
4) Is the fixed or the movable electrode insulated on the igniter block? Why?
5) If a spark plug is used, draw a sketch showing its construction.
6) How far apart are the spark plug points?
7) Why are the points on the spark plug separated and those on the igniter block brought together?
8) Why is it necessary to clean the motor cylinder occasionally?
9) Why grind the valves?
10) What causes carbon to collect in the cylinder?
11) How is the carbon best removed?
12) What happens if a piston ring is broken or stuck?

13) What happens if the valves are not seating properly?
14) What happens if the oil line is stopped up?
15) What happens if bearings are too loose?
16) What happens when bearings are too tight?
17) What are shims?
18) What happens if the governor spring gets weak?
19) What happens if the governor sticks?
20) What is the result if the valve stem sticks?
21) What causes the valves to open too late or too early?
22) About when should the valves open and close on a small stationary engine?
23) What happens if the fuel pipe is partially clogged?
24) What is the effect when the air valve is closed?
25) What is the result if the carburetor is not fastened to the intake manifold with an air-tight joint?
26) The feed to carburetors on most tractors and automobiles is controlled by means of a float. What happens if the float becomes soaked full of gasoline? How remedied?
27) What is the effect of using dirty water in the cooling system?

PART VI

BELTS AND BELTING

CHAPTER XXX

KINDS OF BELTS AND BELT LACES

295. Methods of Connecting Machines. There are three common methods of connecting machines—(1) by shaft, known as direct-connected; (2) by gear wheels, the one on the driving machines being known as the driver and the one on the driven machine being known as the follower, and (3) by belts, in which case the names of the machines are those given when gears are used as connectors.

296. Four Kinds of Belts. There are four common forms of belts—chain, canvas, rubber and leather. Chain belts, except for slight wear in link joints, remain constant in length; hence, need no tightening as they grow old. The other three materials named, however, stretch, and, consequently, belts made from them need tightening from time to time to prevent their slipping. The usual method of tightening is to cut the belt, remove a piece and fasten the ends together.

Canvas, rubber and leather belts may be cemented together. However, the result with canvas belts is not very satisfactory. When rubber cement is used, a rubber belt, if not too old, may be cemented successfully. However, the method of fastening the ends of a belt is applicable principally to leather belts.

297. Cement Splice. The most satisfactory splice is one which keeps the belt at the joint the same in shape and general conditions as at any other point. Such a splice is made by squaring the ends (Fig. 327), and then carefully dressing the joining surface, as indicated in Fig. 328, making the thickness at the squared end as thin as possible — a feather edge.

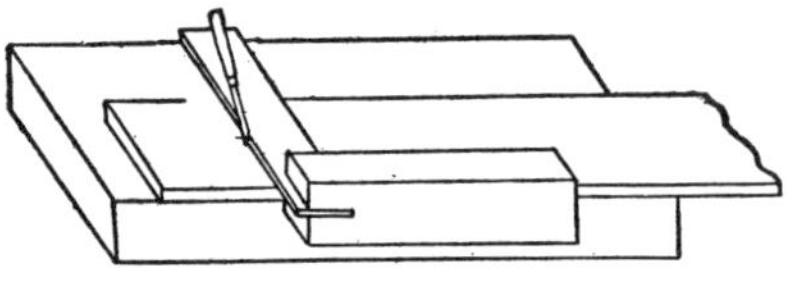

FIG. 327. Squaring a belt.

A cement splice can easily be made without removing belt from pulleys. Tighten belt with a belt clamp (Fig. 329), fitting it squarely on the belt.

The length of the splice should be 1″ greater than the width of the belt, up to 12″, which is regarded as the maximum length for splicing a belt, no matter how wide it is. When the clamp has pulled the belt to the desired tension, cut one end to make the lap 1″ longer than the width of the belt. Lay the end of the belt on a board, the end of the two coinciding, and plane the lap joint with a sharp, small plane until it has the shape shown in Fig. 328.

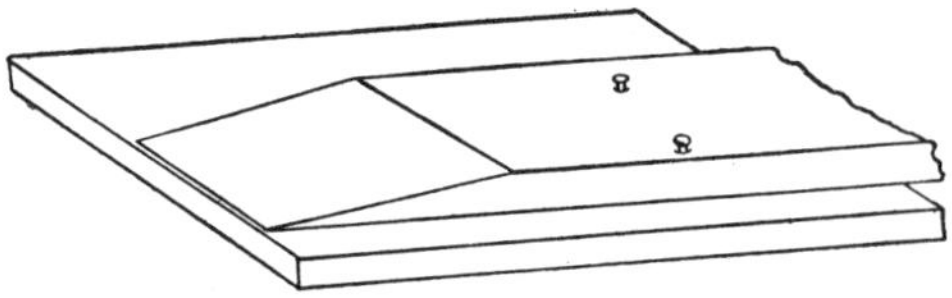

FIG. 328. Tapering for glue-joint.

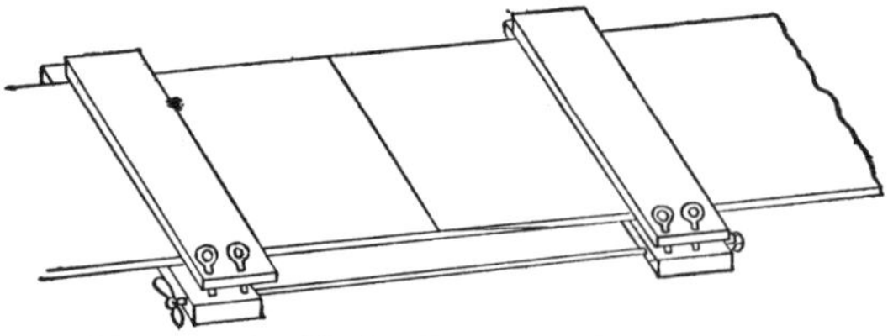

FIG. 329. Belt clamped for gluing.

298. Cementing Belt. The surfaces may be joined with any good belt cement procurable at leather and harness shops. Tack the belt at the joint down to a board, and then securely clamp it to the board to dry for at least twenty-four hours (Fig. 330). When the clamps are removed and the tacks withdrawn, the belt is ready for service. The particular advantage of this splice is that it forms a continuous belt with no extensions to interfere with smooth-running.

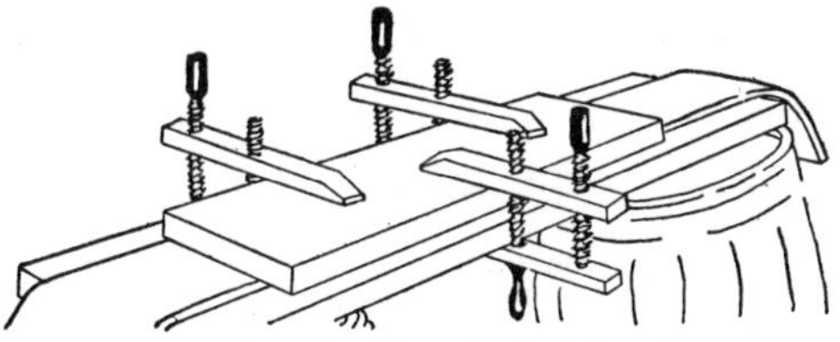

FIG. 330. A glue-joint in clamps.

A canvas belt is usually laced, altho it may be cement-spliced. If so, however, the joint should be cut, as shown in Fig. 331.

299. Laced Joints. These are common for leather belts up to 6″ to 10″ in width. A laced joint is made by calculating the length desired and cutting the belt a little short of this length to allow for stretching.

300. The Process of Lacing. Projects in belt-lacing may be selected from the practical problems of the farm as belts need tightening. It will be well to precede the first lacing of a belt in service by the lacing together of two scrap pieces of belt. Holes are punched in both ends of the belt. Thru these is drawn a lace, usually a strip of untanned hide known as rawhide, in some manner to fasten the two ends securely together and to permit the lacing to pass over the pulleys with as little thumping and wearing as possible. Laced joints are usually classed as single-cross-laced and double-cross-laced, of which the former is the most used except for heavy belts.

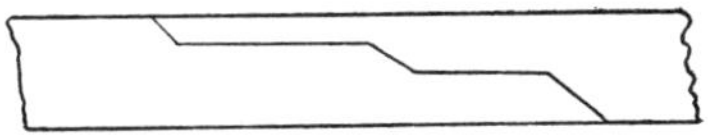

FIG. 331. Joint on canvas belt.

Single-cross lacing gets its name from the fact that a single strand of lacing, or whang, joins the holes punched to receive it, and, also, because these strands cross each other on the side opposite the pulley but once, as shown in Fig. 332.

Patent Belt Fastenings. Many patented belt fastenings are on the market. Some of them are very good, and most of them can be applied in less time than it takes to lace a belt. The pattern which is easily applied and removed consists of a series of metal loops extending thru each end of the belt, thru which a rawhide stick is passed (Fig. 337).

CHAPTER XXXI

PROJECTS IN LACING BELTS

301. Single-Cross Lacing; One Row of Holes Punched on Each End. (Fig. 332.)

Tools and Stock: A 6″ leather belt or (for practice) two short pieces of 6″ belting, 56″ of lace, belt punch, square and knife.

Note: A narrower belt can be laced by modifying the following instructions accordingly:

Working Instructions: Square the ends of the belt to make its length 1″ less than that calculated or measured.

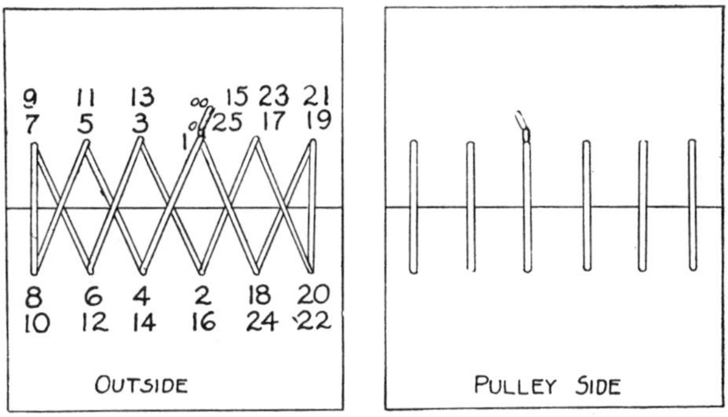

FIG. 332. Single-cross lacing; one row of holes.

Square a pencil line across each end of the belt 1″ from the end and punch 3/16″ holes to dimensions given in *A*, Fig. 333. Point the end of the lace and pass it thru hole 00 (Fig. 332) from the outside, leaving 1/2″ of the end protruding. Pass the lace up thru hole 0 and down thru hole 1, then across to hole 2 and over to hole 3, continuing to pass the lace down thru the odd-numbered holes from the outside of the belt and up thru the even-numbered holes. Continue the lacing, passing thru the holes in rotation, finally returning to hole No. 1, which is also marked 15 and 25. The lacing will now be double. Care must be taken to pass the lacing back to 7 the first time it comes thru 8 in order to get it double at the end.

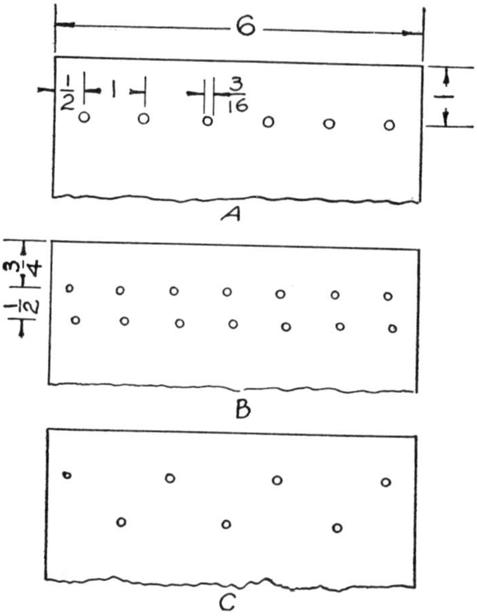

FIG. 333. Position of holes for various laces.

It should be tight and straight. In passing thru a hole the second time or the third, as in case of hole No. 1, use an awl to enlarge the hole slightly. After passing the end of the lace thru hole No. 1, coax it thru holes 0 and 00, leaving the end extending with the first one. Pull these ends thru and level with the belt, cut half-way thru the lacing at an angle with the lace. This forms a notch in each end of the lace to hold it from slipping thru to the pulley side of the belt.

302. Single-Cross Lacing; Two Rows of Holes Punched on Each End.

Note: The instructions given below are for a 6″ belt. It will be noted by referring to Fig. 334 that the lacings on the pulley side of the belt do not lap one on another. The holes being staggered, cause the lacings to lie singly, which is a decided advantage in overcoming noise in running, and wear.

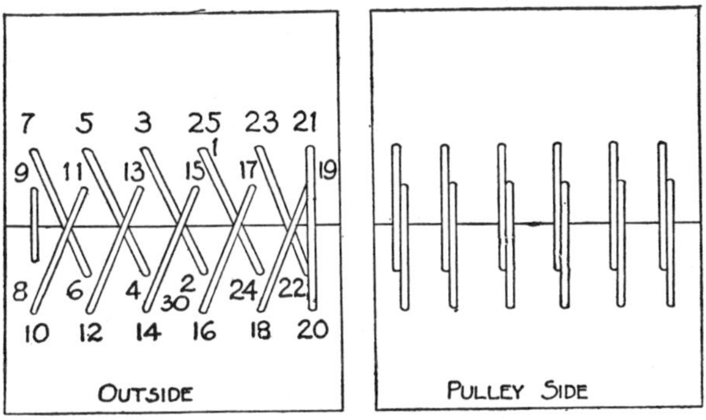

FIG. 334. Single-cross lacing; two rows of holes.

Working Instructions: Punch two rows of holes with a belt punch parallel to the end of the belt. The diameter should be about two-thirds the size of the lace to be used. The first row is placed about 3/4″ from the end of the belt, and the second row about 1-1/2″ from the end. In case the belt is old, these distances are increased slightly. The holes are from 3/4″ to 1″ apart with one-half this distance separating the end holes from the edges of the belt. Determine these outside distances first and then divide up the intervening space so that the distances between points will be as nearly as possible 3/4″ (*B*, Fig. 333). Beginning with the end points on the first row from the end of the belt, punch a hole at every other point. Only one-half the number of holes may be used, as indicated in *C*, Fig. 333. This will make a less substantial lacing. To lace the belt, place a lace thru the middle holes from the pulley side—holes 1 and 2 (Fig. 334)—allowing the two ends of the lace extending on the side of the belt opposite the pulley to be as nearly as possible the same length. The end which extends thru hole No. 2 is put thru hole No. 3, then thru holes Nos. 4, 5, 6, 7 and 8, passing thru the first row of holes on one part of the belt and thru the second row on the other part; then to No. 9, crossing the belt joint, and back thru holes Nos. 10, 11, 12, 13 and 14; then thru hole No. 15, and, finally, thru a tie hole, No. 16, when the end should be cut off about 3/8″ from the belt. The second end of the lacing should follow a similar course, and, upon its return, should go thru hole No. 2, and, finally, thru the tie hole, No. 30. Note that on the side opposite the pulley, the large crosses or plies are over the short ones. This is desirable to reduce friction and wear. Always pull the lacing taut, but do not buckle the belt.

303. Double-Cross Lacing; One or Two Rows of Holes Punched on Each End. For this problem, two laces rather than one must be used. It is not deemed necessary to give detailed instructions for a double-cross lacing, as the instructions given for Problem 1 and Problem 2 apply, except as indicated below.

Double-cross lacing is similar to single-cross lacing except that two strands of lace are drawn thru each hole and that the holes are spaced twice as far apart across the belt. It is necessary that the two strands be drawn equally tight.

This method of lacing a belt is quicker than the single-cross lacing, but is more bulky and, consequently, is noisier and causes more vibration. It is particularly adaptable to the canvas belt because it does not weaken the material as the single-cross lace does, since there are only half as many holes. These should be punctures rather than cut holes, to still further preserve the strength of the material.

304. The Wire Belt Lacing. Wire lacing is now generally used. It is strong, and the strands are not as large as

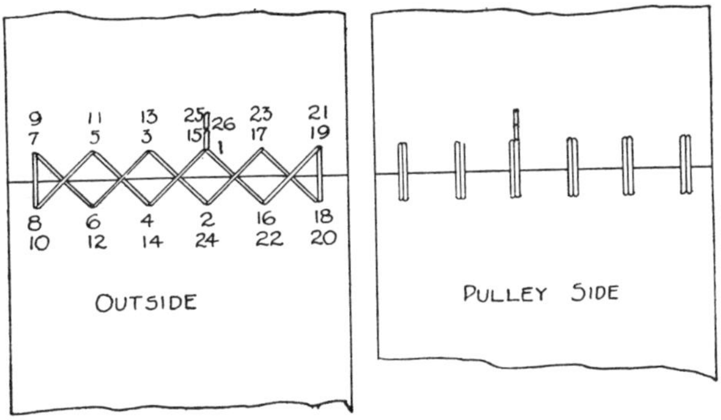

FIG. 335. Wire lacing.

rawhide lacing. The holes are placed nearer the ends of the belt and nearer together, also. The end holes are about 1/4″ from the edge of the belt, and the remaining holes about 1/4″ apart. The row of holes is about 5/16″ from the end of the belt.

A No. 18 soft copper wire may be used for lacing. If it is hard, it can be annealed by heating it to red and plunging in water.

There are now several good makes of patented wire lacing on the market. These are made up from several metals in a proportion which will give a maximum degree of service. Generally, they will be found superior to the copper wire. When using patented wire lacing, care should be taken to follow the directions which are given on the box in which it comes. The size and length of lacing should be selected according to the width of the belt.

When lacing, start at hole No. 1 and pull one-half the wire thru. Then, using the end extending on the pulley side, lace as indicated by Nos. 1, 2, 3, 4, etc., in Fig. 335, returning thru No. 15. Now, use the other end which is protruding on the outside of the belt thru hole No. 2, and pass it thru 16, 17, 18, etc., returning to 25. The ends are now in the same holes,

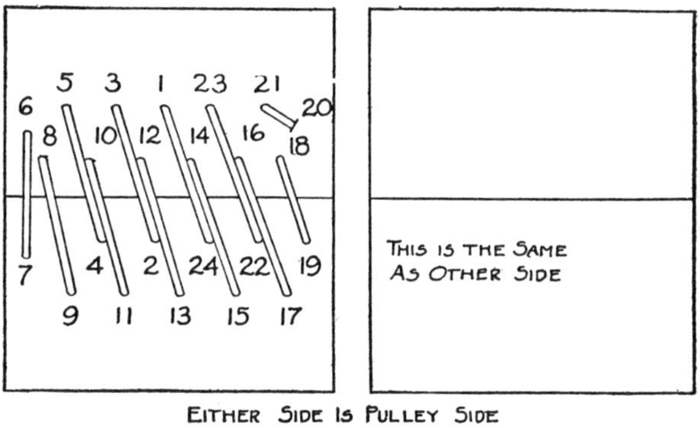

FIG. 336. The Annan lacing.

but in opposite directions. To fasten the ends, make a small hole with a nail, as shown by No. 26, and pass both ends thru this. Make another small hole and pull the wire which is now on the pulley side up on the outside. Cut both ends about 1/2″ from the surface of the belt. Make square hooks on the ends of the wires and clinch them thru the belt in a similar manner to that indicated for the hinge lace in Fig. 337.

Pliers are used for pulling the wire thru when lacing. It is better to take hold of the wire at the extreme end so as to avoid nicking it in order to get the maximum durability in the lacing.

305. The Annan Lacing. This lacing (named after the man who designed it) is very satisfactory, and has the advantage of making the belt reversible on the pulley if necessary, as the lacings on both sides are the same. Besides, the lacings do not cross; thus, the disadvantage of a double thickness of lace is avoided. Fig. 336 shows the steps in making the lacing.

Start the lace as for the single-cross lacing, and continue by

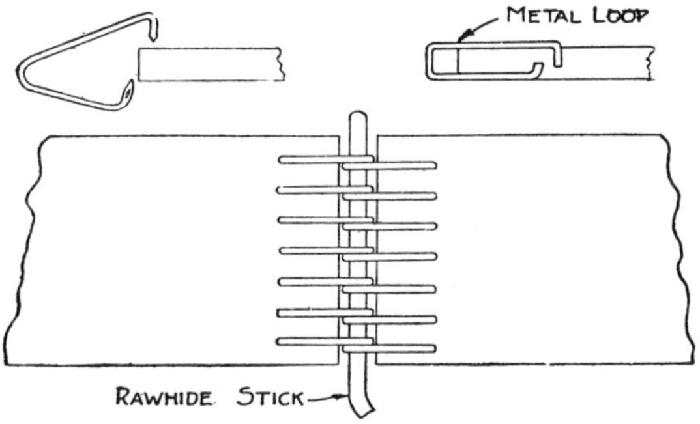

FIG. 337. Hinged belt lacing with wire hooks.

following thru holes as numbered, fastening the last end of the belt at hole 21.

306. The Hinge Belt Lacing. Hinge lacing consists of using practically the same layout of holes as described for the single-cross lacing, but the lace is brought between the edges of the belt where the ends come together and thru the next hole from the opposite side of the belt. In this manner, the plies form a sort of a hinge between the belt ends. They tend to chafe at this point, however, and, consequently, have a short life; therefore, this lacing is no longer popular. Fig. 337 shows method of lacing.

307. Belt-Hook Joint. Belt hooks are obtainable in various sizes and shapes. Some are made to the required shape and are inserted into slits made in the ends of the belt, while others are bent to shape and fitted, as shown in Fig. 338.

FIG. 338. Wire hooks used in lacing.

PART VII

FARM HOME LIGHTING AND SANITARY EQUIPMENT

CHAPTER XXXII

FARM LIGHTING AND FARMHOUSE HEATING

308. Necessity for Good Light. During the long winter nights, those on the farm who would spend a part of the evening in reading the current events of the day, studying the various farm problems, and planning for the next year's work, feel the need of a modern lighting system. On farms where there are boys and girls in school and where they are required to prepare lessons at night, there should be the best lights possible. Shortsightedness in school children is a very common defect, which increases with age. It is due principally to poor school room and home lighting.

A good lighting system improves the sanitary condition in the home and makes for better health and higher efficiency. The farmer should give a great deal of throught and attention to the proper lighting of his buildings. The dairy farmer, especially, should have his house and barns well lighted. A well-lighted barn and dairy makes possible the production of a higher quality of products, makes work more pleasant and decreases the danger from fires, thus reducing the insurance rate.

309. The Cheapest Light. Probably the old-fashioned flat-wick kerosene lamp is the cheapest from the standpoint of cost of fuel. This is not true when one considers the cost of operation, however. Again, a consideration of the poor quality of the light produced by this lamp, its effect on the eyes, its danger, and the fact that no workman can do his best work under poor lighting conditions, makes this pioneer means of home-lighting an expensive one.

The kerosene tubular lamp is an improvement over the flat-wick type in the amount of illumination, especially when it is provided with a mantle which improves the quality and increases the amount of light produced.

310. A More Modern Lighting Plant. The farmer who would install a truly modern lighting system in his home has four kinds of plants from which to make his selection, namely, the electric, acetylene, gasoline gas and Blau gas plants.

311. Electric Lighting Plants. (Fig. 339.) There are definite advantages that the electric light has over other forms of lighting that are recognized by every one. It is clean, safe, its cost is not prohibitive, and it does not make the air impure.

Where the power for electric lights can be secured at a reasonable price from power-distribution lines passing the farm, the situation is ideal. Many farmers do not care to be burdened with the chore of looking after a lighting plant.

Until recent years, there were few unit plants on the market; that is, an engine and generator built together. Most of the generators were formerly belt-driven by a small engine that could be easily used for some other purpose. There is a number of unit plants on the market that are arranged with a belt pulley for power purposes. Some farmers use a power windmill to drive the generator.

In the installation of a small low-voltage electric plant, be sure that all wire is of ample size. The mistake is often made of using the same size wire as used in wiring city residences where a higher voltage is used. All wiring should be properly inspected to see that it meets all insurance requirements. The National Board of Fire Underwriters of Chicago will provide rules for this work.

In operating a small electric plant, pay especial attention

FIG. 339. Farm electric plant.

to the care of the storage batteries. The upkeep and replacement cost of the storage battery is the most expensive item in the cost of operating an electric plant.

312. Acetylene Lighting Plants. Many farmers purchase the acetylene light plant because it is cheaper to operate than the electric plant and requires less attention. Most farmers like the outdoor type of plant best, because it is safe, easily charged, easily cleaned out, and where a 100-pound capacity plant is secured, it does not require re-charging oftener than three or four times during the year. Any acetylene plant that is constructed or located so that the gas will escape into a closed room is dangerous. Acetylene gas is a

FIG. 339-*a*. Gasoline gas generator.

little more dangerous than gasoline; both must be handled with great care.

313. Gasoline Gas Lights. Most of the gasoline equipments are either of the small portable-lamp type or the one by which the gas is piped thru small tubes to the individual lamp. These types of gasoline lamps are objectionable from an insurance standpoint. Only where the gas is produced outside of the building (Fig. 339-*a*) and piped in like ordinary city gas, is the gasoline system really safe. The greatest danger of gasoline lights comes from taking gasoline inside the house.

From a standpoint of economy, the gasoline gas lamps are really cheaper than either acetylene or electric lamps.

314. Blau Gas Lights. Blau gas is an oil gas that is liquified under high pressure. It is freed from all poisonous gases and is practically non-explosive. It is sold in tubes similar to presto-lite—twenty pounds of gas to the tube. The light produced by Blau gas is quite satisfactory and not prohibitive in price.

315. Farmhouse Heating. A well-heated house makes for comfortable living. It has been only during rather recent years that much development has been made in farmhouse heating. Many progressive farmers are now installing systems of heating that will maintain an even temperature thruout the house, and provide an abundance of fresh air. Heating and ventilation go hand-in-hand.

The modern heating system is located in the basement. It keeps the litter and dirt from the main floors, which are difficult to keep clean when fuel and ashes are handled over them in caring for a stove.

316. The Hot-Air System. There are two types of hot-air systems found on the market. One is the pipeless furnace, which is essentially a special type of stove located in the basement and surrounded by a jacket which carries the heat to the rooms above. A down shaft is provided to keep the air in circulation. This type of furnace can be easily installed in any home already built that is provided with a basement or cellar. The other type of hot-air plant is provided with large pipes that carry the hot air direct to the various rooms. These pipes, or "leaders", as they are sometimes called, must run as direct to the rooms to be heated as possible, and they should be wrapped with asbestos to prevent loss of heat. A house can be heated more quickly with hot air than with water or steam, but it will cool off more quickly when the fires die down. During extremely cold, windy weather, it is difficult with a hot-air system to heat rooms on the side of a house from which the wind is blowing.

317. Steam and Hot-Water Systems. The steam-heating system can be installed as a single-pipe or a two-pipe system. The hot-water heating is a two-pipe system. The two systems are quite similar as far as installation is concerned, and can be installed fairly easily in a house already built. The hot-water system works on the principle of water being lighter when hot than when cold. The heated water rises to the various radiators, the heat is given off in the rooms, and the water at a lower temperature flows back to the boiler. Care must be observed in installing the pipes to get proper circulation.

Most steam systems are for low-pressure steam. The steam is generated in the boiler; it rises thru the pipes to the radiators, where it loses its heat, and is condensed and flows back to the boiler. In the one-pipe system, the condensed steam flows back to the boiler thru the same pipe thru which the live steam flows to the radiator.

A house can be heated much more quickly with steam than with hot water, but in a hot-water system the water will hold the temperature more uniformly and a more even heat is maintained. This is the big advantage of the hot-water system over all other systems.

The installation of most lighting and heating equipment should be left to an experienced man. To install a pipeless furnace, however, is not a very great task, and can be done by a person with little experience.

CHAPTER XXXIII

Farm Water Supply and Sewage Disposal

318. Importance of Sanitation on the Farm. It is high time that every farmer give serious thought to the sanitation problems of farm life. Water is thought to be cheap and thus little value is put upon it; this is the chief cause of neglect. Many shallow farm wells are contaminated due to poor protection at the top, poor surface drainage, seepage and general neglect. Cistern water is often made unfit to drink by impurities washing in from the roof due to lack of a good filter, or to one improperly cared for. It is sometimes impure because the cistern is not properly built and seepage water gets in.

The first consideration for health on the farm should be a pure and wholesome water supply of capacity to take care of all the needs of the place. A deep well is about the safest source of water supply. Shallow wells and cisterns, however, can be made safe by proper protection at the top, careful surface drainage, and by preventing the entrance of seepage water. For cisterns, the water should be collected only after the roof has been thoroly washed off. A well-built filter, cleaned out and refilled with filtering material at regular intervals, will go a long way toward purifying such water.

319. Simplest Water System. The simplest system of water supply is an ordinary suction, or force, pump attached to a sink in the kitchen. The pipe leads from the pump thru the floor and into the well or cistern. The source of water for a system of this kind must be near the house and not very deep. For satisfactory service, there should not be more than twenty-five feet between the pump cylinder and the lowest level of the water. A drain must be provided to take off all waste water from the sink. Such a system can be easily installed.

320. Gravity System. The simplest gravity system is one that has a small tank located in the attic and is connected by means of a pipe to a force pump in the kitchen. Such a system makes possible the installation of all other plumbing equipment. Fig. 340 shows a system with a sixty-gallon tank in the attic. Water is pumped to the tank by means of a force pump and a small gasoline engine. The overflow from the storage tank runs to the stock tank in the lot. A good feature of this system is that all of the water for stock is pumped thru the house tank, thereby keeping it always fresh and cool. In Fig. 340 is shown also the installation of complete plumbing connections. Where there is a hill or slight elevation near the house, a tank can be placed on the ground. The concrete tank shown in Fig. 341 is a farm storage tank. It is large enough to supply the house, hog house, hog wallows, barns and garage, all of which are provided with faucets. With the tank placed on the ground and provided with a good foundation, there is no danger of supports giving away as with an elevated tank and the danger of the pipes that lead to the tank freezing is eliminated. Where a satisfactory means of elevating the tank is at hand, the gravity system is the most satisfactory for average farm conditions. A tank supported by concrete or masonry walls is a very good arrangement. A room underneath the tank can thus be provided to be used as a milk house.

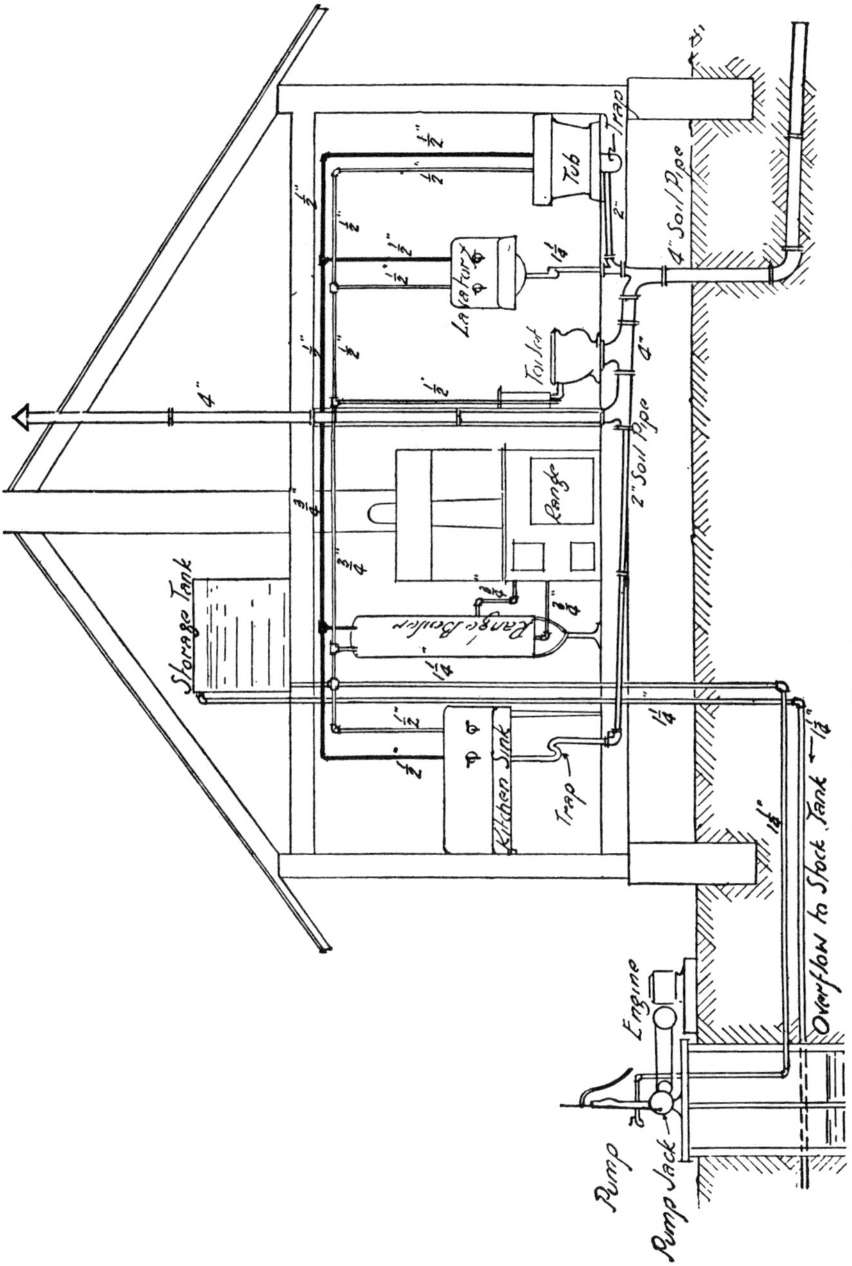

FIG. 340. Gravity water system.

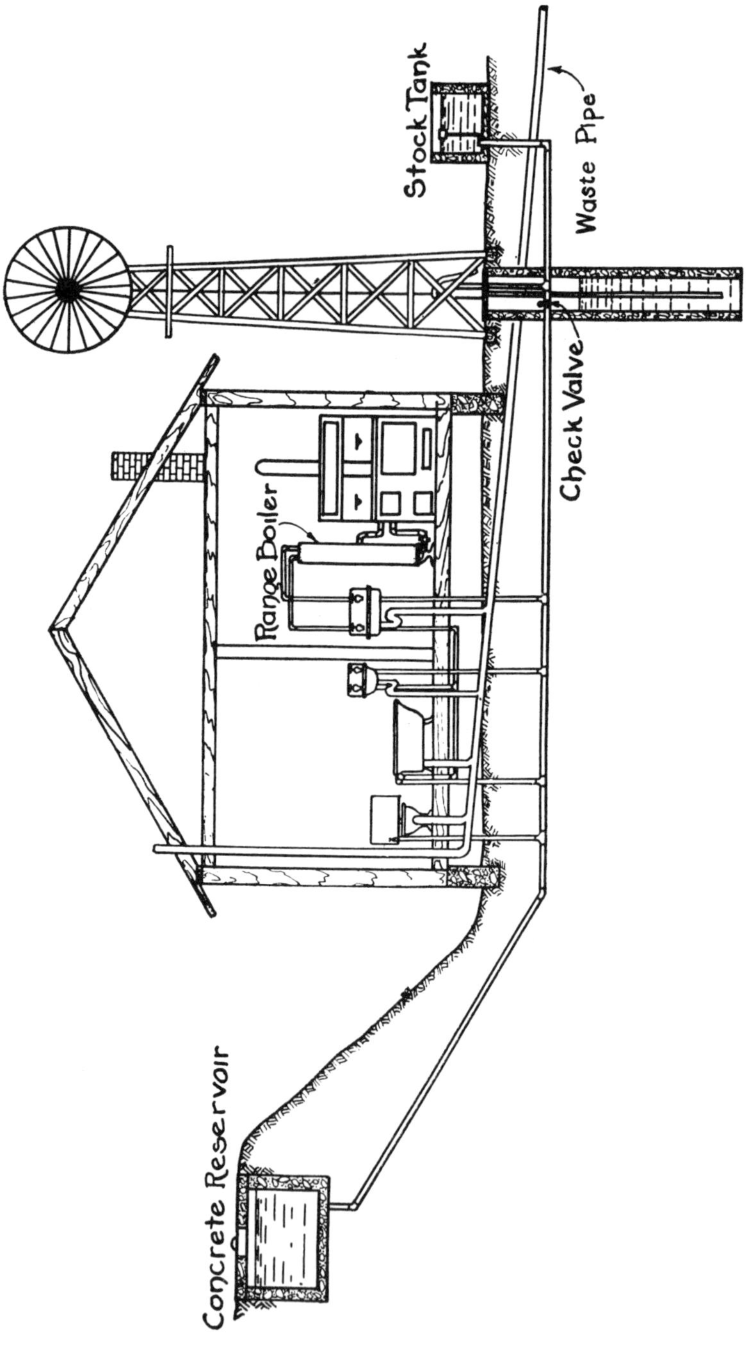

FIG. 341. Concrete reservoir for water storage.

321. Water Air-Pressure System. This system, shown in Fig. 342, is usually called the hydro-pneumatic system. In it the water is stored in an air-tight steel tank and is forced thru the pipes to the fixtures by air pressure. As the water is used, the pressure is gradually reduced. In some systems of this type there is both a water and an air pump. The most common type is equipped with only a water pump with air intake. To operate the system, the tank is filled with air, the water is pumped in, and the air pressure increases as the volume of the air decreases. Only about two-thirds to three-fourths of the volume of the tank is effective for water storage. This is one of the principal objections to this system, because to avoid pumping so often, an extremely large tank must be provided if the water requirements are very large. However, with electric power available, an automatic control can be provided and a smaller tank be used. Complete equipment for a system of this kind includes an air-tight tank, a force pump, pressure gauges, and other fittings, and plumbing fixtures.

322. Hydraulic Ram. Where there is a large quantity of water with sufficient fall, a hydraulic ram is the cheapest means of providing water pressure in the home. The first cost is small, there is practically no upkeep, and it will run continuously without any attention. Under ordinary conditions, a ram will elevate about one-seventh of the water that flows to it thru the drive pipe. A rule that can be used to determine the approximate amount of water that will be delivered with a certain flow is: Multiply the number of gallons of flow per minute by the number of feet of vertical fall between the source of water and the ram. Divide this by the

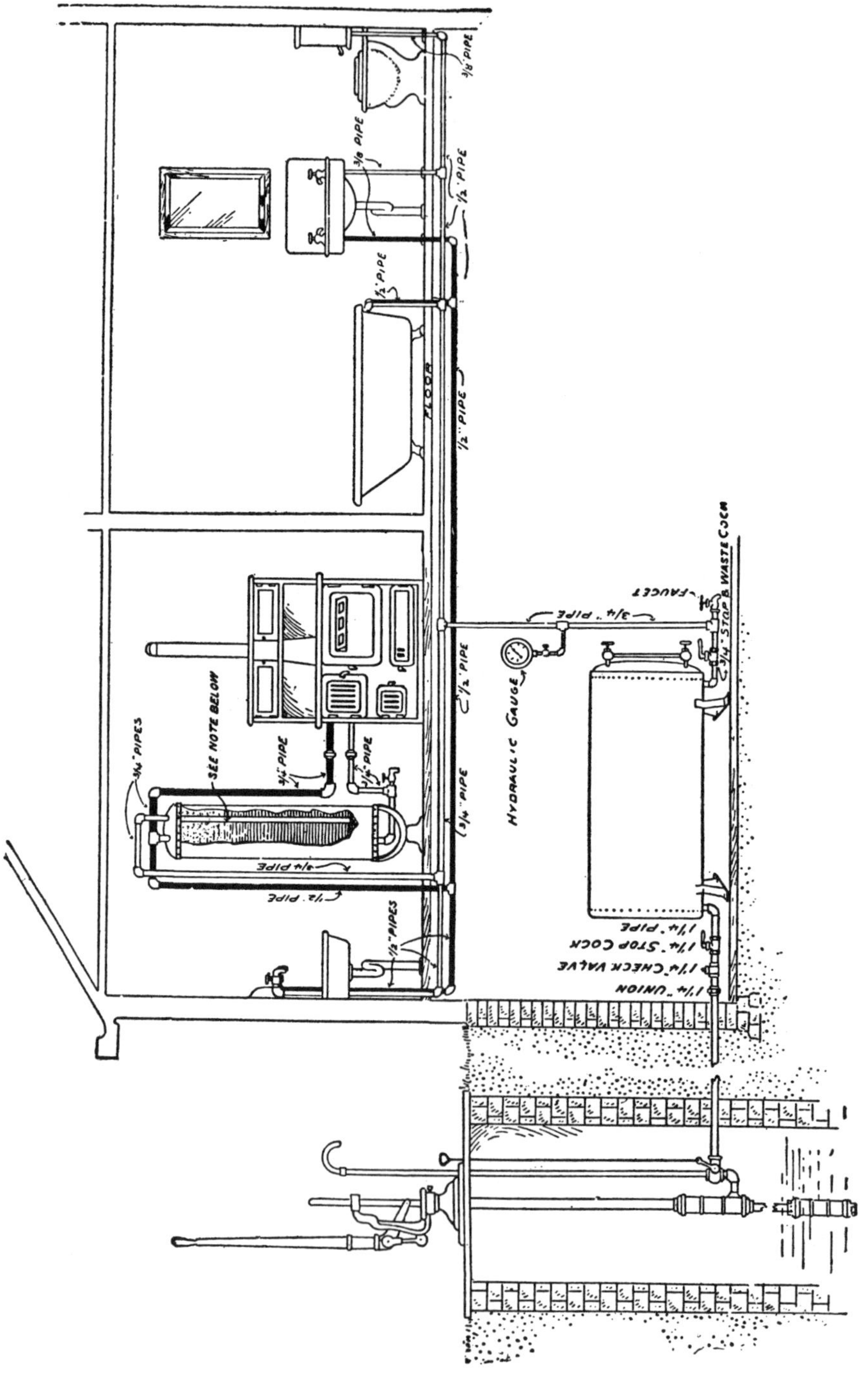

FIG. 342. Hydro-pneumatic water system.

height it is desired to elevate the water, and reduce the result by one-third to take care of friction and losses in the pipes. The remainder will be the quantity of water delivered. For example, if the flow is 4 gallons per minute, the fall is 9 feet and the water is to be elevated 24 feet, we have four times 9 equals 36; 36 divided by 24 equals 1-1/2; reduce this by 1/3, and we have 1 gallon per minute delivered, or 1,440 gallons per 24 hours.

323. Selecting a System. In selecting a water system, many make the mistake of installing one that does not furnish sufficient water. It is much better to have a cistern or tank with greater capacity than actually needed than to have one too small. The same is true in selecting a pressure tank for the hydro-pneumatic system or an air tank for the fresh-water system. The first cost will be a little greater, but the expense will be less in the end. As a basis for estimate, one must remember that after a modern water system is installed, much more water will be used than before. For each person, one should estimate at least 25 or 30 gallons per day; for each cow, 15 gallons; for horses, 10 gallons, and hogs and sheep, 3 gallons per day, allowing for an additional supply to care for chickens, for watering the garden, washing the car or buggy, sprinkling the lawn, etc.

324. The Septic Tank. No modern water system is complete without proper disposal of the waste water and sewage. Oftentimes the sewer is simply tile that leads down to the field or into a ditch or small stream. This method of sewage disposal is not sanitary, nor is it safe from a standpoint of health. If a large stream is at hand, into which to discharge the sewage, it can be used with safety; a small creek, however, would soon become contaminated.

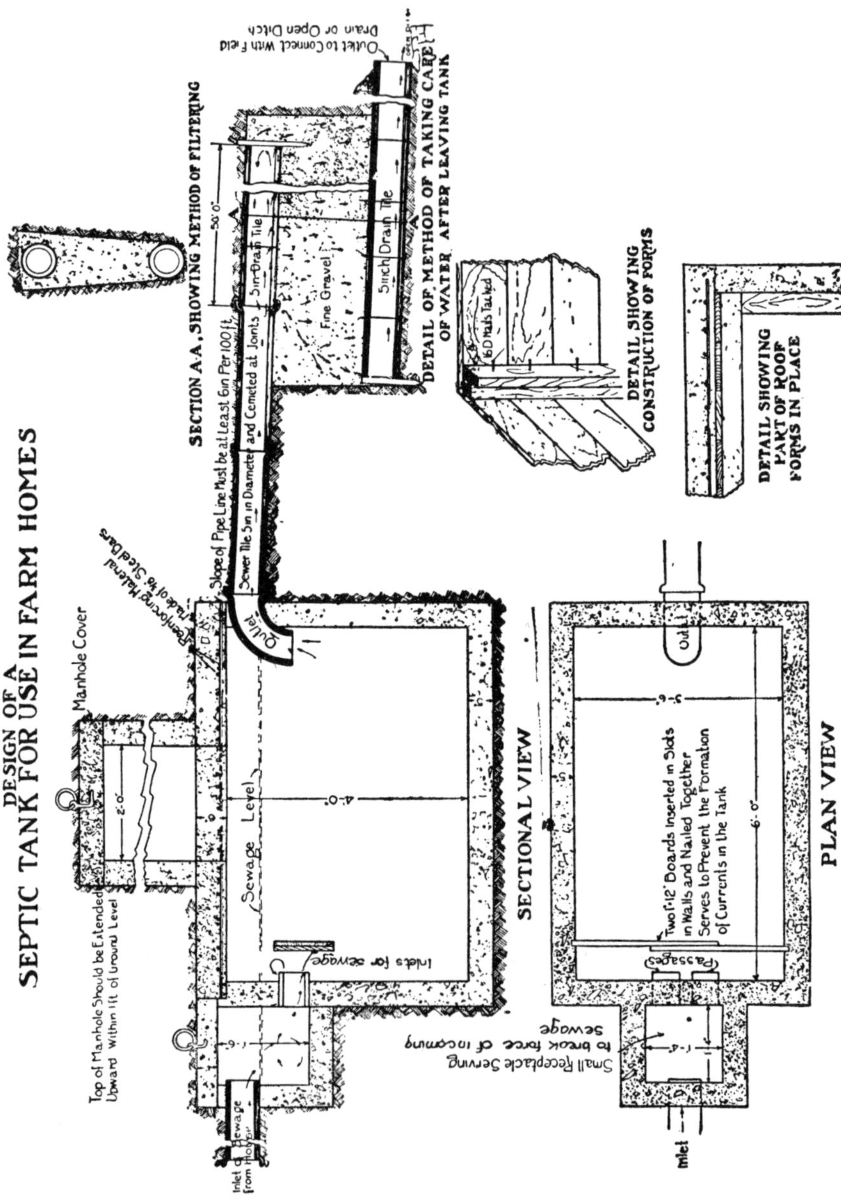

FIG. 343. One-chamber septic tank.

The septic tank is a means of disposal of sewage from the farm home. The septic tank alone will not purify sewage; it will partially purify it and put it in condition to be completely purified by means of a filter or thru a system of tile. The septic tank illustrated in Fig. 343 is a one-chambered tank. Its action is as follows: In the septic tank the sewage is acted on by bacteria—minute organisms that thrive under conditions where there is neither air nor light. The solids in the sewage are broken down and put into solution. It must be remembered that only one or less than one per cent of the sewage is solids—the rest is all water. Soon a thick leathery scum forms on the surface of the tank; this indicates that it is working properly. The solid part that is not dissolved settles to the bottom of the tank. It is necessary to clean this out every few years.

To completely purify this sewage, it is discharged onto a filter or into a system of tile arranged to allow it to filter away into the soil. In the filter or in the surface soil, there are billions of bacteria that thrive in the presence of air and light. These are called the nitrifying bacteria. They completely purify the sewage. This is nature's method of purification.

325. The Art of Plumbing. Plumbing has been called a sanitary art and defined as the art of placing in buildings, pipes and other apparatus used for introducing water supply and for removing wastes.

The Plumber as a Specialist: In big jobs in large building work, there are special plumbers for doing the heavy roughing-in work, putting in the large pipes and the general network of smaller pipes. Then there are other plumbers to do the finishing work.

There are certain essentials in handling a house-plumbing job. The man in charge should be thoroly competent to see that the connections are properly made. A plumbing job that is poorly finished may be a source of a great deal of danger, and should be thoroly inspected. Simplicity in the laying out of piping and fixtures will tend to eliminate plumbing troubles. The principles of drainage must be ever in mind when installing a plumbing system. All supply pipes, as well as drains, must be installed so they have an outlet and with a gradual slope toward this outlet. There must be no low points or pockets where water will collect when the system is drained. Such a defect would cause stoppage in drain pipes, and the supply pipes, when exposed, would freeze at these points. Main soil pipe made of 4″ pipe should extend 5′ from outside of the cellar wall to act as a sewer connection into the house and thru the roof. This pipe should be straight from the cellar to the roof. All fixtures should discharge thru the main soil pipe, and should be provided with traps thoroly ventilated to prevent the escape of sewer gas into the house. In some plumbing jobs, an additional ventilation pipe is carried from each trap into a main 2″ pipe which is independent of the soil pipe and is also carried thru the roof. This prevents leakage of the seal or trap.

Plumbing materials and fixtures should be of good quality, simple in design, with all joints and connections made air- and water-tight. They should be of entirely non-absorbent material.

All plumbing should be as nearly accessible as possible. Removable wooden panels over the soil pipe and other main pipes are worth considering. Fixtures near main drain and all bath and kitchen fixtures should be open work. Free access of air and light should also be obtained. Boxed-in sinks and bath tubs are insanitary because dirt and moisture are bound to collect around the base.

326. Materials Used for Plumbing. For sinks, the solid porcelain is the most expensive. The iron enamel is just about as good as the solid porcelain and can be obtained much cheaper. For laundry equipment, the slate, reinforced concrete and enameled iron can be used. Slate tubs for laundry are very satisfactory. The most sanitary equipments are those which are in one piece with all parts properly rounded. The general equipment is usually listed as to quality as No. 1, No. 2 and No. 3. No. 1 is usually guaranteed and is very expensive; No. 2 is very satisfactory. It is usually not advisable to buy the No. 3 quality.

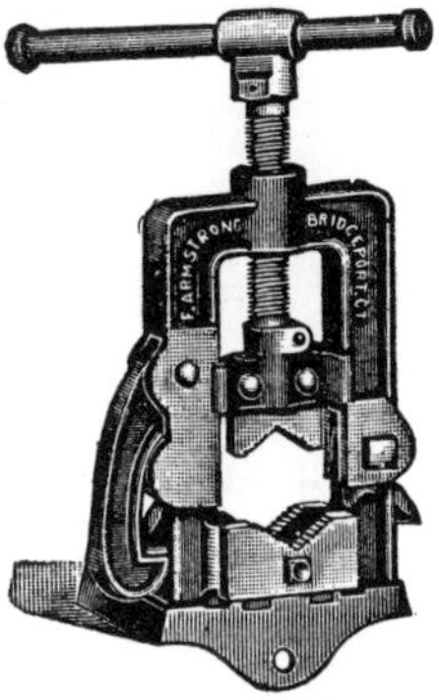

FIG. 344. Pipe vise.

The person who would do the simple plumbing jobs herein described should become familiar with the more common plumbing tools and their uses; also, the various pipe fittings required. The following tools are needed for even the simplest job: Vise, cutter, die-stock and dies, wrenches, reamer or half-round file, and rule.

327. Pipe Vise. The hinged type of vise (Fig. 344) with gravity pawl is about the best to secure. The reversible type may be secured. The latter can be thrown open either to the right or to the left, with a clutch on either side to engage the pawl. Such a vise has a distinct advantage when cutting a pipe which has fittings that will not pass thru the frame of an ordinary vise.

328. Pipe Cutters. Pipe cutters (Fig. 345) are divided into two general types—the three-cutter wheel and the one-cutter wheel types. The one-cutter wheel can be secured with solid back or with two rollers; the latter type is probably in

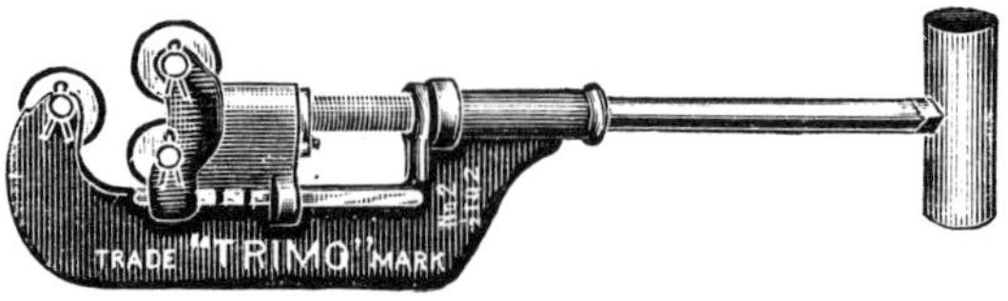

FIG. 345. Three-wheel pipe cutter.

most general use. The three-cutter wheel type has the advantage of being used in close quarters. This type of cutter forms a burr on the outside of the pipe which must be re-

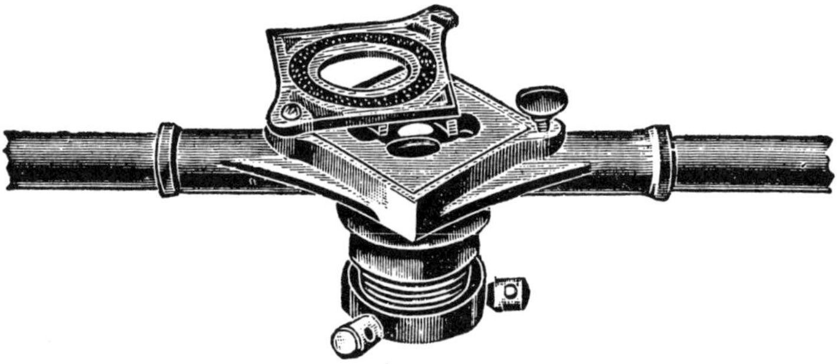

FIG. 346. Stock and die.

moved with a file before the threads can be cut. The pipe does not need to be reamed out, however.

329. Die-stocks and Dies. It must be remembered that a different die is used for threading a pipe than for threading a bolt. The pipe thread is a taper thread, making possible a tight joint. The solid type of die is most commonly used (Fig. 346). A number of dies for different-sized pipe can be secured and used in the same stock. The adjustable type of die is used in a special stock. A ratchet stock is sometimes used.

330. Pipe Wrenches. The Trimo and Stillson wrenches are the two types of wrenches in most common use. At least two sizes of wrenches should be provided—one for small pipes and fittings and one for larger sizes. For extremely large

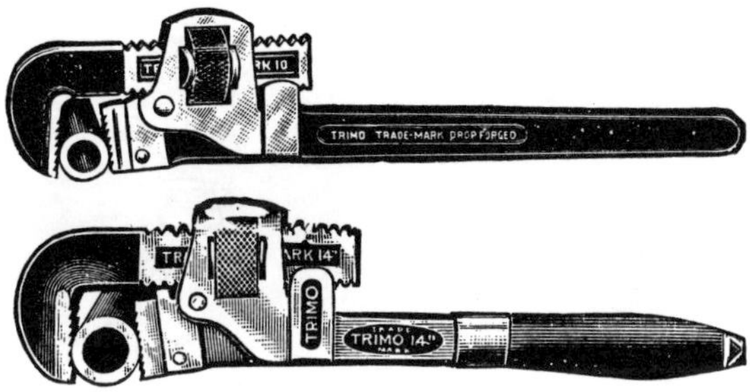

FIG. 347. Pipe wrench.

pipe, chain tongs are usually used. (See Fig. 347 for picture of pipe wrenches. Fig. 347-*a* shows many of these tools in a group.)

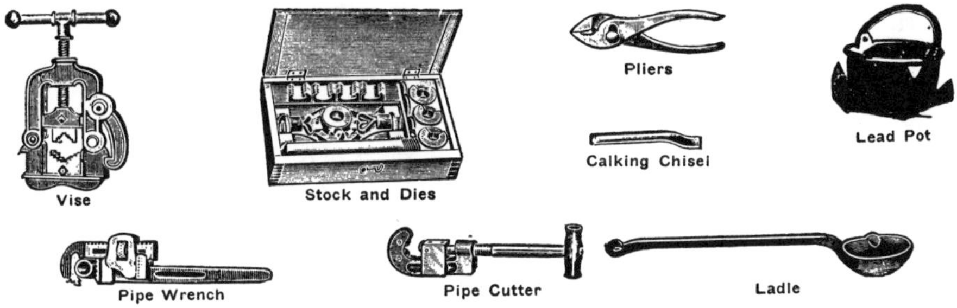

FIG. 347-*a*. Several common plumbing tools.

331. Reamers. The reamer is used to remove the burr formed on the inside of pipe by cutting the pipe. A reamer fitted in a hand wheel is quite satisfactory. A one-half round or a round file can be used.

332. Rule. A folding rule should be provided. For a neat job of pipefitting, careful measuring is necessary.

333. Pipe Fittings. Pipe fittings are used in joining one pipe to another, to change direction, to reduce size, and to

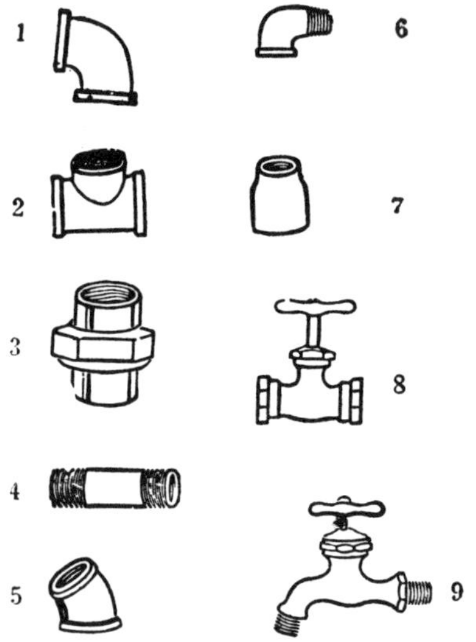

FIG. 348. Fittings for supply pipes:

1. Elbow.
2. Tee.
3. Union.
4. Nipple.
5. 45° elbow.
6. Street elbow.
7. Reducer.
8. Valve.
9. Faucet.

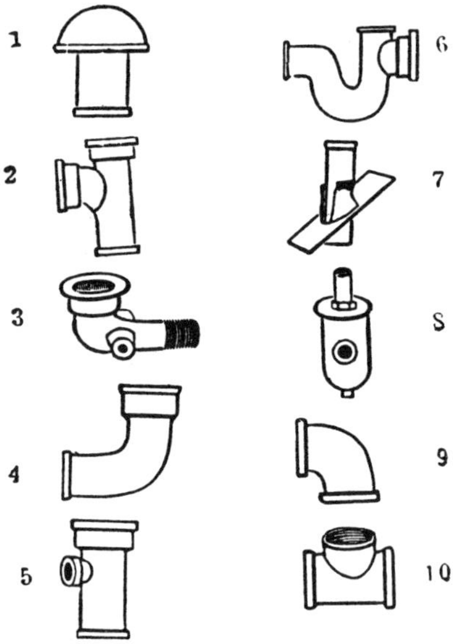

FIG. 348-*a*. Fittings for waste pipes:

1. Ventilating cap.
2. Sanitary T-branch.
3. Closed bend.
4. Quarter bend.
5. Tapped T-branch.
6. Trap with hand hole.
7. Roof flange.
8. Drum trap.
9. 90° elbow.
10. Tee.

branch off. Fittings are made of malleable, cast and wrought iron; the latter are usually galvanized. There are also brass and nickel fittings for special uses. Figs. 348 and 348-*a* give the names of the principal fittings for supply and waste pipes.

CHAPTER XXXIV

Drainage and Pipe-Fitting

334. Fitting Pipe Handle for Lawn Roller.

(Fig. 349.) (See concrete project, Sec. 146.)

Requirements: To cut, thread and assemble pipe and fitting to form a handle of proper dimension for a concrete roller as outlined under Concrete Projects, Sec. 146.

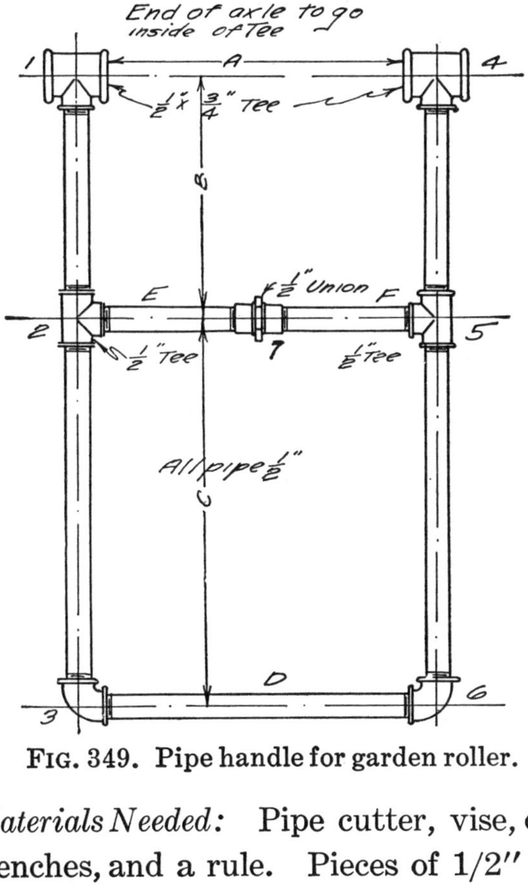

Fig. 349. Pipe handle for garden roller.

Tools and Materials Needed: Pipe cutter, vise, die-stock and die, wrenches, and a rule. Pieces of 1/2″ pipe, lengths depending on requirements of particular handle; two

1/2″ elbows, two 1/2″ tees, one 1/2″ union, and two 3/4″ x 1/2″ tees. The latter is to serve as bearings for axle of roller. The size specified is sufficiently large where a 1/2″ pipe is used for axle.

Preliminary Instruction:

335. Measuring Materials for Handle. Extreme care must be observed in making measurements to have the handle fit smoothly. The distances *A* and *B* (Fig. 349) will depend on the length and diameter of roller. The distance *A* should be made about 1/2″ greater than the length of roller. The distance *B* between center of fittings should be about 2″ greater than the radius of roller. The distance *C* should be made a length that will make the roller convenient to operator. Measurements are usually taken from the center of one fitting to the center of the next. To make accurate measurements, each fitting should be made tight before the next piece of pipe is cut. The 1/2″ union can be eliminated if one of the tees in which the cross pipe is threaded has a right-hand thread and the other a left-hand thread.

Working Instructions:

336. Threading Pipe. Place a piece of 1/2″ pipe in the vise. If not threaded, thread it with a right-hand die as follows: Note that proper die is placed in stock; place guide bushing in place; oil end of pipe with lard oil; place bushing end of die-stock on pipe and start die with hands near center of stock by pressing hard on handles and rotating one-fourth turn at a time. After die has taken hold, move hands out to the ends of handle and continue rotating with less pressure. After each complete turn, rotate backward slightly to allow chips to drop. Continue this process until thread of sufficient length is cut. It is often necessary to remove die and try on fitting to get the best results. The fitting should go on at least three threads by hand. Screw fitting No. 1 on end of pipe by means of the pipe wrench.

337. Cutting Pipe. Draw the pipe thru the vise and lay off length *B* with rule. Place pipe cutter on pipe so that the cutting wheel comes on the mark. Drop a little lard oil on pipe and cutting wheel, screw the handle in until cutting wheel begins to cut, then rotate cutter. At each revolution of the cutter, feed the cutter wheel inward by screwing in on handle; continue until pipe is cut off. Place the pipe *B* in vise and thread blank end, after which screw on fitting No. 2.

Proceed by cutting and threading pipe length *C* and screwing into fitting No. 2 and No. 3. Make up other side of handle in the same manner; then cut, thread and assemble pipe lengths *D*, *E* and *F* so that the two sides of handle will be parallel.

After handle is assembled to proper dimension, unscrew union No. 7 and spring handles apart until fittings Nos. 1 and 4 will slip over the ends of axle, after which tighten union.

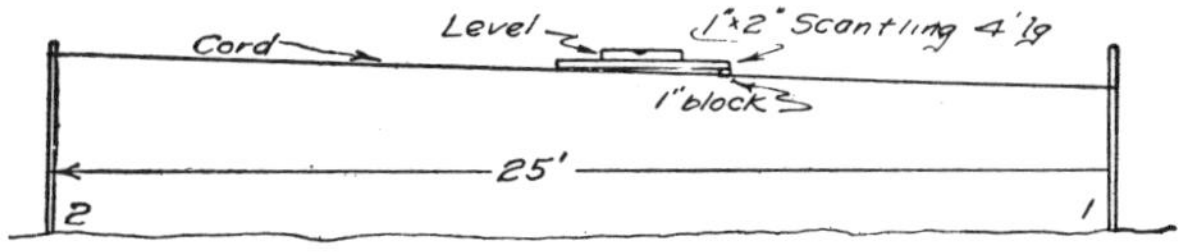

FIG. 350. Establishing a grade for tile.

338. Installing Drain from Kitchen Sink to Sewage Disposal System.

Requirements: To install drain pipe and tile from kitchen sink to outlet or disposal system. (See Figs. 350, 351, 352.)

Tools and Materials Needed: Plumbing tools and tiling spade, hook and scoop, and a carpenter's level are required. Obtain one trap, sufficient 1-1/4″ pipe to carry water from sink to a point 5′ outside house, suitable fittings, white lead, 50′ of 4″ sewer tile, and sufficient farm drain tile to reach outlet.

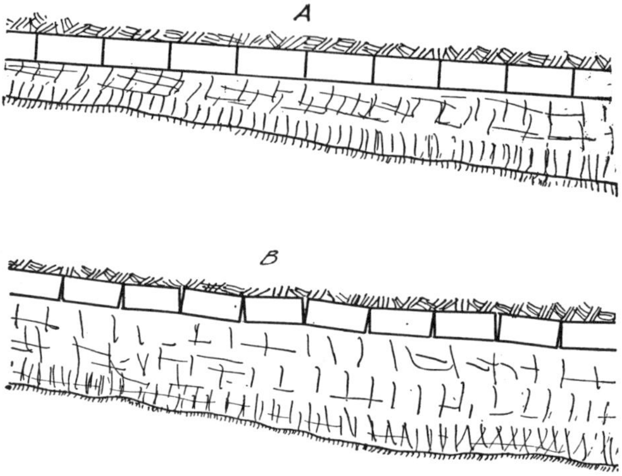

FIG. 351. *A*, tile properly laid; *B*, tile poorly laid.

Preliminary Instruction: The first requirement of every drain is an adequate outlet or point of discharge. This point must be low enough so the tile can be given ample fall to prevent the sewage or water backing up in the drain. It is considered best practice to discharge sewage from sanitary fixtures thru sewer tile direct to septic tank while the kitchen waste water is usually taken care of by ordinary drains. A smooth, uniform grade must be provided for every drain. In farm drainage work, this is usually established by means of a drainage level.

Working Instruction:

339. Establishing Grade Line for Drain. Determine point of outlet and establish a grade line by which to dig the ditch. For a small job such as this, when there is a decided slope of the ground, place the grade parallel to the slope. If the ground is practically level, a grade line can be established by means of an ordinary carpenter's level. Drive in a series of stakes from 4′ to 5′ long at intervals of 25′; for long drains, stakes are placed every 50′. By using long stakes, a guide line to dig by can be placed as the grade is established. If it is desired to have a fall of 1/4″ to the foot, take a straight 1″ x 2″ scantling 4′ long; tack a 1″ block under one end, and fasten to lower side of level with block on lower side. Tie a cord to stake at the outlet at a point about 3′ above the surface of the ground, stretch the cord to the second stake, and test it for grade by placing the level in position so the block will be down grade (Fig. 350). When the bubble of the instrument indicates that it is level, it shows that there is a rise of 1″ to every 4′ along the cord.

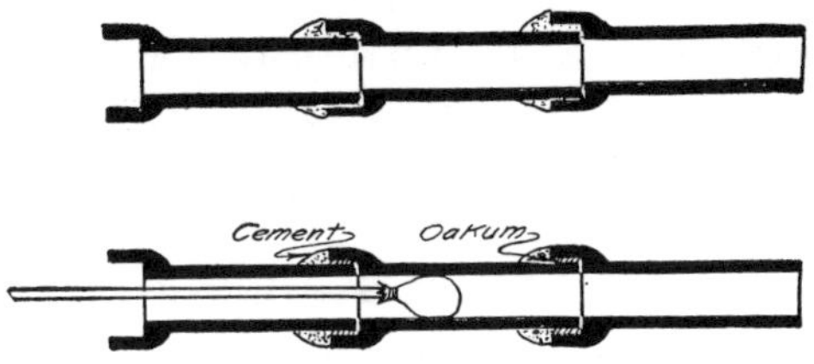

FIG. 352. Sewer tile made tight.

340. Digging Ditch to Grade. Use a gage rod of definite length, and dig ditch so its bottom will be parallel to the cord. If it is desired to have the drain 4′ deep at the outlet, the gage rod should be 7′ long since the cord was placed 3′ above the surface of the ground at the outlet. If the soil is heavy and sticky, an open spade can be used to advantage; use a round-nose spade or a tile scoop for cleaning the bottom of ditch to receive the tile.

341. Laying the Tile. Lay the tile as the ditch is completed, beginning at the outlet. The ordinary farm tile can be laid either by hand or by means of the tile hook. The tile must be made to fit closely together in the ditch (*A*, Fig. 351); this is best accomplished by rotating the tile until it is in place. The sewer tile (Fig. 352) is provided with bell end or bell mouth, and the joints are made tight. Place the tile in place so the direction of flow will be into the bell end; place the spigot end of each tile into the bell end of the preceding tile as it is laid. A small piece of oakum or tarred rope forced in between the spigot and the bell with a flat stick will make possible a smooth job. Place cement mortar in the joint after properly adjusting the tile. The use of a swab, as indicated, is advisable. Place tile to a point 5′ outside of building. Cut, thread and fit pipe to discharge into the sewer that has been laid. The depth to place this pipe and slope to give it will depend upon the sewer outlet.

342. Installing Kitchen Sink and Pump.

Requirements: To install a kitchen sink and pump so that water may be pumped directly from a well or cistern to kitchen (Fig. 353). The installation of drain for this sink is outlined under Secs. 338-341.

Tools and Materials Needed: The tools needed for the project are the same as in Sec. 334. The following materials are needed: Pump, sink, trap and sufficient 1-1/4″ pipe to reach from pump at sink to cistern or well, as illustrated (Fig. 353). Such elbows and couplings as needed and a check valve for suction pipe. White or red lead for making joints.

Preliminary Instruction:

343. Maximum Depth for Pumping Water. It must be remembered that the vertical distance from cylinder of pump to low level of water must be 25′ or less to give satisfaction.

Where there is a likelihood of water in pipe freezing during cold weather, the check valve in suction pipe should be omitted to allow the water to drain back into well. The only

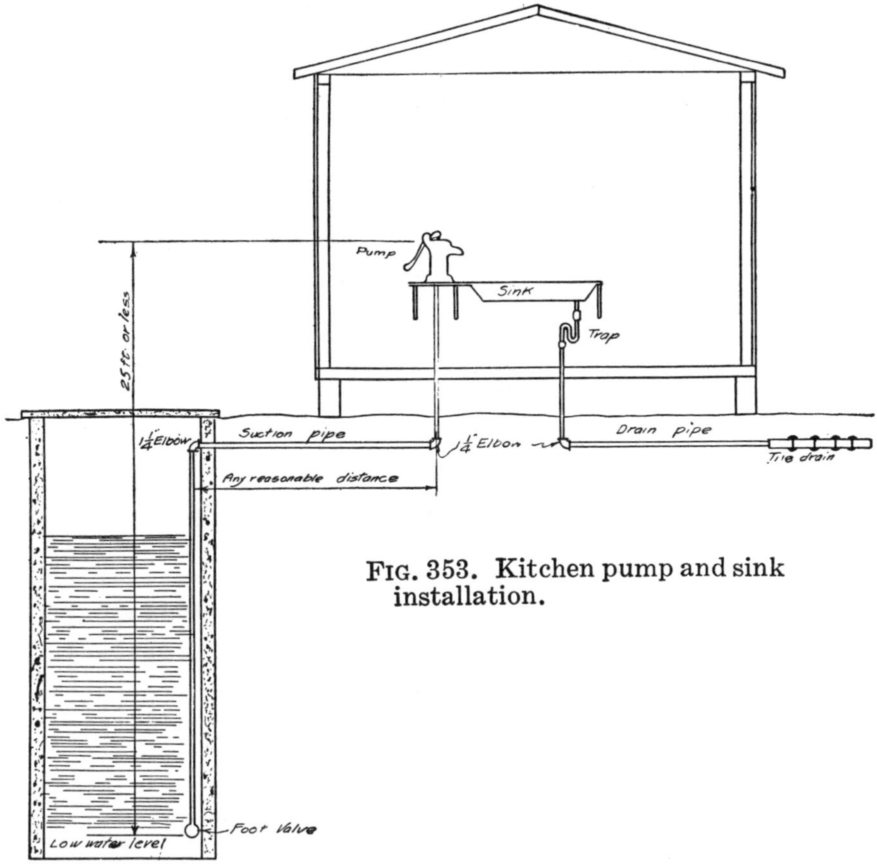

FIG. 353. Kitchen pump and sink installation.

difference in the work in this and the preceding project, Sec. 334, is that the pipe joints must all be made absolutely tight.

Working Instructions:

344. Location of Kitchen Sink. Locate sink in the kitchen so that it will be convenient and have ample light. Most sinks are fastened to a wall by means of hangers or brackets which can be easily installed. Adjust height of sink to convenience of user.

Excavate for pipe from cistern to point underneath sink. If a basement is under house, excavate from cistern to wall. The pipe should be placed below frost line. Take measurements from the cistern to the sink, determining the exact length of each piece of pipe needed and the necessary fittings.

345. Connecting Pipe for Pump. Cut and thread pipe as outlined under Secs. 336, 337. In making the various joints, apply a small amount of white lead to the first three threads in fitting or on the pipe. Begin at the pump and screw each fitting and piece of pipe perfectly tight before beginning on the next.

346. Installing Plumbing in Country Home (Fig. 354).

Requirements: To install rough plumbing, including soil pipe, vent pipes and various drains for fixtures in wall partition while house is under construction. (See Fig. 354.)

Tools and Materials Needed: Plumbing tools, plumber's furnace, ladle and caulking tools. Soil pipe and soil-pipe connections, vent pipes, drains for fixtures and traps. Lead and oakum for joints.

Preliminary Instruction: Every plumbing system should be designed with an idea of simplicity in the layout of piping and fixtures. If possible, the bath room should be directly above the kitchen, and with the laundry room below, as shown in Fig. 354. This will make it possible for one soil pipe to take care of the discharge from fixtures on each floor. Fig. 354-*a* shows a system in a three-story house with a bath room on each floor. The soil pipe should extend from a point 5′ outside the wall, where it connects with the sewer, up thru the house roof. It

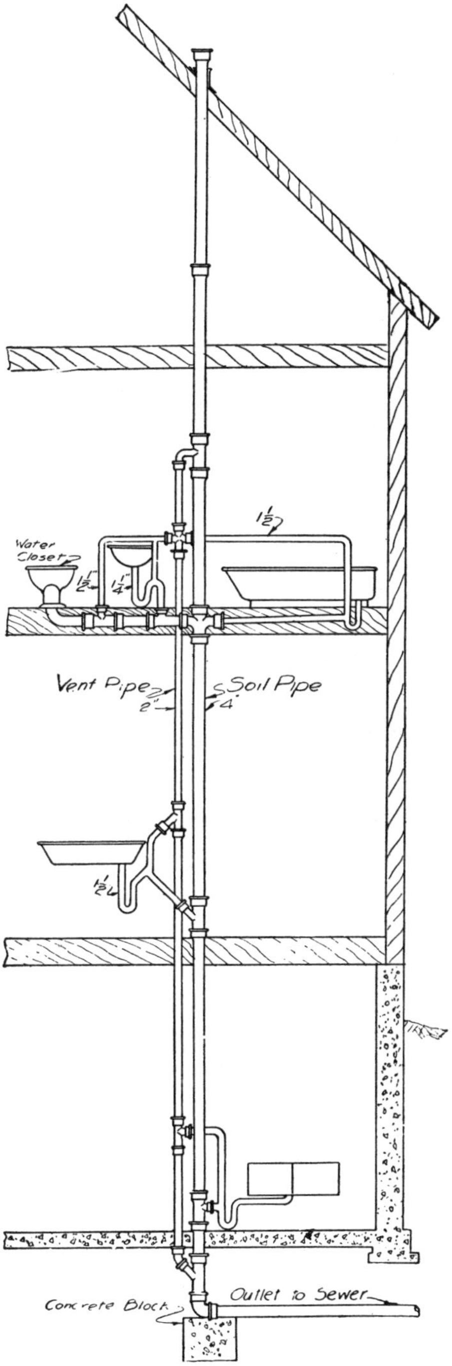

FIG. 354. Waste and ventilating pipe.

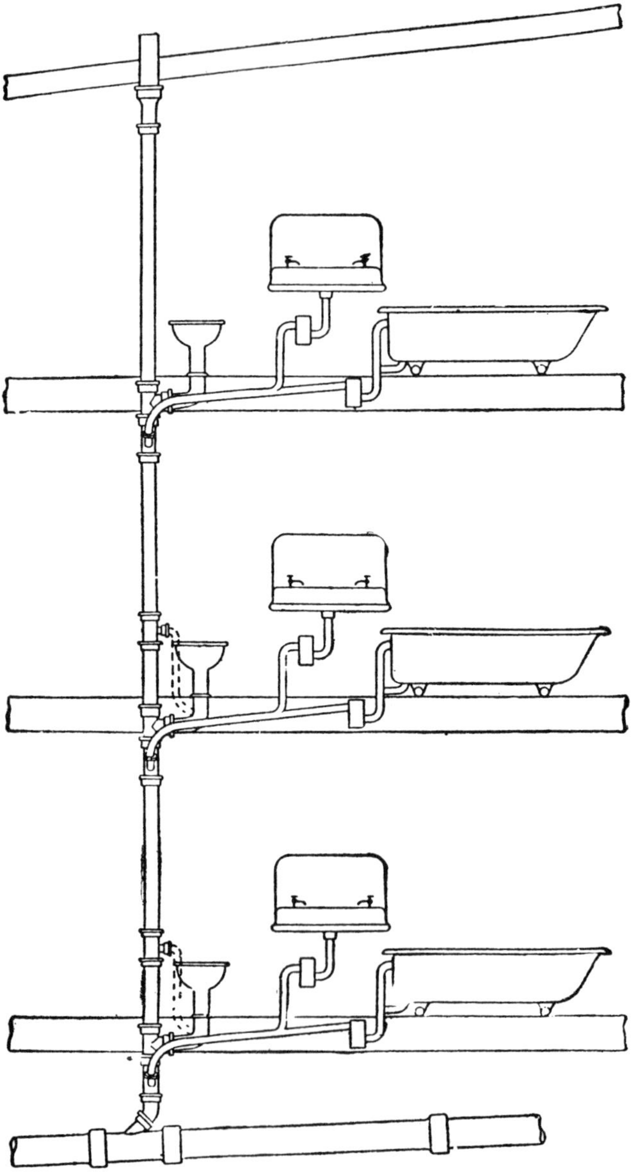

FIG. 354-*a*. Waste pipe without ventilating pipe.

should be straight from cellar to roof. Tight joints are an essential requirement of every plumbing system. Provide a trap for every fixture; the best practice provides a 2″ ventilation pipe with connection to each trap. The location of each fixture should be carefully considered with a view to convenience for the user and to make a simple, efficient layout.

Working Instructions:

347. Sewer Tile. Lay a sewer tile from sewer connection, or from septic tank, to a point 5′ outside of building. Follow instructions as outlined under Secs. 338-341. Make connection of soil pipe with sewer, and extend it to a point in the basement where it will be most convenient to fixtures and where it will pass thru partition to roof.

348. Soil Pipe. The joints of soil pipe are similar to joints of sewer tile. Each section of pipe is provided with a bell end into which is placed the spigot end of the next section. The joints must be perfectly tight; to make them so, oakum and lead are used. The pipe is set in place, a roll of oakum is packed into the bottom of joint, after which molten lead is poured into the joint, filling it completely (Fig. 355). To pour the lead where a joint is made in a horizontal pipe, a sort of collar must be provided with opening at the top. If the oakum is not carefully packed into place, the lead will run thru. After the lead has cooled, pack it solidly into the joint with a hammer and caulking tool. Well-caulked joints are absolutely tight.

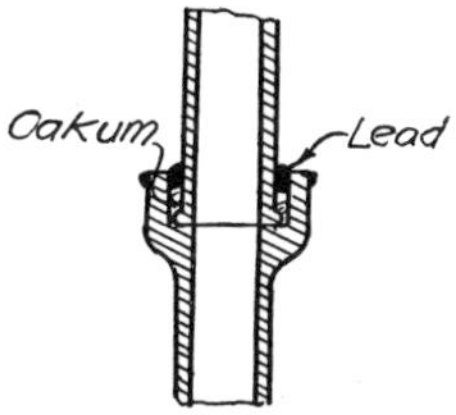

FIG. 355. Soil pipe joint caulked with oakum and lead.

349. Connecting Fixtures and Vents. Provide suitable Ys and Ts for all fixtures, as illustrated. Connect the vent pipe from a point below the bottom fixture and extend it up, and connect back into the soil pipe at a point above the highest fixture. Give all horizontal soil pipes, whether for drainage or ventilation, a fall of at least 1″ to the foot. To support soil pipe, provide suitable concrete or stone footing at the bottom. Support all horizontal lines with suitable hangers to prevent line from getting out of place.

350. Connecting Cast-Iron and Lead Pipe. To make a connection between a cast-iron pipe and a lead pipe, first connect the lead pipe to a brass ferrule by means of a soldered joint; the ferrule is then caulked into the cast-iron hub or bell end, as outlined above.

CHAPTER XXXV

SUPPLEMENTARY PLUMBING PROJECTS

351. Piping Water to Stock Tank.

Requirements: To construct a pipe line from source of water at well or storage tank to stock tank in barnyard, as shown in Fig. 356.

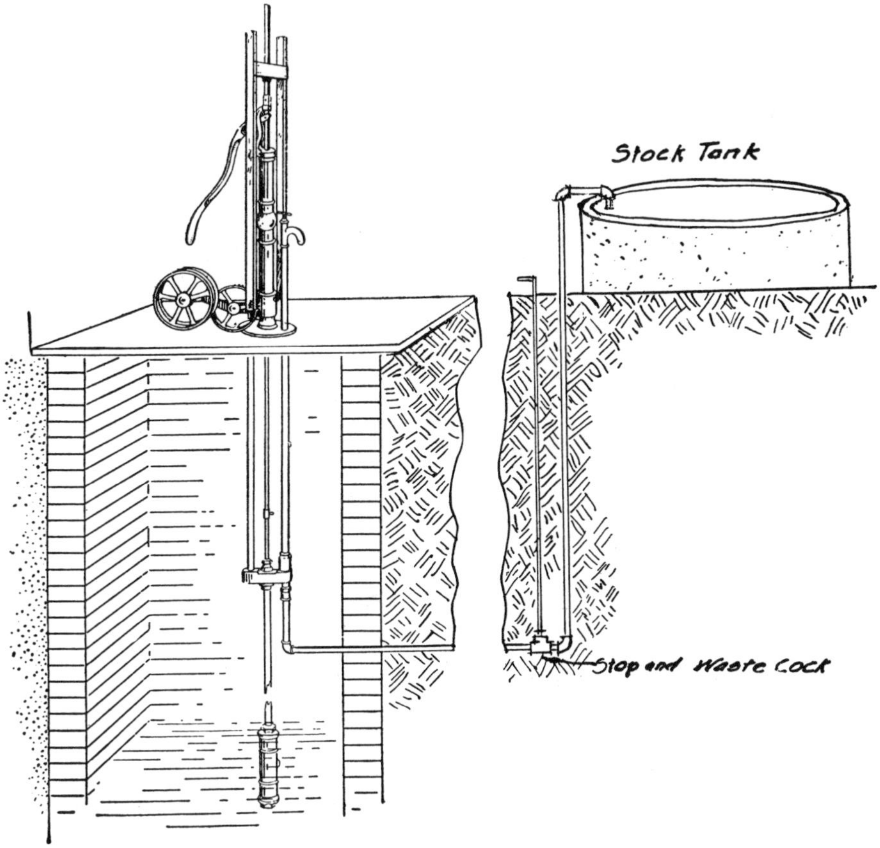

FIG. 356. Piping for stock tank.

Tools and Materials Needed: Plumbing tools, as in Sec. 334. Pipe and fittings determined by particular job.

Instructions:

1) Take measurement for pipe.
2) Cut and thread pipe not threaded.
3) Excavate for pipe line.
4) Connect pipe with fittings above ground.
5) Place pipe in ditch.
6) Provide cut-off and means of draining lines to prevent freezing.

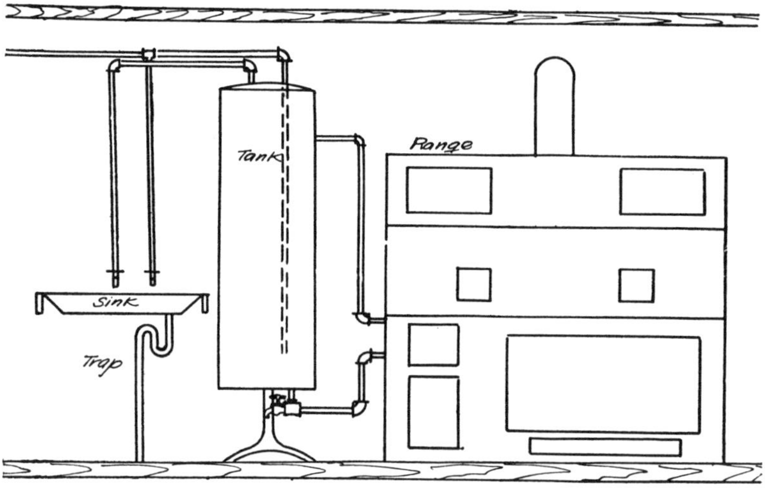

FIG. 357. A hot-water tank installation.

352. Installing Hot-Water Tank with Kitchen Range Having Hot-Water Back.

Requirements: To install a hot-water tank in kitchen with proper connection to water supply, and to hot-water back in kitchen range, as shown in Fig. 357.

Tools and Materials Needed: Tools as in Sec. 334. Materials dependent on particular job. Tank, hot-water back, pipe fittings and white lead or pipe cement.

Instructions:

1) Locate tank so it is out of the way and convenient for connection to mains and to range.

2) Take measurements for pipe. Cut and thread pipe not threaded.
3) Tap main water line with a tee.
4) Make all connections.

Note: Cold water must enter at the bottom of the tank, and hot water is drawn off at the top. Remember, also, that the bottom connection from water back must enter tank at the bottom, and the top connection must enter the tank several feet above the bottom and at a point above the back so the water will rise on being heated and will have proper circulation.

353. To Make a Stock Water Heater.

Requirements: To make a stock water heater when steam pressure and a supply of water under pressure is available. (See Fig. 358.)

Tools Needed: Plumbing tools as in Sec. 334. One breast drill and 1/8″ bit.

Materials Needed: 3′ of 1-1/2″ galvanized pipe, 4-1/2′ of 1/2″ galvanized pipe, three 1/2″ cut-off valves, two 1/2″

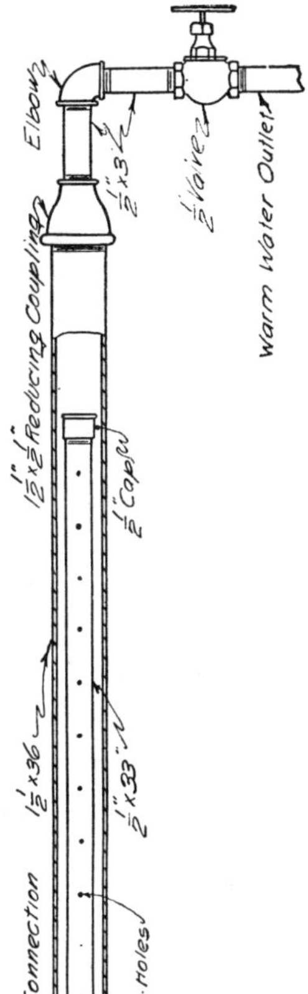
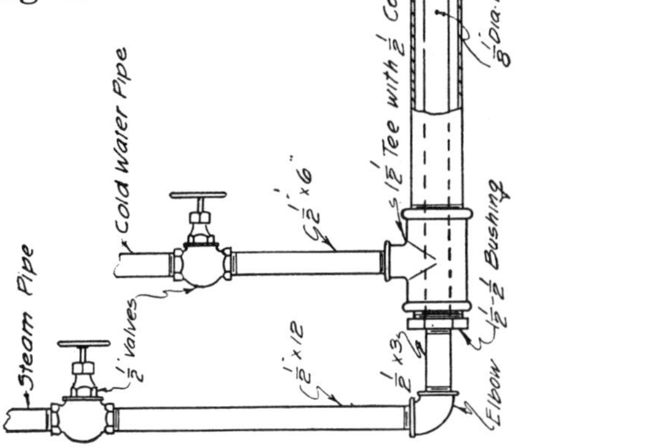

FIG. 358. Stock water heater.

elbows, one 1/2″ cap, one 1-1/2″ to 1/2″ bushing, one 1-1/2″ x 1/2″ tee, one 1-1/2″ to 1/2″ coupling reducer, one 1-1/2″ x 3″ nipple.

Instructions:

1) Cut and thread all pipe to dimension indicated on plan.
2) Drill 1/8″ holes at 3″ intervals on opposite sides of 1/2″ pipe.
3) Assemble 1/2″ steam pipe in following order: Screw 12″ pipe into valve on steam line, elbow onto 12″ pipe, 3″ nipple into elbow, 1-1/2″ x 1/2″ bushing onto nipple, 33″ pipe into opposite side of bushing, screw cap on end of pipe.
4) Assemble water jacket as follows: Screw tee on 1-1/2″ bushing, connect 6″ nipple into tee, screw valve onto nipple, connect valve to water main. Screw 1-1/2″ pipe into tee, on opposite end screw 1-1/2″ x 1/2″ reducing coupling, connect 3″ nipple, elbow, another 3″ nipple and valve to control flow of warm water.

Note: The temperature and flow of water can be controlled by regulating the flow of steam and cold water. Where a boiler is used in connection with dairy room, this is a good way to heat the water for the cows.

354. Installing a Hydraulic Ram.

Requirements: To install a hydraulic ram for elevating water from a lower to a higher elevation for household consumption, as shown in Fig. 359.

Tools Needed: Plumbing tools as in Sec. 334.
Tiling tools as in Project No. 3, Sec. 338.

Material Needed: Sufficient drive and discharge pipe of proper size and length, with necessary fittings; this depending on the individual installation.

Instructions:

1) Locate position of ram.
2) Make measurements and lay out position of drive pipe and discharge pipe.
3) Excavate for drive and discharge pipes.

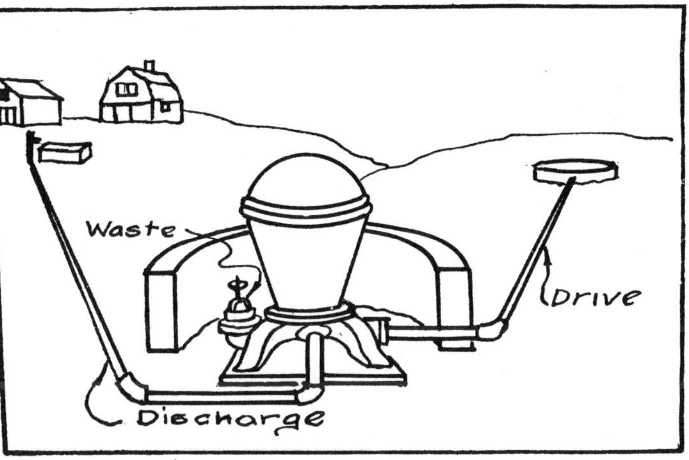

FIG. 359. Hydraulic ram.

4) Proper length and slope of drive pipe depends on particular ram. Secure proper information from manufacturer.
5) Connect drive pipe from ram to source of water.
6) Connect discharge pipe from ram to storage tank.
7) Provide drain for waste water at ram.
8) Cover drive and discharge pipes.
9) Protect ram from high water.

Note: A hydraulic ram is practical only where there is a large quantity of water flowing with several feet fall.

355. Installing Drain Tile at Foundation of House (Fig. 360).

Requirements: To install a drain tile at foundation of house to intercept any seepage water that flows into basement.

Tools and Materials Needed: Tiling tools as in Sec. 338. Sufficient drain tile to extend along side of house and to outlet. Actual amount depending on local conditions.

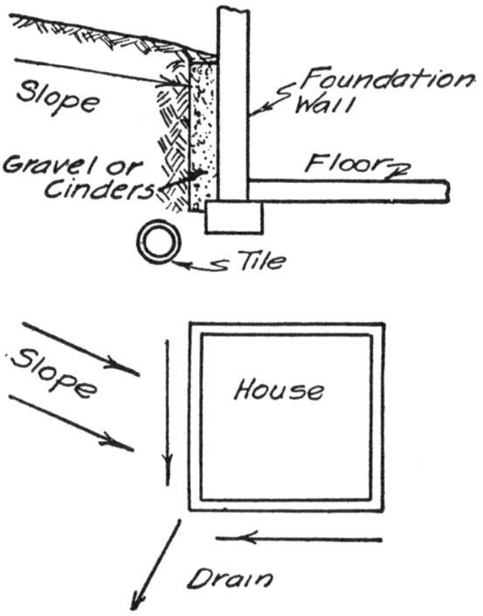

FIG. 360. Location of tile to drain house foundation.

Instructions:

1) Stake out location of drain.
2) Establish grade line.
3) Excavate to grade.
4) Lay tile.
5) Check grade.
6) Back-fill.

Note: Drains should be placed a little below the level of basement floor. If trench above tile is filled with a porous material like gravel, the tile will be much more effective in intercepting the water. This tile should be placed in addition to drains for down-spouting and for basement floor.

356. Additional Jobs on Farm.

a) Install drain to septic tank.
b) Install farm drains.
c) Install tile for down-spouting on barnyard buildings.
d) Install an automatic waterer for stock.
e) Re-charge an acetylene light plant.
f) Put a new pump in a well or cistern.
g) Repair a farm pump.
h) Construct and install a filter.

PART VIII

ROPE AND HARNESS WORK ON THE FARM

CHAPTER XXXVI

CONSTRUCTION AND USE OF ROPE

357. The Need for Rope Work. A working knowledge in the use of rope is of value to every one on the farm. Rope is used in a great many ways, and often much time may be saved by knowing how to make a simple splice, or tie a satisfactory knot or hitch for a particular purpose. Accidents are often averted by knowing how to tie the right knot for the right place. To become expert in tying and splicing rope requires a great deal of practice. One can learn this kind of work only by actually doing it. The work outlined under this head is to give the reader an idea of the principal knots and splices and their applications. Practice work is grouped into several projects. The student should not expect to make progress in rope work without carrying thru these projects.

358. Materials of Which Rope Is Made. The greater part of rope is made from either manilla or sisal fiber. Manilla fiber, a product of the Philippine Islands, is obtained from a plant similar to the banana. The sisal fiber, from which most binder twine is made, a product of Yucatan, is secured from a plant similar to the American aloe. The two kinds of rope are ordinarily known as hemp rope. The sisal is neither as strong nor as durable as manilla fiber. A distinguishing characteristic of the best quality manilla fiber is its glossy appearance. The poorer quality of manilla is of a brownish color, and its glossy characteristic is only slight. Sisal has a dead, lifeless color. The difference between the two might be compared with enamel paint and flat paint. Cotton rope is little used at present, altho, at one time, it was used almost exclusively in some localities.

359. How Rope Is Made. In the actual process of making a rope, the fibers are twisted right-handed into yarns; several yarns are twisted right-handed into a strand, and the strands are twisted left-handed into a rope.

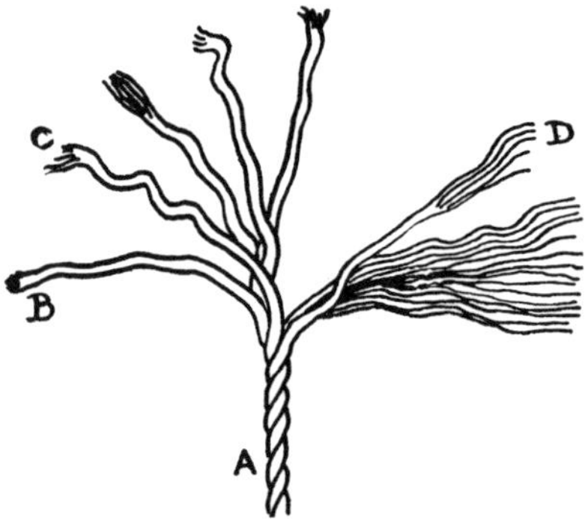

FIG. 361. Parts of rope: *A*, rope; *B* and *C*, strands; *D*, fiber twisted into yarn.

360. Rope Terms.

Fiber — material as obtained from plant.

Yarn—twisted fiber.

Thread—two or more small yarns twisted together left-handed. (Usually cotton, wool and silk.)

String or *Twine*—same as thread, but made of a little larger yarns. (Jute and hemp also used.)

Strand—same as string, but with larger yarns, for making rope.

Cord—two or more threads or strings twisted together.

Rope—two or more strands twisted together right-handed.

Hawser—a rope of three strands.

Shroud-laid—a rope of four strands.

Cable—three hawsers twisted together left-handed.

Standing part—long end of rope not used.

Bight—is formed when the rope is turned back on itself, forming the letter *U*.

End—part used in leading.

Loop—is formed by crossing the sides of a bight.

Lay—to twist the strands of a rope together.

Unlay—to untwist the strands of a rope.

Relay—to twist strands together that have become untwisted.

Whip—to bind the end of the rope to prevent raveling.

Splice—to join two ends of a rope by interweaving the strands.

Crown splice—to interweave the strands at the end of a rope.

Pay—to paint, tar or grease a rope to resist moisture.

Haul—to pull on a rope.

Taut—drawn tight or strained.

361. **Care and Treatment of Rope.** A new rope that is kinky when unwound can best be straightened out by drawing it across the floor or over a sod-covered field. If it is very stiff, it should be immersed in raw linseed oil, tallow or lard, and boiled. This treatment not only makes the rope more pliable, but serves as a lubricant, preventing internal wear. The wear inside a rope is the result of the fibers slipping back and forth over each other, frequently caused by using a pulley that is too small. This wear in a rope can be easily seen by pulling the strands apart. Often a rope is greatly weakened before the wear is noticed. External wear is the result of drawing the rope over rough surfaces which tears the fibers. This source of wear can be easily detected and removed. Where it is desired to protect the rope from dampness, as well as to prevent external wear, the application of an exterior coating such as tallow, graphite, beeswax, or black lead and tallow, will lengthen the life of a rope. Always keep rope in a

dry place. If it does get wet, stretch to dry it. Do not allow the end of the rope to unravel.

362. Requirements of a Good Knot. The three requirements of a good knot have been stated as follows: (*a*) Rapidity with which it can be tied, (*b*) its ability to hold fast when pulled tight, (*c*) the readiness with which it can be untied.

363. Theory of Knots and Splices. Method of making various types of knots can be acquired only by practice. The method of making many good knots is obtained by close observation. There are no very definite rules that one can follow. The following principles should be kept in mind:

"The principle of a knot is that no two parts which move in the same direction, if the rope were to slip, should lie alongside of and touch each other."* . . . "A knot or hitch must be so devised that the tight part of the rope must bear on the free end in such a manner as to pinch and hold it, in a knot against another tight part of the rope, or in a hitch against the object to which the rope is attached."†

The student should try to apply these two principles until they are thoroly mastered.

*Wm. Kent, *Mechanical Engineers' Hand Book.*
†Howard W. Riley, *Cornell Reading Course.*

CHAPTER XXXVII

WHIPPING AND MAKING END KNOTS, END SPLICES

364. Tools and Materials Needed for Rope Work. *Tools and Materials Needed:* A knife and a large nail or marlin spike (Fig. 362) which can be whittled out of a piece of hard wood, are the only tools needed for this work. A few pieces of 3/8″ rope and some pieces of cord will complete the equipment.

FIG. 362. Marlin spike.

365. Treatment of Raveled Ropes. In ropes that are raveled, the strands should be twisted and carefully relaid to the point where the knot is to be formed. In unlaying the end of a new rope in preparation for making a knot, care must

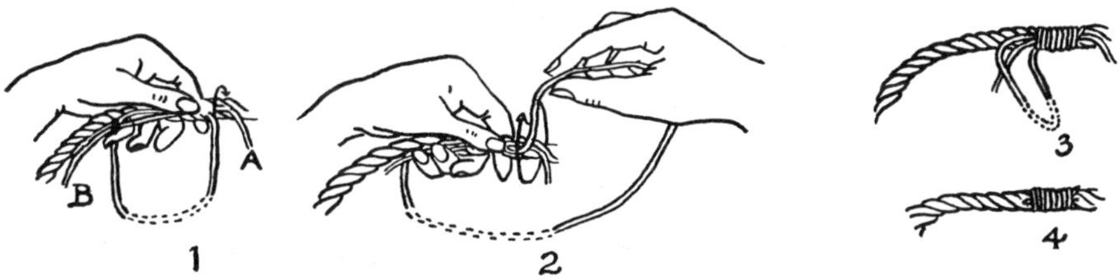

FIG. 363. Whipping end of rope.

be taken not to untwist the strands. Neither whipping nor down crowns can be called knots, but they serve the purpose of a knot and can be used to advantage where it is desirable to have a knot on the end of a rope.

366. Whipping. Place the piece of cord on the rope, allowing one end to hang loosely over the end of the rope about 2″ (*A*, Fig. 363). Make a loop by passing the other

(*B*) end of the string along the rope to make a loose end of about 2″. Hold the rope and cord with left hand, as shown in 2, Fig. 363. Grasp the loop of cord with the right hand and wrap it tightly down the rope over itself, as shown in third sketch. When wrapped as much as desired, draw up the loop by pulling on the ends *A* and *B*. This will complete the job of whipping.

367. Crown Knot. The crown knot (Fig. 364) in itself is of little value, but it is the first step in making a crown or end splice. First unlay several inches of rope, then bring strand No. 1 between strands Nos. 2 and 3, forming a loop, as shown in sketch 1. Pass strand No. 2 across the loop, as shown in sketch 2. Pass strand No. 3 over strand No. 2 and thru the loop. Pull the strands down tightly and complete the crown.

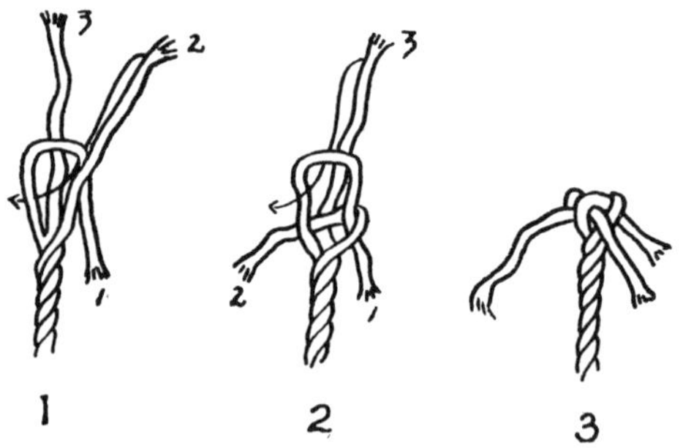

FIG. 364. Crown knot.

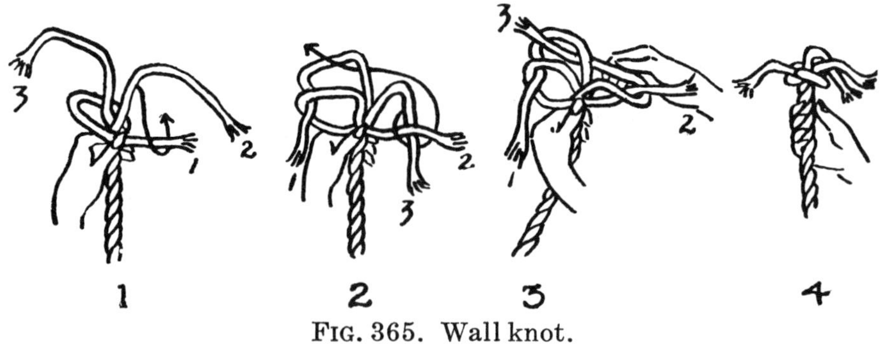

FIG. 365. Wall knot.

368. Wall Knot (Fig. 365). Unlay several inches of rope as in previous case. Hold rope with left hand and with right hand bring strand No. 1 around, forming a loop as in 1. Strand No. 2 is passed around No. 1, as indicated by arrow in 1. Strand No. 3 is passed around No. 2 and up thru loop formed by No. 1, as indicated in 2 and 3. The loose ends are then drawn up, as shown in 4.

369. Wall and Crown Knot (Fig. 366). As the name would imply, the knot is a combination of the two previous knots. The wall knot is made and then the crown knot, as shown in 1 and 2, Fig. 366.

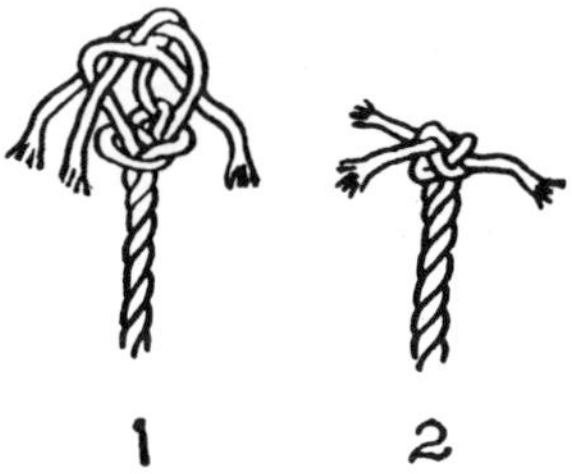

FIG. 366. Wall and crown knot.

370. Manrope Knot. (Fig. 367.) This knot is also a combination of the wall and crown knot, but is made just the reverse of the wall and crown knot. The crown knot is first made and the wall knot drawn down over it.

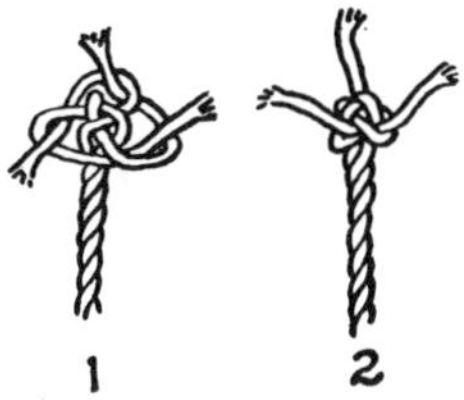

FIG. 367. Manrope knot.

371. Matthew Walker Knot (Fig. 368). This is a very permanent end knot. It is made by first making a loosely-constructed wall knot, then by passing *A* thru the loop with *B*, *B* thru the loop with *C*, and *C* thru the loop with *A*, as shown in 1, Fig. 368. When drawn up tight, we have knot, as shown in 2, Fig. 368.

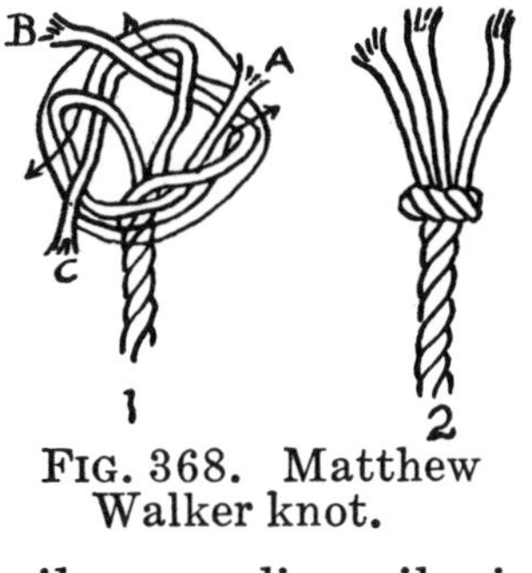

FIG. 368. Matthew Walker knot.

372. End or Crown Splice (Fig. 369). This is one of the best end fastenings for lead ropes. It is made by making a crown knot and then splicing back the loose ends. A large nail or marlin spike is best for weaving the loose ends back. Each loose strand is passed over the adjacent strand in a diagonal direction and under the next one, as shown in 1, 2 and 3, Fig. 369.

373. Overhand Knot (Fig. 370). The overhand knot is

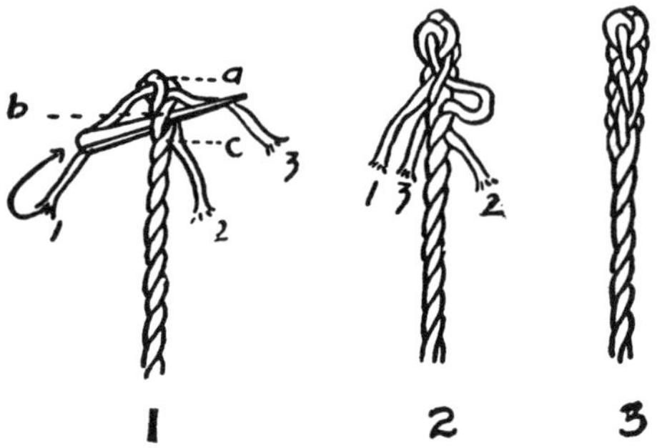

FIG. 369. Crown splice.

FIG. 370. Overhand knot.

one of the most common and the simplest of end knots. It forms a part of many other knots and hitches. It is made by making a loop in the rope and passing one end thru it. Either a right- or left-hand knot may be made.

374. Blood Knot (Fig. 371). This knot is larger than the overhand knot, but made in the same way, except that

FIG. 371. Blood knot.

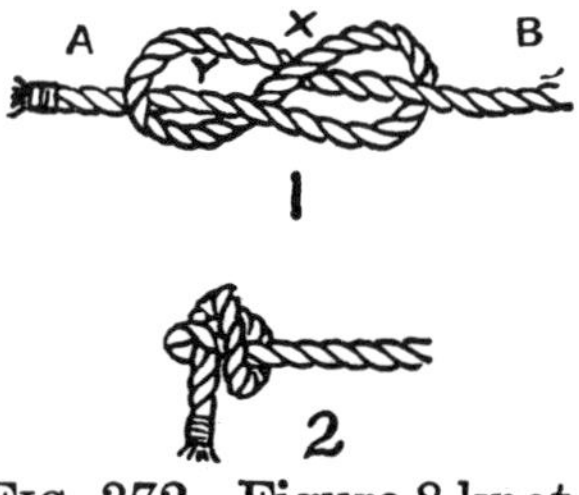

FIG. 372. Figure 8 knot.

the end of the rope is passed thru the loop several times before it is pulled tight. A similar knot is made by the seamstress by rolling the end of the thread between the finger and thumb.

375. Figure 8 Knot (Fig. 372). This knot is a good one to use on the ends of ropes to prevent them from being pulled thru a pulley or a hole. It is made by forming a loop, then passing the short end *A* of the loop over the standing part of the rope *B* at *X* and bringing it back thru the loop at *Y*.

FIG. 373. Stevedore knot.

376. Stevedore Knot (Fig. 373). This knot is the same as the figure 8 knot, but instead of one turn around the standing part of rope, three turns are made, as shown in 1 and 2, Fig. 373.

CHAPTER XXXVIII

TYING KNOTS AND HITCHES

377. Practice in Tying Knots. Whip the ends of each piece of rope. Study each knot carefully, and make the same knot several times for practice with and without sketch. Be sure the knot is correctly tied before attempting a new one.

378. Binder Knot. This knot (Fig. 374) is one of the simplest for fastening two pieces of rope together. It is made by taking the two rope ends, placing them side by side, and tying an overhand knot.

FIG. 374. Binder knot.

379. Square Knot (Fig. 375). This is a smooth knot that is easily tied and easily untied. It is used a great deal for tying packages; also, for fastening the ends of binder twine when threading the binder. To make this knot, first make a right-hand overhand knot, then cross the strand and tie the left-hand overhand knot. This knot will not hold if the two ropes are of different sizes.

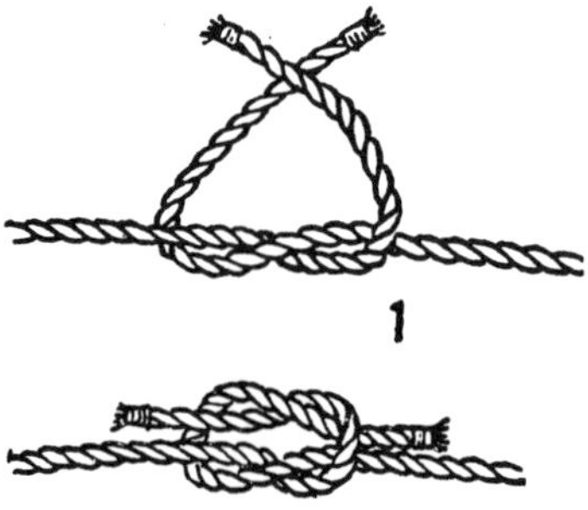

FIG. 375. Square knot.

380. Granny Knot (Fig. 376). The granny knot slips easily and is therefore a very poor knot. The difference between the granny knot and square knot can be easily noted by comparing Fig. 375 and Fig. 376. A great many make the granny knot when attempting to make the square knot.

FIG. 376. Granny knot.

FIG. 377. Surgeon's knot.

381. Surgeon's Knot (Fig. 377). This knot is practically the same as the square knot, except that when making the right-hand overhand knot, the rope is twice wrapped instead of only once. The second part of the knot is completed by making a left-hand overhand as in completing the square knot.

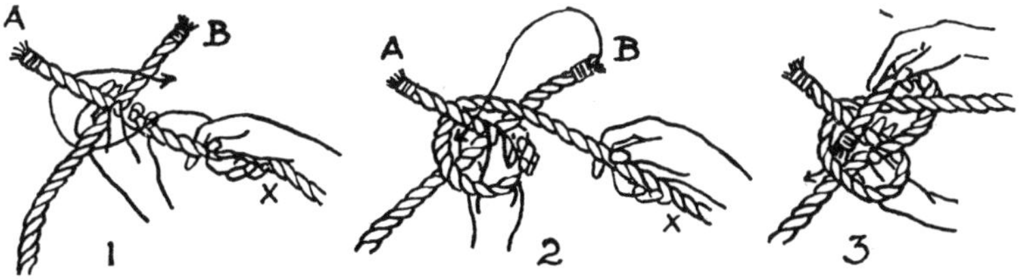

FIG. 378. Weaver's knot.

382. Weaver's Knot (Fig. 378). This knot is one of the best, due to the fact that it holds well, is easily tied and easily untied. To tie this knot, grasp the ends of the rope with left hand, as shown in 1. With end *A* under *B*, grasp rope at *X* and pass it around end *A*, forming a loop as in 2; complete the knot by passing end *B* thru loop as in 3. Draw it up tight.

383. Carrick's Bend (Fig. 379). This knot is used as a fancy knot in braids. It is also a very satisfactory knot to fasten ropes together. In tying this knot, form a loop with the end *Y* under the standing part *A*, as shown in 1. Pass

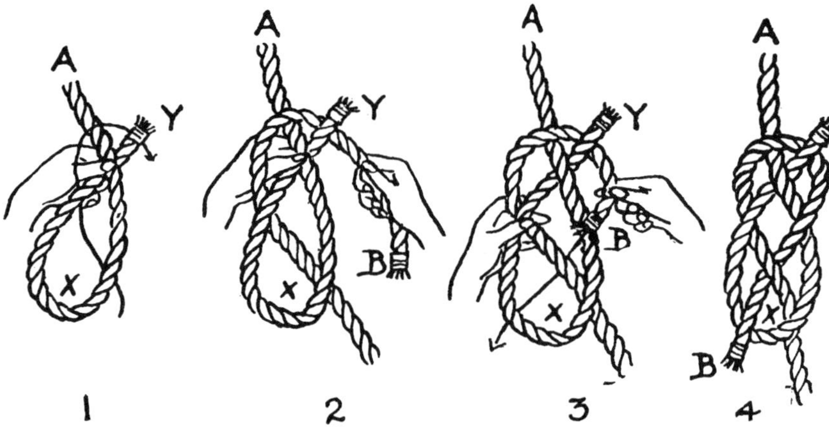

FIG. 379. Carrick's bend.

the other end of rope under the loop *X*, over the standing part *A*, under end *Y*, again over *A*, under standing part *B* and over *A*, the final knot being completed as in 4. When drawn tight, it will assume the shape of a double bowline.

Knots for Fastening Cattle, Tying Hay Ropes, Etc.:

A point to be considered in use of rope is the correct selection of knot for right place; this is especially true where a knot is to be loosened often, or where it is desired to have a knot that will slip.

384. Bowline Knot (Fig. 380). This is one of the best knots for fastening the end of a rope as in hitching. There are several kinds, but the overhand is probably the easiest and quickest to make. To make the knot, form a small loop (*C*) in 1 near the end of the rope, as in Fig. 380. Hold the loop with the left hand, grasp the end *A* with the right hand, pass it thru the loop *C* and around the standing part *B*, and back thru the loop, as in 2 and 3.

385. Double-Rope Bowline Knot (Fig. 381). This knot is quite similar to the knot just described, but is used

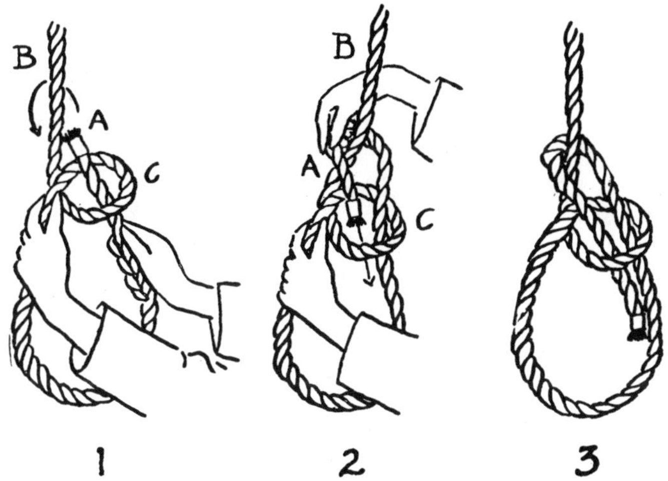

FIG. 380. Bowline knot.

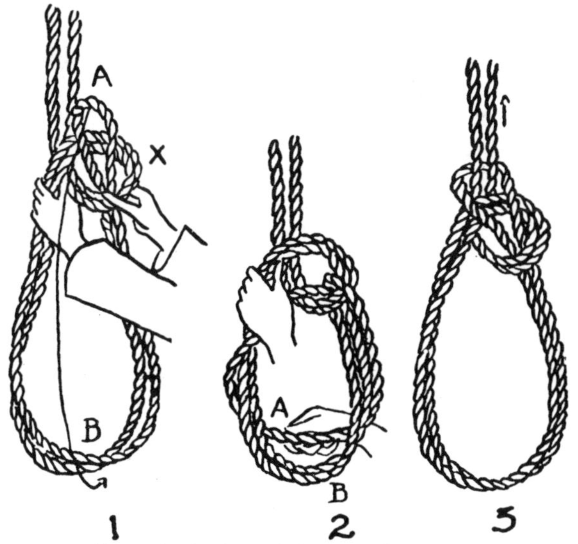

FIG. 381. Double rope bowline.

when made in the middle of a long rope or at the end when doubled. A loop (*X*) is formed and part *A* passed thru as in previous case. Part *A* is drawn thru far enough so that the double loop *B* can be drawn thru it, as shown in 2 and 3. This knot is especially useful in throwing horses and cattle.

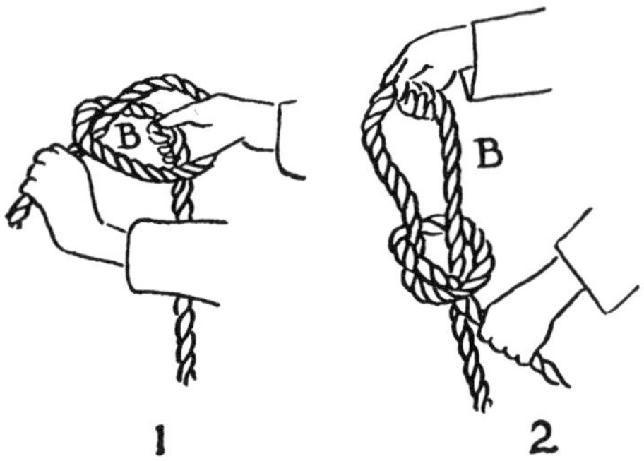

FIG. 382. Slip knot.

386. Slip Knot (Fig. 382). The slip knot is a very common one and often used when a different type of knot would be much more satisfactory. To tie this knot, form a loop, grasp rope *B* and draw it thru, as shown in 1 and 2 in Fig. 382.

387. Manger Knot (Fig. 383). This knot is quite similar to the ordinary slip knot, but much better on account of

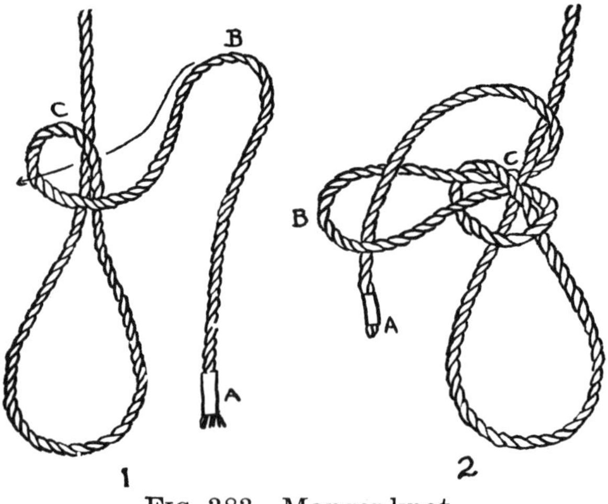

FIG. 383. Manger knot.

being easier to untie. To tie this knot, form a loop *C*, grasp the bight *B* and pass it around the standing part of the rope and thru loop *C*; then complete the knot by bringing end *A* around the standing part and thru *B*.

388. Lariat Knot (Fig. 384). As the name would indicate, this knot is used in forming a lariat. It is tied by first forming an overhand knot near the end of the rope, as at C in 1,

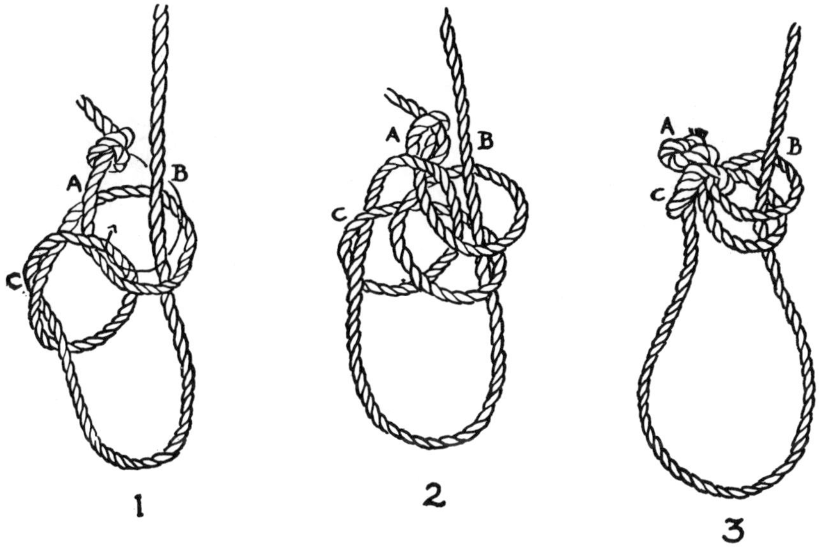

FIG. 384. Lariat knot.

Fig. 384. The end *A* is then passed around the standing part *B* and thru the loop twice. The overhand knot is then drawn tight and the knot is complete.

389. Hangman's Noose (Fig. 385). This is another knot with a slip loop. It is a knot that is easy to tie and holds

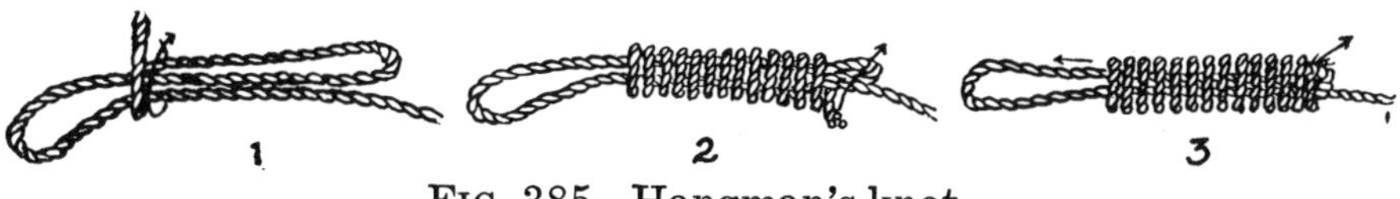

FIG. 385. Hangman's knot.

well. Make a double loop, as in 1; then wind the end of rope back the number of rounds desired, passing it thru loop *Y*, 2. By drawing on the noose, the knot is completed, as in 3.

390. Farmer's Loop (Fig. 386). If it is desired to tie a loop in the middle of a rope when both ends are fastened, the farmer's loop is suitable. It is easily tied and easily untied. Make two turns in rope and hold it, as in 1, Fig. 386. Pass

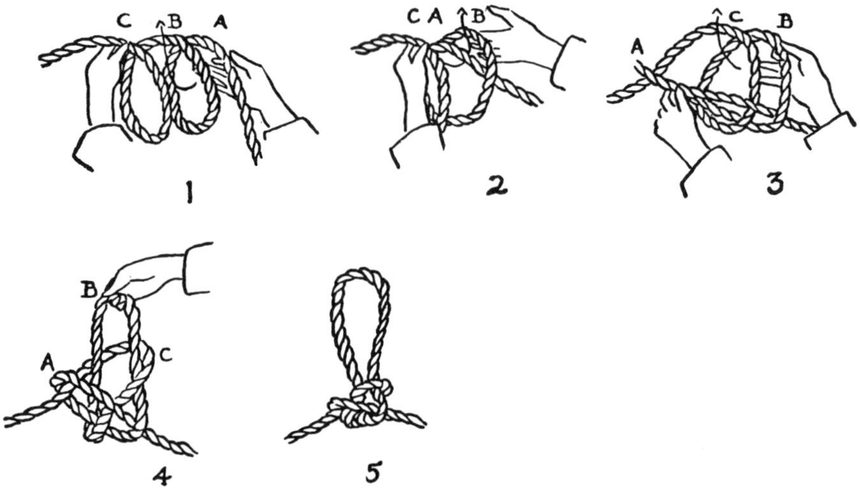

FIG. 386. Farmer's loop.

loop *A* under loop *B* between *B* and *C* in 2. Next pass loop *C* under loop *A*, as in 3. Now, pass *B* under loop *C* and up between *A* and *C* in 4. The knot is completed by drawing the standing part tight.

Temporary Hitches.

Note: A hitch should be selected for a particular use. One should be very careful in making a scaffold hitch where life is in danger. It must be kept in mind that the hitches here outlined are for temporary use.

391. Half Hitch (Fig. 387). The half hitch is one step in making other hitches and knots. It is useful, however, when the standing part of the rope is drawn tight and pinches the end against object tied, as in Fig. 387.

392. Timber Hitch (Figs. 388 and 389). This hitch is one step in advance over the half hitch. The end of the rope is wrapped several times instead of simply drawn under once

FIG. 387. Half hitch.

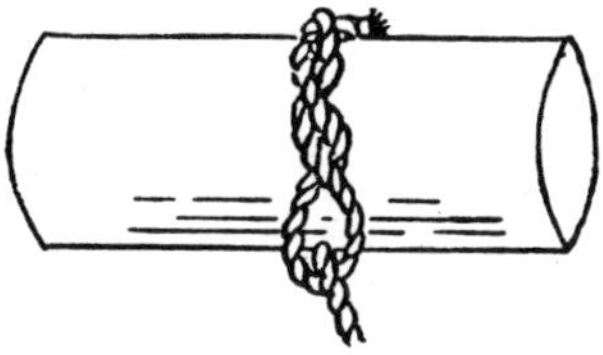

FIG. 388. Timber hitch.

as in the half hitch. A combination of the timber and half hitch is much more secure. (See Fig. 389.)

FIG. 389. Timber and half hitch.

FIG. 390. Rolling hitch.

393. Rolling Hitch (Fig. 390). This hitch is very easily and quickly made, and is a suitable fastening for most any purpose. Wrap rope three times about the object to which it is to be fastened, then make two half hitches about the standing part.

394. Clove Hitch (Fig. 391). This is one of the simplest and yet one of the most secure methods of fastening tent ropes, guy ropes or any rope when there is to be a direct pull against it. There are several methods of making the clove hitch, but probably the farmer's method is best. Cross the arms, the left in front of the right; grasp the rope, as in 1, Fig. 391; then bring the hands to position. shown in 2; then

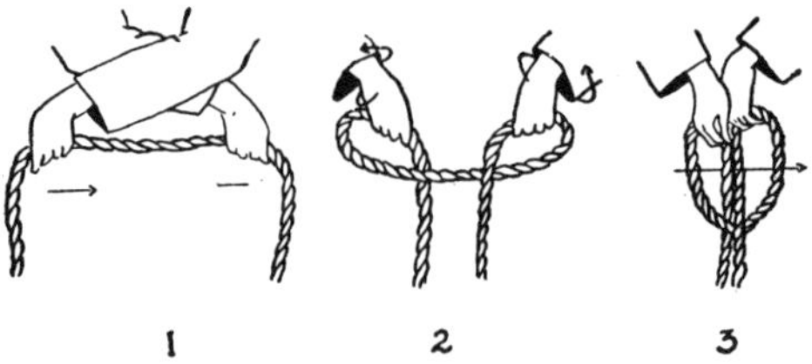

FIG. 391. Clove hitch.

complete the hitch by turning both hands to the right, as in 3.

395. Scaffold Hitch (Fig. 392). The scaffold hitch is a modified form of the clove hitch. Make a rather loose clove

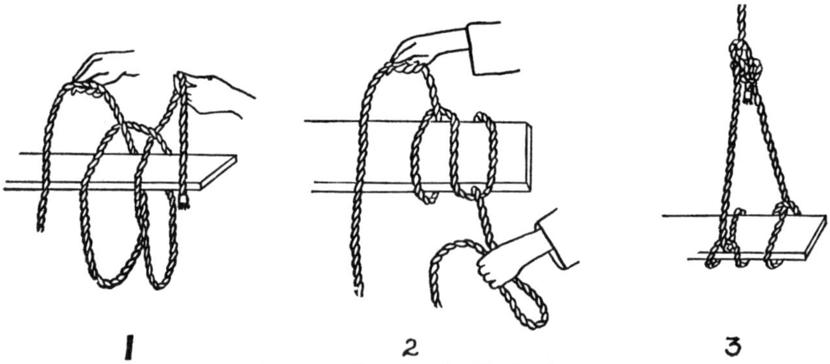

FIG. 392. Scaffold hitch.

hitch and place over the end of scaffold, as in 1, Fig. 392. Draw the ropes tight in opposite direction, turn the plank over and fasten short end to the standing part by means of a bowline knot, as in 3.

396. Blackwall Hitch (Fig. 393). This hitch can be used only when the pull on rope is continuous and a hook is provided. Make a bight in the rope and pass around the hook; the free end is then passed thru the hook, and the standing part passed over it from the opposite side.

397. Sheepshank (Fig. 394). The sheepshank is not a hitch in the same sense as the other hitches described. It is

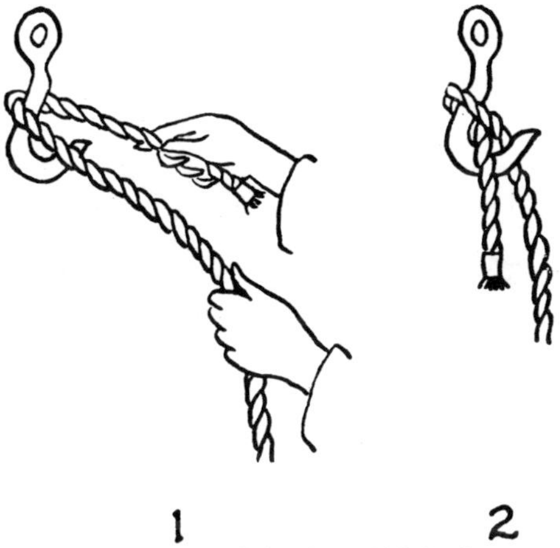

FIG. 393. Blackwall hitch.

used as a means of shortening ropes. To tie this hitch, a loop is formed that is large enough to reduce the rope to desired length (see 1, Fig. 394) and held in the left hand; a half hitch is formed of the standing part of the rope and passed over

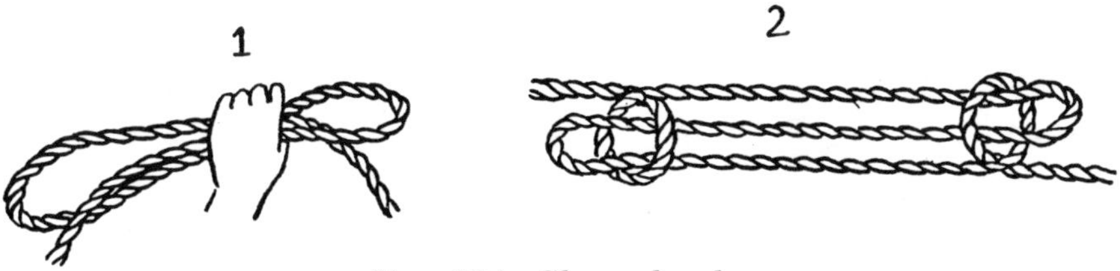

FIG. 394. Sheepshank.

each end of the loop, as in 2. To make this hitch permanent, the standing part is drawn thru the bight at each end of the loop.

Splices:

398. End or Crown Splice. This type of splice has been described under head of means of preventing rope from raveling (Fig. 369).

399. Loop Splice (Fig. 395). This splice is used when a permanent loop is to be constructed at any point of the rope other than the end. The size and location of the loop is first determined, then two strands are raised on the short end and

FIG. 395. Loop splice.

the lead rope passed under them. To complete the splice, two strands in the long part of the rope are raised, as in *a*, 1, Fig. 395; and the short end *b* is passed thru and drawn up, as in 3.

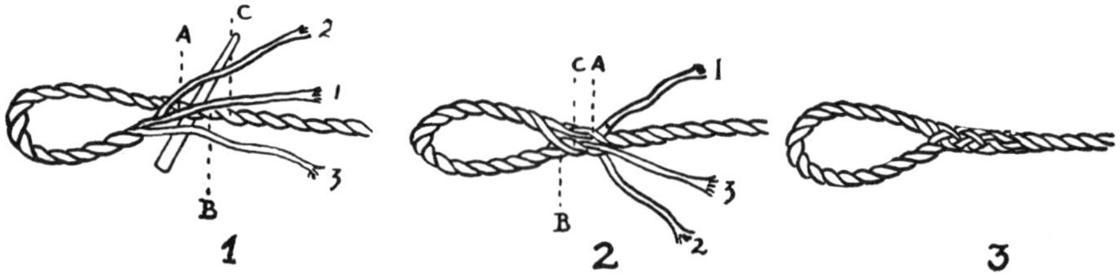

FIG. 396. Eye splice.

400. Eye Splice or Side Splice (Fig. 396). The eye splice is used when it is desired to form a loop at the end of a rope or as a side splice where it is desired to fasten one rope to another at any point other than the end. Unlay the end of the rope for several inches, determine the size of loop to form, then place the two outside strands to straddle the main rope and the center strand to run along the top of the rope, as in 1, Fig. 396. Now, by means of the marlin spike or large nail, raise one of the strands *A* and pass the center strand No. 1 under it. Pass strand No. 2 over *A* and under *B*, and pass strand No. 3 thru from the opposite side so that it comes out where No. 1 enters. Draw all ends up snug and weave in the strands, as described for the end splice.

401. Short Splice (Fig. 397). The short splice is used for joining the two ends of rope together when it is not desired

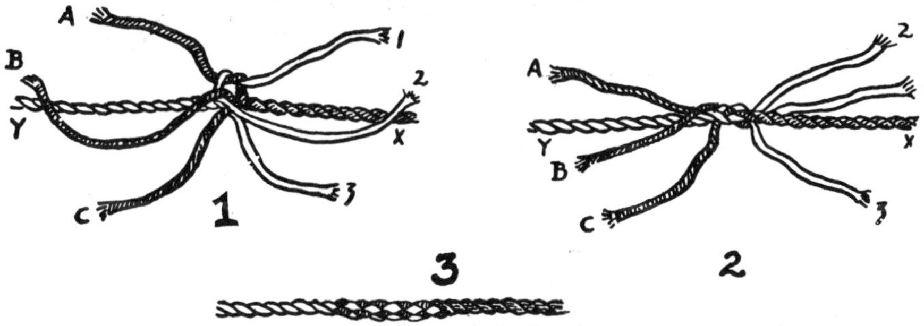

FIG. 397. Short splice.

to draw it thru pulleys. This splice is not as smooth as the long splice, but it is strong and quite easily made. To make the splice, unlay the ends of the two ropes for a sufficient distance, depending on size of rope and load—for a 3/8″ rope, at least 6″. Bring the ends of the rope together so that the strands of one pass alternately between those of the other, as in 1, Fig. 397. Take each pair of strands from opposite sides and tie a right-hand overhand knot, draw the knots tightly and pass each strand diagonally to the left, then weave it in as in making the end splice (1, 2 and 3, Fig. 397).

402. Long Splice (Fig. 398). This type of splice is so nearly the same size as the other part of the rope, that it can be used thru pulleys without hindrance. Every user of rope

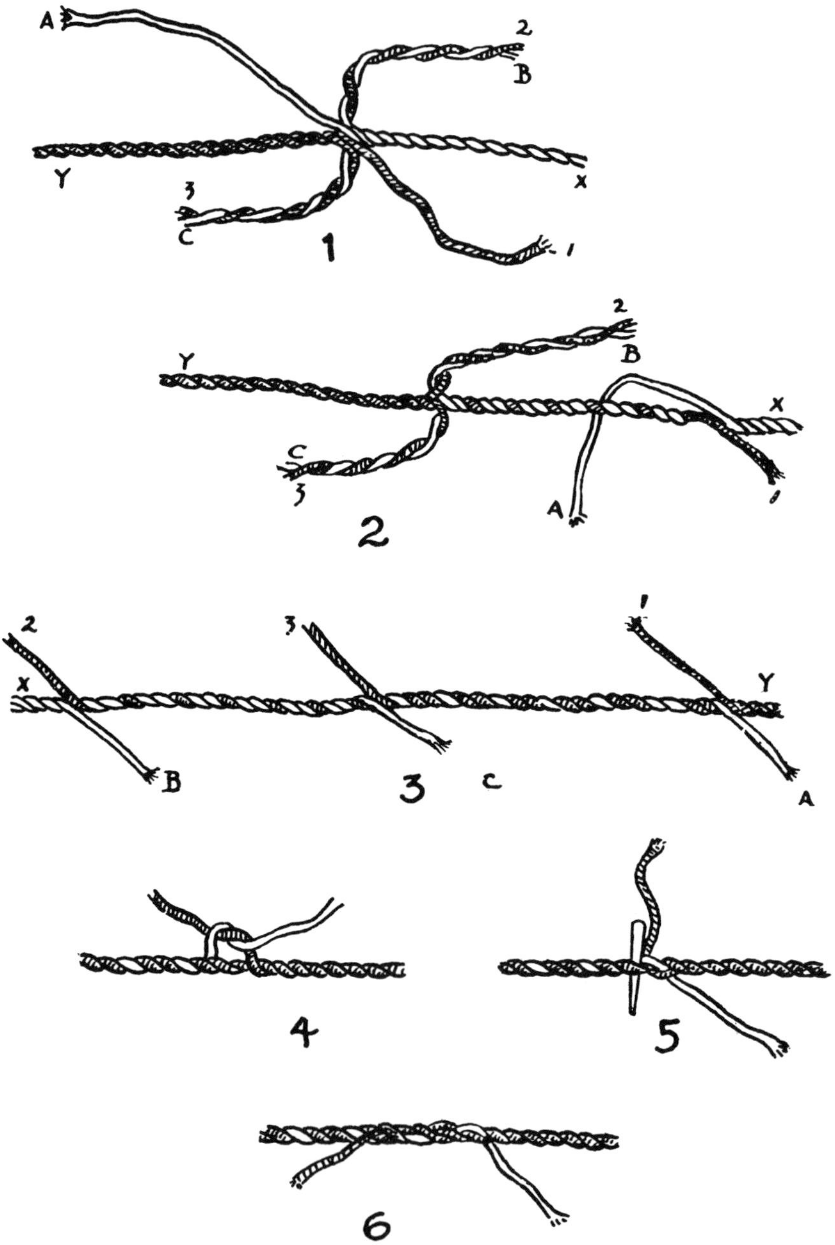

FIG. 398. Long splice.

should know how to make the long splice. Unlay the end of the rope, as in making a short splice. A 1/4″ rope should be unlaid about 12″, a 3/8″ rope 16″, a 1/2″ rope 24″, and a 1″ rope 36″, to obtain best results. Lock the strands as in the beginning of the short splice, pair the strands from each end, as in 1, Fig. 398, twisting two of the pairs together. As for the remaining pair, unlay one strand and relay the other strand in its place. Continue until within a few inches of the end of the relaid strand No. 1, as in 2. Repeat the process with either pair of the other strands. Untwist the last pair; the rope should appear, as in 3, with each strand coming from the left and passing in front of the strands from the right. To complete the splice, tie each pair of strands with a right-hand overhand knot, as in 4. Weave the loose ends into the rope by passing one end over the adjacent strand and under the next, as in 5. Cut the ends of strands off and pound down the uneven ends to make finished splice, as in 6.

CHAPTER XXXIX

PROJECTS IN ROPE WORK

403. Making a Halter.

Preliminary Instructions: There will be 12′ or more of rope needed for this project. Temporary halters are much more satisfactory for leading an animal than is a rope placed about the animal's neck. To make a temporary

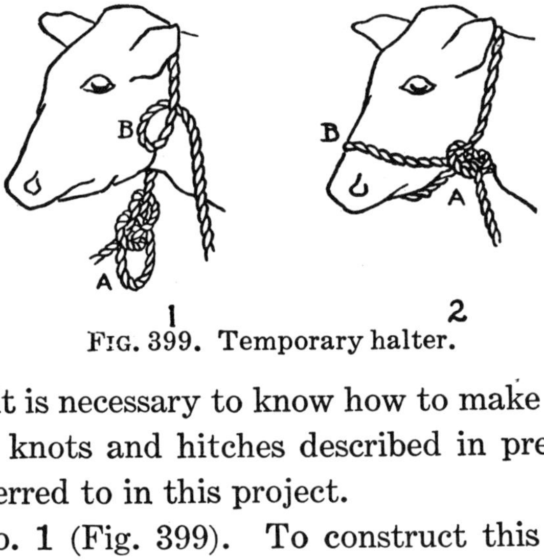

FIG. 399. Temporary halter.

halter, it is necessary to know how to make a few of the various knots and hitches described in previous pages and referred to in this project.

Halter No. 1 (Fig. 399). To construct this halter, first make a loop in the end of the rope *A*, tying it with a simple overhand bowline, as described in Sec. 389. Pass the end of rope with loop about animal's neck and form a second loop *B* in the standing part of the rope thru which draw loop *A* and place around the animal's nose. The slack is drawn out with the free end of the rope, as in 2.

Halter No. 2 (Fig. 400). This type of temporary halter is usually called the Hackamore. It is used for leading either cattle or horses, and is made by passing one end of the rope about the animal's neck and tying with a bowline knot. A half hitch is thrown in the standing part of the rope and passed over the animal's nose, as in 1, Fig. 400; a second half

FIG. 400. Temporary halter (Hackamore).

hitch is made below the first and passed over the nose, as in 2. The first half hitch is wrapped about the second and passed over the aninal's head, as in 3. To complete the halter, the standing part of the rope is passed thru the loop *C* below the half hitch, as indicated in 4.

404. An Adjustable Halter (Fig. 401).

Preliminary Instructions: To make a satisfactory adjustable halter, it is necessary to be familiar with the method of making the eye splice, loop splice and end splice. The size of rope to use will depend on the use of halter. Most halters are made from 1/2″ to 3/4″ rope. The length of rope needed is 12′.

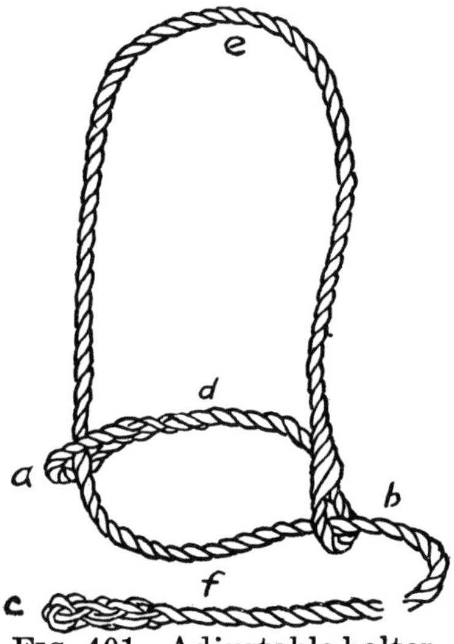

FIG. 401. Adjustable halter.

Working Instructions:

1) Make an eye splice in end of rope as at *a*, Fig. 401 This splice should be only large enough to allow the standing part of rope to pass thru it freely.
2) Measure from the loop of the eye splice the distance (*d*) that will be required to reach nearly around the animal's nose. At this point make a loop splice (*b*) with loop the same size as that of the eye splice.
3) Pass the standing end of the rope thru loop *a* and loop *b*.
4) Complete halter by making end splice on end *c*.

405. Making a Non-Adjustable Halter (Fig. 402).

Note: The only difference between this halter and the one described in Sec. 404 is that the head piece and nose piece are made of definite length, depending on the head dimensions of the particular animal for which the halter is made.

1) Determine the necessary length of head piece and nose piece by measuring animal's head.

2) Make loop splice (*b*, Fig. 402), leaving *c* long enough to form nose piece.
3) Side splice end of *c* into standing part of rope at *a*, making head piece *d* of suitable size.
4) Thread end *c* thru loop *b*.
5) Make end splice *e* in end of standing part of rope to complete the halter.

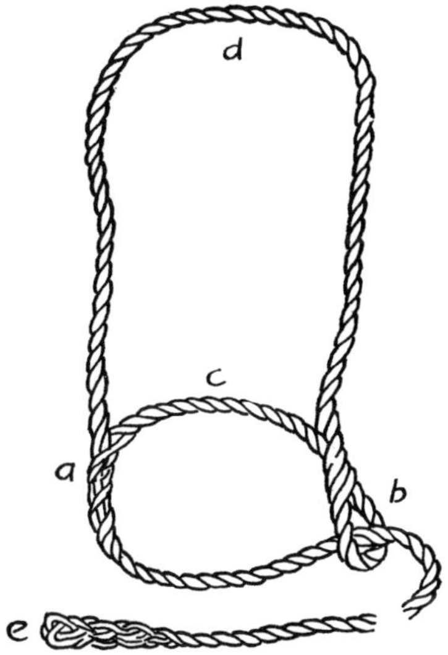

FIG. 402. Non-adjustable halter.

406. The Trip Rope (Fig. 403).

Materials Needed: Thirty feet of 1/2″ rope, three 2″ rings, and two heavy straps with buckles to go around ankles.

Preliminary Instructions: In handling young horses, it is sometimes very essential to have some means of tripping them when the horse does not obey the command of the trainer. Knee pads should be provided when the trip rope is used.

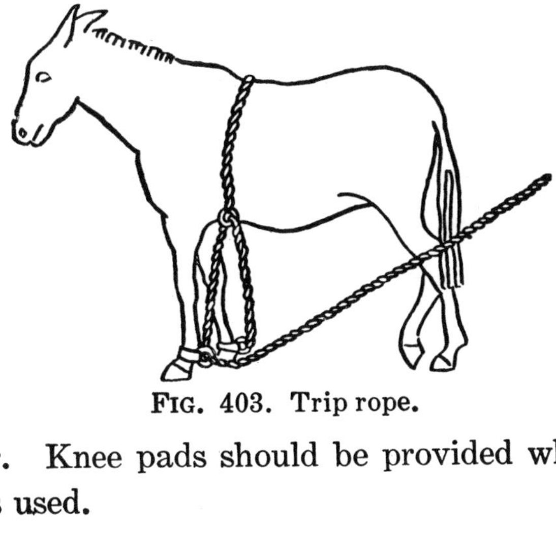
FIG. 403. Trip rope.

Working Instructions:

1) Place ankle straps on front ankles with a ring on each strap.
2) Place surcingle with ring at bottom around horse just back of shoulders, or tie around the body at this point a piece of rope, using a single bowline knot.
3) Take long rope provided, pass thru ring on ankle strap of near foot, up thru ring at bottom of surcingle, and down

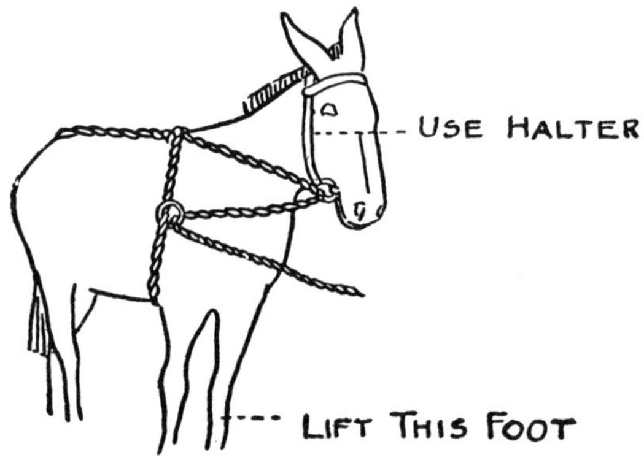

FIG. 404. Throwing rope.

to other ankle ring where it is tied. The trip is then ready to use by pulling on standing part of long rope.

407. Throwing or Casting Rope (Fig. 404).

Materials Needed: Thirty feet of 1/2″ rope and straps.

Preliminary Instructions: In handling horses, it is sometimes necessary to throw the animal for the purpose of an operation or otherwise. To avoid chafing or burning the animal with a rope, straps should be provided for those places where a rope would rub.

Working Instructions:

1) Tie a double rope bowline knot, as described in Sec. 385, in middle of rope to serve as crupper.

2) Adjust crupper in place, run to withers and tie a square knot (Sec. 379).
3) Pass rope about body at withers just back of front legs; tie with another square knot, forming a surcingle and

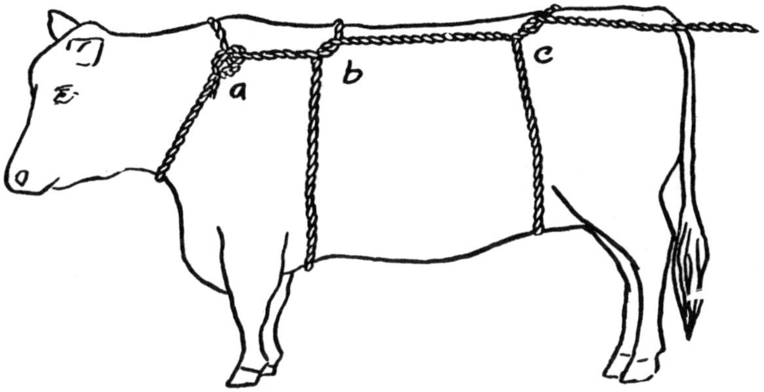

FIG. 405. Casting rope.

crupper properly adjusted to the animal. Provide ring or girth, as shown in Fig. 404.
4) Run the free end of the rope from top of surcingle thru the ring in halter back thru ring on girth. The rope is then ready for use.
5) Instead of rope under No. 3, a regular crupper and surcingle may be used.
6) To use rope, lift the front foot of the animal on the side opposite that on which the rope is passed and pull on the free end of the rope.

408. Rope for Casting Cattle (Fig. 405).

Material Needed: Thirty-five feet of 1″ rope.

Preliminary Instructions: The instruction for throwing a horse should be kept in mind in throwing a cow or steer. Care must be observed to avoid hurting the animal. One need be acquainted only with the bowline knot and the simplest half hitches to adjust a rope for throwing cattle.

Working Instructions:

1) Place one end around the animal's neck and tie rope with a bowline knot (*a*, Fig. 405).
2) Pass the rope about the animal's body just back of the fore legs, forming a half hitch at withers, as shown at *b*, Fig. 405.
3) Pass the rope about the body (*c*) at the hips, forming another half hitch.
4) If a cow is to be thrown, the rope should be placed just in front of the udder.
5) To throw the animal, pull to rear and toward side upon which it is to be thrown.

CHAPTER XL

HARNESS REPAIR

409. The Importance of Good Harness. Nothing adds more to the appearance of a well-groomed horse than a neat, clean and properly-fitting harness. A good set of harness not only adds to the appearance of a team, but makes the team more efficient in its operation. A first-class teamster will take pride in keeping his team properly fitted. Such negligence as allowing the harness to be bound up with pieces of baling wire and with binder twine is inexcusable. Often the hame straps are allowed to loosen, the breeching to hang too low, resulting in sore shoulders and chafed sides and back.

The farmer cannot afford to neglect the care and upkeep of his harness. In fact, each farmer should be provided with a simple harness repair outfit and keep on hand a few supplies for adding a strap by sewing or riveting where one is worn.

The life of a harness can be greatly increased by systematic care. The practice of oiling the harness at least once a year should not be overlooked. Take the harness apart and wash it thoroly in warm, soft water and soap; allow it time to dry; then apply a coat of good quality harness oil. Allow the oil to soak in before it is rubbed off. Before the harness is reassembled, each part should be gone over carefully and needed repairs made. This work can easily be done on the farm on rainy days.

410. The Harness Room. A conveniently-located harness room is of great value in caring for the harness. It is very objectionable to store the harness in most stables due to the effect of the moisture and the ammonia from the manure. When the stable is kept thoroly cleaned and is well ventilated, harness can be kept with little damage and are thereby much more conveniently located for use.

411. Harness Oil. Be careful not to use a mineral oil for the harness or leather belts. Mineral oils will cause the leather to dry out and crack. Buy only standard brands found on the market. A good oil can be made by melting three pounds of tallow without letting it boil, and gently adding one pound of neat's-foot oil. Stir continuously until cold so that it will be perfectly mixed. Color by adding a little lampblack.

412. Repair Leather. Leather for repairing can be bought from any harness shop. It is best to buy a fairly large piece, as it can be secured much more cheaply that way. Some men buy a half hide, and, thereby, secure some of both the best quality leather from the back of the hide and the poorer, cheaper belly leather. The latter can be used where there is little strain.

413. Equipment for Harness Work. A clamp is needed for holding the work. This can easily be made at home. Some men prefer a vise to a clamp. A common type of clamp is illustrated and described under woodwork. (Fig. 86.) In addition to the clamp, the repair outfit should consist of the following: One dozen sewing needles, different sizes; a sharp knife, half dozen awls, ball of shoe thread, two awl handles, one revolving punch, one small riveter with rivets. The entire repair outfit can be purchased for less than $2. Instead of shoe thread and wax, the prepared thread can be secured. An advantage of the shoe thread and wax is that it can be prepared to meet the requirement of the special job.

414. Splicing Worn Harness Strap.

Requirements: To make a satisfactory splice that will be smooth and not chafe, and if used thru a ring, will not catch or bind. It must also be strong enough to resist the force applied to it.

Materials Needed: Suitable leather strip for repair, thread, wax.

Tools Needed: Clamp (such as shown in Fig. 86), one selected awl, two selected needles, one sharp knife.

415. Preparing Strap for Sewing. Prepare the worn strap for splice by cutting away the worn part. Thin the ends down with a sharp knife to a gradual taper for about 3″. If the strap is one that can be shortened, it is then ready for splicing; otherwise, an insert will have to be prepared and a double splice made. Small wire tacks are useful in holding the straps together while the stitching is being done. Prepare thread for sewing by waxing it. To do this, the thread must first be broken with a ragged end. Pull the thread out of the center of the ball, hold it on the knee, and roll it to take out the twist. When the twist is out, give the string a pull and it should break with long ragged ends. Give the end a twist around the first finger of the left hand and draw it thru the right hand. When about 6′ have been drawn out, throw the center over a hook in the wall and pull until the ends are about even and each about 3′ long. Keep the string tight with the left hand, and with the right hand rub it on the knee as before and break it. Repeat this until the required number of strands have been secured, depending on the work to be done. Make the ends of the strands slightly uneven in length to provide a long tapering point for threading the needle. Wax the free ends before twisting. Twist the thread carefully and wax it thoroly. Put the two needles on the thread ready for sewing.

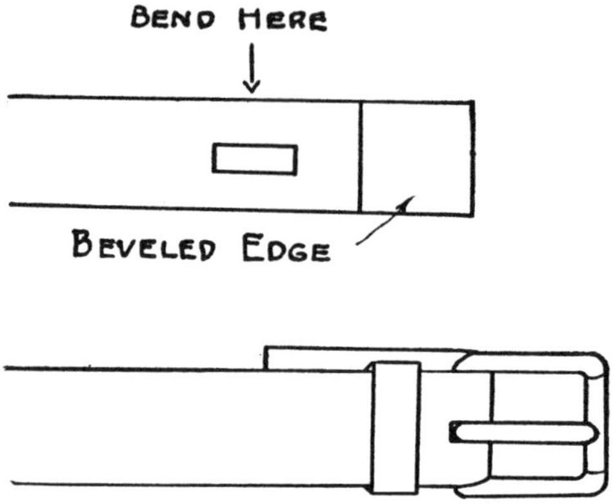

FIG. 406. Sewing buckle or strap.

416. Sewing the Splice. Put the splice in the clamp, using extreme care to keep edges perfectly even. Mark off holes a definite distance apart. Make hole with the awl, insert needle and draw the thread half way thru, leaving one needle on each side. Make another hole with the awl, insert the needle thru and draw the thread thru a few inches; then put the other needle thru the same hole from the other side and pull both threads up tight, being careful to avoid knots. Continue this process along both sides and across the ends of the splice. To do a good job, keep the stitches straight and of uniform length. To complete the job, draw the ends of the thread out between the splice and tie.

417. Sewing Buckle and Ring on Harness Strap. Suitable buckle, ring and strap for the work intended are the required materials for this job. The proper selection of strap and buckle for the particular job is very essential. The buckle should be slightly wider than the strap to insure ease in buckling and to reduce the amount of wear on the strap. The strap should be prepared for sewing as in preceding exercise. Fig. 406 illustrates this operation.

418. Instructions for Sewing Buckle. If strap is wider than buckle, trim it down until it is a very little nar-

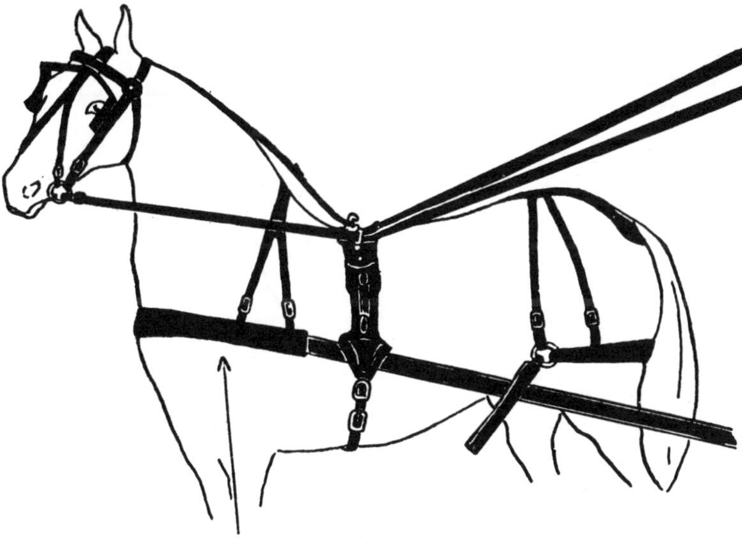

FIG. 407. Single harness, breast collar type.

rower than the buckle. Double end of strap back thru buckle at least 2″ for a 1″ strap; cut a slot for the tongue of buckle long enough to move the tongue thru 180 degrees. Next shave the inner surface of the end of the strap to a beveled edge to make a smooth joint when it is sewed. Cut a narrow strap of leather to pass around the strap, as shown (Fig. 406), to hold the opposite end of the strap when buckled. Put buckle in place, fold strap back, and clamp tightly in sewing clamp. Proceed to sew, as in preceding problem. Riveting and sewing can often be employed together on such work.

419. Overhauling a Set of Harness (Figs. 407 and 408).

Preliminary Instructions: Soap and water, oil, harness dressing and metal polish must be provided for this work. Harness in poor repair means a loss of time during the busy season. Inspect and repair all harness before the

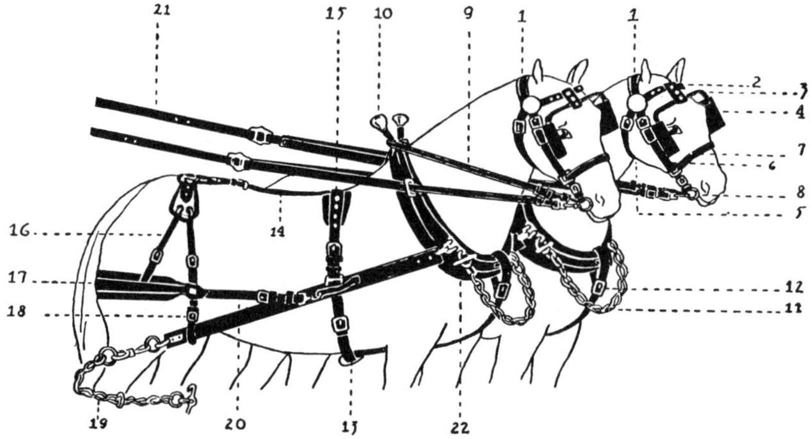

1-BRIDLE CROWNPIECE, 2-BROWBAND, 3-BLINDSTAY, 4-BLINDS, 5-THROATLATCH, 6-CHEEKPIECE, 7-NOSEBAND, 8-BIT, 9-REIN, 10-HAMES, 11-NECKYOKE CHAINS, 12-BREAST STRAP, 13-BELLYBAND, 14-BACKSTRAP, 15-SADDLE, 16-HIPSTRAPS, 17-BREECHING, 18-LAZY-STRAP, 19-HEELCHAIN, 20-HOLDING BACK STRAP, 21-LINES, 22-COLLAR

FIG. 408. Double harness.

spring season work begins. The best time to do this is when the weather is bad and outside work cannot be done to advantage. To keep the harness in best condition, they should be gone over at least twice each year.

Working Instructions: First take the harness apart so that each strap, buckle and ring can be carefully inspected. Carefully clean with a little warm soft water. If the harness is very dirty, soak for a few minutes in warm water; then scrub with a brush, using soap freely; wipe and hang up to dry. When dried, apply oil, prepared as outlined in Sec. 411, or a special harness oil. Make several applications and rub the oil into the leather to get the best results. To give the harness a good, glossy, black finish, it is necessary to apply some good standard harness dressing as recommended by the harness-maker. Ordinary black shoe polish may be used, but would probably be a little more expensive than the material prepared for the purpose. After application, rub vigorously with a polishing cloth to get the best results. To clean the metal mountings, use some form of metal polish or cleansing compound, like Old Dutch Cleanser or Bon Ami. Careful polishing is a big factor in giving the harness a good appearance. Lastly, put harness back together, making all necessary repairs, adding new straps, buckles or rings where needed, following instructions outlined in Secs. 415-418.

420. Adjusting Harness to Horse. Every one who handles a team should realize the importance of a well-fitted harness. A poorly-fitted harness not only hinders the horse in working, but is liable to make a balker out of a good worker, and, in addition, is liable to damage the horse by causing a sore mouth, shoulders or back. Well-fitted harness insures more work done during the busy season.

421. The Bridle. The fitting of the bridle will depend on the individual animal. Adjust the check pieces so that the bit will not hang too low in the mouth or so high that it will raise the corners of the mouth, thereby causing soreness. Each part of the bridle should fit snugly, but not so tight as to cause pinching. The blinds should fit snugly up to the head. Do not adjust the throat latch too tight.

422. The Collar. Pay especial attention to the collar, as it must bear the load. Test the fittings of the collar by pressing it back against the shoulder when the horse is holding its head in working position. The collar should have an even contact against all parts of the shoulder and have ample space at the wind pipe for the place of one's hand. Collars often need to be readjusted after the animal has been worked a while in the spring, due to its losing flesh. Adjust breast collar to a height where it will neither hinder movement nor interfere with breathing.

423. Hames. After the collar is adjusted, adjust the hames at the top to fit the collar and then buckle or tie as tightly as possible at the bottom.

424. Other Adjustments. All other parts of the harness should be adjusted to make them fit snugly, neither too tight nor too loose. Adjust the breeching the proper height. Fit the saddle to the back at the low place just back of the withers. Adjust the crupper strap, back straps, hip straps, holding back straps and traces to proper length in the order mentioned.

Note: Avoid accidents in hitching the team to implement or vehicle by taking down the lines and adjusting them first.

INDEX